Your Study of
The
Doctrine and Covenants Made Easier

Part 3
Section 94 through Section 138
Official Declaration—1
Official Declaration—2

Second Edition

David J. Ridges

Your Study of
The

Doctrine and Covenants Made Easier

Part 3
Section 94 through Section 138
Official Declaration—1
Official Declaration—2

Second Edition

David J. Ridges

CFI, an imprint of

Springville, Utah

© 2020 David J. Ridges
All rights reserved.

No part of this book may be reproduced in any form whatsoever, whether by graphic, visual, electronic, film, microfilm, tape recording, or any other means, without prior written permission of the publisher, except in the case of brief passages embodied in critical reviews and articles.

This book is not an official publication of The Church of Jesus Christ of Latter-day Saints. The opinions and views expressed herein belong solely to the author and do not necessarily represent the opinions or views of Cedar Fort, Inc. Permission for the use of sources, graphics, and photos is also solely the responsibility of the author.

ISBN 13: 978-1-4621-3897-5

Published by CFI, an imprint of Cedar Fort, Inc.
2373 W. 700 S., Springville, UT, 84663
Distributed by Cedar Fort, Inc., www.cedarfort.com

Library of Congress Control Number: 2020945612

Cover design by Shawnda T. Craig
Cover design © 2020 Cedar Fort, Inc.

Printed in the United States of America

10 9 8 7 6 5 4 3 2 1

Printed on acid-free paper

Dedication

*To my wife, Janette, who
is my greatest blessing.*

Contents

Preface 1
Introduction 3
Sections
    94 5
    95 8
    96 13
    97 16
    98 23
    99 39
    100 42
    101 46
    102 71
    103 80
    104 91
    105 103
    106 112
    107 114
    108 135
    109 137
    110 152
    111 161
    112 164
    113 173
    114 176
    115 178
    116 182
    117 185

SECTIONS

118	189
119	193
120	197
121	197
122	207
123	210
124	231
125	254
126	256
127	257
128	259
129	269
130	271
131	277
132	280
133	307
134	323
135	326
136	330
137	334
138	338
Official Declaration—1	349
Official Declaration—2	354

SOURCES ... 357

ABOUT THE AUTHOR ... 361

PREFACE

The Doctrine and Covenants is the Savior's book to us in our day. It teaches the "doctrines" and "covenants" necessary to live a righteous, rewarding life, which can bring joy and satisfaction during mortality, as well as exaltation in the eternities. In the October 1986 general conference of the Church, in reference to the importance of understanding the doctrines of the gospel, Elder Boyd K. Packer said:

> True doctrine, understood, changes attitudes and behavior. The study of the doctrines of the gospel will improve behavior quicker than a study of behavior will improve behavior. ("Little Children," *Ensign*, Nov. 1986)

Briefly put, "doctrines" are the teachings of the plan of salvation, the answers to questions about the meaning and purpose of life, instructions, rules, and commandments that, if followed, will lead to salvation. In D&C 10:62, the Lord tells His people that He is going to "bring to light the true points" of His doctrine. The Doctrine and Covenants does this.

This book is a brief, to-the-point guide to a better understanding of the doctrines of the gospel. The style is somewhat conversational to help you feel as if you were being guided through the Doctrine and Covenants by a teacher. It is designed to give you instant understanding of basic doctrines and principles, as well as to provide you with a background for deeper understanding and testimony.

INTRODUCTION

I have had a number of friends who have told me that they "don't get much out of reading the Doctrine and Covenants." This study guide is intended to remedy that. Through background and setting notes for each section, plus brief in-the-verse notes, along with the help of the Holy Ghost, I hope you will be enabled to feel and relive the excitement and effects of these revelations on the Prophet Joseph Smith and the early participants in the Restoration and see how they apply to you. Indeed, a key to understanding and enjoying studying the Doctrine and Covenants is seeing the application of its doctrines and teachings in your own life and in the lives of your family and friends. There are boundless applications and blessings available to us directly from the Savior through the study of this book of scripture. This study guide points them out.

As was the case with the first edition, this second edition comes in three volumes. This is part three. This new three-volume set contains many updates and much additional historical information based on research made available through the Joseph Smith Papers Project. I have used the 2013 edition of the Doctrine and Covenants, as published by The Church of Jesus Christ of Latter-day Saints, as the basic text. References to the Bible come from the King James Version, also as published by The Church of Jesus Christ of Latter-day Saints. JST references refer to the Joseph Smith Translation of the Bible.

Every verse of the Doctrine and Covenants from section 94 through section 138 and Official Declarations 1 and 2 are included in this volume. All the remaining verses of the Doctrine and Covenants are contained in parts one and two of this three-volume study guide set. All three volumes have background and setting notes for each section, as well as brief notes of explanation between and within the verses to clarify and help you learn and grow in your appreciation and understanding of this sacred volume of scripture. The notes within the verses are printed in italics and enclosed in brackets in order to make it easy for you to distinguish between the actual scripture text and my teaching comments.

Notes between the verses are indented and printed in a different font than the scripture text. **Bold** is often used to highlight things for teaching purposes.

You may be aware, as mentioned above, that, as a result of recent research for the Joseph Smith Papers Project, there are a number of changes to the section headings in the 2013 printing of the Doctrine and Covenants compared to previous editions. Such adjustments, most of them minor, have been made to 78 sections. One example of this is found in sections 39 and 40, where the name "James Covel" is now used rather than "James Covill." Another example of these Joseph Smith Papers Project research-based changes is this: If you are using an edition of the Doctrine and Covenants prior to the 2013 edition, you will see a number of corrected or added dates for the sections in this study guide. For example, prior to the 2013 edition of the Doctrine and Covenants, the date given for section 80 is March 1832. Based on recent research, the date is now given as March 7, 1832. Furthermore, at the time I wrote the first edition of this study guide, the then-current research for when living the Word of Wisdom became a temple recommend requirement was documented as being in the 1930s under President Heber J. Grant. However, current research has established it as being in 1919, shortly after President Grant became the Prophet. The Second Edition of *Doctrine and Covenants Made Easier* incorporates these changes as well as adding hundreds of additional helps and clarifications to assist you in your study.

This study guide is designed to be a user-friendly, "teacher in your hand" introductory study of this portion of the Doctrine and Covenants, as well as a refresher course for more advanced students of the scriptures. It is also designed to be a quick-reference resource that will enable readers to look up a particular passage or block of scripture for use in lessons, talks, or personal study as desired. It is my hope that you will incorporate some of the notes given in this study guide into your own scriptures, whether paper copy or on digital devices, to assist you in reading and studying this portion of the Doctrine and Covenants in the future. Thus, your own scriptures will become one of your best tools in your continued study of the gospel.

—David J. Ridges

SECTION 94

Background

This revelation was given through the Prophet Joseph Smith on August 2, 1833, at Kirtland, Ohio. Prior to the publication of the 2013 edition of the Doctrine and Covenants, the date for this revelation was given as May 6, 1833. However, recent research has proved this to be incorrect. You can see, though, that the order in which the revelations appear in the Doctrine and Covenants has not been changed.

Perhaps you've noticed that many of the revelations contained in the Doctrine and Covenants were given in Kirtland, Ohio, or the surrounding communities. In fact, sixty-three of them were, which constitutes over 40 percent of the Doctrine and Covenants. You can verify this by going to the front of your Doctrine and Covenants and browsing through the "Chronological Order of Contents," looking to the far right of the page to see how many revelations were given during a specific month for that location.

There is a lesson to be learned from this. On occasion, you may hear someone wonder why the Lord required the Saints to put so much work and effort into building up the Kirtland area when they were only going to be there for about five years (see D&C 64:21). But when you see what happened in this area—the receiving of these revelations, the building of the Kirtland Temple, the appearance of the Savior in it, the appearance of Moses, Elias, and Elijah restoring priesthood keys (see D&C 110), and the gathering and strengthening of valiant converts to provide a firm foundation (see D&C 58:7) for the spreading of the gospel into all the world—you understand the wisdom of the Lord in having Kirtland as "a strong hold . . . for the space of five years" (D&C 64:21). It temporarily became a vital hub for missionary work and for the education of a strong core of faithful members in the ways of the Lord.

You may know of several strong and faithful members who have been guided by the Lord to locate in a particular area for a season, and then, after renovating their homes and yards just the way they wanted them, they were transferred by an employer to another location or were compelled to relocate for other reasons. Years later, they look back and see that they were strengthened by each move and are now in a position to do more good than would otherwise have been possible.

At this point in Church history, the Saints have a little over three years left in Kirtland before they will be driven out, especially by apostates.

As you can see from the heading

to this section in your Doctrine and Covenants, as well as in verses 13 and 14, Hyrum Smith, Reynolds Cahoon, and Jared Carter are appointed to be the building committee that supervises the construction work required by the Lord for this area now.

Instructions for the layout of a "Zion" city and the eventual formation of the first stake of the Church in Kirtland will be given in verse 1, next.

1 AND again, verily I say unto you, my friends, a commandment I give unto you, that **ye shall commence a work of laying out and preparing a beginning and foundation of the city of the stake of Zion, here in the land of Kirtland,** beginning at my house [*beginning at the site for the building of the Kirtland Temple*].

The first stake of the Church, the Kirtland Stake, was officially organized on February 17, 1834.

2 And behold, **it must be done according to the pattern which I have given unto you.**

The Prophet Joseph Smith received the layout for a typical "city of Zion" by revelation. It was a plan for a city, one mile square, which would accommodate from fifteen to twenty thousand residents. It was the basic plan for the layout of Kirtland, and the Prophet sent it to the brethren in Missouri in late June 1833. It is described in the 1989 Institute of Religion's Church history manual as follows:

"Late in June 1833 the Prophet sent a plan for the building up of the city of Zion and its accompanying temple to the Saints in Missouri. The city was designed for fifteen to twenty thousand people and 'was to be one mile square, with ten-acre blocks, divided into one-half-acre lots, one house to the lot.' A complex of twenty-four 'temples' was to be built and used as houses of worship. The schools were to be located on two central city blocks. Lands on the north and south of the city were to be used for barns, stables, and farms. The farmer, as well as the merchant and mechanic, was to live in the city to enjoy all the social, cultural, and educational advantages. Unfortunately, mob interference prevented the implementation of this plan, although many of its basic ideas were later used by the Latter-day Saints in northern Missouri, Nauvoo, Illinois, and in hundreds of other settlements in the West" (*Church History in the Fulness of Times*, 1989, 130).

You can read more about this in *The Joseph Smith Papers, Documents, Volume 3: February 1833–March 1834*, 208–11.

Next, beginning in verse 3, the Lord specifies that a building is to be built next to the site of the

SECTION 94

Kirtland Temple for the use of the First Presidency in receiving revelations and conducting the business of the Church.

3 And **let the first lot on the south** [*of the temple site*] **be consecrated** [*set aside*] **unto me for the building of a house for the presidency** [*the First Presidency*], for the work of the presidency, in obtaining revelations; and for the work of the ministry of the presidency, in all things pertaining to the church and kingdom.

> In verses 4–9, the Savior gives specific instructions for constructing this headquarters building for the First Presidency and outlines worthiness guidelines for entering it. You will notice that these are similar to the requirements for entering holy, dedicated Church buildings today.

4 Verily I say unto you, that **it shall be built fifty-five by sixty-five feet in the width thereof and in the length thereof**, in the inner court.

5 And there shall be a lower court and a higher court, according to the pattern which shall be given unto you hereafter.

6 And **it shall be dedicated unto the Lord** from the foundation thereof, according to the order of the priesthood, according to the pattern which shall be given unto you hereafter.

7 And **it shall be wholly dedicated unto the Lord for the work of the presidency.**

8 And **ye shall not suffer** [*permit*] **any unclean thing to come in unto it**; and **my glory shall be there, and my presence shall be there.**

9 **But if there shall come into it any unclean thing, my glory shall not be there; and my presence shall not come into it.**

> The second lot to the south of the temple site is to be set aside for a building in which Church publications could be printed and in which Joseph Smith and his scribes could continue work on the translation of the Bible (the Joseph Smith Translation of the Bible, or JST).

10 And again, verily I say unto you, **the second lot on the south shall be dedicated unto me for the building of a house unto me, for the work of the printing of the translation of my scriptures** [*the Joseph Smith Translation of the Bible (JST)*], **and all things whatsoever I shall command you.**

11 **And it shall be fifty-five by sixty-five feet** in the width thereof and the length thereof, in the

inner court; and there shall be a lower and a higher court.

12 And **this house shall be wholly dedicated unto the Lord** from the foundation thereof, for the work of the printing, in all things whatsoever I shall command you, **to be holy, undefiled**, according to the pattern in all things as it shall be given unto you.

> Verses 13–15 instruct that the three men of the Church building committee are to have their homes near the printing office.

13 And **on the third lot** [*south of the temple site*] **shall my servant Hyrum Smith receive his inheritance.**

14 And **on the first and second lots on the north** [*north of the temple site*] **shall my servants Reynolds Cahoon and Jared Carter receive their inheritances—**

15 **That they may do the work** which I have appointed unto them, **to be a committee to build mine houses**, according to the commandment, which I, the Lord God, have given unto you.

> Having given the above instructions for a building for the First Presidency and a printing office, the Lord instructs the Saints to delay actually beginning construction until He tells them to move ahead.

16 **These two houses are not to be built until I give unto you a commandment concerning them.**

> Although neither of these two buildings was actually built since constructing the temple took all the members' time and resources and then the Saints were driven out, this revelation did lay the foundation for building church office buildings in Salt Lake City, Utah, as well as establishing facilities for Church publications.
>
> Thus, we see the Lord preparing the faithful Saints in the present for the future. He does much of the same thing with us.

17 And now **I give unto you no more at this time.** Amen.

SECTION 95

Background

> This revelation was given through the Prophet Joseph Smith on June 1, 1833, in Kirtland, Ohio.
>
> Applying the teachings, doctrines, and principles found in the Doctrine and Covenants in our own lives gives life and deep meaning to our study of this sacred volume of scripture. This section provides an excellent example of such application.
>
> In December 1832, the Lord commanded the Saints to build

a temple in Kirtland (see D&C 88:119). It was not to be the same kind of temple as those we build now, where sacred ordinances are performed for the living and the dead, and where a temple recommend is required for entering. Rather, it was to be a building where the Saints could meet, where revelations could be given, where the School of the Prophets could meet, and so forth.

As you can see, section 95 was given on June 1, 1833, five months after the commandment to build the Kirtland Temple. Because of poverty and perhaps a lack of understanding of the importance of this temple, nothing had yet been done as far as actually beginning construction was concerned.

As you study this revelation, you will see that the Saints are severely chastised by the Lord for this lack of action on their part (verses 2–3). This gives us an opportunity to observe how the Lord disciplines His children. We will thus be taught a lesson in parenting skills or skills for effectively supervising others.

Among the steps used by the Lord in disciplining, we see Him:

1. Reassuring them that He loves them (verse 1).

2. Informing them that they are in trouble (verse 2).

3. Not leaving them guessing as to what they have done wrong. Rather, He tells them exactly what the problem is (verse 3).

4. Explaining why it is a problem (verses 4–8).

5. Giving them a way to get out of the trouble they're in (verse 13).

We will note these steps as we proceed. No doubt, you will be able to see others also. As usual, we will use **bold** type to point things out.

Step 1

1 **VERILY, thus saith the Lord unto you whom I love**, and **whom I love I also chasten** [*scold, reprove; the fact that the Lord scolds us as needed is proof that He loves us; so also with parents*] **that their sins may be forgiven**, for with the chastisement I prepare a way for their deliverance in all things out of temptation, and **I have loved you** [*I have always loved you*]—

Step 2

2 Wherefore, **ye must needs be chastened and stand rebuked** before my face;

Step 3

3 For **ye have sinned against me a very grievous** [*serious*] **sin, in that ye have not considered the great commandment** in all

things, that **I have given unto you concerning the building of mine house** [*the Kirtland Temple—see D&C 88:119*];

Step 4

4 **For the preparation wherewith** [*the temple is to be built in preparation for the following:*] **I design** [*plan*] **to prepare mine apostles** [*a broad reference; those who have been called to preach the gospel—the Quorum of the Twelve Apostles will not be organized until February 1835*] **to prune my vineyard** [*to cut out false doctrines and philosophies, to shape and form people's lives with the gospel throughout the world*] **for the last time** [*before the Second Coming; see Jacob 5:71*], **that I may bring to pass my strange act** [*as prophesied by Isaiah—see Isaiah 28:21; the Restoration, the "marvelous work and a wonder"—2 Nephi 27:26*], **that I may pour out my Spirit upon all flesh—**

5 **But behold, verily I say unto you, that there are many who have been ordained among you**, whom I have called **but few of them are chosen** [*to have true power in doing the work of the Lord*].

6 **They who are not chosen** [*to be effective tools in the hand of the Lord*] **have sinned** a very grievous sin, **in that they are walking in darkness at noon-day** [*they are not living the gospel when it is "shining" all around them*].

7 And **for this cause** [*this reason*] **I gave unto you a commandment that you should call your solemn assembly** [*including building a temple in which to hold solemn assemblies—D&C 88:70–119*], **that your fastings and your mourning might come up into the ears of the Lord of Sabaoth** [*the Savior—see notes for D&C 87:7 in part 2 of this series*], **which, by interpretation, is the creator of the first day, the beginning and the end.**

President Spencer W. Kimball gave a few details about "solemn assemblies" and some of the reasons for holding them. He said that they "have been known among the Saints since the days of Israel. They have been of various kinds but generally have been associated with the dedication of a temple or a special meeting appointed for the sustaining of a new First Presidency or a meeting for the priesthood to sustain a revelation, such as the tithing revelation to President Lorenzo Snow. . . .

"Each of the presidents of the Church has been sustained by the priesthood of the Church in solemn assembly down to and including President Harold B. Lee, who was sustained October

6, 1972" (in Conference Report, April 1974, 64–65; or "What Do We Hear?" *Ensign,* May 1974, 45).

8 Yea, verily I say unto you, **I gave unto you a commandment that you should build a house** [*the Kirtland Temple*], **in the which house I design** [*plan*] **to endow** [*bless*] **those whom I have chosen with power from on high** [*which will include the appearance of the Savior, Moses, Elias, and Elijah—see D&C 110*];

> Next, in verse 9, the Master explains that these are some of the reasons why He wants these Saints to remain in the Kirtland area for a period of time, even though He has already told them that it will only be for about five years (see D&C 64:21).

9 For **this is the promise of the Father unto you; therefore** [*for this reason*] **I command you to tarry** [*to remain in the Kirtland area for a time*], even as mine apostles at Jerusalem [*see Acts 1:4*].

10 Nevertheless [*in spite of these wonderful promises*], **my servants sinned** a very grievous sin; and **contentions arose in the school of the prophets** [*in spite of the commandment given in D&C 88:123–24 to "love one another" and to "cease to find fault one with another"*]; **which was very grievous unto me, saith your Lord**; therefore I sent them forth to be chastened.

11 Verily I say unto you, **it is my will that you should build a house** [*the temple*]. **If you keep my commandments you shall have power to build it.**

12 **If you keep not my commandments, the love of** [*the blessings of*] **the Father shall not continue with you, therefore you shall walk in darkness.**

> In the context of verse 12, above, "the love of the Father" means "the blessings of the Father," which are earned by obedience to His commandments. You may wish to read "Divine Love," an article by then Elder Russell M. Nelson in the February 2003 *Ensign,* in which he teaches this concept of the Father's love.

Step 5

13 **Now here is wisdom** [*this is how you can get out of the trouble you are in*], **and the mind of the Lord—let the house be built**, not after the manner of the world, for I give not unto you that ye shall live after the manner of the world;

> The Saints responded quickly to this revelation, and the day after they received it, they began digging trenches for the foundation of the temple.

14 Therefore, **let it be built after the manner which I shall show unto three of you**, whom ye shall appoint and ordain unto this power.

> The promise of the Lord, given to Joseph Smith, Frederick G. Williams, and Sidney Rigdon in verse 14, above, was marvelously fulfilled according President Williams. He said:
>
> "Joseph [Smith] received the word of the Lord for him to take his two counselors, [Frederick G.] Williams and [Sidney] Rigdon, and come before the Lord, and He would show them the plan or model of the house to be built. We went upon our knees, called on the Lord, and the building appeared within viewing distance, I being the first to discover it. Then all of us viewed it together. After we had taken a good look at the exterior, the building seemed to come right over us" (in *Teachings of Presidents of the Church: Joseph Smith* [2007], 271). When the temple was nearing completion, President Williams said it looked like the building he had seen in vision to the smallest detail, and he could not tell the difference between the temple he saw in vision and the temple as built (Tait and Rogers, "A House for Our God," *Revelations in Context*, 167).
>
> Next, in verses 15–17, the Savior gives the dimensions for the building of the Kirtland Temple as well as the uses for various parts of the building.

15 And the size thereof shall be **fifty and five feet in width**, and let it be **sixty-five feet in length**, in the inner court thereof.

16 And **let the lower part of the inner court be dedicated unto me for your sacrament offering**, and for your **preaching**, and your **fasting**, and your **praying, and the offering up of your most holy desires unto me**, saith your Lord.

17 And **let the higher part of the inner court be dedicated unto me for the school of mine apostles** [*the School of the Prophets*], **saith Son Ahman** [*the Son of God*]; or, in other words, Alphus; or, in other words, Omegus [*another form of "Alpha and Omega," the first and last letters of the Greek alphabet, meaning Christ*]; even Jesus Christ your Lord. Amen.

> "Ahman," used in verse 17, above, is the name of God in the pure language. This is explained by Elder Orson Pratt as follows (**bold** added for emphasis):
>
> "There is one revelation that this people are not generally acquainted with. I think it has never been published, but probably it will be in the Church History. It is given in questions and answers. The first

question is, **'What is the name of God in the pure language?'** The answer says, **'Ahman.'** 'What is the name of the Son of God?' Answer, 'Son Ahman—the greatest of all the parts of God excepting Ahman'" (*Journal of Discourses*, 2:342).

SECTION 96

Background

This revelation was given to the Prophet Joseph Smith on June 4, 1833, in Kirtland, Ohio.

In the heading to this section in your Doctrine and Covenants, the "French farm" (103 acres) is mentioned. Some months prior to this revelation, the Church had purchased some farms for the purpose of settling the members and establishing the Kirtland Stake. The Prophet Joseph Smith spoke of this in his history. He said (**bold** added for emphasis):

"*March 23* [1833].—A council was called for the purpose of appointing a committee to purchase land in Kirtland, upon which the Saints might build a Stake of Zion. Brother Joseph Coe and Moses Dailey were appointed to ascertain the terms of sale of certain farms; and Brother Ezra Thayre to ascertain the price of **Peter French's farm**. The brethren agreed to continue in prayer and fasting for the ultimate success of their mission. After an absence of about three hours Brothers Coe and Dailey returned and reported that Elijah Smith's farm could be obtained for four thousand dollars; and Mr. Morley's for twenty-one hundred; and **Brother Thayre reported that Peter French would sell his farm for five thousand dollars**. The council decided to purchase the farms, and appointed Ezra Thayre and Joseph Coe to superintend the purchase; and they were ordained under the hands of Sidney Rigdon, and set apart as general agents of the Church for that purpose" (*History of the* Church, 1:335).

The Peter French farm had a good stone quarry and the facilities needed for making brick. Thus, it was an ideal tract of land on which to build the temple and other buildings and homes associated with the establishing of Kirtland as a temporary gathering place for the Saints. About fifteen hundred members had gathered to Kirtland by this time.

At the time of this revelation, a committee of high priests had met to consider a number of issues associated with the dividing up of the French farm for a temple site and for lots upon which members could settle and build homes. One issue was who should be in charge. Since these men could not agree on the matter, they agreed to ask the Lord through the Prophet.

You will see answers to this and other matters as we study this section.

1 BEHOLD, I say unto you, **here is wisdom, whereby ye may know how to act concerning this matter,** for **it is expedient** [*urgent, necessary*] in me **that this stake** [*the Kirtland Stake*] that I have set for the strength of Zion **should be made strong.**

2 Therefore, **let my servant Newel K. Whitney** [*the bishop in Kirtland*] **take charge** of the place which is named among you, upon which I design to build mine holy house.

3 And again, **let it be divided into lots, according to wisdom** [*you decide and use wisdom and common sense*], for the benefit of those who seek inheritances, **as** it shall be **determined in council** among you.

> Verse 3, above, is a good example of the use of councils in the Church for making decisions and taking action to move the work of the Lord ahead. The council process can lead to revelation. As you know, councils, such as ward councils, are still a vital part of the Church today.

4 Therefore, take heed that ye **see to this matter** [*move ahead on this*], and that portion that is necessary to benefit mine order [*the United Order or United Firm in Kirtland—see D&C 92:1*], **for the purpose of bringing forth my word to the children of men** [*the ultimate purpose of the Church*].

A quote from the 2018 *Doctrine and Covenants Student Manual,* chapter 37, helps us understand verse 4, above.

"A portion of the property was to be used to benefit the Lord's 'order, for the purpose of bringing forth [His] word to the children of men' (D&C 96:4). This had reference to the United Order, or United Firm. 'A subset of the United Firm, the Literary Firm, was responsible for publishing the revelations' [see D&C 70]. 'That portion' [D&C 96:4] to be devoted to bringing forth God's word may refer either to acreage allotted for building a print shop or to land-sale proceeds that could be used to support such a printing operation" (in *The Joseph Smith Papers, Documents, Volume 3: February 1833–March 1834,* 111, note 277).

5 For behold, verily I say unto you, **this** [*referring to the last phrase in verse 4, above*] **is the most expedient in me** [*the most important thing of all*], **that my word should go forth unto the children of men** [*people*], for the purpose of subduing the hearts of the children of men for your good. Even so. Amen.

Next, in verses 6–9, the Lord instructs that John Johnson should be invited to join the United Firm in the Kirtland area. Brother and Sister Johnson joined the Church in the spring of 1831, after Sister Johnson's arm was miraculously healed in Kirtland when Joseph Smith commanded in the name of Jesus Christ that she be made whole.

Joseph and Emma accepted the Johnson's invitation to live with them in their spacious farm home in Hiram, Ohio, about thirty miles southeast of Kirtland. They moved in on September 12, 1831. They lived there until September 1832, and the Johnson home became the headquarters of the Church during that time. The Prophet received many revelations while there, including section 76, which deals with the three degrees of glory and perdition. It was also while living at the Johnson home that Joseph was tarred and feathered by a mob (on the night of March 24, 1832). John Johnson heard the noise of the mob and went outside to help the Prophet but was knocked down and suffered a broken collarbone. He was later administered to by David Whitmer and was immediately healed.

The above brief background about John Johnson gives added meaning to the phrase "whose offering I have accepted" in verse 6, next.

6 And again, verily I say unto you, it is wisdom and expedient in me, that my servant **John Johnson whose offering I have accepted**, and whose prayers I have heard, unto whom I give a promise of eternal life [*exaltation*] inasmuch as [*if*] he keepeth my commandments from henceforth—

7 For **he is a descendant of Joseph and a partaker of the blessings of the promise made unto his fathers** [*in other words, he is an heir to the blessings of Abraham, Isaac, and Jacob (see Abraham 2:9–11) if he lives worthy of them (verse 6, above)*]—

8 Verily I say unto you, it is expedient in me that he **should become a member of the order** [*the United Firm, operating under the law of consecration*], that he may assist in bringing forth my word unto the children of men.

9 Therefore **ye shall ordain him unto** [*set him apart for*] **this blessing**, and he shall seek diligently to take away incumbrances [*the financial obligations*] that are upon the house named among you, that he may dwell therein. Even so. Amen.

Just a quick note about the term *ordain* as used in verse 9, above. Perhaps you've noticed that the vocabulary of the Church gradually developed over many years. For example, the words *intelligence*, *spirits,* and *souls* were used interchangeably early on (see Abraham 3:18–23). Whereas now we use *intelligence* to mean what we were before spirit birth, *spirit* means that which leaves the body at death, and *soul* means the "spirit and the body" (see D&C 88:15).

The term *ordain* was used interchangeably in the early days of the restored Church to mean ordained to the priesthood as well as being set apart to a calling or assignment in the Church. For example, Emma Smith was "ordained" to be an instructor in the Church (D&C 25:7). Whereas, now, the term *ordained* is used in reference to priesthood offices, and *set apart* is used for all other callings that are accompanied by the laying on of hands. This includes serving in a stake presidency, in a Relief Society presidency, as a missionary, and many other such callings.

SECTION 97

Background

This revelation dealing with the situation of the members in Missouri was given through the Prophet Joseph Smith on August 2, 1833, in Kirtland, Ohio. As requested by the Lord (D&C 88:77–80, 117–41), the members in Missouri had started a School of the Elders with Parley P. Pratt as the teacher. Of this he wrote:

"A school of Elders was . . . organized, over which I was called to preside. This class, to the number of about sixty, met for instruction once a week. The place of meeting was in the open air, under some tall trees, in a retired place in the wilderness, where we prayed, preached and prophesied, and exercised ourselves in the gifts of the Holy Spirit. Here great blessings were poured out, and many great and marvelous things were manifested and taught. The Lord gave me great wisdom, and enabled me to teach and edify the Elders, and comfort and encourage them in their preparations for the great work which lay before us. I was also much edified and strengthened" (*Autobiography of Parley P. Pratt*, 93–94).

Mob violence broke out against the members in Independence, Missouri, on July 20, 1833. The home of W. W. Phelps (who would later write "Praise to the Man" and other Church hymns) was destroyed along with the Church's printing press (underway with the printing of the Book of Commandments). Bishop Edward Partridge was taken to the town square of Independence and tarred and feathered, as was Brother Charles Allen. A brief account of these events is given in *History of the Church* as follows:

"On the 20th of July, the mob collected, and demanded the discontinuance of the Church printing establishment in Jackson county, the closing of the store, and the cessation of all mechanical labors. The brethren refused compliance, and the consequence was that the house of W. W. Phelps, which contained the printing establishment, was thrown down, the materials taken possession of by the mob, many papers destroyed, and the family and furniture thrown out of doors.

"The mob then proceeded to violence towards Edward Partridge, the Bishop of the Church, as he relates in his autobiography:

"'I was taken from my house by the mob, George Simpson being their leader, who escorted me about half a mile, to the court house, on the public square in Independence [Missouri]; and then and there, a few rods from said court house, surrounded by hundreds of the mob, I was stripped of my hat, coat and vest and daubed with tar from head to foot, and then had a quantity of feathers put upon me; and all this because I would not agree to leave the county, and my home where I had lived two years.

"'Before tarring and feathering me I was permitted to speak. I told them that the Saints had suffered persecution in all ages of the world; that I had done nothing which ought to offend anyone; that if they abused me, they would abuse an innocent person; that I was willing to suffer for the sake of Christ; but, to leave the country, I was not then willing to consent to it. By this time the multitude made so much noise that I could not be heard: some were cursing and swearing, saying, 'call upon your Jesus,' etc.; others were equally noisy in trying to still the rest, that they might be enabled to hear what I was saying.

"'Until after I had spoken, I knew not what they intended to do with me, whether to kill me, to whip me, or what else I knew not. I bore my abuse with so much resignation and meekness, that it appeared to astound the multitude, who permitted me to retire in silence, many looking very solemn, their sympathies having been touched as I thought; and as to myself, I was so filled with the Spirit and love of God, that I had no hatred towards my persecutors or anyone else.'

"Charles Allen was next stripped and tarred and feathered, because he would not agree to leave the county, or deny the Book of Mormon. Others were brought up to be served likewise or whipped" (*History of the Church,* 1:390–91).

The Prophet Joseph Smith later reflected on the tarring and feathering of Edward Partridge and Charles Allen as follows:

"When Bishop Partridge, who was without guile, and Elder Charles Allen, walked off, coated like some unnamed, unknown bipeds, one of the sisters cried aloud: '*While you,* who have done this wicked deed, must suffer the vengeance of God, they, having endured persecution, can rejoice, for henceforth for them, is laid up a crown eternal in the heavens.'

"Surely this was a time for awful reflection; man, unrestrained, like the brute beast, may torment the body; but God will punish the soul!" (*History of the Church*, 1:390–93).

Some of the local leaders of the Church in Missouri even offered themselves to the mob if they would leave the other members in peace. We read:

"It was at this point, too, that several of the brethren stepped forward and offered themselves as a ransom for the Church, expressing themselves as being willing to be scourged or to die if that would appease the anger of the mob against the Saints. The mob would not accept the sacrifice of the brethren, however, but renewed their threats of violence against the whole Church. The brethren who offered themselves as a ransom for the Saints were John Corrill, John Whitmer, William W. Phelps, Algernon S. Gilbert, Edward Partridge, and Isaac Morley" (*History of the Church,* footnote 5, 1:394–95).

On July 23, 1833, local leaders of the Church were forced to sign an agreement stating that the Saints would leave Jackson County. The Prophet recorded: "On the same day (July 23rd), while the brethren in Missouri were preparing to leave the county, through the violence of the mob, the corner stones of the Lord's House were laid in Kirtland, after the order of the Holy Priesthood" (*History of the* Church, 1:400).

It is significant that, with the slow communication methods of the day, the Prophet Joseph Smith had no way of knowing what had so recently transpired among the members in Missouri. This revelation is another witness that he was truly a prophet of God, as it addresses the causes of these troubles, of which he had not yet heard by communication from Missouri.

First, in this section, the Savior addresses the members in Kirtland and assures them that the faithful among the membership of the Church in Missouri will not lose their eternal reward, regardless of what happens to the Church in general in Zion. Notice as He begins this revelation that we are taught that "hearing" the voice of the Spirit is essentially the same as hearing the literal voice of the Lord.

1 **VERILY I say unto you my friends** [*the faithful in Kirtland*]**, I speak unto you with my voice, even the voice of my Spirit**, that I may show unto you my will **concerning your brethren in the land of Zion** [*Jackson County,*

Missouri], **many of whom are truly humble and are seeking diligently to learn wisdom and to find truth.**

2 Verily, verily I say unto you, **blessed are such, for they shall obtain** [*among other things, they will obtain exaltation*]; **for I, the Lord, show mercy unto all the meek**, and upon all whomsoever I will, that I may be justified when I shall bring them unto judgment. [*In other words, all will receive the opportunity to know of the mercy and kindness of God. And because the Lord is completely fair, all who are faithful will ultimately receive their reward of exaltation in celestial glory regardless of the seemingly unfair things that happen to them on earth.*]

> Next, in verses 3–5, the Master expresses His pleasure with the work of Parley P. Pratt as the director of the "school in Zion."

3 Behold, I say unto you, **concerning the school in Zion** [*School of the Elders*]**, I, the Lord, am well pleased** that there should be a school in Zion, and **also with my servant Parley P. Pratt, for he abideth in me** [*he carefully stays true to the teachings and commandments of God as he teaches this School of the Elders*].

4 **And inasmuch as** [*if*] **he continueth to abide in me** [*continues to remain faithful*] **he shall continue to preside over the school** in the land of Zion until I shall give unto him other commandments.

5 And **I will bless him with a multiplicity of blessings, in expounding** [*explaining and teaching*] **all scriptures and mysteries** [*basics of the gospel, which are a "mystery" to most inhabitants of the world—see Bible Dictionary under "Mystery"*] **to the edification** [*building up and enlightenment*] **of the school, and of the church in Zion.**

> Next, in verses 6–7, the Savior tells those in the School of the Elders that He will give them another chance to repent, but if they don't, the "ax" is about to fall.

6 And **to the residue of the school** [*the others who are attending this school*]**, I, the Lord, am willing to show mercy; nevertheless, there are those that must needs be chastened** [*punished if they don't repent*]**, and their works shall be made known.**

7 **The ax is laid at the root of the trees**; and **every tree** [*trees are often symbolic of people in the scriptures*] **that bringeth not forth good fruit** [*that does not repent and live righteously*] **shall be hewn down and cast into the fire** [*will

be destroyed; can also mean that they will be turned over to Satan to suffer for their sins]. I, the Lord, have spoken it.*

Next, the Savior again assures those who are doing their best to live the gospel that they are not included in the chastisement He has just given.

8 Verily I say unto you, **all among them who know their hearts are honest, and are broken, and their spirits contrite, and are willing to observe their covenants by sacrifice—yea, every sacrifice which I, the Lord, shall command—they are accepted of me.**

Did you notice the answer in verse 8, above, to a question that often comes up in gospel discussions; namely, whether we can know if we are doing alright in the eyes of God? The answer is yes.

The Lord goes on to use beautiful imagery to describe the growth and productivity of faithful members of the Church who are willing to grow under the direction of God.

9 For **I, the Lord, will cause them to bring forth** [*produce*] **as a very fruitful tree which is planted in a goodly land, by a pure stream, that yieldeth much precious fruit.**

Next, the topic turns to the building of a temple in Zion. Verses 10–17 provide a short course in financing temple construction and in the value and blessings of temple attendance.

10 Verily I say unto you, that **it is my will that a house** [*a temple*] **should be built unto me in the land of Zion**, like unto the pattern which I have given you.

11 Yea, **let it be built speedily, by the tithing of my people.**

12 Behold, **this is the tithing and the sacrifice which I, the Lord, require at their hands**, that there may be **a house** [*temple*] **built unto me for the salvation of Zion—**

13 **For a place of thanksgiving** for all saints, and for a place **of instruction** for all those who are called to the work of the ministry in all their several callings and offices;

14 **That they may be perfected in the understanding of their ministry, in theory**, in **principle**, and in **doctrine**, in **all things pertaining to the kingdom of God on the earth**, the keys of which kingdom have been conferred upon you.

Next, in verses 15–17, we see the reason for requiring temple recommends for entrance into our holy temples.

15 And **inasmuch as [*if*] my people build a house unto me** in the name of the Lord, **and do not suffer any unclean thing to come into it**, that it be not defiled, **my glory shall rest upon it**;

16 Yea, and **my presence shall be there**, for **I will come into it**, and **all the pure in heart that shall come into it shall see God.**

> There are many ways to interpret the phrase "shall see God" in verse 16, above. First, when the conditions are right and it is in harmony with His will, people can literally see God. Another way of "seeing" the Lord is through studying the scriptures. Example: "The scriptures shall be given . . . they will hear my voice, and shall see me" (D&C 35:20–21). Yet another meaning of "seeing" God is to have a firm testimony of His existence, through the power of the Holy Ghost.
>
> In D&C 88:68, we learn that "the days will come that you shall see him; for he will unveil his face unto you, and it shall be **in his own time**, and **in his own way**, and **according to his own will.**"

17 **But if it be defiled I will not come into it**, and my glory shall not be there; for I will not come into unholy temples.

> In verses 18–19, next, the promise is given that if the members of the Church in Zion repent and live according to the laws and commandments given above, Zion will be established. This will require truly living in accordance with celestial law, including the law of consecration, which is the law upon which Zion will be built. See D&C 105:5.

18 And, now, behold, **if Zion do these things she shall prosper, and spread herself and become very glorious, very great, and very terrible** [*frightening to enemies who would like to destroy the Church*].

19 And **the nations of the earth shall honor her**, and shall say: Surely Zion is the city of our God, and surely Zion cannot fall, neither be moved out of her place, for God is there, and the hand of the Lord is there;

20 **And he hath sworn by the power of his might to be her salvation and her high tower** [*symbolic of protection*].

> The "high tower" spoken of in verse 20, above, calls to mind the imagery of a watch tower, built onto the city wall in ancient times, from which danger could be seen while yet far off. Thus, "high tower" symbolizes safety and protection from God, who sees danger coming and warns and protects against it. Another way to say it is that those who exercise their

agency so that they live within the safe haven of the gospel walls and protection will come under the safety and protection of God.

Next, the Savior gives us His definition of *Zion*. You will see that it is primarily a condition of the heart. Thus, in effect, Zion can be wherever we are, if we are pure in heart. Zion is wherever the Saints are gathered, if they are pure in heart.

21 Therefore, verily, thus saith the Lord, let Zion rejoice, for **this is Zion—THE PURE IN HEART**; therefore, let Zion rejoice, while all the wicked shall mourn.

Sometimes confusion arises with respect to the word *Zion*. This is because there are so many different meanings to it in addition to the basic definition given in verse 21, above. The Bible Dictionary gives a number of definitions as follows:

Zion

"The word *Zion* is used repeatedly in all the standard works of the Church, and is defined in latter-day revelation as 'the pure in heart' (D&C 97:21). Other usages of Zion have to do with a geographical location. For example, Enoch built a city that was called Zion (Moses 7:18–19); Solomon built his temple on Mount Zion (1 Kgs. 8:1; cf. 2 Sam. 5:6–7); and Jackson County, Missouri, is called Zion in many of the revelations in the D&C, such as 58:49–50; 62:4; 63:48; 72:13; 84:76; 104:47. The city of New Jerusalem, to be built in Jackson County, Missouri, is to be called Zion (D&C 45:66–67). The revelations also speak of 'the cause of Zion' (D&C 6:6; 11:6). In a wider sense all of North and South America are Zion (HC 6:318–19). For further references see 1 Chr. 11:5; Ps. 2:6; 99:2; 102:16; Isa. 1:27; 2:3; 4:3–5; 33:20; 52:1–8; 59:20; Jer. 3:14; 31:6; Joel 2:1–32; Amos 6:1; Obad. 1:17, 21; Heb. 12:22–24; Rev. 14:1–5; and many others. (In the N.T., *Zion* is spelled *Sion*.)"

Next, in verses 22–24, the Savior foretells the destructions that will go forth upon the earth because of wickedness. He informs us that people will become tired of the constant barrage of negative news (verse 23) and that things will not get better until the Second Coming and Millennium (end of verse 23).

22 For behold, and lo, **vengeance cometh speedily upon the ungodly as the whirlwind**; and who shall escape it?

23 **The Lord's scourge shall pass over by night and by day**, and **the report thereof** [*the news*] **shall vex all people**; yea, **it shall not be stayed** [*it won't be stopped*] **until the Lord come;**

24 **For the indignation of the Lord is kindled against their**

abominations [*gross wickedness*] and all their wicked works.

> In verses 25–26, next, the members in Jackson County are, in effect, told that if they repent, Zion can still be established at this time. But if they fail to repent, they will be subject to "sore affliction."

25 Nevertheless, **Zion shall escape if she observe to do all things whatsoever I have commanded her.**

26 But if she observe not to do whatsoever I have commanded her, I will visit [*punish*] **her according to all her works, with sore affliction, with pestilence, with plague, with sword, with vengeance, with devouring fire.**

> Yet again, in verses 27–28, the Savior invites these Saints to repent and do much better at living according to the laws and commandments upon which Zion can be successfully built. If they do, they will be spared further serious affliction and can remain in Missouri. He is giving them one more chance. Otherwise, it will be far in the future when Zion will be established in Missouri.

27 Nevertheless, let it be read this once to her ears, that I, the Lord, have accepted of her offering; and **if she sin no more none of these things shall come upon her;**

28 And I will bless her with blessings, and multiply a multiplicity of blessings upon her, and upon her generations forever and ever, saith the Lord your God. Amen.

> Unfortunately, too many of the members in Missouri failed to repent sufficiently for the above blessings to be provided in 1833. Parley P. Pratt wrote the following:
>
> "This revelation [section 97] was not complied with by the leaders and Church in Missouri as a whole (notwithstanding many were humble and faithful); therefore, the threatened judgment was poured out to the uttermost, as the history of the five following years will show" (*Autobiography of Parley P. Pratt*, 96).

SECTION 98

Background

This revelation was given through the Prophet Joseph Smith on August 6, 1833, at Kirtland, Ohio, and primarily concerned the difficulties between the old settlers in Missouri and the newly arrived members of the Church there.

In 1833, the original settlers of Missouri had become greatly concerned about the large influx of Latter-day Saints coming into their state. Shortly after the Lord revealed in July 1831 (section 57) that the city of Zion as well as a temple were to be built in Independence, Missouri, hundreds of members began gathering to Jackson county. By summer of 1833, it appears that more than 1,200 Saints had settled there. (For more information, see *The Joseph Smith Papers, Documents, Volume 3: February 1833–March 1834*, ed. Gerrit J. Dirkmaat and others [2014], 121.)

There were obviously significant lifestyle differences and differences in religious beliefs between the two groups, which led the old settlers to form mobs and persecute the members of the Church, often with the encouragement of local ministers of other churches.

Sections 97 and 98 go together and were sent from Kirtland at the same time—August 6, 1833—in a letter from the Prophet to the Saints in Missouri. The members in Missouri had already suffered mob violence, beginning on July 20, 1833 (see background information for section 97 in this study guide). There was much sentiment on the part of many members in Jackson County to retaliate and get revenge for the atrocities already committed against them (see heading to section 98 in your Doctrine and Covenants).

While section 98 is often referred to as a revelation giving the laws and principles of self-defense, which it definitely is, it can also be considered a revelation on character development and self-control.

If we hope to someday become like our Father in Heaven, we must develop self-control. Otherwise, we would never succeed in being sufficiently patient with our own spirit children whom we send to worlds to undergo the training and lessons that we are now undergoing. Without self-control and the other character traits that go along with it, including love, patience, and the ability to forgive, we would quite likely prematurely destroy the worlds we create for our spirit children. In other words, we would never qualify to become gods.

We will first go through the entire section, **bolding** some of the words and phrases that exemplify the Christlike character traits we need to develop if we are to become gods. We will also bold things that show how this mortal life is a test or proving ground. Then we will repeat the section and add notes and commentary.

1 VERILY I say unto you my friends, fear not, let your hearts be comforted; yea, rejoice evermore, and in everything give thanks;

2 **Waiting patiently** on the Lord, for your prayers have entered into the ears of the Lord of Sabaoth, and are recorded with this seal and testament—the Lord hath sworn and decreed that they shall be granted.

3 Therefore, he giveth this promise unto you, with an immutable covenant that they shall be fulfilled; and all things wherewith you have been afflicted shall work together for your good, and to my name's glory, saith the Lord.

4 And now, verily I say unto you **concerning the laws of the land, it is my will that my people should observe to do all things whatsoever I command them**.

5 **And that law of the land which is constitutional**, supporting that principle of freedom in maintaining rights and privileges, **belongs to all mankind, and is justifiable before me**.

6 **Therefore, I, the Lord, justify you**, and your brethren of my church, **in befriending that law which is the constitutional law of the land**;

7 And as pertaining to law of man, whatsoever is more or less than this, cometh of evil.

8 I, the Lord God, make you free, therefore ye are free indeed; and the law also maketh you free.

9 Nevertheless, when the wicked rule the people mourn.

10 **Wherefore, honest men and wise men should be sought for diligently, and good men and wise men ye should observe to uphold**; otherwise whatsoever is less than these cometh of evil.

11 And I give unto you a commandment, that ye shall **forsake all evil and cleave unto all good**, that ye shall **live by every word which proceedeth forth out of the mouth of God**.

12 For he will give unto the faithful line upon line, precept upon precept; and **I will try you and prove you herewith**.

13 And whoso layeth down his life in my cause, for my name's sake, shall find it again, even life eternal.

14 Therefore, be not afraid of your enemies, for I have decreed in my heart, saith the Lord, that **I will prove you in all things**, whether you will abide in my covenant, even unto death, that you may be found worthy.

15 For **if ye will not abide in my covenant ye are not worthy of me**.

16 Therefore, **renounce war and proclaim peace**, and seek diligently to turn the hearts of the children to their fathers, and the hearts of the fathers to the children;

17 And again, the hearts of the Jews unto the prophets, and the prophets unto the Jews; lest I come and smite the whole earth with a curse, and all flesh be consumed before me.

18 Let not your hearts be troubled; for in my Father's house are many mansions, and I have prepared a place for you; and where my Father and I am, there ye shall be also.

19 Behold, I, the Lord, am not well pleased with many who are in the church at Kirtland;

20 For they do not forsake their sins, and their wicked ways, the pride of their hearts, and their covetousness, and all their detestable things, and observe the words of wisdom and eternal life which I have given unto them.

21 Verily I say unto you, that I, the Lord, will chasten them and will do whatsoever I list, if they do not repent and observe all things whatsoever I have said unto them.

22 And again I say unto you, if ye observe to do whatsoever I command you, I, the Lord, will turn away all wrath and indignation from you, and the gates of hell shall not prevail against you.

23 Now, I speak unto you concerning your families—**if men will smite you, or your families, once, and ye bear it patiently and revile not against them, neither seek revenge, ye shall be rewarded**;

24 **But if ye bear it not patiently, it shall be accounted unto you as being meted out as a just measure unto you.**

25 And again, **if your enemy shall smite you the second time**, and you revile not against your enemy, and **bear it patiently**, your reward shall be an hundred fold.

26 And again, **if he shall smite you the third time**, and ye **bear it patiently**, your reward shall be doubled unto you four-fold;

27 And these three testimonies shall stand against your enemy if he repent not, and shall not be blotted out.

28 And now, verily I say unto you, if that enemy shall escape my vengeance, that he be not brought into judgment before me, then ye shall see to it that ye warn him in my name, that he come no more upon you, neither upon your family, even your children's children unto the third and fourth generation.

29 And then, if he shall come upon you or your children, or your children's children unto the

third and fourth generation, I have delivered thine enemy into thine hands;

30 And then **if thou wilt spare him**, thou shalt be rewarded for thy righteousness; and also thy children and thy children's children unto the third and fourth generation.

31 Nevertheless, thine enemy is in thine hands; and if thou rewardest him according to his works thou art justified; if he has sought thy life, and thy life is endangered by him, thine enemy is in thine hands and thou art justified.

32 Behold, this is the law I gave unto my servant Nephi, and thy fathers, Joseph, and Jacob, and Isaac, and Abraham, and all mine ancient prophets and apostles.

33 And again, this is the law that I gave unto mine ancients, that they should not go out unto battle against any nation, kindred, tongue, or people, save I, the Lord, commanded them.

34 And if any nation, tongue, or people should proclaim war against them, they should first lift a standard of peace unto that people, nation, or tongue;

35 And if that people did not accept the offering of peace, neither the second nor the third time, they should bring these testimonies before the Lord;

36 Then I, the Lord, would give unto them a commandment, and justify them in going out to battle against that nation, tongue, or people.

37 And I, the Lord, would fight their battles, and their children's battles, and their children's children's, until they had avenged themselves on all their enemies, to the third and fourth generation.

38 Behold, this is an ensample unto all people, saith the Lord your God, for justification before me.

39 And again, verily I say unto you, if after thine enemy has come upon thee the first time, he repent and come unto thee praying thy forgiveness, **thou shalt forgive him**, and shalt hold it no more as a testimony against thine enemy—

40 And so on unto the second and third time; and **as oft as thine enemy repenteth** of the trespass wherewith he has trespassed against thee, thou shalt **forgive him**, until seventy times seven.

41 And if he trespass against thee and repent not the first time, nevertheless thou shalt **forgive him**.

42 And if he trespass against thee the second time, and repent not, nevertheless thou shalt **forgive him**.

43 And if he trespass against thee the third time, and repent not, thou shalt also **forgive him**.

44 But if he trespass against thee the fourth time thou shalt not forgive him, but shalt bring these testimonies before the Lord; and they shall not be blotted out until he repent and reward thee four-fold in all things wherewith he has trespassed against thee.

45 And if he do this, thou shalt **forgive him with all thine heart**; and if he do not this, I, the Lord, will avenge thee of thine enemy an hundred-fold;

46 And upon his children, and upon his children's children of all them that hate me, unto the third and fourth generation.

47 But if the children shall repent, or the children's children, and turn to the Lord their God, with all their hearts and with all their might, mind, and strength, and restore four-fold for all their trespasses wherewith they have trespassed, or wherewith their fathers have trespassed, or their fathers' fathers, then **thine indignation shall be turned away**;

48 And vengeance shall no more come upon them, saith the Lord thy God, and their trespasses shall never be brought any more as a testimony before the Lord against them. Amen.

Having gone through section 98 pointing out the instructions that when followed lead to character development (including self-control), we will now repeat section 98 adding notes and commentary.

To begin with, the Savior calls these early members His "friends," which is a term of closeness and endearment. And, at the end of verse 1, He counsels them to develop the character trait of gratitude. As you have perhaps noticed, those who have gratitude live a much more pleasant and peaceful life, regardless of their circumstances and what is going on around them. In fact, all commandments are given for our good and to promote inner peace, happiness, and joy, here as well as hereafter. And the Lord specifically commanded us to show gratitude (see D&C 59:21).

Section 98 repeated, with notes and commentary added

1 **VERILY I say unto you my friends**, fear not, let your hearts be comforted; yea, rejoice evermore, and **in everything give thanks**;

As we watch the Master school and help His "children" (Mosiah 5:7) move toward exaltation, we see Him next counsel them to have patience and reassure them that their prayers are heard. Those who do not have patience often develop bitterness toward God. Perhaps you've noticed that things usually happen according to the timetable of the Lord rather than according to the demands of people.

2 Waiting patiently on the Lord, for your prayers have entered into the ears of the Lord of Sabaoth [*the Savior, "the creator of the first day, the beginning and the end"—see D&C 95:7*], and are recorded with this seal and testament—[*covenant—see Bible Dictionary under "Covenant"*]—**the Lord hath sworn** [*promised*] **and decreed that they shall be granted.**

If you were to stop at the end of verse 2, above, and fail to read verse 3, next, you would miss the connection between what we ask for in prayer and what we get from the Lord. A major lesson here is that we get what is best for us rather than simply what we ask for.

3 Therefore, he giveth this promise unto you, with an immutable [*unchangeable*] covenant that they shall be fulfilled; and **all things wherewith you have been afflicted shall work together for your good,** and to my name's glory [*His work and "glory" is "to bring to pass the immortality and eternal life of man"—see Moses 1:39*], saith the Lord.

As we approach verses 4–6, next, wherein the Saints are counseled to support the laws of the land and the Constitution of the United States, it is helpful to remember that the members of the Church in Missouri had not been protected by the laws of the land thus far. In fact, the Prophet Joseph Smith recorded his thoughts on how the Missouri Saints had been treated by civil authorities and others who should have sustained and invoked the laws of the land in behalf of all citizens, including members of the Church. He recorded:

"In the course of this day's wicked, outrageous, and unlawful proceedings, many solemn realities of human degradation, as well as thrilling incidents were presented to the Saints [in Missouri]. An armed and well organized mob, in a government professing to be governed by law, with the Lieutenant Governor (Lilburn W. Boggs), the second officer in the state [of Missouri], calmly looking on, and secretly aiding every movement, saying to the Saints, 'You now know what our Jackson boys can do, and you must leave the county;' and all the justices, judges, constables, sheriffs, and military officers, headed by such western missionaries and clergymen as the Reverends McCoy, Kavanaugh, Hunter, Fitzhugh, Pixley, Likens, and Lovelady, consisting of Methodists, Baptists, Presbyterians, and all the different sects of religionists that inhabited that country, with that great moral reformer, and register of the land office at Lexington, forty miles east, known as the head and father of the Cumberland Presbyterians, even the Reverend Finis Ewing, publicly publishing that 'Mormons were the common enemies of mankind, and ought to be destroyed'—all these solemn realities were enough to melt the heart of a savage; while there was not a *solitary offense* on record, or proof, that a Saint had broken the law of the land" (*History of the Church*, 1:391–92).

As you will see, in verses 4–6, despite all of these violations and the lack of help from the government and laws of the land, the Lord still counsels the Saints to support the constitutional laws of the land.

4 And now, verily I say unto you **concerning the laws of the land**, it is my will that my people should observe to do all things whatsoever I command them.

5 And **that law of the land which is constitutional, supporting that principle of freedom in maintaining rights and privileges, belongs to all mankind, and is justifiable before me.**

6 Therefore, **I, the Lord, justify you, and your brethren of my church, in befriending that law which is the constitutional law of the land;**

You may wish to read D&C 101:77–80, in which the Lord gives His reasons for inspiring the writers of the Constitution of the United States. In verse 7, next, it implies that the Missouri mobbers were not abiding by the constitutional laws established by God, therefore, their behaviors were evil.

7 And **as pertaining to law of man, whatsoever is more or less than this** [*the Constitution*], **cometh of evil.**

In verses 8–10, next, we are all given counsel about exercising our right to vote and about supporting good and wise political leaders.

8 **I, the Lord God, make you free** [*we were all given the freedom by the Lord to exercise moral agency—see D&C 29:35*], **therefore ye are free indeed** [*we truly are free to make choices*]; **and the law also maketh you free** [*good laws that adhere to the principles found in the Constitution allow people freedom and accountability—see D&C 101:77–78*].

9 Nevertheless, when the wicked rule the people mourn.

10 **Wherefore** [*for this reason*], **honest men and wise men should be sought for diligently** [*for public office*], and **good men and wise men ye should observe to uphold**; otherwise whatsoever is less than these cometh of evil.

> Next, the topic turns to what God expects and requires of those who desire to be His true followers, regardless of circumstances. In other words, the distressed Saints in Missouri cannot use the wicked behavior of others to justify evil behavior on their part.

11 And I give unto you a commandment, that **ye shall forsake all evil and cleave unto all good, that ye shall live by every word which proceedeth forth out of the mouth of God.**

> Verses 12–15, next, teach about the support of the Lord and the personal growth that will come to all who apply verse 11 in their lives, regardless of what those around them do. They will continue to grow and make progress toward eternal exaltation in celestial glory.

12 For **he will give unto the faithful line upon line, precept upon precept** [*principle upon principle*]; **and I will try you and prove** [*test*] **you herewith.**

13 And **whoso layeth down his life in my cause, for my name's sake, shall find it again, even life eternal** [*a scriptural term meaning exaltation*].

> In verses 14–15, we are given to understand that the real enemy is not those who might even go so far as to kill us. Rather, it is the breaking of our covenants that we have made with God to live the gospel.

14 Therefore, **be not afraid of your enemies**, for I have decreed in my heart, saith the Lord, that **I will prove you in all things, whether you will abide in my covenant, even unto death, that you may be found worthy.**

15 For **if ye will not abide in my covenant ye are not worthy of me** [*in other words, if we do not do our best to keep our covenants, regardless of pressures to break them, we will not be found worthy of exaltation*].

> Next, in verses 16–18, among other things, we are taught that true Saints strive to be peacemakers. However, sometimes our efforts to make peace and "renounce war" are not successful because of the behavior of others. Under those circumstances, there are rules and principles concerning self-defense, which the Lord will give us in verses 23–48.

16 Therefore, **renounce war** and **proclaim peace**, and **seek diligently to turn the hearts of the children to their fathers** [*among other things, perhaps including teaching the gospel so that people's hearts turn toward the ancient "fathers" or prophets*], and the hearts of the fathers to the children [*implying, among other things, the tying or binding of generations together; the sealing power will be restored by Elijah in section 110, as he restores the keys of sealing families together to Joseph Smith and Oliver Cowdery*];

> Continuing the message given in verse 16, above, the Savior informs us that the day will come when our brothers and sisters of the tribe of Judah (the Jews) will have their hearts softened. Large numbers of them will accept the gospel of Jesus Christ as their hearts are also turned "unto the prophets."

17 And again, **the hearts of the Jews unto the prophets, and the prophets unto the Jews**; lest I come and smite the whole earth with a curse, and all flesh be consumed before me.

> President Ezra Taft Benson spoke of the Jews and verse 17, above, as follows:
>
> "In Jacob's blessing to Judah, he declared: 'Judah is . . . as an old lion: who shall *rouse* him up?' (Gen. 49:9; italics added.) We come as messengers bearing the legitimate authority to arouse Judah to her promises. We do not ask Judah to forsake her heritage. We are not asking her to leave father, mother, or family. We bring a message that Judah does not possess. That message constitutes 'living water' from the fountain of living water.
>
> "Our prophet, Joseph Smith, was given a commandment by the Lord to turn 'the hearts of the Jews unto the prophets, and the prophets unto the Jews.' (D&C 98:17.) We are presently sending our messengers to every land and people whose ideology permits us entrance. We have been gathering Joseph's descendants for 146 years. We hope you, who are of Judah, will not think it an intrusion for us to present our message to you. You are welcome to come to our meetings. We display no crosses. We collect no offerings. We honor your commitment to your unique heritage and your individuality. We approach you in a different way than any other Christian church because we represent the restored covenant to the entire house of Israel.
>
> "Yes, we understand the Jews, as David Ben-Gurion said. We understand them because we belong to the same house of Israel. We are your brothers—Joseph. We look forward to the day of fulfillment of

God's promise when 'the house of Judah shall walk with the house of Israel' (Jer. 3:18.)" ("A Message to Judah from Joseph," *Ensign,* December 1976, 72).

Before we leave verse 17, above, take another look at the last half of the verse. A major doctrine we gain from it is that the primary purpose of the creation of this earth is to provide the opportunity for exaltation for Father's spirit children. If the "hearts of the children" were not turned to their "fathers," and the "hearts of the fathers to the children" (verse 16, above), this purpose would not be fulfilled. Temple work for the dead would not take place. The gospel of Christ would not be here; thus, all would turn to wickedness, and all would be "consumed" (verse 17) at the Second Coming, leaving none on earth during the Millennium to do temple work for the dead.

In verse 18, next, the Savior comforts the faithful, assuring them that there is plenty of room in celestial glory for all who qualify to come there.

18 **Let not your hearts be troubled**; for **in my Father's house are many mansions**, and **I have prepared a place for you; and where my Father and I am, there ye shall be also.**

The phrase "many mansions," found in verse 18, above, is often used to teach the doctrine that there are different degrees of glory. But in the context of verse 18, it seems to be saying that there are "many mansions" within the Father's "house," or, in other words, there is room for the "innumerable" (D&C 76:67) righteous people who will return to His presence to live forever.

Although this section deals primarily with the plight of the members in Missouri, the Lord sees similar lack of faithfulness, pride, and so forth among the members in Kirtland. We would do well to check our own lives against the concerns of the Lord spoken of in verses 19–22. The promise given at the end of verse 22 can also apply to us.

19 Behold, **I, the Lord, am not well pleased with many who are in the church at Kirtland**;

20 For **they do not forsake their sins, and their wicked ways**, the **pride** of their hearts, and their **covetousness**, and **all their detestable things**, and **observe the words of wisdom and eternal life** [*the knowledge and counsel already given them by the Lord*] **which I have given unto them.**

21 **Verily** [*listen up—what comes next is important*] I say unto you, that **I, the Lord, will chasten them and will do whatsoever I**

list [*whatever is necessary to purify them*], **if they do not repent and observe all things whatsoever I have said unto them.**

22 And again I say unto you, **if ye observe to do whatsoever I command you, I, the Lord, will turn away all wrath and indignation** [*punishments*] from you, **and the gates of hell shall not prevail against you** [*will not ultimately win against you*].

> It is important to understand that there is a difference between being punished by the "indignation" (verse 22, above) of God, because of sin and wickedness on our part, and being tried and proven "in the furnace of affliction," which can come upon the righteous even though they are living the gospel. The punishments of God are designed to stop the downward spiral in the lives of people who have turned to sin. Trials and tribulations that come upon the righteous are designed to solidify progress already made and to provide more growth toward godhood.
>
> Next, in verses 23–48, the Savior will give these beleaguered Saints the laws of self-defense that He gave to the ancient prophets, including Nephi, Abraham, Isaac, Jacob, and Joseph (see verse 32). As mentioned in the background notes to this section in this study guide, section 98 is well-known for this counsel regarding self-defense. As you read, pay close attention to how much self-control is required in order to obey this law. Also, be aware that the first, second, and third offense scenarios given in verses 23–26 are not life-and-death situations when someone is threatening to kill you or your family and is raising a gun to shoot you. Such cases are dealt with in the last half of verse 31.

The Lord's Law of Self-Defense

The First Offense

23 Now, I speak unto you concerning your families—if men will smite you, or your families, once, and ye **bear it patiently and revile not against them, neither seek revenge, ye shall be rewarded** [*by the Lord*];

> The reward spoken of at the end of verse 23, above, could include the peace and satisfaction of having exercised self-control, freedom from personal hatred, the developing of additional Christlike virtues, the peace and calm that are given to the obedient by the Holy Ghost, and so forth.
>
> Verse 24, next, may sound somewhat harsh, but remember that we are dealing with the high laws and expectations that pertain to those who wish to become "Zion" people. Behaviors expected of "Zion" people are the

same behaviors required of gods, or, in other words, "celestial" (D&C 105:5). Gods must be patient with their children and exercise much self-control.

24 But **if ye bear it not patiently, it shall be accounted unto you as being meted out as a just measure unto you** [*in other words, you deserve what you get*].

The Second Offense

25 And again, **if your enemy shall smite you the second time**, and you **revile not** against your enemy, and **bear it patiently**, your **reward shall be an hundred fold**.

The Third Offense

26 And again, if he shall smite you **the third time**, and ye **bear it patiently**, your **reward** shall be doubled unto you four-fold;

27 **And these three testimonies shall stand against your enemy if he repent not**, and shall not be blotted out.

> As indicated in verse 28, next, the Lord does not always "smite" the enemies of the righteous upon the first offense, nor the second, nor the third. Sometimes He never does during their mortal lives. This can be hard at times for the righteous to understand and difficult for them to bear. The Savior reminds us in D&C 64:21 that the reason He often holds back is that He may yet save more of the wicked if He gives them more chances to repent.
>
> Also, in verses 28–31, next, we are told that there are circumstances under which we are justified in fighting against our enemies. Captain Moroni used these principles in defending his people against their enemies (see Alma 46:12–13, 18; see also Alma 43–63).

28 And now, verily I say unto you, **if that enemy shall escape my vengeance**, that he be not brought into judgment before me, **then ye shall see to it that ye warn him in my name**, that he come no more upon you, neither upon your family, even your children's children unto the third and fourth generation.

29 And **then, if he shall come upon you** or your children, or your children's children unto the third and fourth generation, **I have delivered thine enemy into thine hands** [*you may go ahead and defend yourselves*];

> Did you see what happened between verse 29, above, and verse 30, next? Even though we are justified in defending ourselves, as stated in verse 29, there is a great reward for us and

our posterity if we still forgive as indicated in verse 30. The good examples given by patient and forgiving parents or grandparents continue to live on and influence their children and grandchildren down through the ages.

30 And **then if thou wilt spare him, thou shalt be rewarded** for thy righteousness; and **also thy children** and **thy children's children** unto the third and fourth generation.

> As previously mentioned, immediate danger to life and limb are covered by a different law. It is given in the last half of verse 31, next.

In Case of Immediate Danger to Life and Limb

31 **Nevertheless, thine enemy is in thine hands; and if thou rewardest him according to his works thou art justified** [*in other words, if you chose to extract justice from your enemy, at this point, you are not being wicked*]; **if he has sought thy life, and thy life is endangered by him, thine enemy is in thine hands and thou art justified** [*you may take immediate action; in other words, you do not give him the first three shots at point blank range*].

> In verses 32–38, the Master informs us that the laws of self-defense given in this revelation are those that He gave the righteous in ancient times, and they apply to nations as well as individuals.

32 Behold, **this is the law I gave unto my servant Nephi, and thy fathers** [*ancestors*], **Joseph,** and **Jacob,** and **Isaac,** and **Abraham,** and **all mine ancient prophets and apostles**.

33 And again, **this is the law that I gave unto mine ancients**, that **they should not go out unto battle against any nation, kindred, tongue, or people, save** [*unless*] **I, the Lord, commanded them**.

34 And **if any nation, tongue, or people should proclaim war against them**, they should **first lift a standard of peace** unto that people, nation, or tongue;

35 And **if that people did not accept** the offering of peace, **neither the second nor the third time**, they should **bring these testimonies before the Lord;**

36 **Then I, the Lord, would** give unto them a commandment, and **justify them in going out to battle** against that nation, tongue, or people.

> Those individuals and nations who adhere to these laws are entitled to special help from the Lord in battle.

37 And **I, the Lord, would fight**

their battles, and their children's battles, and their children's children's, until they had avenged themselves on all their enemies, to the third and fourth generation.

38 Behold, **this is an ensample** [*example; a precedent that may be safely followed*] **unto all people, saith the Lord your God, for justification before me** [*if you want to be justified in self-defense*].

> President David O. McKay summarized the doctrine of self-defense as follows:
>
> "There are, however, two conditions which may justify a truly Christian man to enter—mind you, I say enter, not begin—a war: (1) An attempt to dominate and to deprive another of his free agency, and (2) Loyalty to his country. Possibly there is a third, viz., Defense of a weak nation that is being unjustly crushed by a strong, ruthless one.
>
> "Paramount among these reasons, of course, is the defense of man's freedom. An attempt to rob man of his free agency caused dissension even in heaven....
>
> "To deprive an intelligent human being of his free agency is to commit the crime of the ages....
>
> "So fundamental in man's eternal progress is his inherent right to choose, that the Lord would defend it even at the price of war. Without freedom of thought, freedom of choice, freedom of action within lawful bounds, man cannot progress....
>
> "The greatest responsibility of the state is to guard the lives, and to protect the property and rights of its citizens; and if the state is obligated to protect its citizens from lawlessness within its boundaries, it is equally obligated to protect them from lawless encroachments from without—whether the attacking criminals be individuals or nations" (in Conference Report, April 1942, 72–73).

In verses 39–48, next, the Savior provides a summary of His laws of self-defense, emphasizing the importance of forgiving our enemies.

39 And again, verily I say unto you, **if** after thine enemy has come upon thee **the first time, he repent and come unto thee praying thy forgiveness, thou shalt forgive him**, and **shalt hold it no more as a testimony against thine enemy** [*this is, among other things, strong counsel not to hold grudges*]—

40 And so on unto the second and third time; and **as oft as thine enemy repenteth of the trespass wherewith he has trespassed against thee, thou shalt forgive**

him, until seventy times seven [*in effect, with no limits*].

> Remember we said earlier that these laws are those that gods follow. Verse 40, above, is similar to Mosiah 26:30, which says:
>
> "Yea, and as often as my people repent will I forgive them their trespasses against me."
>
> The extreme importance of our developing the ability to forgive others is obvious in light of the fact that Jesus repeats these laws yet again as this revelation draws to a close.

41 And **if he trespass against thee and repent not the first time, nevertheless thou shalt forgive him.**

42 And if he trespass against thee **the second time, and repent not, nevertheless thou shalt forgive him.**

43 And if he trespass against thee **the third time, and repent not, thou shalt also forgive him.**

> After so many offenses without repentance on the part of the offender, the matter is to be turned over to the Lord (compare with D&C 64:9–11).

44 But **if he trespass against thee the fourth time thou shalt not forgive him**, but shalt **bring these testimonies before the Lord**; and **they shall not be blotted out until he repent and reward thee** [*make restitution*] fourfold in all things wherewith he has trespassed against thee.

> Paying back "four fold" (verse 44, above) is most likely a reference to the laws of restitution given by Moses to the children of Israel. For example, if a man robbed a sheep from another, he was to restore four sheep as part of his repentance (see Exodus 22:1).
>
> Yet again, the importance of our forgiving others with all our heart is emphasized in verse 45, next.

45 And if he do this, **thou shalt forgive him with all thine heart**; and if he do not this, I, the Lord, will avenge thee of thine enemy an hundred-fold [*in other words, if he or she does not repent and make restitution, he or she will answer to the Lord in His own due time*];

> Verse 46 shows the natural consequence of bad example on the part of parents. It is natural that the pattern set by the parents influences their children down through the generations. But verses 47–48 teach that this chain can be broken at any time by righteous offspring (compare with Ezekiel 18).

46 And **upon his children, and upon his children's children of all them that hate me, unto the third and fourth generation.**

47 But if the children shall repent, or the children's children, and turn to the Lord their God, **with all their hearts** and with all their might, mind, and strength, **and restore four-fold for all their trespasses wherewith they have trespassed**, or wherewith their fathers have trespassed, or their fathers' fathers, then **thine indignation** [*your justifiable anger*] **shall be turned away**;

48 And vengeance shall no more come upon them, saith the Lord thy God, and **their trespasses shall never be brought any more as a testimony before the Lord against them.** Amen.

> The wording in the last half of verse 48, above, pertaining to the fact that we should forgive and forget when people ask us for forgiveness is similar to the rules that the Lord follows, as given in D&C 58:42–43 (**bold** added for emphasis).

D&C 58:42–43

42 Behold, he who has repented of his sins, the same is forgiven, and I, the Lord, remember them no more.

43 By this ye may know if a man repenteth of his sins—behold, he will confess them and forsake them.

SECTION 99

Background

This revelation was given through the Prophet Joseph Smith to John Murdock on August 29, 1832, at Hiram, Ohio. At the time of this revelation, Brother Murdock had been a widower with four living children for about fifteen months. His three oldest children were still under his care, and the fourth, a one-year-old daughter, had been adopted by Joseph and Emma Smith.

John Murdock was born on July 15, 1792. Thus, he was about thirteen and a half years older than Joseph Smith. Early in life, John had a vision in which he was asked if he were participating in the ordinances of the gospel. He was not. This led him to earnestly search for a religion that made gospel ordinances an important part of worship.

As he pursued his search for such a church, he joined several different religions, being ultimately disappointed with each. First, he joined a Lutheran sect but eventually decided that they did not follow the Bible. Next, he affiliated with the Presbyterians, then the Baptists, and after that, the Methodists. By 1827, he and his wife of just over three years, Julia, were residing in the Kirtland, Ohio, area where he had joined the Cambellite faith started by Alexander Campbell. However, he gradually became disappointed with them, too, because many Cambellites did not believe in the gift of the Holy Ghost as spoken of in the scriptures.

By the time Parley P. Pratt, Oliver Cowdery, Ziba Peterson, and Peter Whitmer Jr. came through the Kirtland, Ohio, area in the winter of 1830, preaching the restored gospel as they traveled to teach the Lamanites on the western frontier (D&C 32), John had decided that all religions were wrong because they had departed from the teachings of the Bible.

As a result, when he heard of the four missionaries and that they taught the restoration of the ancient church, he traveled twenty miles to hear them for himself. He read the Book of Mormon and knew it was true. Parley P. Pratt baptized him on November 5, 1830. He had already been baptized by immersion twice in other churches, but this time he felt the power and authority of the true priesthood and forgiveness of sins.

At the time of their baptism, John and his wife, Julia, had three children, and she was expecting twins. On April 30, 1831, she gave birth to a girl and a boy. Julia died six hours afterward. John named the girl Julia Murdock and the boy Joseph Smith Murdock. Emma Smith also gave birth the same day, but her twins, a girl, Louisa, and a boy, Thaddeus, lived only about three hours and died. In deep sorrow, John gave his twins to Joseph and Emma to raise.

On June 7, 1831, John Murdock was called to serve a mission to Missouri with Hyrum Smith (see D&C 52:8). Upon returning home, he found that his little son, Joseph, had died as a result of exposure after a mob broke into the home (March 24, 1832) where Joseph and Emma Smith were staying. The Prophet had stayed up late caring for little Joseph Smith Murdock, who was sick with the measles. The mob broke in and dragged the Prophet out over the frozen ground to tar and feather him. The door was left open, and the resulting cold air led to the baby's death.

Sometime during the winter of 1832–1833, John Murdock received a vision of the Savior. He said, "I saw the form of a man, most lovely, the visage of his face was sound and fair as the sun. His hair a bright silver grey, curled in most majestic form, His eyes a keen penetrating blue, and the skin of his neck a most beautiful white and he was covered from the neck to the feet with a loose garment, pure white, whiter than any garment I have ever before seen. His countenance was most penetrating, and yet most lovely" (Typescript of the journal of John Murdock, 18).

In section 99, Brother Murdock is called on another mission, this

SECTION 99

time to the "eastern countries" (verse 1). He will preach in the Kirtland area from September 1832 to April 1833, at which time he will depart on a mission to New York. He will serve for a year with his companion Zebedee Coltrin.

John will participate in Zion's Camp, serve a mission to New York beginning on March 5, 1835, and will marry Amoranda Turner on February 4, 1836, in New York. They will have no children. He will help settle Far West, Missouri, in 1836 and will serve on the high council there. His wife will die on August 16, 1837. He will marry Electa Allen on May 3, 1838, and they will have three children.

He will be ordained bishop of the Nauvoo Twentieth Ward on August 20, 1842, and will be called to serve a mission to the East in November 1844. His wife will die on October 16, 1845. He will marry Sarah Zuflet on March 13, 1846. They will have two children. In May 1846, he will go west with the Saints and serve as a high councilor, a bishop in Salt Lake City, and a delegate to the House of Representatives in 1849. John will be called to serve a mission to Australia and will serve for about two years, after which he will be released by President Brigham Young, who will gently tell him his missionary days are over and to come home permanently and be at peace. He will be called as a patriarch, serving many Saints in Utah County for thirteen years. He will reside in Lehi, Utah, from 1854 to 1867 and will die faithful to the Church on the Prophet Joseph Smith's birthday, December 23, 1871, at the age of seventy-nine in Beaver County, Utah.

We will now proceed with this revelation to John Murdock, given August 29, 1832.

1 BEHOLD, thus saith the Lord unto my servant John Murdock— **thou art called to go into the eastern countries** from house to house, from village to village, and from city to city, **to proclaim mine everlasting gospel** unto the inhabitants thereof, in the midst of persecution and wickedness.

> In verses 2–3, next, we are taught a simple truth, along with John Murdock, that when people receive the missionaries, they receive the Lord.

2 And **who receiveth you receiveth me**; and you shall have power to declare my word in the demonstration of my Holy Spirit [*you will have the help of the Holy Ghost in your teaching*].

3 And **who receiveth you as a little child** [*with pure, simple faith*], **receiveth my kingdom**; and blessed are they, for they shall obtain mercy.

4 And **whoso rejecteth you shall be rejected of my Father** and his house; and you shall **cleanse your feet** in the secret places [*not in public, which would stir people up against you unnecessarily*] by the way **for a testimony against them.**

> When we see the phrase "I come quickly," as in verse 5, next, we probably should not think of it as meaning "soon." Rather, we should know that when the Second Coming begins, there will be no more time for repenting, since He will come "quickly" or "suddenly" (D&C 133:2) when He comes.

5 And behold, and lo, **I come quickly** to judgment, to convince all of their ungodly deeds which they have committed against me, as it is written of me in the volume of the book [*perhaps meaning "in the scriptures," as in 2 Nephi 26:18, 1 Thessalonians 5:3, Mark 13:36, and so forth, but we don't know for sure*].

> As we approach verse 6, next, it is helpful to remember that although Brother Murdock had given the twins to Joseph and Emma to raise after Julia's death, he still had three older children whose ages would range from about seven down.

6 And now, verily I say unto you, that **it is not expedient** [*necessary*] **that you should go** [*on your mission to the East—verse 1*] **until your** [*three older*] **children are provided for,** and sent up kindly [*suitably, appropriately*] unto the bishop of Zion [*to Bishop Edward Partridge in Missouri who arranged for the children to be cared for by Latter-day Saint families there*].

> Next, in verses 7–8, we are reminded of another gospel principle—the Lord leaves many things up to our own choosing. There are many situations in which either choice would be righteous, and the Lord will support us in whichever we choose. You may wish to cross-reference these verses with D&C 58:26–28. In this case, the Savior is telling Brother Murdock, who loves missionary work, that after a few years he may settle down and stay home, or he may continue going on missions throughout his life.

7 And **after a few years, if thou desirest of me, thou mayest go up also unto the goodly land**, to possess thine inheritance;

8 **Otherwise thou shalt continue proclaiming my gospel until thou be taken** [*until the end of your life*]. Amen.

SECTION 100

Background

This revelation was given to the Prophet Joseph Smith and Sidney Rigdon on October 12, 1833, at Perrysburg in southwestern New

York, which was located about one hundred and forty miles northeast of Kirtland.

Having left Kirtland on October 5, 1833, they were going on a mission to Canada, preaching along the way. They returned home to Kirtland and their families on November 4, 1833. The Prophet recorded:

"*October 5.*—I started on a journey to the east, and to Canada, in company with Elders Rigdon and Freeman Nickerson, and arrived the same day at Lamb's tavern, in Ashtabula; and the day following, the Sabbath, we arrived in Springfield, whilst the brethren were in meeting, and Elder Rigdon spoke to the congregation. A large and attentive congregation assembled at Brother Rudd's in the evening, to whom we bore our testimony. We continued at Springfield until the 8th of October, when we removed to Brother Roundy's at Elk Creek; and continuing our journey on the evening of the 9th, we arrived at a tavern, and on the 10th, at Brother Job Lewis' in Westfield where we met the brethren according to previous appointment, and spoke to them as the Spirit gave utterance, greatly to their gratification.

"On the 11th of October, we left Westfield, and continuing our journey, staid that night with a man named Nash . . . with whom we reasoned, but to no purpose. On the 12th, arrived at Father Nickerson's, at Perrysburg, New York, where I received the following revelation [section 100]" (*History of the Church*, 1:416–17, 419–20).

In footnote 6, for *History of the Church*, 1:419, we are informed of an entry made by the Prophet in his private journal, in his own handwriting, on October 11, 1833. He said, "I feel very well in my mind. The Lord is with us, but have much anxiety about my family" (Joseph's journal, 7. See also *The Joseph Smith Papers, Documents, Volume 3: February 1833– March 1833*, 321–23).

Having received this revelation in section 100, Joseph and Sidney then continued to Canada where they preached for over a week, baptizing fourteen people.

Knowing that Joseph was worried about being away from his family, we hear the Lord's answer to his concern, next, in verse 1.

1 VERILY, thus saith the Lord unto you, **my friends** Sidney and Joseph, **your families are well; they are in mine hands**, and I will do with them as seemeth me good; for in me there is all power.

We will pause for just a moment to consider the significance of the Lord's calling these brethren His "friends" in verse 1 and elsewhere in the Doctrine and Covenants. While many religions teach that God is unapproachable and that it is blasphemous and demeaning to God to even think that one could have a tender relationship with Him, others believe that it is proper and appropriate for one to think of God as being approachable and near. The debate continues among other groups, but the answer is given here by pure revelation. "Friends" is a term of closeness, approachability, and endearment.

2 Therefore, follow me, and **listen to the counsel which I shall give unto you.**

3 Behold, and lo, **I have much people in this place, in the regions round about**; and **an effectual door shall be opened** [*Joseph and Sidney are opening an effective door for future missionary work in Canada as well as in New York*] **in the regions round about in this eastern land.**

> Verse 3 is prophetic. Many converts will come from Canada through this "door," including John Taylor, who will eventually serve as the third president of the Church.

4 **Therefore** [*for this reason*], **I, the Lord, have suffered you to come unto this place** [*have permitted and requested you to come here, even though you are needed at home*]; **for thus it was expedient in me** [*it was necessary*] **for the salvation of souls.**

5 Therefore, verily I say unto you, **lift up your voices unto this people; speak the thoughts that I shall put into your hearts, and you shall not be confounded** [*confused and stopped*] before men;

> Verse 6, next, contains a promise that can apply to all of us as we serve in our callings to teach and preach. It happens often to missionaries, to teachers in the classroom, to speakers in sacrament meetings and so forth.

6 For **it shall be given you in the very hour, yea, in the very moment, what ye shall say.**

> When the Spirit of the Lord helps us, as stated in verse 6, above, things often go very well, and it could be tempting to take glory to ourselves and become prideful. In verses 7–8, next, we are reminded that we must remain humble and speak with reverence about the blessings we receive.

7 But a commandment I give unto you, that **ye shall declare whatsoever thing ye declare** in my name, **in solemnity of heart, in the spirit of meekness** [*in humility*], in all things.

8 And I give unto you this promise, that **inasmuch as ye do this the Holy Ghost shall be shed**

forth in bearing record unto all things whatsoever ye shall say.

> Next, in verses 9–11, Sidney Rigdon is given specific instructions by the Savior regarding his role compared to the role of the Prophet. He is to represent the Prophet to the people, whereas, Joseph is to represent the Lord to him. It is vital for Sidney not to begin thinking that he is the prophet.

9 And it is expedient in me that you, my servant **Sidney, should be a spokesman unto this people**; yea, verily, I will ordain you unto this calling, even to be **a spokesman unto my servant Joseph.**

10 And **I will give unto him** [*Joseph Smith*] **power to be mighty in testimony.**

11 And **I will give unto thee** [*Sidney Rigdon*] **power to be mighty in expounding** [*teaching and explaining*] **all scriptures**, that **thou** [*Sidney*] **mayest be a spokesman unto him**, and **he** [*Joseph*] **shall be a revelator unto thee**, that thou mayest know the certainty of all things pertaining to the things of my kingdom on the earth.

12 Therefore, **continue your journey and let your hearts rejoice**; for behold, and lo, I am with you even unto the end.

> As this revelation concludes, the Savior gives counsel regarding the status of Zion in Jackson County, Missouri. At this time in 1833, acts of mob violence are commonly occurring there, and the members of the Church will soon be driven from Jackson County.
>
> In late August 1833, Orson Hyde and John Gould (verse 14) had been sent from Kirtland on the dangerous journey to Jackson County with instructions to the Missouri Saints.
>
> First, in verse 13, next, we learn that Zion will someday be redeemed. However, she will be "chastened for a little season." From our vantage point in time, we see that this "little season" was to last many years. The day will yet come when the prophecies about building Zion and the New Jerusalem in Missouri will be fulfilled (see 3 Nephi 20:22; 21:23–25; Ether 13:2–6; D&C 45:65–69; 84:2–4).

13 And now I give unto you a word concerning Zion. **Zion shall be redeemed, although she is chastened for a little season.**

14 Thy brethren, my servants **Orson Hyde and John Gould, are in my hands**; and inasmuch as they keep my commandments they shall be saved.

> A quote from the 2018 *Doctrine and Covenants Student Manual* helps us understand verse 14, above.

"In late August 1833 the Prophet Joseph Smith sent Orson Hyde and John Gould to Jackson County, Missouri, with letters and other documents to comfort the suffering Church members there. These two men returned to Kirtland, Ohio, on November 25, 1833, with the unfortunate news that attacks on the Saints in Jackson County had resumed. (See *The Joseph Smith Papers, Documents, Volume 3: February 1833–March, 1834*, 325, note 39.)"

There is an important message for all of us in verse 15, next. This message is particularly helpful at times when things are not going as we expected and prayed for.

15 Therefore, **let your hearts be comforted**; for **all things shall work together for good to them that walk uprightly**, and to the sanctification of the church.

16 **For I will raise up unto myself a pure people, that will serve me in righteousness** [*the reason for the delay in building up Zion at this time in Jackson County*];

17 And **all that call upon the name of the Lord, and keep his commandments, shall be saved** [*in celestial glory*]. Even so. Amen.

SECTION 101

Background

This revelation was given to the Prophet Joseph Smith on December 16 and 17, 1833, at Kirtland, Ohio. It explains why the members of the Church in Missouri had been driven from their homes in Zion.

Beginning in July 1833, mobs began attacking the Saints in Zion (Jackson County, Missouri), destroying their homes and driving them from the county. During the night of Thursday, October 31, 1833, "a mob of about fifty horsemen attacked the Whitmer Settlement on the Big Blue River west of Independence. They unroofed thirteen houses and nearly whipped to death several men, including Hiram Page, one of the eight witnesses of the Book of Mormon" (*Church History in the Fulness of Times*, 135–36).

On November 25, 1833, Joseph Smith learned that mobs had driven the Saints from Jackson County. This news caused him great sorrow. On December 10, 1833, he wrote a letter to the Church leaders in Missouri in which he said:

"I have always expected that Zion would suffer some affliction, from what I could learn from the commandments which have been given.... I know that Zion, in the own due time of the Lord will be redeemed; but how many will be the days of her purification, tribulation and affliction, the Lord has kept hid from my eyes; and when I enquire concerning this subject, the voice of the Lord is, Be still, and know that I am God! All those who suffer for my name shall reign with me, and he that layeth down his life for my sake, shall find it again. Now, there are two things of which I am ignorant, and the Lord will not shew them [unto] me; . . . why God hath suffered so great calamity to come upon Zion; and what the great moving cause of this great affliction is: And again, by what means he will return her back to her inheritance" (in *Manuscript History of the Church*, vol. A-1, page 393, josephsmithpapers.org). Joseph continued praying for answers, and finally, on December 16 and 17, he received this revelation now known as section 101.

By the time of this revelation, most Church members in Jackson County had fled across the Missouri River into Clay County, Missouri, where local citizens helped them by offering shelter, food, clothing, and work as much as their own circumstances permitted. The Saints lived in abandoned slave cabins, built crude shacks, and lived in tents throughout the rest of the winter. Members of the mobs in Jackson County called the citizens of Clay County "Jack-Mormons" because they were friendly toward the Mormons.

Needless to say, this was a great disappointment to the members of the Church. They had anticipated that Zion would be built up at this time in Missouri and looked forward to being a part of it. As we look back, we see that many were doing well at living the gospel as required to establish a Zion society. But many were not (see verse 41). They had been warned many times by the Lord that they must do better at being true followers of Christ if they were to establish Zion. They were warned in D&C 97:26 that if they did not repent and do better at being true Saints, they would be subject to "sore affliction, with pestilence, with plague, with sword, with vengeance, with devouring fire."

This should be somewhat sobering and thought-provoking to us since we are constantly being counseled by the Lord to do better at keeping the Sabbath Day holy, avoiding the evils that surround us, studying the scriptures, carrying out our ministering sisters and ministering brothers service, and so forth.

Because section 101 is such a major revelation in the Doctrine and Covenants and contains such significant doctrine, counsel, and perspective, we will take extra time here to give a somewhat detailed overview. If you "stand back" and look at it as a whole, you will see that the Lord begins by explaining why these Saints have been driven from their lands and homes (verses 1–8). He then holds out hope to them (verse 9) and gives them perspective, telling them that the day is coming when troubles and punishments will be poured out upon the whole earth because of wickedness, which will ultimately open the doors for His people to build up the Church (verses 10–11).

Perspective of future blessings can provide strength and encouragement to endure present troubles. The Savior next takes the minds and hearts of these battered Saints into the future, showing them the gathering of Israel (verses 12–13), the comforting of the faithful who have been persecuted (verses 14–16), giving assurance that Zion will yet be established (verses 17–21), and promising that the faithful among them will participate in the glory that will accompany His Second Coming (verses 22–35). This blessing will come upon the faithful Saints, whether living or dead (see D&C 88:96–98). In addition, the faithful will have all their questions answered at the beginning of the Millennium (verse 32).

Continuing to give perspective, the Savior reminds the members in Missouri, as well as those in the Kirtland area, that the highest joys and blessings come to the faithful in the next life, and that one should work even more diligently to care for the soul than for physical life (verses 36–38). A major role and obligation of true Saints is to be the "salt of the earth," which includes being a good example to others regardless of circumstances (verses 39–40).

Next, in verses 41–62, the Master Teacher sets the stage and then gives a parable, which once again explains why the Saints in Missouri were driven out, thus failing to establish Zion at this time. The Savior continues by emphasizing the work of gathering that must continue and by reviewing the parable of the wheat and the tares, implying that the "tares" among the Missouri Saints were the cause of the members being driven out of Jackson County (verses 63–66). Tares will be found among the Church membership until the Second Coming, but it's comforting to know that the "tares" in the Church often convert to "wheat."

Even though the members of the Church have been driven out of Jackson County, all members are given another opportunity to demonstrate their faith in the Lord by continuing to purchase land in Jackson County (verses 67–75). This may be one of the most difficult tests of all for the members at this time in history (see verse 75).

Another very difficult issue was the fact that the Saints were not protected by the Constitution, because local and state officials in Missouri refused to enforce the constitutional rights of the Latter-day Saints.

Thus, the value and importance of the Constitution of the United States was in doubt in the minds of many. In verses 76–80, the Savior leaves no doubt as to the validity and importance of this inspired document.

In verses 81–95, Jesus gives instructions that the Saints themselves are to adhere to the constitutional laws of the land and are to follow those laws in attempting to get redress and justice.

Finally, in verses 96–101, the Church is given specific instructions regarding land and property in Missouri owned by members.

With this overview as background, we will now begin our verse-by-verse study of this section. As stated previously, in verses 1–8 the Lord gives the reasons for the Saints not being allowed to establish Zion at this time. Remember that this revelation was given to Joseph Smith in Kirtland, Ohio, informing him and others about the situation in Jackson County.

1 VERILY I say unto you, **concerning your brethren** [*the members of the Church in Jackson County, Missouri*] **who have been** afflicted, and persecuted, and **cast out from the land of their inheritance**—

2 **I, the Lord, have suffered** [*permitted*] **the affliction** to come upon them, wherewith they have been afflicted, **in consequence of their transgressions**;

> Note the encouragement given in verse 3, next. This can apply to all of us who diligently and humbly repent as needed.

3 **Yet I will own them**, and **they shall be mine** in that day when I shall come to make up my jewels [*when He assigns people to celestial glory*].

4 Therefore, **they must needs be chastened** [*scolded and punished for wrongdoing*] **and tried** [*tested*], even as Abraham, who was commanded to offer up his only son [*see Genesis 22:1–14; Hebrews 11:17–19*].

5 For **all those who will not endure chastening** [*those who will not accept correction from God*], **but deny me, cannot be sanctified**.

> Remember that the laws upon which Zion is to be established are the same laws that apply to the celestial kingdom (see D&C 105:5). Harmony, purity, and pleasantness are among these laws. We would all do well to seek to avoid succumbing to the sins and tendencies listed in verses 6–8, next.

6 Behold, I say unto you, there were **jarrings**, and **contentions**, and **envyings**, and **strifes**, and **lustful and covetous desires**

among them; therefore **by these things they polluted their inheritances** [*in other words, they ruined their opportunity to build a Zion society*].

7 They were slow to hearken unto the voice of the Lord their God; therefore, the Lord their God is slow to hearken unto their prayers, to answer them in the day of their trouble.

8 In the day of their peace they esteemed lightly my counsel; but, in the day of their trouble, of necessity they feel after me.

> Verse 9, next, assures that the law of mercy can still be made active in behalf of those who have fallen short through the sins mentioned in verses 6–8, above.

9 Verily I say unto you, notwithstanding [*in spite of*] **their sins, my bowels** [*a scriptural term meaning the deepest center of feeling and tenderness*] **are filled with compassion towards them**. I will not utterly cast them off; and in the day of wrath I will remember mercy.

> Next, in verses 10–11, we are taught that the days will come when the wicked who persecute the righteous will feel the wrath of God. This is one of the "signs of the times" (prophecies that will be fulfilled in the last days before the Second Coming). One of many references to this is found in D&C 88:89–91.

10 I have sworn [*promised*], and the decree hath gone forth by a former commandment which I have given unto you [*see D&C 1:13–14*], **that I would let fall the sword of mine indignation** [*righteous anger*] **in behalf of my people**; and even as I have said, it shall come to pass.

11 Mine indignation is soon to be poured out without measure [*without limits*] **upon all nations**; and this will I do when the cup of their iniquity [*their wickedness*] is full.

> Some people get impatient, hoping that the Lord will smite the wicked now. They have apparently missed the last of verse 11, above, where it says, in effect, that the wicked will feel the anger of God when "the cup of their iniquity is full," meaning when they have become extremely wicked.
>
> Next, the Savior gives counsel as to how we can be saved, and foretells the gathering of Israel and the rewarding of the righteous.

12 And in that day [*when pestilence, plagues, natural disasters, and so forth are poured out upon the earth because of wickedness*] **all who are found upon the**

watch-tower [*who have gathered to the gospel and joined with the prophets who watch for and defend against evil*], **or in other words, all mine Israel** [*all of Israel who have come to Christ*], **shall be saved.**

13 And they that have been scattered shall be gathered [*this would be especially comforting to the Saints in Jackson County who have been "scattered" from their homes and lands in Zion*].

14 And all they who have mourned shall be comforted.

15 And all they who have given their lives for my name shall be crowned.

16 Therefore, let your hearts be comforted concerning Zion; for all flesh is in mine hands; be still and know that I am God.

Next, we are taught that the location for the city of Zion, the New Jerusalem, has not been changed. It will yet be built in Independence, Jackson County, Missouri.

Doctrine
Zion, New Jerusalem will yet be built in Jackson County, Missouri.

17 Zion shall not be moved out of her place, notwithstanding [*even though*] her children [*the members of the Church in Jackson County in 1833*] are scattered.

By the way, did you know that the Garden of Eden was located where the city of Zion will be built? Joseph Fielding Smith taught this as follows:

"In accord with the revelations given to the Prophet Joseph Smith, we teach that the Garden of Eden was on the American continent located where the City Zion, or the New Jerusalem, will be built. When Adam and Eve were driven out of the Garden, they eventually dwelt at a place called Adam-ondi-Ahman, situated in what is now Daviess County, Missouri" (*Doctrines of Salvation,* 3:74).

18 They that remain [*likely meaning the righteous remnant of Israel in the last days who are gathered to the gospel*]**, and are pure in heart, shall return, and come to their inheritances** [*will help build the city of Zion*]**, they and their children, with songs of everlasting joy, to build up the waste places of Zion—**

19 And all these things [*will take place in order*] **that the prophets might be fulfilled** [*in order that the prophecies about Zion given by the Lord's prophets might be fulfilled*].

In verses 20–21, next, the Savior tells these early Saints that as the latter-day gathering of Israel goes forth, the day will come when stakes of Zion will be added as gathering places for the Lord's people throughout the world. We are witnessing the fulfillment of this prophecy on a grand scale in our day!

20 And, behold, **there is none other place appointed** than that which I have appointed; neither shall there be any other place appointed than that which I have appointed, **for the work of the gathering of my saints—**

21 **Until the day cometh when there is found no more room for them**; and then **I have other places which I will appoint unto them, and they shall be called stakes**, for the curtains or the strength of Zion.

> The counsel given at the end of verse 22, next, applies to all of us as we prepare to meet the Savior (verse 23), whether it is at His Coming or when we die, if we pass away before He comes.

22 Behold, it is my will, that **all they who call on my name, and worship me according to mine everlasting gospel, should gather together, and stand in holy places** [*such as temples, righteous homes, church, seminaries and institutes of religion, associating with righteous friends, and so forth*];

Doctrine
Everyone will see the Savior when He comes again. This includes those who have already died and are in the spirit world.

23 And **prepare for the revelation which is to come** [*the Second Coming*], **when the veil** [*which keeps us from seeing heaven and the spirits around us, etc.*] of the covering of my temple, in my tabernacle, **which hideth the earth, shall be taken off**, and **all flesh shall see me together** [*at the same time*].

> Orson Pratt taught that it will not only be those living at the time of the Second Coming who will see the coming Lord. The dead will also see Him. Elder Pratt said (**bold** added for emphasis):
>
> "The second advent of the Son of God is to be something . . . accompanied with great power and glory, something that will not be done in a small portion of the earth like Palestine, and seen only by a few; but it will be an event that will be seen by all—all flesh shall see the glory of the Lord; when he reveals himself the second time, every eye, **not only those living at that time in the flesh, in mortality on the earth, but also the very dead themselves**" (*Journal of Discourses*, 18:170; also quoted in the 1981

Doctrine and Covenants Student Manual, 241).

Revelation 1:7 teaches that "every eye shall see him" and that even those who crucified Him will see His coming. We will quote the verse here:

Revelation 1:7

7 Behold, he cometh with **clouds** [*from heaven in glory*]; and every eye shall see him, and they *also* which pierced him [*those who crucified Him*]: and all [*the wicked*] kindreds of the earth shall wail because of him. Even so, Amen.

Watch now as the Savior takes the minds of these Saints into a "high mountain," high above their present troubles and concerns, and gives them perspective and details about His Second Coming (verses 23, 25, 32–34), the destruction of all "corruptible" things (verse 24), and the Millennium (verses 25–31, 35).

Since we understand that animals, birds, fish, and so forth, are not capable of sin, we interpret "every corruptible thing" in verse 24, next, as being a symbolic statement that anything that would disturb the peace and righteousness on earth as the thousand years of peace begins will be destroyed at the time of the Second Coming.

Doctrine

All things that do not belong on earth during the Millennium (including wicked people, pornographic materials, the occult, things that promote evil, destroy peace, and so forth) will be burned by the glory of the coming Christ. See D&C 5:19.

24 And every corruptible thing, both of man, or of the beasts of the field, or of the fowls of the heavens, or of the fish of the sea, that dwells upon all the face of the earth, **shall be consumed;**

25 And also that of **element shall melt with fervent heat;** and **all things shall become new** [*"the earth will be renewed and receive its paradisiacal glory"—tenth article of faith*]**, that my knowledge and glory may dwell upon all the earth.**

Doctrine

There will be peace on earth during the Millennium.

26 And **in that day** [*during the Millennium*] the enmity [*animosity*] of man, and the enmity of beasts, yea, **the enmity of all flesh, shall cease** from before my face [*in other words, the Millennium will truly be a time of peace*].

It appears from verse 27, next, that among other things, because of personal righteousness during the Millennium, people will be close enough to the Spirit to know what they may ask for and thus will have their requests granted (compare with D&C 46:30; 50:30).

27 And in that day whatsoever any man shall ask, it shall be given unto him.

People sometimes wonder whether Satan will literally be bound by God's power during the Millennium so he can't even try to tempt, or if he will go about tempting but no one will listen. The answer is given in verse 28, next.

Doctrine
Satan will not be allowed to tempt mortals on earth during the Millennium.

28 And in that day [*during the Millennium*] **Satan shall not have power to tempt any man.**

Occasionally someone refers to 1 Nephi 22:26 and asserts that it will be "because of the righteousness of his people" that "Satan has no power" during the Millennium. In other words, Satan will still be here, tempting and attempting to lead people astray, but no one will follow him. Joseph Fielding Smith addressed this issue as follows:

"There are many among us who teach that the binding of Satan will be merely the binding which those dwelling on the earth will place upon him by their refusal to hear his enticings. This is not so. He will not have the privilege during that period of time to tempt any man. (D. & C. 101:28)" (*Church History and Modern Revelation*, 1:192).

Next, in verses 29–31, the Savior teaches these Saints who are refugees from mob violence and have lost loved ones that there will be no death as we know it (in the sense of mourning, having funerals, burying loved ones, and so forth) during the Millennium. During the thousand years of peace, people will die but will be resurrected in the "twinkling of an eye" (verse 31).

29 And there shall be no sorrow because there is no death [*as we have come to know it, burying loved ones in graves until we meet again*].

30 In that day [*during the Millennium*] **an infant shall not die until he is old; and his life shall be as the age of a tree;**

The "age of a tree," as given at the end of verse 29, above, means one hundred years old (see Isaiah 65:20). Elder Joseph Fielding Smith taught (**bold** added for emphasis):

"When Christ comes the saints who are on the earth will be quickened and caught up to meet him. This does not mean that those who are living in mortality at that time will be changed and pass through the resurrection, for mortals must remain on the earth until after the thousand years are ended. A change, nevertheless, will come over all who remain on the earth; they will be quickened so that they will not be subject unto death until they are old. **Men shall die when they are one hundred years of age**, and the change shall be made suddenly to the immortal state. Graves will not be made during this thousand years. . . . death shall come as a peaceful transition from the mortal to the immortal state" (*Way to Perfection*, 298–99, 311).

31 And **when he dies he shall not sleep**, that is to say **in the earth** [*he will not be buried in a grave*], **but shall be changed in the twinkling of an eye**, and shall be caught up, and his rest shall be glorious.

Doctrine

All of our questions will be answered at the beginning of the Millennium, including how the earth was created, how long it took, the role of dinosaurs, and so forth (see verses 32–34).

32 Yea, verily I say unto you, **in that day when the Lord shall come, he shall reveal all things—**

33 Things which have passed, and hidden things which no man knew, **things of the earth, by which it was made**, and the purpose and the end thereof—

34 **Things most precious**, things that are above, and things that are beneath, things that are in the earth, and upon the earth, and in heaven.

Apostle Bruce R. McConkie taught us what "reveal all things" (verse 32) includes:

"All things are to be revealed in the millennial day. The sealed part of the Book of Mormon will come forth; the brass plates will be translated; the writings of Adam and Enoch and Noah and Abraham and prophets without number will be revealed. We shall learn a thousand times more about the earthly ministry of the Lord Jesus than we now know. We shall learn great mysteries of the kingdom that were not even known to those of old who walked and talked with the Eternal One. We shall learn the details of the creation and the origin of man."

Elder McConkie concluded that in the millennial day, "Nothing in or on or over the earth will be withheld" (*The Millennial Messiah: The Second Coming of the Son of Man*, 676.

Next, in verses 35–38, the Savior gives us a brief lesson in eternal perspective.

35 And **all they who suffer persecution for my name, and endure in faith**, though they are called to lay down their lives for my sake **yet shall they partake of all this glory** [*spoken of in verses 23–34, above*].

36 Wherefore, **fear not even unto death**; for **in this world your joy is not full, but in me your joy is full**.

> In verse 37, next, we are counseled not to make physical well-being a priority over spiritual well-being.

37 Therefore, **care not for the body, neither the life of the body; but care for the soul, and for the life of the soul**.

38 And **seek the face of the Lord always, that in patience ye may possess your souls, and ye shall have eternal life** [*"eternal life," as used in the scriptures, always means "exaltation" in the highest degree of glory in the celestial kingdom, or, in other words, becoming gods and living in our own family units forever*].

> One of the things we are taught in verses 39–40, next, is that when we make covenants with God, we are covenanting to be the "salt of the earth." In other words, we commit to be an influence for good and to spread the gospel by word and deed throughout our lives.

39 **When men** are called unto mine everlasting gospel, and **covenant with an everlasting covenant, they are accounted as the salt of the earth** and the savor of men [*they add pleasantness and goodness to people's lives*];

40 **They are called to be the savor of men**; therefore, **if that salt of the earth lose its savor** [*if they do not keep these covenants to live the gospel and be an influence for good, etc.*], behold, **it is thenceforth good for nothing** only to be cast out and trodden under the feet of men.

> Next, in verses 41–42, the Lord specifically addresses the issue of the Saints' having been driven out of Jackson County.

41 Behold, **here is wisdom** [*counsel*] **concerning the children of Zion** [*the members who were driven out of Zion in Jackson County, Missouri*], even **many, but not all**; they **were found transgressors, therefore they must needs be chastened** [*corrected and disciplined*]—

42 **He that exalteth himself** [*is prideful*] **shall be abased** [*humbled*], **and he that abaseth** [*humbles*] **himself shall be exalted** [*strengthened and supported by the Lord*].

SECTION 101

Next, the Savior gives a parable explaining why the Saints were driven from Jackson County. This parable is a strong witness of the fact that Joseph Smith was a prophet of God. It consists of verses 44–62.

As with all parables, there can be different levels of meaning and interpretation. As we go through it, we will provide one possible interpretation. You will likely see additional possibilities.

Parable

43 And now, I will show unto you a parable, that you may know my will **concerning the redemption of Zion.**

44 A certain nobleman [*Christ—see verse 52*] had a **spot of land** [*Zion, in Jackson County, Missouri*], **very choice; and he said unto his servants** [*members of the Church who were called to go to Zion*]: **Go ye unto my vineyard** [*Jackson County*], **even upon this very choice piece of land** [*Zion*], **and plant twelve olive-trees** [*establish Latter-day Saint settlements*];

Twelve, in scriptural symbolism, means "God's divine organization and work." Thus, twelve in verse 44, above, would not literally mean twelve settlements but rather communities that represent God and His work.

45 And set **watchmen** [*prophets; Church leaders*] round about them, and build a **tower** [*temple*], that **one** [*the local leaders of the Church*] **may overlook the land round about** [*may see and spot approaching danger, especially spiritual dangers*], **to be a watchman upon the tower** [*to guard against the evils and dangers of the world*], **that mine olive-trees** [*covenant Israel; the members and their new settlements*] **may not be broken down when the enemy shall** [*not if but when dangers come*] **come to spoil** and take upon themselves the fruit of my vineyard.

46 Now, **the servants of the nobleman** [*the Saints who went to Missouri*] went and did as their lord commanded them [*moved to the land of Zion*], and planted the olive-trees [*established Latter-day Saint settlements*], and **built a hedge round about** [*established their territory*], and **set watchmen** [*local leaders of the Church*], and **began to build a tower** [*began to build a temple*].

Remember that the Lord had already designated the site for this temple (see D&C 57:3), and the Prophet Joseph Smith had already dedicated it (see D&C 84:3).

Watch now, as the parable continues, how the members

in Zion rationalized away the importance of the temple and began making their own rules and priorities rather than obeying the Lord's commandments.

47 And **while they were yet laying the foundation thereof** [*of the temple; they did lay the cornerstones of the temple*]**, they began to say among themselves: And what need hath my lord of this tower?**

48 **And consulted for a long time** [*began procrastinating*]**, saying among themselves: What need hath my lord of this tower, seeing this is a time of peace?** [*See verse 8.*]

49 **Might not this money be given to the exchangers?** [*Couldn't we make better use of this money?*] For **there is no need of these things.**

> Remember, the Lord said in verse 41 that some were faithful but others were not. This obviously led to disharmony, "jarrings and contentions" (verse 6), which are not compatible with the celestial laws and principles upon which Zion was to be established (D&C 105:5).
>
> As we see, beginning with verse 50, next, because of such lack of harmony and unity with respect to commitments and covenants each of them had already made with the Lord, they lost His help, which

opened the door to mob violence against them and the failure to establish Zion at that time.

50 And **while they were at variance one with another they became very slothful, and they hearkened not unto the commandments of their lord.**

51 **And the enemy came by night** [*symbolizing that they did not expect trouble*]**, and broke down the hedge** [*broke through the inadequate defenses of the Saints, spiritually as well as physically*]**; and the servants of the nobleman** [*the members of the Church in Zion*] **arose and were affrighted, and fled; and the enemy** [*the mobs, symbolic of Satan*] **destroyed their works, and broke down the olive-trees** [*destroyed the Saints' settlements in Zion*]**.**

> Next, the Lord chastens these members for failing to obey His commandments and establish Zion.

52 Now, **behold, the nobleman, the lord of the vineyard, called upon his servants, and said** unto them, **Why! what is the cause of this great evil?**

53 **Ought ye not to have done even as I commanded you, and**—after ye had planted the vineyard, and built the hedge

round about, and set watchmen upon the walls thereof—**built the tower also, and set a watchman upon the tower, and watched for my vineyard, and not have fallen asleep, lest the enemy should come upon you?**

> Verse 54, next, gives us strong reason to carefully study and heed the words of our living prophets!

54 And behold, **the watchman upon the tower would have seen the enemy while he was yet afar off**; and **then ye could have made ready** and kept the enemy from breaking down the hedge thereof, **and saved my vineyard from the hands of the destroyer.**

> Next, beginning with verse 55, Joseph Smith is instructed to gather a small army from the members in the Kirtland area and elsewhere, which will become known as Zion's Camp. They are to march to Missouri to help the Saints there.

55 And **the lord of the vineyard** [*Christ*] **said unto one of his servants** [*Joseph Smith—see D&C 103:21*]: **Go and gather together the residue of my servants** [*in the Kirtland area*], **and take** all the strength of mine house, which are **my warriors**, my young men, and they that are of middle age also among all my servants, who are the strength of mine house, save [*except*] those only whom I have appointed to tarry [*those who are to remain behind to lead the Church while Joseph and the others march the nine hundred miles to Missouri*];

56 **And go ye** straightway [*right away*] **unto the land of my vineyard** [*Jackson County, Missouri*], and **redeem my vineyard**; for it is mine; **I have bought it with money** [*the Saints in Zion had paid for their properties and had legal title to the lands from which they were driven*].

> As you can see, verse 57, next, contains terms and symbolism of warfare in ancient times.

57 **Therefore, get ye straightway** [*right away*] **unto my land; break down the walls of mine enemies; throw down their tower, and scatter their watchmen.**

> Have you noticed that there is a significant lesson in the timing of the Lord in these verses? We see the phrase "by and by" in verse 58, next. And in verses 59–60, we see the servant asking, in effect, when will Zion be redeemed? And the Lord answers, "When I will." One of the lessons we must learn is that when the Lord commands, we must obey—now. In some cases, people basically say that they will obey after they see the blessings and make sure that they make the

effort to obey worthwhile. That is not how it works.

In this case, the Saints are told what to do "straightway" (verses 56–57, 60, 62), but the desired results will take place "when I will" (verse 60)—in other words, in the Lord's due time.

58 And inasmuch as they gather together against you, avenge me of mine enemies, **that by and by** [*eventually, in the Lord's due time*] **I may come with the residue** [*perhaps meaning the righteous remnant of Israel—compare with 3 Nephi 5:24; Ether 13:10*] **of mine house and possess the land.**

59 **And the servant said unto his lord: When shall these things be?**

60 And he said unto his servant: **When I will**; go ye straightway, and **do all things whatsoever I have commanded you;**

In verse 61, next, the Savior compliments and gives approval to His prophet, Joseph Smith. At the end of verse 62, we see that it will be a long time before Zion will be established in Missouri.

61 And **this shall be my seal** [*the Lord's approval and covenant*] **and blessing upon you** [*Joseph Smith—see verse 55*]—**a faithful and wise steward in the midst of mine house, a ruler in my kingdom.**

62 And **his servant went straightway, and did all things whatsoever his lord commanded him**; and **after many days all things were fulfilled.**

In the *Doctrine and Covenants Student Manual,* 1981 edition, page 243, which is used by the institutes of religion of the Church, a quote by Sidney B. Sperry is given in which he explains the above parable as follows:

"It would seem that the parable is to be interpreted in this way: the nobleman is the Lord, whose choice land in His vineyard is Zion in Missouri. The places where the Saints live in Zion are the olive trees. The servants are the Latter-day Saint settlers, and the watchmen are their officers in the Church. While yet building in Zion, they become at variance with each other and do not build the tower or Temple whose site had been dedicated as early as August 3, 1831. Had they built it as directed, it would have been a spiritual refuge for them, for from it the Lord's watchmen could have seen by revelation the movements of the enemy from afar. This foreknowledge would have saved them and their hard work when the enemy made his assault.

"But the Saints in Missouri were slothful, lax, and asleep. The enemy came, and the Missouri persecutions were the result. The Lord's people were scattered and much of their labors wasted. The Almighty rebuked His people, as we have already seen, but He commanded one of His servants (v. 55), Joseph Smith (103:21), to gather the 'strength of Mine house' and rescue His lands and possessions gathered against them.

"Subsequently, the Prophet and his brethren in the famous Zion's Camp did go to Missouri in 1834 in an attempt to carry out the terms of the parable. Before they went, additional revelation was received (see 103:21–28) concerning the redemption of Zion. The brethren were instructed to try to buy land in Missouri, not to use force; and if the enemy came against them, they were to bring a curse upon them. Zion was not redeemed at that time but we may look for it in the not-too-distant future. Verily, it will be redeemed when the Lord wills it (*Compendium*, 521–22)."

That same manual goes on to say:

"Though Joseph Smith followed the Lord's instructions to gather together the 'strength of my house' (D&C 103:22) by organizing Zion's Camp to go forth to redeem Zion, the Lord's purpose in sending them and his will concerning the redemption of Zion were not fully understood by his people. The redemption of Zion did not take place at that time. When the servant in the parable asked when the land would be possessed, the Lord responded, 'When I will' (D&C 101:60).

"The parable further states that all things will be fulfilled 'after many days' (v. 62), which passage indicates that a long period of time will pass before Zion will be redeemed. The redemption of Zion still had not taken place even after the Saints had been expelled from Missouri and from Nauvoo. The Lord then told Brigham Young that 'Zion shall be redeemed in mine own due time' (D&C 136:18). The redemption of Zion (meaning, the city of New Jerusalem in Missouri) is still future, although of course it is much closer now than it was when the Saints first sought to regain their inheritance in the land of Zion.

"The time of Zion's redemption is referred to in Doctrine and Covenants 58:44; 105:15, 37. Compare the parable in Doctrine and Covenants 101 with those given in Isaiah 5:1–7 and Matthew 21:33–46."

The Savior now changes the subject to the importance of continuing the work of gathering the Saints in many different locations. In verse 63, next, He implies that all the Saints can learn wisdom if they are willing to listen more effectively than they have in the past.

63 Again, verily I say unto you,

I will show unto you wisdom in me concerning all the churches [*groups, branches, wards, stakes, and the like*], **inasmuch as** [*if*] **they are willing to be guided in a right and proper way for their salvation—**

64 **That the work of the gathering** together of my saints **may continue**, that I may build them up unto my name upon holy places [*note that this is plural; in other words, there are now many gathering places for the Saints*]; **for the time of harvest is come** [*it is time for the prophesied last days gathering of Israel*], and my word must needs [*must*] be fulfilled.

> Next, the Lord refers to the parable of the wheat and the tares (Matthew 13:24–30, 36–43). Tares are undesirable weeds that are hard to distinguish from wheat when both are young and growing together. But, when they both mature, it is easy to tell the wheat from the tares. The wheat symbolizes the righteous members of the Church and the tares represent the wicked among them.

65 Therefore, **I must gather together my people, according to the parable of the wheat and the tares, that the wheat may be secured** [*through righteous living and keeping covenants*] **in the garners** [*anciently, barns; symbolically to be gathered to celestial exaltation*] **to possess eternal life** [*exaltation*]**, and be crowned with celestial glory, when I shall come** in the kingdom of my Father **to reward every man according as his work shall be** [*this is often referred to as the "law of the harvest"; in other words, what you plant is what you will harvest*];

66 While **the tares shall be bound** in bundles, and **their bands made strong** [*the time will come for the unrepentant in which the law of justice cannot be satisfied by the law of mercy; in other words, the wicked will be "bound" by their sins*]**, that they may be burned with unquenchable fire.**

> You may wish to reread the parable of the wheat and the tares in Matthew 13:24–30, 36–43. Additional helps for understanding it are given in D&C 86.
>
> The commandment for these early Saints to continue to gather in various places is given in verse 67, next, but in verse 68, they are cautioned not to hurry so much that they are poorly prepared.

67 Therefore, **a commandment I give unto all the churches, that they shall continue to gather together unto the places which I** have appointed.

68 **Nevertheless,** as I have said

unto you in a former commandment [D&C 58:56; 63:24], **let not your gathering be in haste, nor by flight; but let all things be prepared before you.**

> It may be a bit of a surprise at this point that the Lord is going to ask the members of the Church to continue donating money to purchase land in Missouri, including in Jackson County (verses 70–71). However, when we realize that faith and obedience are some of the most important lessons we can learn in this life, we soon see that humble obedience is the key issue here, not whether or not these early members of the Church will be permitted to build Zion in Missouri during their lifetime.

69 And **in order that all things be prepared before you, observe** [*keep*] **the commandment which I have given concerning these things—**

70 **Which saith**, or teacheth, to **purchase all the lands with money, which can be purchased** for money [*which are for sale*], **in the region round about the land** which I have appointed to be the land **of Zion**, for the beginning of the gathering of my saints;

71 **All the land which can be purchased in Jackson county, and the counties round about, and leave the residue** [*the rest of what needs to be done*] **in mine hand.** [*In other words, do what you've been commanded to do and leave the rest to the Lord.*]

> In verses 72–73, next, the Lord gives more specific detail about what the members of the Church should do in order to qualify for Him to take it from there. You will see that these things are to be done with wisdom and order, not helter-skelter—a most important principle that must be followed in building up the Lord's Church on earth.

> With hindsight made possible by histories kept by early members, we note that many of those who originally moved to Missouri to establish Zion came poorly prepared, apparently thinking that if they came, God would provide. This was counter to the instructions given them in D&C 58:56 and 63:24, and, if repeated, would go against the instructions given in verse 72, here.

72 Now, verily I say unto you, **let all the churches** [*the wards and branches throughout the Church*] **gather together all their moneys** [*their donations*]; **let these things be done in their time** [*in a timely manner*]**, but not in haste**; and observe to have all things prepared before you.

73 And **let honorable men be appointed, even wise men, and**

send them to purchase these lands.

Verse 74, next, may mean that the Lord is inviting the wards and branches already established in the eastern United States and Canada to likewise buy lands upon which they can settle, thus establishing Zion communities in various locations. This seems to be a part of the fulfillment of verse 21, which indicates that stakes will become gathering places for Zion people. Perhaps you have noticed that we often refer to stakes as "stakes of Zion," in our gospel vocabulary today.

However, verse 74 could also mean that members of the Church in "eastern countries" should pool their resources and buy land in and around Jackson County and then settle there, thus building Zion.

74 And **the churches in the eastern countries** [*generally meaning areas in the United States and Canada, which are north and east of Ohio*], when they are built up, if they will hearken unto this counsel they **may buy lands and gather together upon them; and in this way they may establish Zion.**

The Lord gives an interesting perspective in verse 75, next. We generally see the poverty of these early members and feel sorry for them as they scrape together donations from their meager means in order to obey God's commandments on financial matters. Yet, in verse 75, the Savior informs us that these Saints had more than enough money among them to purchase the needed land in Missouri at this time!

No doubt, there is an important lesson for us here. It is that with our means, no matter how small or large, plus the help of the Lord (see verse 71), we can accomplish what He asks the Church to do financially.

75 **There is even now already in store sufficient, yea, even an abundance** [*there is more than enough*], **to redeem Zion**, and establish her waste places, **no more to be thrown down, were the churches, who call themselves after my name, willing to hearken to my voice** [*if the members of the Church who claim to be the Lord's people were willing to be obedient on this matter*].

Perhaps you have occasionally wondered (as many of us have) whether you would have been a faithful member of the Church had you lived in the days of these Saints. It may be that one way to tell is whether we are generous with our donations to the Church today.

Next, the topic switches to the Constitution of the United States of America. These Saints have not been protected from mobs and atrocities committed against them. Thus, the importance and validity of the Constitution has come into serious question in the hearts and minds of many of them. We will now be taught important doctrine by the Savior regarding the inspiration that went into the framing of the Constitution.

First, in verse 76, He counsels adherence to constitutional law as the Saints seek redress and compensation for their losses in Missouri.

Doctrine

The Constitution of the United States is an inspired document.

76 And again I say unto you, those who have been scattered by their enemies [*the members of the Church who lived in Jackson County, Missouri*], it is my will that they **should continue to importune for redress** [*compensation; amends, satisfaction*]**, and redemption, by the hands of those who are placed as rulers and are in authority over you—**

77 **According to the laws and constitution** of the people, **which I have suffered** [*caused*] **to be established** [*the Savior inspired the writing of the Constitution*], and should be maintained for the rights and protection of all flesh, **according to just and holy principles;**

We are taught about the basic purposes and goals of the Constitution as an inspired document, in verses 78–79, next. As you will see, the preservation of individual moral agency and accountability are key principles. These are principles over which the War in Heaven was fought (see Moses 4:3).

78 **That every man may act** in doctrine and principle pertaining to futurity, **according to the moral agency which I have given unto him** [*we were given agency way back in our premortal existence—see D&C 29:35*]**, that every man may be accountable for his own sins in the day of judgment.**

79 Therefore**, it is not right that any man should be in bondage one to another.**

80 And **for this purpose have I established the Constitution of this land, by the hands of wise men whom I raised up unto this very purpose, and redeemed the land by the shedding of blood.**

Did you notice what kind of men the Lord used to frame the Constitution (in verse 80, above)? They were great men whom the Lord sent to earth at that time for that exact purpose! Undoubtedly, they were among the "noble and great ones" seen by Abraham as recorded in Abraham 3:22.

Perhaps you have noticed that some current historians seem to delight in "dethroning" our founding fathers as heroes. They take pleasure in pointing out their faults and shortcomings, as if to say, "They weren't that great." Verse 80, above, quickly puts things back into proper perspective, and shows that these commentators and historians are wrong.

By the way, did you know that most of these great men are now members of the Church? The signers of the Declaration of Independence, many of whom helped write the Constitution, appeared to Wilford Woodruff in the St. George Utah Temple and requested that their temple work be done. Their baptisms were performed on August 21, 1877. We will get some details about this from Wilford Woodruff, who was serving at the time as the president of the St. George Temple. He said:

"I will here say, before closing, that two weeks before I left St. George, the spirits of the dead gathered around me, wanting to know why we did not redeem them. Said they, 'You have had the use of the Endowment House [in Salt Lake City] for a number of years, and yet nothing has ever been done for us. We laid the foundation of the government you now enjoy, and we never apostatized from it, but we remained true to it and were faithful to God.' These were the signers of the Declaration of Independence, and they waited on me for two days and two nights. I thought it very singular, that notwithstanding so much work had been done, and yet nothing had been done for them. The thought never entered my heart, from the fact, I suppose, that heretofore our minds were reaching after our more immediate friends and relatives. I straightway went into the baptismal font and called upon brother McCallister to baptize me for the signers of the Declaration of Independence, and fifty other eminent men, making one hundred in all, including John Wesley, Columbus, and others; I then baptized him for every President of the United States, except three [Buchanan, Van Buren, and Grant]; and when their cause is just, somebody will do the work for them (*Journal of Discourses*, 19:229–30).

It is interesting to note that the "fifty other eminent men" included Benjamin Franklin, Daniel Webster, Henry Clay, John Wesley, and Benito Juarez. Also, after the work was done for these men, Sister Luc Bigelow Young was baptized for seventy prominent women, including Martha Washington and Elizabeth Barrett Browning (see Richard Cowan, *Temples to Dot the Earth*, 79–80).

Next, in verses 81–84, Jesus compares the situation of the Missouri Saints and their unsuccessful attempts to get help and protection from civil authorities to the parable of the woman and the unjust judge, which was given by Him and recorded in Luke 18:1–8. The main point of this parable is given in Luke 18:1 as follows:

Luke 18:1

1 AND he spake a parable unto them to this end [*in other words, the main point is*], **that men ought always to pray, and not to faint** [*not give up; not give up on the Lord*];

Notice that the Savior repeats the main point of this parable in the last part of verse 81, next.

81 Now, unto what shall I liken the children of Zion [*the members of the Church who were driven out of Jackson County*]? **I will liken** [*compare*] **them unto the parable of the woman and the unjust judge, for men ought always to pray and not to faint, which saith—**

82 There was in a city a judge which feared not God, neither regarded man.

83 And there was a widow in that city, and she came unto him, saying: Avenge me of mine adversary.

84 And he would not for a while [*implying that it will be a considerable time before the Saints return to build up Zion*], but afterward he said within himself: Though I fear not God, nor regard man, yet **because this widow troubleth me I will avenge her, lest by her continual coming she weary me.**

In verses 85–92, next, the Master teaches how this parable applies to these discouraged Saints.

85 **Thus** [*to this parable*] **will I liken the children of Zion** [*the Saints driven from Zion*].

86 **Let them importune at the feet of the judge** [*let them formally request of the local civil authorities in Jackson County to insure them their rights as citizens*];

87 And **if he heed them not** [*if they do not receive justice, protection and their civil rights from local government officials*], **let them importune at the feet of the governor** [*let them go to the governor of the state*];

88 And **if the governor heed them not, let them importune at the feet of the president** [*of the United States*];

The Saints did ask for redress and help from both Presidents Andrew Jackson (in 1834) and Martin Van

Buren (on November 29, 1839—see *Church History in the Fulness of Times*, 220) but to no avail. Late in 1839, the Prophet and Elias Higbee traveled to Washington D.C. and met with President Van Buren. Joseph recorded this interview with the President of the United States as follows:

"During my stay I had an interview with Martin Van Buren, the President, who treated me very insolently, and it was with great reluctance he listened to our message, which, when he had heard, he said: *"Gentlemen, your cause is just, but I can do nothing for you;"* and *"If I take up for you I shall lose the vote of Missouri."* His whole course went to show that he was an office-seeker, that self-aggrandizement was his ruling passion, and that justice and righteousness were no part of his composition. I found him such a man as I could not conscientiously support at the head of our noble Republic. I also had an interview with Mr. John C. Calhoun, whose conduct towards me very ill became his station. I became satisfied there was little use for me to tarry, to press the just claims of the Saints on the consideration of the President or Congress, and stayed but a few days, taking passage in company with Porter Rockwell and Dr. Foster on the railroad and stages back to Dayton, Ohio" (*History of the Church,* 4:80).

After the Saints have done all in their power through legal means to right the wrongs against them, the Lord will take over (verses 89–91). Remember, though, that He will intervene when the timing is right (verse 90).

89 And **if the president heed them not, then will the Lord arise and come forth out of his hiding place, and in his fury vex the nation**;

90 **And in his hot displeasure,** and **in his fierce anger, in his time** [*when the time is right, according to the will and wisdom of the Lord*], **will cut off those wicked, unfaithful, and unjust stewards, and appoint them their portion among hypocrites, and unbelievers;**

91 Even **in outer darkness,** where there is weeping, and wailing, and gnashing of teeth [*symbolic of the extreme misery of those who reject the Savior's Atonement and thus are punished for their own sins*].

The "outer darkness" spoken of in verse 91, above, is not the outer darkness we often associate with the final fate of the sons of perdition. Rather, it refers more to the wicked who will end up in the telestial kingdom and who will first be turned over to Satan to be punished for their own sins (thus, the "weeping, and wailing, and gnashing of teeth") because they rejected the pleas of the Saints for redress and justice and, ultimately, the Savior's Atonement for their sins (see Alma 40:13; D&C 19:15–17).

Many people tend to look forward to the punishment of the wicked and gain considerable satisfaction in realizing that they will someday get what they deserve. However, as we draw closer and closer to the Lord, we will have more of a tendency to follow the counsel given in verse 92, next.

92 Pray ye, therefore, that their ears may be opened unto your cries, **that I may be merciful unto them, that these things may not come upon them.**

Next, the Savior gives us a general lesson in the principle of accountability and explains that the civil authorities mentioned in verses 86–88 must be given a chance to respond positively to the requests for redress from the Saints in order for them to be held accountable for their responses to fair claims from citizens.

93 What I have said unto you must needs be [*the members must take their complaints to the government authorities as instructed; this is a basic principle that goes with agency, knowledge and accountability*], **that all men may be left without excuse** [*in order for all to be held accountable*];

94 That wise men and rulers may hear and know that which they have never considered [*in other words, they will be surprised when they see the hand of the Lord in behalf of the righteous—compare with Isaiah 52:10*];

As the Savior continues to tell why the Saints must follow His instructions, He explains that the world will look upon the restoration of the gospel and the faithful members of the Church as "strange" or unusual.

95 That I may proceed to bring to pass my act, my strange act [*the restoration of the gospel—see D&C 95:4*], and perform my work, **my strange work** [*Isaiah 28:21*], **that men may discern between the righteous and the wicked** [*the Restoration will provide the people of the world with a choice between good examples and bad examples*], saith your God.

In verses 96–99, the displaced members who had lived in Jackson County are instructed not to sell their lands and properties in Zion, even though they have been driven out and prospects for returning look doubtful. This was a difficult test for them.

Oliver Cowdery failed this test. On April 12, 1838, he was excommunicated from the Church. One of the charges brought against him was selling land in Jackson County, Missouri, in direct opposition to the counsel of the Lord on this matter (*Church History in the Fulness of Times*, 186–87).

96 And again, I say unto you, **it is contrary to my commandment and my will that my servant Sidney Gilbert should sell my storehouse** [*the store (D&C 58:37) that he established in Independence, Jackson County, Missouri*], **which I have appointed unto my people, into the hands of mine enemies.**

97 **Let not that which I have appointed be polluted by mine enemies, by the consent of those who call themselves after my name** [*by those who claim to be faithful members of the Church*];

98 For **this is a very sore and grievous sin against me, and against my people** [*against the faithful members of the Church*], **in consequence of those things which I have decreed and which are soon to befall the nations.**

99 Therefore, **it is my will that my people should claim, and hold claim upon that which I have appointed unto them** [*do not sell their properties in Jackson County, which they own by legal deed, according to the laws of the land*], **though they should not be permitted to dwell thereon** [*even if they do not get to return and live there again*].

Finally, in verses 100–101, the Savior tells the members who were driven from their land and homes in Jackson County that there is still a chance for them to return if they will repent sufficiently and live the higher laws required of a Zion people.

100 Nevertheless, **I do not say they shall not dwell thereon; for inasmuch as** [*if*] **they bring forth fruit and works meet for my kingdom** [*if they demonstrate that they are willing to live the celestial laws upon which Zion is to be built (D&C 105:5)*] **they shall dwell thereon.**

101 **They shall build, and another shall not inherit it; they shall plant vineyards, and they shall eat the fruit thereof** [*compare with Isaiah 65:21*]. **Even so. Amen.**

It appears that the opportunity to return to their lands in Jackson County was dependent not only on the faithfulness of the Saints who had been displaced, but also upon the faithfulness of the general membership of the Church at that time, particularly in Ohio and the eastern United States and Canada.

Members throughout the Church had been instructed (D&C 101:69–

73) to donate money for additional purchase of land in Jackson County. Many were slow to do so or did not contribute at all.

When it came to gathering men, as instructed in D&C 101:55–57, to march to Jackson County and help the members return to their lands there, many would not go. We will study more about this when we get to section 103. Suffice it to say, at this point, that the Lord initially requested an "army" of five hundred (D&C 103:30). Recruiting efforts, which lasted a month, yielded an army of 207.

SECTION 102

Background

Perhaps you've noticed that most sections in the Doctrine and Covenants are revelations to Joseph Smith, or are, through him, given to others. Section 102 is a record of the minutes taken by Elders Oliver Cowdery and Orson Hyde of the organization of the first high council of the Church on February 17, 1834, at Kirtland, Ohio. These minutes were revised by Joseph Smith the next day and presented the following day to the high council. They unanimously accepted them. Verses 30–32 were added to the minutes later in preparation for this section to be included in the 1835 publication of the Doctrine and Covenants. They explain the difference between local high councils and the Council of the Twelve Apostles.

In this section, many of the principles and procedures followed in modern-day membership councils are given by the Lord. You can read details about membership councils (formerly referred to as "disciplinary councils") in the General Handbook, Section 32, which has been revised and was made available to all members on the Church's website in 2020.

Before we study section 102 verse by verse, we will give a bit more background.

It is important to distinguish between this first "high council" for which the First Presidency of the Church served as the presidency and stake high councils as they are organized today. In our day, a stake presidency serves as the presidency of the high council in their stake.

It is interesting to watch the gradual development of various levels of organization within the Church from the time of the Restoration to the present day. It is wonderful evidence of ongoing revelation.

The first stake in the Church was organized in Kirtland, Ohio, on February 17, 1834. The First Presidency of the Church, with Joseph Smith as the president, served as the stake presidency. In conjunction with the organizing of this first stake of Zion, a high council was called. Some of section 102 applies only to this first high council (verses 9–10), but much of it applies to stake high councils today.

The Prophet Joseph Smith taught that the high council is organized according to the pattern used by the Saints in ancient times. He said:

"I then declared the council organized according to the ancient order, and also according to the mind of the Lord" (*History of the Church*, 2:32–33).

One of the primary functions of the first high council of the Church was to serve as a second level of judiciary; in other words, to handle difficult issues that could not be settled satisfactorily by local leaders such as bishoprics and branch presidencies (see verse 2). Decisions of the bishopric could be appealed to the high council, and decisions of the high council could be appealed to the first presidency (verse 27).

As we proceed to study this section, we will emphasize, among other things, procedures that apply to high councils as well as to membership councils today. Remember, this section is the minutes kept by Oliver Cowdery and Orson Hyde for the meeting during which this high council was organized and was later revised by Joseph Smith.

1 THIS day [*February 17, 1834*] a general council of twenty-four high priests assembled at the house of Joseph Smith, Jun., by revelation, and **proceeded to organize the high council of the church of Christ, which was to consist of twelve high priests, and one or three presidents as the case might require.**

Next, the purpose of this high council is given.

2 **The high council was appointed** by revelation **for the purpose of settling important difficulties** [*including serious transgressions on the part of individual members*] **which might arise in the church, which could not be settled by the church or the bishop's council** [*conducted by a bishop and his counselors*] **to the satisfaction of the parties.**

We see in verse 3, next, that this high council consisted of a presiding presidency and twelve high priests to serve as high councilors.

3 **Joseph Smith, Jun.** [*president of the Church*]**, Sidney Rigdon** [*first counselor in the First Presidency*] **and Frederick G. Williams** [*second counselor in the First Presidency*] **were acknowledged presidents** [*sustained, as required by D&C 26:2*] **by the voice of the council; and Joseph Smith, Sen.** [*the Prophet's father*]**, John Smith, Joseph Coe,**

John Johnson, Martin Harris, John S. Carter, Jared Carter, Oliver Cowdery, Samuel H. Smith, Orson Hyde, Sylvester Smith, and Luke Johnson**, high priests, **were chosen to be a standing council** [*one that continues to function on an on-going basis*] **for the church**, by the unanimous voice of the council.

> Proper procedure in the Church is to allow the person who has been called the opportunity to accept or turn down the position. This is demonstrated next in verse 4.

4 **The above-named councilors were then asked whether they accepted their appointments, and whether they would act in that office according to the law of heaven**, to which they all answered that they accepted their appointments, and would fill their offices according to the grace of God bestowed upon them.

5 **The number composing the council** [*the group attending this meeting where this high council was selected*]**, who voted in the name and for the church in appointing the above-named councilors were forty-three**, as follows: nine high priests, seventeen elders, four priests, and thirteen members.

> According to verse 6, next, in order to conduct and conclude any official business, a minimum of seven high councilors must be in attendance at a high council meeting.

6 Voted: that **the high council cannot have power to act without seven of the above-named councilors**, or their regularly appointed successors are present.

> Verse 6, above, does not apply in the case of a stake disciplinary council. Twelve high priests must be present, in addition to the stake president and two other high priests (usually his counselors). If any of the high councilors cannot be in attendance, other high priests may be asked to fill in (see verse 7, next). If the stake president cannot attend, the disciplinary council cannot be held unless a General Authority gives permission for one of the stake president's counselors to take his place.

7 **These seven shall have power to appoint other high priests**, whom they may consider worthy and capable **to act in the place of absent councilors**.

> Next, instructions are given for replacing high councilors. As you will see, the stake president and his counselors nominate the replacements.

8 Voted: that **whenever any vacancy shall occur** by the

death, removal from office for transgression, or removal from the bounds of this church government [*if a high councilor moves to a location outside the jurisdiction of this high council*], of any one of the above-named councilors, **it shall be filled by the nomination of the president or presidents**, and sanctioned [*sustained*] by the voice of a general council of high priests, convened for that purpose, to act in the name of the church.

> Next, in verses 9–10, instructions are given that apply only to the president of the Church and his counselors. Remember that at this early stage in the growth of the Church, the First Presidency was also the stake presidency for the Kirtland Stake, the first stake in the Church.

9 **The president of the church**, who is also the president of the council [*the Kirtland Stake high council*], **is appointed by revelation, and acknowledged** [*sustained—see D&C 26:2*] **in his administration by the voice of the church** [*by the general membership of the Church*].

> Next, in verse 10, these early Saints are reminded that the president presides over the entire Church. This is nothing unusual to us because we are used to it. However, we must realize that it was not the normal thing among various religious groups and sects in Joseph Smith's day. Many Christian churches of his day had their own local leaders and did not have a strong central organization. Thus, many of the converts to the Church were not accustomed to having one central leader with strong authority over all local units of the Church.

10 And **it is according to the dignity of his** [*the president of the Church*] **office that he should preside over the council of the church** [*the whole Church*]; **and it is his privilege to be assisted by two other presidents** [*the counselors in the First Presidency*], appointed after the same manner that he himself was appointed.

> Verse 11, next, applies both to the First Presidency of the Church as well as to stake presidencies. Again, in order to understand how important these specific organizational instructions are, we must be aware that such strong organizational rules were not common among religions in the Prophet's day, nor are they generally common among many religious organizations in our day.

11 And **in case of the absence of one or both of those** [*counselors*] who are appointed to assist him, **he has power** [*authority*] **to preside over the council without an**

assistant; and **in case he himself is absent, the other presidents** [*his counselors*] **have power to preside in his stead, both or either of them.**

> Verse 12, next, foreshadows the establishment of many stakes as the Church grows.
>
> Beginning with verse 12 and continuing through verse 33, procedures and instructions are given that apply directly to stake membership councils (formerly called disciplinary councils). You will see the reason for drawing numbers (verse 12, next) when you read verse 17. As you will see in verse 34, the members of this first high council did draw numbers that arranged them in order from one to twelve for purposes of disciplinary councils.

12 **Whenever a high council of the church of Christ is regularly organized**, according to the foregoing pattern, it shall be the duty of the twelve councilors to **cast lots by numbers**, and thereby ascertain who of the twelve shall speak first, commencing with number one and so in succession to number twelve.

13 **Whenever this council convenes to act upon any case** [*in other words, whenever a stake membership council is convened*], the twelve councilors shall consider whether it is a difficult one or not; if it is not [*if it is not a difficult or complex case*], **two only** of the councilors **shall speak upon it** [*make a recommendation as to what the decision of the council should be*], according to the form above written.

14 But **if** it is thought to be **difficult, four** shall be appointed; and **if more difficult, six**; but in no case shall more than six be appointed to speak [*make recommendations as to what the outcome of the council should be*].

> The importance of preserving the worth of the individual (D&C 18:10) is a basic principle of the gospel of Jesus Christ. Verse 15, next, shows this principle in action. Half of the high councilors are assigned to make sure that the individual is treated with respect during the proceedings.

15 **The accused, in all cases, has a right to half of the council, to prevent insult or injustice.**

16 And **the councilors appointed to speak** [*the two, four, or six—verses 13–14, above*] before the council **are to present the case, after the evidence is examined** [*make their recommendation as to what disciplinary action should be applied to the person appearing before the council, after the whole council has examined and discussed*

the case together], **in its true light before the council**; and every man is to speak according to equity and justice [*personal biases and prejudices are to be set aside*].

17 **Those councilors who draw even numbers**, that is, 2, 4, 6, 8, 10, and 12, are the individuals who **are to stand up in behalf of the accused, and prevent insult and injustice.**

> The high councilors mentioned in verse 17, above, are not "defense attorneys." Membership councils in the Church are not like courts of civil law in which there are prosecuting attorneys and defense attorneys. Rather, the six high councilors who are to "stand up in behalf of the accused" are responsible to stand up for him or her in the sense of insuring respect, courtesy, and fairness.
>
> In most disciplinary councils held today, there are not "accusers" and "accused" (verse 18, next). Rather, a member has already confessed serious transgression and desires help in repenting and doing whatever is necessary to put things back in order with God. However, in cases where a member is accused of serious sin and does not confess (if guilty), both the person or persons who claim to know of the transgression and the accused are to be heard by the council.

18 In all cases **the accuser and the accused shall have a privilege of speaking for themselves before the council, after the evidences are heard and the councilors who are appointed to speak on the case have finished their remarks**.

> Verse 19, next, instructs that the stake president is to make the final decision as to what disciplinary action is to be taken by the council and that his decision is to be presented to the other members of the membership council for their sustaining vote.
>
> In the case of a bishop's membership council, the bishop makes the final decision and presents it to his counselors for sustaining.

19 After the evidences are heard, the councilors, accuser and accused have spoken, **the president shall give a decision** according to the understanding which he shall have of the case, and call upon **the twelve councilors** to **sanction the same by their vote.**

20 **But should the remaining councilors, who have not spoken** [*who were not part of the two, four, or six (verses 13–14) who were chosen to make recommendations as to the outcome of the council*], **or any one of them** [*any council member*], after hearing the evidences and

pleadings impartially, **discover an error in the decision of the president**, they can manifest it, and **the case shall have a re-hearing** [*in other words, unless the decision of the stake president is sustained unanimously at this point by the other council members, the council must be continued*].

21 And **if, after a careful rehearing, any additional light is shown upon the case, the decision shall be altered accordingly.**

If, after rehearing, which would include the discussion of any new evidence or points of view, nothing basically has changed, then the decision can be given based on the majority (verse 22) of council members sustaining it. In practice, few stake presidents go ahead with a decision unless it is sustained unanimously by the council members.

22 **But in case no additional light is given, the first decision shall stand, the majority of the council having power to determine the same.**

Verse 23, next, applies directly to the prophet in this context, but obviously can apply within their stewardships to stake presidents and bishops.

23 **In case of difficulty respecting doctrine or principle**, if there is not a sufficiency written to make the case clear to the minds of the council, **the president may inquire and obtain the mind of the Lord by revelation.**

Verses 24–25 apply primarily to the early days of the Church, before there were stakes in other locations.

24 **The high priests, when abroad, have power to call and organize a council** [*a membership council*] after the manner of the foregoing, to settle difficulties, **when the parties or either of them shall request it.**

25 And **the said council** of high priests **shall have power to appoint one of their own number to preside** over such council for the time being.

Membership councils today follow the same practice, given in verse 26, next, of reporting the results of disciplinary action to the First Presidency.

26 **It shall be the duty of said council to transmit, immediately, a copy of their proceedings**, with a full statement of the testimony accompanying their decision, **to the** high council of the seat of the **First Presidency of the Church.**

If a member is dissatisfied with

the result of a bishop's council, it can be referred to the stake president with a request that a stake membership council be convened. Likewise, if a member is not satisfied with the outcome of a stake membership council, he or she may appeal it to the First Presidency as indicated in verse 27, next.

27 Should the parties or either of them be dissatisfied with the decision of said council, **they may appeal to** the high council of the seat of **the First Presidency of the Church**, and have a re-hearing, which case shall there be conducted, according to the former pattern written, as though no such decision had been made.

> In order to prevent the time and energies of the high council from being consumed by frivolous arguments and disagreements among members, the Lord gives the instruction in verses 28–29, next.

28 This council of high priests abroad is only to be called on the most difficult cases of church matters; and no common or ordinary case is to be sufficient to call such council.

29 The traveling or located high priests abroad have power to say whether it is necessary to call such a council or not.

> Verses 30–33, next, distinguish between the authority of the Twelve Apostles, which will be organized as a quorum in 1835, and the authority of the high council or high councils referred to in this section.

30 There is a distinction between the high council or traveling high priests abroad, and the traveling high council composed of the twelve apostles, in their decisions.

31 From the decision of the former [*the local high council*] **there can be an appeal; but from the decision of the latter** [*the Apostles*] **there cannot.**

32 The latter can only be called in question by the general authorities of the church **in case of transgression.**

33 Resolved: that the president or presidents of the seat of **the First Presidency of the Church shall have power to determine whether any such case, as may be appealed, is justly entitled to a re-hearing**, after examining the appeal and the evidences and statements accompanying it.

> Among the many things we learn from this section is that the Lord's kingdom is indeed a "house of order" (D&C 132:8).

SECTION 102

Verse 34, next, is a record of the outcome of drawing lots on the part of the first high council. The purpose for this was mentioned previously in verses 15 and 17.

34 The twelve councilors then proceeded to cast lots or ballot, to ascertain who should speak first, and the following was the result, namely: 1, Oliver Cowdery; 2, Joseph Coe; 3, Samuel H. Smith; 4, Luke Johnson; 5, John S. Carter; 6, Sylvester Smith; 7, John Johnson; 8, Orson Hyde; 9, Jared Carter; 10, Joseph Smith, Sen.; 11, John Smith; 12, Martin Harris. After prayer the conference adjourned.

OLIVER COWDERY,
ORSON HYDE, Clerks.

By the way, the first case heard by the Kirtland Stake high council was the case of Brother Curtis Hodges. Ezra Thayer, who later left the Church, brought charges against Brother Hodges. The minutes of this disciplinary council, held on February 19, 1834 (two days after the date of section 102) are available in *History of the Church*, kept by Joseph Smith, as follows:

"To the President of the High Council of the Church of Christ.

"The following charges I prefer against Elder Curtis Hodges, Sen., of this Church: First, for an error in spirit; second, for an error in the manner of his address, which consisted in loud speaking, and a want of clearness in articulation, which was calculated to do injury to the cause of God; and also, for contending that that was a good and proper spirit that actuated him thus to speak—all of which I consider unbecoming in an Elder in this Church, and request a hearing before the High Council.

(Signed) Ezra Thayer.

"Elder Hodges pleaded 'not guilty' of the above charges.

"Father Lions was called on to substantiate the above charges, and his testimony was pointed against Brother Hodges. Brother Story testified that Elder Hodges talked so loud at a prayer meeting that the neighbors came out to see if some one was hurt. At another meeting, he said that Elder Thayer rebuked him for his error, but he did not receive the rebuke; that he raised his voice so high, that he could not articulate so as to be understood; and that his teaching brought a damper upon the meeting, and was not edifying. Brother Erastus Babbitt was then called upon, who testified that Elder Hodges was guilty of hollowing [making noise without value] so loud that in a measure he lost his voice, and uttered but little else distinctly than 'Glory to heaven's King.' His testimony against Brother Hodges was pointed. Brother Truman Wait testified much to the same effect.

"Councilor Oliver Cowdery stood up on the part of the accuser, and opened the case clearly.

"Councilor Joseph Coe stood up on the part of the accused, but could say but a few words.

"The accuser and the accused then spoke for themselves, after which the President arose and laid open the case still more plainly, and gave his decision, which was, that the charges in the declaration had been sustained by good witnesses; also, that Elder Hodges ought to have confessed when rebuked by Elder Thayer; also, if he had the Spirit of the Lord at the meetings, where he hollowed [made so much noise], he must have abused it, and grieved it away. All the Council agreed with the decision.

"Elder Hodges then rose and said he now saw his error, but never saw it before; and appeared to feel thankful that he saw it. He said he had learned more during this trial than he had since he came into the Church; confessed freely his error, and said he would attend to the overcoming of that evil, the Lord being his helper.

"The Council forgave him, and adjourned to the evening of the 20th" (*History of the Church*, 2:34).

SECTION 103

Background

This revelation was given through the Prophet Joseph Smith on February 24, 1834, at Kirtland, Ohio. We will give somewhat more background for this section than usual, in order to help you gain a more detailed understanding and a better feel for what the Saints were going through at this time. It is hoped also that it will better enable you to see how the Lord works with people who have not yet quite caught the vision of what it means to be totally committed to the Church and the covenants they have made to God.

Mob action and violence against the Saints in Jackson County, Missouri, had begun in July 1833. By early November 1833, the members of the Church who had settled in Zion, Jackson County, Missouri, had been driven by mobs from their homes and across the Missouri River to Clay County, Missouri. Though they were kindly received by the citizens of Clay County and were able to subsist there for a brief season, they desired to know what their longer-term future was. As mentioned in the background notes for section 101 in this study guide, being driven out of Zion was a severe blow to these Saints. In section 101, the Lord gave them the reasons they had been driven out, as well as some instructions for the future.

SECTION 103

By the winter of 1834, the Saints determined to send two men to Kirtland to counsel with the Prophet Joseph Smith and the members there about their situation in Missouri. Elder Parley P. Pratt wrote about this as follows:

"After making our escape into the county of Clay—being reduced to the lowest poverty—I made a living by day labor, jobbing, building, or wood cutting, till some time in the winter of 1834, when a general Conference was held at my house, in which it was decided that two of the Elders should be sent to Ohio, in order to counsel with President Smith and the Church at Kirtland, and take some measures for the relief or restoration of the people thus plundered and driven from their homes. The question was put to the Conference: 'Who would volunteer to perform so great a journey?'

"The poverty of all, and the inclement season of the year made all hesitate. At length Lyman Wight and myself offered our services, which were readily accepted. I was at this time entirely destitute of proper clothing for the journey; and I had neither horse, saddle, bridle, money nor provisions to take with me; or to leave with my wife, who lay sick and helpless most of the time.

"Under these circumstances I knew not what to do. Nearly all had been robbed and plundered, and all were poor. As we had to start without delay, I almost trembled at the undertaking; it seemed to be all but an impossibility; but 'to him that believeth all things are possible.' [Mark 9:23.] I started out of my house to do something towards making preparation; I hardly knew which way to go, but I found myself in the house of brother John Lowry, and was intending to ask him for money; but as I entered his miserable cottage in the swamp, amid the low, timbered bottoms of the Missouri river, I found him sick in bed with a heavy fever, and two or three others of his family down with the same complaint, on different beds in the same room. He was vomiting severely, and was hardly sensible of my presence. I thought to myself, 'well, this is a poor place to come for money, and yet I must have it; I know of no one else that has got it; what shall I do?' I sat a little while confounded and amazed. At length another Elder happened in; at that instant faith sprung up in my heart; the Spirit whispered to me, 'is there anything too hard for the Lord?' I said to the Elder that came in: 'Brother, I am glad you have come; these people must be healed, for I want some money of them, and must have it.'

"We laid hands on them and rebuked the disease; brother Lowry rose up well; I did my errand, and readily obtained all I asked. This provided in part for my family's sustenance while I should leave them. I went a little further into the woods of the Missouri bottoms, and came to a camp of some brethren, by the name of Higbee, who owned some horses; they saw me coming, and, moved by the Spirit, one of them said to the other, 'there comes brother Parley; he's in want of a horse for his journey—I must let him have old Dick;' this being the name of the best horse he had. 'Yes,' said I, 'brother, you have guessed right; but what will I do for a saddle?' 'Well,' says the other, 'I believe I'll have to let you have mine.' I blessed them and went on my way rejoicing.

"I next called on Sidney A. Gilbert [actually, A. Sidney Gilbert—see D&C 53, heading], a merchant, then sojourning in the village of Liberty—his store in Jackson County having been broken up, and his goods plundered and destroyed by the mob. 'Well,' says he, 'brother Parley, you certainly look too shabby to start a journey; you must have a new suit; I have got some remnants left that will make you a coat,' etc. A neighboring tailoress and two or three other sisters happened to be present on a visit, and hearing the conversation, exclaimed, 'Yes, brother Gilbert, you find the stuff and we'll make it up for him.' This arranged, I now lacked only a cloak; this was also furnished by brother Gilbert.

"Brother Wight was also prospered in a similar manner in his preparations. Thus faith and the blessings of God had cleared up our way to accomplish what seemed impossible. We were soon ready, and on the first of February we mounted our horses, and started in good cheer to ride one thousand or fifteen hundred miles through a wilderness country. We had not one cent of money in our pockets on starting.

"We travelled every day, whether through storm or sunshine, mud, rain or snow; except when our public duties called us to tarry. We arrived in Kirtland early in the spring, all safe and sound; we had lacked for nothing on the road, and now had plenty of funds in hand. President Joseph Smith and the Church in Kirtland received us with a hospitality and joy unknown except among the Saints; and much interest was felt there, as well as elsewhere, on the subject of our persecution (*Autobiography of Parley P. Pratt,* 107–9).

Elders Pratt and Wight arrived in Kirtland on February 22, 1834. Two days later, the Kirtland Stake high council, which had been organized for less than a week—see D&C 102, met in the home of the Prophet Joseph Smith and heard the report of these two brethren concerning the plight of the Saints in Missouri. That same day, section 103 was received.

As you will see, this revelation reviews two major reasons that the Saints were driven out of Jackson County (verses 1–4), encourages these members of the Church to do better at keeping all the commandments the Lord has given about being a Zion people, and warns of the consequences if they do not (verses 5–10). It also teaches a lesson about the blessings that will come after faithfully enduring tribulation (verses 11–14), explains part of the parable given in D&C 101:43–62 in which Joseph Smith is told to lead men to Missouri (verses 15–21), instructs Joseph Smith to begin gathering this army of men (verse 22), and instructs all members of the Church to continue contributing money and purchasing land in Zion (verse 23). In addition, it explains that some will lose their lives in the cause of redeeming Zion (verses 24–28), sends eight men (four companionships) on brief missions to gather funds and recruit men to serve in what will become known as Zion's Camp—the name of the small army that is to march to Zion (verses 29–40)—and gives specific instructions as to how many men are needed and what to do if that number cannot be obtained (verses 30–34).

Near the end of February, the eight men listed, including the Prophet (verses 37–40), left on recruiting missions to gather funds and men for Zion's Camp. They traveled throughout the eastern United States, visiting the various branches of the Church there, but had little success. The Prophet expressed his concern about the lack of support for Zion's Camp in a letter written by the First Presidency to Orson Pratt (verse 40), who was still in the East recruiting. The Prophet wrote:

"Kirtland, April 7, 1834.

"Dear Brother Orson:—We received yours of the 31st ultimo in due course of mail, and were much grieved on learning that you were not likely to succeed according to our expectations. Myself, Brothers Newel, Frederick and Oliver, retired to the translating room, where prayer was wont to be made, and unbosomed our feelings before God; and cannot but exercise faith yet that you, in the miraculous providences of God, will succeed in obtaining help. The fact is, unless we can obtain help, I myself cannot go to Zion, and if I do not go, it will be impossible to get my brethren in Kirtland, any of them, to go; and if we do not go, it is in vain for our eastern brethren to think of going up to better themselves by obtaining so goodly a land, (which now can be obtained for one dollar and one quarter per acre,) and stand against that wicked mob; for unless they do the will of God, God will not help them; and if God does not help them, all is vain.

"Now the fact is, this is the head of the Church and the life of the body; and those able men, as members of the body, God has appointed to be hands to administer to the necessities of the body. Now if a man's hand refuses to administer to the necessities of his body, it must perish of hunger; and if the body perish, all the members perish with it; and if the head fail, the whole body is sickened, the heart faints, and the body dies, the spirit takes its exit, and the carcase remains to be devoured by worms.

"Now, Brother Orson, if this Church, which is essaying to be [claiming to be] the Church of Christ will not help us, when they can do it without sacrifice, with those blessings which God has bestowed upon them, I prophesy—I speak the truth, I lie not—God shall take away their talent, and give it to those who have no talent, and shall prevent them from ever obtaining a place of refuge, or an inheritance upon the land of Zion; therefore they may tarry, for they might as well be overtaken where they are, as to incur the displeasure of God, and fall under His wrath by the way side, as to fall into the hands of a merciless mob, where there is no God to deliver, as salt that has lost its savor, and is thenceforth good for nothing, but to be trodden under foot of men" (*History of the Church*, 2:48).

The Camp of Israel (later known as Zion's Camp) left for the thousand-mile journey to Missouri on May 1, 1834, from Kirtland. Many groups of recruits joined along the way, coming from the surrounding country, including Indiana and Illinois. Even though the total number of recruits for Zion's Camp was below the initial five hundred requested in this revelation (verse 30), a number of strong and valiant Saints were among its numbers. Many future leaders of the Church would come from this group. The average age of the recruits was 29, the age of the Prophet Joseph Smith at the time. The youngest member was 16, and the oldest, 79. Ultimately, there were 207 men, 11 women, 11 children, and 25 baggage wagons in Zion's Camp.

We will now proceed to study section 103 verse by verse. First, the Lord refers to the Prophet and others in Kirtland as His "friends," a term of closeness and endearment. He informs them that He will now tell them what to do regarding the plight of the Saints in Missouri, about which they have just heard from Parley Pratt and Lyman Wight.

1 VERILY I say unto you, **my friends**, behold, **I will give unto you a revelation and commandment, that you may know how to act** in the discharge of your duties **concerning the salvation and redemption of your brethren, who have been scattered on the land of Zion**;

Next, in verse 2, we are reminded again that the Lord does things according to His own timetable and wisdom. Although this is sometimes a difficult lesson to accept, especially when we have a need or want that we would like fulfilled now, it is a vital concept to accept. Otherwise, we are likely to become bitter toward the Lord and lose our faith and testimony.

2 Being driven and smitten by the hands of mine enemies, on whom I will pour out my wrath without measure **in mine own time.**

> Next, even though it is a difficult lesson, especially if you are the victim, we are reminded that the wicked are sometimes allowed to persecute the righteous in order that there be sufficient evidence against them to convict them on Judgment Day. If the Lord were to intervene every time a person chooses to be wicked, the whole system of moral agency would be defeated, and there would be no real agency. This is the first reason the Lord gives in this revelation as to why the wicked were allowed to drive the Saints from Jackson County.

3 For **I have suffered them thus far** [*allowed the mobbers to do what they have done so far*], **that they might fill up the measure of their iniquities** [*in order that their agency choices might convict them on Judgment Day—compare with Alma 14:11*], **that their cup might be full** [*in order that their punishments might be fair*];

> The second reason for the Lord's allowing the persecution of the Saints in Missouri is given next in verse 4.

4 And **that those who call themselves after my name** [*who claim to be the people of the Lord*] **might be chastened** [*disciplined because of their sins*] **for a little season with a sore** [*severe*] **and grievous chastisement, because they did not hearken altogether unto the precepts** [*specific rules and instructions about living in Zion*] **and commandments which I gave unto them.**

> In verses 5–10, next, the Savior explains what can happen if the members of the Church do much better from now on and also what will happen if they don't.

5 But verily I say unto you, that **I have decreed a decree which my people shall realize** [*which will be fulfilled in behalf of the persecuted Saints*], **inasmuch as** [*if*] **they hearken from this very hour unto the counsel which I,** the Lord their God, **shall give unto them.**

6 Behold **they shall,** for I have decreed it, **begin to prevail** [*win*] **against mine enemies from this very hour.**

> Did you notice the important statement by the Savior, in verse 6, above, as to whose enemies the enemies of the Lord's people are?

Next, in verse 7, the Master again emphasizes the importance of adhering to all His words, not just picking and choosing from among His teachings. This lesson applies to all of us.

7 And **by hearkening to observe** [*obey*] **all the words which I, the Lord their God, shall speak unto them, they shall never cease to prevail** until the kingdoms of the world are subdued under my feet, and the earth is given unto the saints, to possess it forever and ever [*in other words, such Saints will "inherit the earth" (Matthew 5:5) and will live on the earth forever as their celestial kingdom—D&C 130:9–11*].

8 **But inasmuch as they keep not my commandments, and hearken not to observe all my words**, the kingdoms of **the world shall prevail against them.**

9 For **they were set to be a light unto the world, and to be the saviors of men;**

10 And **inasmuch as they are not the saviors of men, they are as salt that has lost its savor, and is thenceforth good for nothing but to be cast out and trodden under foot of men.**

Next, in verses 11–14, the Savior specifically says that the Saints who have been driven off their land will return. But it will be after much tribulation. Also, note how the Lord includes the rest of the members of the Church (verse 13). In other words, they too must live the gospel according to the laws of Zion (the laws of the celestial kingdom—see D&C 105:5). Without verse 14, we would not have the complete context of the Savior's promise that they "shall return" (verse 11), and thus might be inclined to claim that the Lord did not fulfill His promise to these Saints (see verse 31 and compare with D&C 58:31–33).

11 But verily I say unto you, **I have decreed that your** [*referring to the members in the Kirtland area*] **brethren** [*in Missouri*] **which have been scattered shall return** to the lands of their inheritances, and shall build up the waste places of Zion.

12 For **after much tribulation**, as I have said unto you in a former commandment [*D&C 58:2–4*], **cometh the blessing.**

13 Behold, **this is the blessing which I have promised after your tribulations** [*the members in Kirtland and other locations besides Missouri*], **and the tribulations of your brethren** [*the Saints in Missouri*]—**your redemption, and the redemption of your brethren, even their restoration to the land of**

Zion, to be established, no more to be thrown down.

14 Nevertheless, if they pollute [*through personal sin and unworthiness*] **their inheritances they shall be thrown down**; for I will not spare them if they pollute their inheritances.

15 Behold, I say unto you, **the redemption of Zion must needs come by power** [*the power of God, which will come only if they fulfill the requirements given in verse 7, above*];

16 **Therefore** [*because Zion can only be redeemed by the power of God*], **I will raise up unto my people a man** [*Joseph Smith*], **who shall lead them like as Moses led the children of Israel** [*compare to D&C 107:91*].

17 For **ye are the children of Israel**, and of **the seed** [*descendants*] **of Abraham**, and **ye must needs be led out of bondage by power**, and with a stretched-out arm [*scriptural symbolism for the power of God*].

18 And **as your fathers** [*ancestors*] **were led at the first, even so shall the redemption of Zion be.**

19 **Therefore, let not your hearts faint** [*don't get discouraged*], for I say not unto you as I said unto your fathers: Mine angel shall go up before you, **but not my presence.**

> Note, in comparison to the last phrase in verse 19, above, that the Savior promises that His presence will accompany the Saints who eventually go to redeem Zion (verse 20).
>
> Also, don't miss the phrase "in time" in verse 20, next. As you have no doubt already noticed, there are many hints in these verses that the redemption of Zion will take longer than most Saints perhaps anticipated.

20 But I say unto you: **Mine angels shall go up before you, and also my presence**, and **in time ye shall possess the goodly land.**

> Next, the Savior provides the interpretation as to who the "servant" is in verse 55 of section 101.

21 Verily, verily I say unto you, that **my servant Joseph Smith, Jun. is the man to whom I likened the servant** to whom the Lord of the vineyard spake **in the parable** [*D&C 101:43–62*] which I have given unto you.

> In verse 22, next, the Prophet Joseph Smith is instructed to proceed to gather the men for the march of Zion's Camp. It has been over two months since the

revelation was given (section 101) in which he was alerted that this time would come.

22 **Therefore let my servant Joseph Smith, Jun. say** unto the strength of my house, my young men and the middle aged—**Gather yourselves together unto the land of Zion**, upon the land **which I have bought with money that has been consecrated unto me** [*in other words, the Saints, with money they had consecrated to the Lord under the law of consecration, had legally purchased the lands from which they had been driven, and they had legal deeds to that property*].

Next, the members of the Church in all locations are counseled to continue contributing money for the purpose of purchasing land in Jackson County, Missouri, in spite of the fact that the Missouri Saints had been driven off their land. This is a real test of faith and obedience!

23 And **let all the churches** [*the branches of the Church*] **send up wise men with their moneys, and purchase lands even as I have commanded them.**

One possible interpretation of "curse" as used in verses 24–26 is to be cursed in the sense that the righteous obedience of the Saints will bring down condemnation from God against their enemies until their enemies or their children, grandchildren, or later posterity stop fighting against truth and righteousness.

Another possible meaning of the word is that the Lord will "hide [his] face from them" (Deuteronomy 32:20) such that they will not receive His blessings and protections (see Deuteronomy 32:20–25).

Yet another possible meaning of curse is that the Saints and their leaders would actively pray that the Lord would stop their enemies and that He would curse their enemies by smiting them in various ways.

24 And **inasmuch as** [*if*] **mine enemies come against you to drive you from my goodly land**, which I have consecrated to be **the land of Zion, even from your own lands after these testimonies** [*after you have fulfilled these commandments*], **which ye have brought before me against them, ye shall curse them;**

25 **And whomsoever ye curse, I will curse**, and ye shall avenge me of mine enemies.

26 And **my presence shall be with you** even in avenging me of mine enemies, unto the third and fourth generation of them that hate me.

The phrase "unto the third and fourth generation of them that hate me," in verse 26, above, shows that hatred and wickedness on the part of the parents normally spreads to their children, grandchildren, and so forth. However, any of them or their posterity can "break the chain" by turning to God (see Ezekiel 18, especially verses 14–17).

Verses 27–28, next, emphasize the necessity of total dedication to the Lord at all costs if one desires exaltation.

27 Let no man be afraid to lay down his life for my sake; for whoso layeth down his life for my sake shall find it again [*will find eternal life, exaltation*].

28 And whoso is not willing to lay down his life for my sake is not my disciple [*true follower*].

In verse 29, next, Sidney Rigdon is instructed to go on a brief recruiting mission to the eastern United States, explaining to the members of the Church there what the Lord has said concerning that which must be done to redeem Zion. He is to urge them to keep the commandments and instructions of the Lord given in the above verses respecting the redemption of Zion. Lyman Wight will be assigned to go with him (verse 38).

29 It is my will that my servant Sidney Rigdon shall lift up his voice in the congregations in the eastern countries, in **preparing the churches to keep the commandments which I have given** unto them **concerning the restoration and redemption of Zion.**

In verse 30, Parley P. Pratt and Lyman Wight are instructed not to go back to the Saints in Clay County until recruits have been gathered to join the cause of Zion's Camp. Parley will go on a brief recruiting mission with Joseph Smith (verse 37) and, as mentioned above, Lyman will go with Sidney Rigdon (verse 38). Five hundred men are to be sought for to join Zion's Camp, as the small army of Saints will be called.

30 It is my will that my servant Parley P. Pratt and my servant **Lyman Wight should not return to the land of their brethren** [*the Saints temporarily staying in Clay County, Missouri—across the Missouri River from Jackson County*], **until they have obtained companies** [*of "soldiers" for Zion's Camp*] **to go up unto the land of Zion,** by tens, or by twenties, or by fifties, or by an hundred, **until they have obtained** to the number of **five hundred** of the strength of my house [*of the able-bodied men who are members of the Church*].

Next, in verse 31, the Lord makes

an understatement. It is somewhat similar to the understatement made by Abraham, when his life was in imminent danger. Abraham said, "I, Abraham, saw that it was needful for me to obtain another place of residence" (Abraham 1:1).

31 Behold this is my will; ask and ye shall receive; but **men do not always do my will.**

> In verses 32–34, the Lord tells them what to do if they cannot get five hundred men to join Zion's Camp.

32 Therefore, **if you cannot obtain five hundred**, seek diligently that peradventure [*perhaps*] you may obtain **three hundred.**

33 And **if ye cannot obtain three hundred**, seek diligently that peradventure ye may obtain **one hundred.**

34 **But** verily I say unto you, a commandment I give unto you, that **ye shall not go up unto the land of Zion until you have obtained a hundred** of the strength of my house, to go up with you unto the land of Zion.

> Do you realize that, as members of the Church, we have both the privilege and the obligation to pray for our living prophet? We see this principle in verses 35–36, next.

35 Therefore, as I said unto you [*in Matthew 7:7, D&C 4:7, and so forth*], ask and ye shall receive; **pray earnestly that peradventure my servant Joseph Smith, Jun., may go with you**, and preside in the midst of my people, and organize my kingdom upon the consecrated land, and establish the children of Zion upon the laws and commandments which have been and which shall be given unto you.

36 **All victory and glory is brought to pass unto you through your diligence, faithfulness, and prayers of faith.**

> In verses 37–40, the Savior organizes companionships for brief recruiting missions for Zion's Camp.

37 Let my servant **Parley P. Pratt** journey with my servant **Joseph Smith, Jun.**

38 Let my servant **Lyman Wight** journey with my servant **Sidney Rigdon.**

39 Let my servant **Hyrum Smith** journey with my servant **Frederick G. Williams.**

40 Let my servant **Orson Hyde** journey with my servant **Orson Pratt**, whithersoever my servant Joseph Smith, Jun., shall counsel them, in obtaining the fulfilment of these commandments which

I have given unto you, and leave the residue in my hands. Even so. Amen.

By the way, Oliver Cowdery and Sidney Rigdon did not march with Zion's Camp to Missouri. Rather, they were left behind in Kirtland to lead the Church there in the absence of the Prophet and other brethren. Among their responsibilities was supervising the ongoing construction on the Kirtland Temple.

SECTION 104

Background

This revelation concerning the United Firm (see headings to sections 78 and 82 in the 2013 edition of the Doctrine and Covenants) was given to the Prophet Joseph Smith on April 23, 1834. The exact location is not recorded, although the Prophet had just returned to Kirtland the day before, on April 22, 1834 (see *History of the Church*, 2:54). The setting was likely that of a council meeting of members belonging to the United Firm, which was in financial difficulties.

By way of background, we will quote from the 2018 Doctrine and Covenants Student Manual, chapter 40:

"In March and April of 1832, the Lord commanded the Prophet Joseph Smith and a small group of priesthood leaders in Ohio and Missouri to organize the United Firm (also referred to as the United Order). They covenanted to consecrate property to the Church and to work together to manage the Church's storehouses and printing business (see D&C 78:1–3; 82:11–12). In addition, United Firm members 'supervised farms and residential real estate, an ashery, a tannery, a stone quarry, a sawmill, and a brick kiln' (in *The Joseph Smith Papers, Documents, Volume 2: July 1831– January 1833*, ed. Matthew C. Godfrey and others [2013], 498). The profits made from these businesses were to be used to finance the work of building Zion as well as to provide income to United Firm members (see D&C 82:17–19).

"By April 1834 the United Firm was experiencing serious financial problems. Because of mob violence in Missouri in 1833, William W. Phelps's printing office in Jackson County had been destroyed and Sidney Gilbert was forced to close his storehouse. Consequently, neither the printing office nor the store could produce income for the firm, but the firm still had to repay the debts it had acquired to establish and supply these businesses. In Ohio, United Firm members increasingly became indebted to New York companies as they borrowed money to supply the Kirtland storehouse and to purchase land and a new printing press in Kirtland. In addition, some of the firm's members 'manifest[ed] a covetous spirit toward the firm's property for which they were responsible' (in *The Joseph Smith Papers, Documents, Volume 4: April 1834–September 1835*, 20). Because of these difficulties, 'members of the Kirtland branch of the United Firm met on 10 April 1834 and decided "that the firm should be [dissolved] and each one" receive a stewardship, or property, to oversee and manage' (in *The Joseph Smith Papers, Documents, Volume 4: April 1834–September 1835*, 21; see also *The Joseph Smith Papers, Journals, Volume 1: 1832–1839*, ed. Dean C. Jessee and others [2008], 38). About two weeks later the Prophet Joseph Smith received the revelation recorded in Doctrine and Covenants 104, which contained further instructions from the Lord regarding the United Firm and its properties."

The United Firm was originally set up based upon the laws and principles of the law of consecration.

1 VERILY I say unto you, my friends, **I give unto you counsel, and a commandment, concerning all the properties which belong to the order** [*the United Firm, headquartered in Kirtland*] **which I commanded to be organized and established, to be a united order,** and an everlasting order for the benefit of my church, and **for the salvation of men until I come—**

Beginning with verse 2, next, the Lord explains that those called to belong to the United Firm must be faithful and keep their covenants. If so, they would receive the high blessings that attend living according to the law of consecration. But those who were not faithful and violated the covenants made when joining the United Firm were subject to the "buffetings of Satan" (verse 9).

2 **With promise immutable** [*not subject to being revoked*] **and unchangeable, that inasmuch as those whom I commanded were faithful they should be blessed with a multiplicity of blessings;**

3 **But inasmuch as** [*if*] **they were not faithful they were nigh unto cursing.**

In verse 4, next, we are shown two major stumbling blocks to living the law of consecration.

4 **Therefore, inasmuch as some of my servants have not kept the commandment, but have broken the covenant through covetousness,** and **with feigned words** [*pretended sincerity*]**, I have cursed them with a very sore and grievous curse.**

The seriousness of breaking the covenant made (as in D&C 78:11;

SECTION 104

82:15) in order to participate in the United Firm is pointed out in verses 5–9, next.

5 For I, the Lord, have decreed in my heart, that **inasmuch as any man belonging to the order shall be found a transgressor**, or, in other words, **shall break the covenant with which ye are bound** [*compare with D&C 78:11–12; 82:15*], **he shall be cursed in his life, and shall be trodden down by whom I will** [*in other words, will not receive the protection from enemies which would otherwise be available from the Lord*];

6 For **I, the Lord, am not to be mocked in these things**—

As you will see in verse 7, next, even if the United Firm is dissolved because of the transgressions and selfishness of some participants, those who did strive to keep their covenants and live the law of consecration would ultimately receive their reward in heaven.

7 **And all this that the innocent among you** [*those who did their best to live according to the law of consecration*] **may not be condemned with the unjust; and that the guilty among you may not escape**; because **I, the Lord, have promised unto you a crown of glory** [*a scriptural term symbolizing exaltation*] **at my right hand** [*the covenant hand, symbolizing those who made and kept covenants with God*].

8 Therefore, **inasmuch as** [*if*] **you are found transgressors, you cannot escape my wrath in your lives.**

9 Inasmuch as ye are cut off for transgression, **ye cannot escape the buffetings of Satan** until the day of redemption.

The "buffetings of Satan" are described by Bruce R. McConkie as follows:

"To be turned over to the buffetings of Satan is to be given into his hands; it is to be turned over to him with all the protective power of the priesthood, of righteousness and of godliness removed, so that Lucifer is free to torment, persecute, and afflict such a person without let [interference] or hindrance" (*Mormon Doctrine*, 108).

Verse 10, next, points out that repentance and forgiveness are still available to transgressors who have not kept their covenants in the United Order. However, if they refuse to repent, the leaders of the Church are authorized to subject them to Church discipline, including excommunication if needed, which will turn them over to the buffetings of Satan.

10 And **I now give unto you power** from this very hour, that

if any man among you, of the order [*who belongs to the United Firm*], **is found a transgressor and repenteth not** of the evil, that **ye shall deliver him over unto the buffetings of Satan**; and he shall not have power to bring evil upon you.

> Next, in verses 11–18, the Savior gives a brief review of the principles of "stewardship" and accountability as they relate to the United Firm and the law of consecration. These principles also apply to our lives and what we do with the blessings (stewardships) we are given by the Lord.

11 It is wisdom in me; therefore, a commandment I give unto you, that **ye shall organize yourselves and appoint every man his stewardship;**

12 **That every man may give an account unto me of the stewardship which is appointed unto him.**

13 For **it is expedient** [*necessary*] **that I, the Lord, should make every man accountable, as a steward over earthly blessings**, which I have made and prepared for my creatures.

> Next, in verses 14–16, the Savior explains that He is the Creator and that all things belong to Him. In other words, we are stewards over things that belong to God and are thus obligated to use them as He would.

14 **I, the Lord, stretched out the heavens, and built the earth** [*created the heaven and the earth—Genesis 1:1*], my very handiwork; and **all things therein are mine.**

15 And **it is my purpose to provide for my saints, for all things are mine.**

16 **But it** [*providing for the Saints—verse 15, above*] **must needs be done in mine own way**; and behold **this is the way** [*the laws, rules, and attitudes inherent in the law of consecration*] **that I, the Lord, have decreed to provide for my saints, that the poor shall be exalted** [*strengthened and nourished spiritually and physically*], **in that the rich are made low** [*kept humble and generous*].

> Perhaps you have heard some people claim that the earth is not capable of supporting the large populations that are upon it and that are yet coming. Verse 17, next, answers that concern.

17 For **the earth is full, and there is enough and to spare**; yea, I prepared all things, and have given unto the children of men to be agents unto themselves.

> As you can see, referring back to

SECTION 104

verse 17, above, the real problem when it comes to poverty and starvation is man's mismanagement of the natural resources that God has placed upon the earth. It is the selfishness, greed, malicious destruction of resources, and oppression that cause the problems we see in the world around us, not the lack of preparation on the part of God to provide for all His children whom He will send to this earth.

Verse 18, next, explains the importance of generosity and sharing with others, as a major component of the law of consecration.

18 Therefore, **if any man shall take of the abundance which I have made, and impart not his portion** [*refuse to use his means for the benefit of others*], **according to the law of my gospel** [*including the law of consecration; see D&C 42:30*], **unto the poor and the needy, he shall, with the wicked, lift up his eyes in hell, being in torment** [*as was the case with the selfish rich man in the parable given by the Savior—see Luke 16:22–23*].

Remember, as explained in the background notes at the beginning of this section, that the United Firm in Kirtland was to be dissolved and reorganized at this time as instructed by the Lord. One of the lessons we learn from this is that the Lord gives us opportunities to live higher laws, but when we fail, He patiently has us live according to other laws that, if obeyed, will lead eventually to our being able to live higher celestial laws.

Beginning with verse 19, next, the Savior gives instructions for the dividing up of the properties of the Kirtland United Firm among the members of that order.

19 And now, verily I say unto you, **concerning the properties of the order—**

20 **Let** my servant **Sidney Rigdon have** appointed unto him **the place where he now resides, and the lot of the tannery** [*Sidney Rigdon's father was a tanner, therefore, Sidney had some training in tanning leather for leather goods*] **for his stewardship, for his support while he is laboring in my vineyard**, even as I will, when I shall command him.

According to verse 21, next, the principle of common consent (sustaining—see D&C 26:2) is to be applied to this distribution of property among the members of the Kirtland United Firm.

21 And **let all things be done according to** the counsel of the order, and **united consent or voice of the order**, which dwell in the land of Kirtland.

22 And **this stewardship and**

blessing, I, the Lord, confer upon my servant Sidney Rigdon for a blessing upon him, and his seed [*posterity*] after him;

23 And I will multiply blessings upon him, inasmuch as he will be humble before me.

24 And again, **let** my servant **Martin Harris have** appointed unto him, for his stewardship, **the lot of land which my servant John Johnson obtained in exchange for his former inheritance**, for him and his seed after him;

25 And inasmuch as he is faithful, I will multiply blessings upon him and his seed after him.

26 And **let** my servant **Martin Harris devote his moneys for the proclaiming of my words**, according as my servant Joseph Smith, Jun., shall direct.

27 And again, **let** my servant **Frederick G. Williams have the place upon which he now dwells.**

28 And **let** my servant **Oliver Cowdery have the lot which is set off joining the house, which is to be for the printing office**, which is lot number one, and **also the lot upon which his father resides.**

29 And **let** my servants **Frederick G. Williams and Oliver Cowdery have the printing office** and all things that pertain unto it.

30 And this shall be their stewardship which shall be appointed unto them.

31 And inasmuch as they are faithful, behold I will bless, and multiply blessings upon them.

32 And this is the beginning of the stewardship which I have appointed them, for them and their seed after them.

33 And, inasmuch as they are faithful, I will multiply blessings upon them and their seed after them, even a multiplicity of blessings.

34 And again, **let** my servant **John Johnson have the house in which he lives, and the inheritance**, all **save** [*except*] **the ground which has been reserved for the building of my houses** [*see D&C 94:3, 10, 16*], which pertains to that inheritance, and those lots which have been named for my servant Oliver Cowdery.

35 And inasmuch as he is faithful, I will multiply blessings upon him.

36 And **it is my will that he should sell the lots that are laid off** [*designated*] **for the building up of the city of my saints**, inasmuch as it shall be made known to him by the voice of the Spirit, and according to the counsel of the order, and by the voice of the order.

37 And this is the beginning of the stewardship which I have appointed unto him, for a blessing unto him and his seed after him.

38 And inasmuch as he is faithful, I will multiply a multiplicity of blessings upon him.

39 And again, **let** my servant **Newel K. Whitney** [*the bishop in the Kirtland area*] **have** appointed unto him **the houses and lot where he now resides, and the lot and building on which the mercantile establishment stands** [*the Newel K. Whitney Store*]**, and also the lot which is on the corner south of the mercantile establishment, and also the lot on which the ashery is situated.**

40 And all this I have appointed unto my servant Newel K. Whitney for his stewardship, for a blessing upon him and his seed after him, for the benefit of the mercantile establishment of my order which I have established for my stake in the land of Kirtland.

41 Yea, verily, this is the stewardship which I have appointed unto my servant N. K. Whitney, even this whole mercantile establishment, him and his agent, and his seed after him.

42 And inasmuch as he is faithful in keeping my commandments, which I have given unto him, I will multiply blessings upon him and his seed after him, even a multiplicity of blessings.

43 And again, **let** my servant **Joseph Smith, Jun., have** appointed unto him **the lot which is laid off for the building of my house** [*the Kirtland Temple—see D&C 95:8*], **which is forty rods long** [*a rod is 16.5 feet long*] **and twelve wide, and also the inheritance upon which his father now resides**;

44 And this is the beginning of the stewardship which I have appointed unto him, for a blessing upon him, and upon his father.

45 For behold, **I have reserved an inheritance for his father, for his support**; therefore he shall be reckoned in the house of my servant Joseph Smith, Jun.

46 And I will multiply blessings upon the house of my servant Joseph Smith, Jun., inasmuch as he

is faithful, even a multiplicity of blessings.

> When the United Firm was first organized, there was one group, and the Saints in Kirtland, as well as the Saints in Missouri, belonged to it. In verses 47–51, next, the Savior instructs that the members in Kirtland and those in Missouri were to become separate, independent organizations at this time.

47 And now, a commandment I give unto you concerning Zion [*in Missouri*], that **you shall no longer be bound as a united order to your brethren of Zion**, only on this wise [*except as follows*]—

48 After you are organized, **you shall be called the United Order of the Stake of Zion, the City of Kirtland.** And **your brethren** [*in Missouri*], after they are organized, **shall be called the United Order of the City of Zion.**

49 And **they shall be organized in their own names**, and in their own name; and they **shall do their business in their own name**, and in their own names;

50 And **you shall do your business in your own name**, and in your own names.

> In verses 51–53, next, the Lord explains why they are to divide these two groups into two separate organizations.

51 And **this I have commanded to be done for your salvation, and also for their salvation, in consequence of their being driven out and that which is to come.**

52 **The covenants being broken through transgression,** by **covetousness** and **feigned words** [*see verse 4, above*]—

53 **Therefore, you are dissolved as a united order with your brethren**, that you are not bound only up to this hour unto them, only on this wise, as I said, by loan as shall be agreed by this order in council, as your circumstances will admit and the voice of the council direct.

> Beginning with verse 54, next, the Lord gives instructions to those in Kirtland as to what is to be done with the stewardships He distributed, starting with verse 19 of this section. First, He reminds them that all things belong to Him and that they are to be faithful stewards over them.

54 And again, **a commandment I give unto you concerning your stewardship which I have appointed unto you.**

55 Behold, **all these properties are mine,** or else your faith is vain

[*otherwise, your faith in God would be of no value*], and ye are found hypocrites, and the covenants which ye have made unto me are broken;

56 And **if the properties are mine, then ye are stewards**; otherwise ye are no stewards.

57 But, verily I say unto you, **I have appointed unto you to be stewards** over mine house, even stewards indeed.

> One of the things the Savior requires these Saints to do with the proceeds from their stewardships is to print the "fulness of my scriptures" and the revelations that He had given and would yet give (verse 58, next). This would no doubt include the Doctrine and Covenants (published in Kirtland in 1835), as well as the Joseph Smith Translation of the Bible (see D&C 104, footnote 58a). It could also include the book of Moses and the book of Abraham, which were first published in Church periodicals and later became part of the Pearl of Great Price.
>
> The Savior explains the importance of making the fullness of the scriptures and the revelations available to all to read and study. One of the purposes is to prepare us to live with Him someday.

58 And **for this purpose I have commanded you to organize yourselves, even to print my words, the fulness of my scriptures**, the **revelations which I have given unto you, and which I shall, hereafter, from time to time give unto you**—

59 **For the purpose of building up my church and kingdom on the earth**, and **to prepare my people for the time when I shall dwell with them**, which is nigh at hand.

> Another instruction from the Savior is that the Saints in the Kirtland area are to organize two separate funds, a "treasury" (verses 60–66) that is to be called the "sacred treasury" (verse 66) and "another treasury" (verse 67), into which surplus money from individual stewardships is to be placed.

60 And ye shall **prepare** for yourselves **a place for a treasury**, and consecrate it unto my name.

61 And ye shall **appoint one among you to keep the treasury**, and he shall be ordained unto this blessing.

> Verse 62, next, explains that the funds given to the treasury in Kirtland are to be kept separate from other funds.

62 And **there shall be a seal upon the treasury**, and **all the sacred things shall be delivered into the treasury; and no man**

among you shall call it his own, or any part of it, for **it shall belong to you all** with one accord.

63 And I give it unto you from this very hour; and now see to it, that ye go to and **make use of the stewardship** which I have appointed unto you, **exclusive of the sacred things** [*verse 62, above*], **for the purpose of printing these sacred things** as I have said.

64 And **the avails** [*profits, proceeds—see D&C 104, footnote 64a*] **of the sacred things shall be had in the treasury**, and a seal shall be upon it; and **it shall not be used or taken out of the treasury by any one**, neither shall the seal be loosed which shall be placed upon it, **only** [*except*] **by the voice of the order, or by commandment.**

65 And thus shall ye preserve the avails of the sacred things in the treasury, for sacred and holy purposes.

66 And **this shall be called the sacred treasury of the Lord**; and a seal shall be kept upon it that it may be holy and consecrated unto the Lord.

67 And again, **there shall be another treasury prepared**, and **a treasurer appointed to keep the treasury**, and **a seal shall be placed upon it**;

J. Reuben Clark Jr., of the First Presidency, gave a general conference talk in which he spoke of these funds. He said:

"The Lord created two other institutions besides the [bishop's] storehouse: one was known as the Sacred Treasury, into which was put 'the avails of the sacred things in the treasury, for sacred and holy purposes.' While it is not clear, it would seem that into this treasury were to be put the surpluses which were derived from the publication of the revelations, the Book of Mormon, the Pearl of Great Price, and other similar things, the stewardship of which had been given to Joseph and others. (D. & C. 104:60–66)

"The Lord also provided for the creation of 'Another Treasury,' and into that other treasury went the general revenues which came to the Church, such as gifts of money and those revenues derived from the improvement of stewardships as distinguished from the residues of the original consecrations and the surpluses which came from the operation of their stewardships. (D. & C. 72:11)

"We have in place of the two treasuries, the 'Sacred Treasury' and 'Another Treasury,' the general funds of the Church.

"Thus you will see, brethren, that in many of its great essentials, we have, as the Welfare Plan has now developed, the broad essentials of the United Order" (in Conference Report, October 1942, 56–58).

As you will see in the next verses, the amount of money we donate to the Church for the work of the Lord is not the important thing. The key issue is that we donate according to our ability.

68 And **all moneys that you receive in your stewardships, by improving upon the properties which I have appointed unto you**, in houses, or in lands, or in cattle, or in all things save it be the holy and sacred writings, which I have reserved unto myself for holy and sacred purposes, **shall be cast into the treasury** as fast as you receive moneys, **by hundreds**, or by **fifties**, or by **twenties**, or by **tens**, or by **fives**.

69 Or in other words, if any man among you obtain five dollars let him cast them into the treasury; or if he obtain ten, or twenty, or fifty, or an hundred, let him do likewise;

Since donating to this general fund of the Church is a rather new concept for these Saints, the Lord emphasizes that this is a general fund of the Church and is to be used by the Church only by the sustaining vote of the pertinent members.

70 And **let not any among you say that it is his own; for it shall not be called his, nor any part of it.**

71 And **there shall not any part of it be used, or taken out of the treasury, only by the voice and common consent of the order.**

72 And **this shall be the voice and common consent** [see D&C 26:2] of the order—**that any man among you say to the treasurer: I have need of this** [money from the "other" treasury—verse 67] **to help me in my stewardship**—

73 If it be five dollars, or if it be ten dollars, or twenty, or fifty, or a hundred, **the treasurer shall give unto him the sum which he requires to help him in his stewardship**—

Next, in verses 74–77, warning and instruction are given with respect to how to handle transgressors who are participating in the use of the funds.

74 **Until he be found a transgressor**, and it is manifest before the council of the order plainly [it is clear that he has transgressed] that he is an unfaithful and an unwise steward.

75 But so long as he is in full fellowship, and is faithful and wise in his stewardship, this shall be his token unto the treasurer that the treasurer shall not withhold [*the faithful and worthy Saints are to be helped as needed from this fund*].

76 But in case of transgression, the treasurer shall be subject unto the council and voice of the order [*the vote of the order as to what to do regarding a transgressor*].

77 And **in case the treasurer is found** an **unfaithful** and an **unwise** steward, he shall be subject to the council and voice of the order, and **shall be removed out of his place, and another shall be appointed in his stead** [*in his place*].

> At this point, the Church in Kirtland was heavily in debt. The burden of providing for the steady flow of new converts was exhausting to the financial resources of the Church. In verses 78–86, the Lord gives instructions about dealing with this heavy burden. Note how He stresses that this should be a one-time dilemma for them (verses 83 and 86).

78 And again, verily I say unto you, **concerning your debts—** behold it is my will that **you shall pay all your debts.**

79 And it is my will that you shall **humble yourselves before me, and obtain this blessing by your diligence and humility and the prayer of faith.**

80 And **inasmuch as you are diligent and humble, and exercise the prayer of faith**, behold, **I will soften the hearts of those to whom you are in debt, until I shall send means unto you for your deliverance** [*until the Lord provides the means to pay them*].

81 Therefore **write speedily to New York** and write **according to that which shall be dictated by my Spirit; and I will soften the hearts of those to whom you are in debt**, that it shall be taken away out of their minds to bring affliction upon you.

82 And **inasmuch as** [*if*] **ye are humble and faithful and call upon my name**, behold, **I will give you the victory.**

83 I **give unto you a promise, that you shall be delivered this once** out of your bondage [*the bondage of debt*].

> In verses 84–85, next, the Prophet and the Church leaders in Kirtland are given permission to use the property they were given (beginning with verse 19) as collateral for loans that could help pay off the debts of the Church at this time.

84 **Inasmuch as you obtain a chance to loan money** by hundreds, or thousands, even **until you shall loan enough to deliver yourself from bondage** [*from debt*], **it is your privilege.**

85 And **pledge** [*use for collateral to secure the loans*] **the properties** which I have put into your hands, **this once**, by giving your names by common consent or otherwise, as it shall seem good unto you.

86 **I give unto you this privilege, this once**; and behold, **if you proceed to do the things which I have laid before you**, according to my commandments, all these things are mine, and ye are my stewards, and **the master** [*Christ*] **will not suffer his house to be broken up** [*if these Saints faithfully follow the Lord's instructions given here, the Church will not be broken up*]. Even so. Amen.

SECTION 105

Background

This revelation was given through the Prophet Joseph Smith on June 22, 1834, on the Fishing River in Missouri.

In obedience to the instructions given by the Lord (D&C 103), the Camp of Israel, a small "army" of about 100 men from northeastern Ohio, led by the Prophet Joseph Smith (later referred to as Zion's Camp) had departed from Kirtland in early May 1834 for the purpose of marching to Missouri and, with the promised assistance of Missouri Governor Daniel Dunklin's militia, restoring the displaced Latter-day Saints to their lands in Jackson County. Others, including men from Michigan Territory recruited by Hyrum Smith and Lyman Wight, joined as they marched along and ultimately, 207 men, 11 women, and 11 children had joined the 900-mile march of Zion's Camp. They brought 25 baggage wagons with them, containing clothing and provisions for the journey, as well as for the Saints in Missouri.

Upon arriving near Jackson County, the leaders of Zion's Camp negotiated with Governor Dunklin to have him keep his word. However, he backed out of his agreement, stating as his reason the threat of civil war in his state if he assisted the Latter-day Saints.

Mobbers had gathered together in wild bands, and, on June 19, five leaders of the Missouri mobs had ridden into the camp on Fishing River, bragging that they had four hundred men who would destroy the members of Zion's Camp before morning. What happened next is recorded as follows:

"A few minutes after the Missourians left, a small black cloud appeared in the clear western sky. It moved eastward, unrolling like a scroll, filling the heavens with darkness. As the first ferry load of mobbers crossed the Missouri River to the south, a sudden squall made it nearly impossible for the boat to return to pick up another load. The storm was so intense that Zion's Camp abandoned their tents and found shelter in an old Baptist meetinghouse nearby. When Joseph Smith came in, he exclaimed, 'Boys, there is some meaning to this. God is in this storm.' It was impossible for anyone to sleep, so the group sang hymns and rested on the rough benches. One camp member recorded that during this time the whole canopy of the wide horizon was in one complete blaze with terrifying claps of thunder.

"Elsewhere the beleaguered mobbers sought any refuge they could. The furious storm broke branches from trees and destroyed crops. It soaked and made the mobbers' ammunition useless, frightened and scattered their horses, and raised the level of the Fishing River, preventing them from attacking Zion's Camp. The Prophet recalled, 'It seemed as if the mandate of vengeance had gone forth from the God of battles, to protect His servants from the destruction of their enemies.'

"Two days later, on 21 June, Colonel John Sconce and two associates of the Ray County militia rode into Zion's Camp to learn of the Mormons' intentions. 'I see that there is an Almighty power that protects this people,' Sconce admitted. The Prophet explained that the only purpose of Zion's Camp was to help their brethren be reinstated on their lands and that their intent was not to injure anyone. He said, 'The evil reports circulated about us were false, and got up by our enemies to procure our destruction.' Sconce and his companions were so affected by the stories of the unjust trials and suffering of the Saints that they promised to use their influence to offset feelings against the Mormons (*Church History in the Fulness of Times*, 2003, 148).

From *The Joseph Smith Papers, Documents, Volume 4: April 1834–September 1835*, 71–72, we learn that, in order to calm the minds of Missouri citizens, Joseph Smith along with some other members of Zion's Camp, on June 21, 1834, signed a statement stating that they did not plan "to commence hostilities against any man or body of men," rather were seeking a peaceful way to help the displaced Latter-day Saints to return to their homes and lands in Jackson County.

The next day, on June 22, 1834, the Prophet Joseph Smith held a council with camp members to determine how to proceed from there. During the council, he received the revelation now known as section 105, disbanding Zion's Camp. It was officially disbanded

SECTION 105

in Clay County, Missouri, across the River north of Jackson County, on June 24, 1834.

On the same day as the camp was disbanded, an earlier prophecy given by the Prophet Joseph Smith before Zion's Camp entered Missouri began to be fulfilled. Heber C. Kimball, a member of the Camp and later a member of the First Presidency of the Church, wrote:

"Brother Joseph got up in a wagon and said he would deliver a prophecy. After giving the brethren much good advice, he exhorted them to faithfulness and humility, and said the Lord had told him that there would be scourge come upon the camp in consequence of the fractious and unruly spirits that appeared among them, and they would die like sheep with the rot; still if they would repent and humble themselves before the Lord, the scourge in great measure might be turned away; 'but, as the Lord lives, this camp will suffer for giving way to their unruly temper'; which afterwards actually did take place to the sorrow of the brethren" (Whitney, *The Life of Heber C. Kimball*, 47–48).

As stated above, this prophecy began to be fulfilled at the time the Camp was disbanded on June 24, 1834. According to the 2018 *Doctrine and Covenants Student Manual*, chapter 41, "The camp experienced the beginnings of an outbreak of cholera, causing vomiting and severe diarrhea. As a result, 68 people, including the Prophet Joseph Smith, suffered from the sickness, and 13 members of the camp and 2 other Latter-day Saints who were living in Clay County died (see *The Joseph Smith Papers, Documents, Volume 4: April 1834–September 1835*, 72, note 334)."

As we study the Lord's word here, we will see that His purposes often reach beyond our current circumstances and expectations. This can sometimes cause disappointment and frustration on our part, but if we steadfastly remain true to God and continue in faith, the day will come that we will see as He sees and rejoice that He answered our prayers the way He did.

In verses 1–6, the Savior explains to the members of Zion's Camp (and to the entire Church) why the Missouri Saints cannot be put back on the land of Zion at this time.

1 VERILY I say unto you who have assembled yourselves together **that you may learn my will concerning the redemption of mine afflicted people** [*the members who were driven out of Zion, Jackson County*]—

2 Behold, I say unto you, **were it not for the transgressions of my people**, speaking concerning

the church and not individuals [*in other words, many were living in harmony with the laws required of a Zion people, but too many were not*], **they might have been redeemed even now.**

3 But behold, **they have not learned to be obedient** to the things which I required at their hands, **but are full of all manner of evil, and do not impart of their substance, as becometh saints, to the poor and afflicted among them**;

4 **And are not united according to the union required by the law of the celestial kingdom;**

5 And **Zion cannot be built up unless it is by the principles of the law of the celestial kingdom;** otherwise I cannot receive her unto myself.

6 And **my people must needs be chastened until they learn obedience**, if it must needs be [*if necessary*], by the things which they suffer.

> Next, in verse 7, the Lord explains that He is not referring to all of the leaders of the Church in what He said in verses 1–6, above.

7 **I speak not concerning those who are appointed to lead my people,** who are **the first elders** [*the leaders*] **of my church**, for they are not all under this condemnation;

> Next, in addition to the members in Missouri, the Savior includes the members of the Church in other areas who are failing to live the gospel as they should. As we see, from verse 8, next, some of them, especially those in the eastern United States, have been saying, in effect, that if God does not protect the Saints in Missouri, then they will not plan on moving to Missouri, nor will they waste their money by contributing to the cause of building up Zion in Missouri, even though the Lord commanded it (see D&C 101:69–75; 103:23).

8 But **I speak concerning my churches** [*branches of the Church*] **abroad** [*in other locations*]—**there are many who will say: Where is their God** [*why doesn't God protect them*]? **Behold, he will deliver them in time of trouble, otherwise we will not go up unto Zion, and will keep our moneys.**

> In verses 9–12, next, the Lord gives several reasons for not redeeming Zion by putting the Saints back on their land now.

9 Therefore, **in consequence of the transgressions of my people** [*in all locations of the Church*], **it is expedient in me** [*it is according to the Lord's wisdom*]

that mine elders [*Zion's Camp*] should wait for a little season for the redemption of Zion—

10 **That they themselves may be prepared, and that my people may be taught more perfectly,** and **have experience,** and **know more perfectly concerning their duty, and the things which I require at their hands.**

> According to verses 11–12, next, in addition to the strengthening and preparation mentioned in verses 9 and 10, above, the members of the Church, in order to establish Zion, need the endowment of power that will not be available to them until they finish building the temple in Kirtland, Ohio. This power will come, especially when the Savior, Moses, Elias, and Elijah appear in the Kirtland Temple on April 3, 1836, and priesthood keys are restored (see D&C 110). The "endowment" of "power from on high" spoken of in verses 11–12 should not be confused with the "endowment" that we receive in temples today.

11 And **this** [*the redemption of Zion—verse 9*] **cannot be brought to pass until mine elders are endowed with power from on high.**

12 For behold, **I have prepared a great endowment and blessing to be poured out upon them, inasmuch** [*if*] **as they are faithful and continue** [*endure tribulation*] in humility before me.

13 **Therefore it is expedient in me** [*this is the reason it is wise in the Lord's sight*] **that mine elders should wait for a little season, for the redemption of Zion** [*for Zion to be built up*].

> Next, the Lord says, in effect, that if the Saints will fight and win their personal battles against selfishness and sin (with the help of the Atonement), He will fight the battles necessary to reclaim the land of Zion.

14 For behold, **I do not require at their hands to fight the battles of Zion**; for, as I said in a former commandment [*see D&C 98:37*], even so will I fulfil—**I will fight your battles.**

15 **Behold, the destroyer** [*perhaps meaning destroying angels, such as mentioned in Revelation 7:1–3, the destruction of the wicked by the wicked (Mormon 4:5) or by plagues, pestilences, and so on (D&C 88:87–90)*] **I have sent forth to destroy and lay waste mine enemies**; and not many years hence [*in the future*] they shall not be left to pollute mine heritage, and to blaspheme [*speak disrespectfully of*] my name upon the lands which I have consecrated for the gathering together of my saints.

Did you notice the word "lands" (plural) in verse 15, above? This implies that the scope of this prophecy extends beyond Jackson County to various gathering places of the Saints throughout the whole earth.

Next, in verses 16–19, the Lord gives comforting and encouraging words to those who were faithful in Zion's Camp.

16 Behold, **I have commanded my servant Joseph Smith, Jun., to say unto the strength of my house** [*the members of the Church in the Kirtland area and in the eastern United States*], even my warriors, my young men, and middle-aged, to **gather together** [*Zion's Camp*] **for the redemption of my people**, and throw down the towers of mine enemies, and scatter their watchmen;

17 But **the strength of mine house have not hearkened unto my words** [*including the members of the Church in the eastern United States at the time did not respond with sufficient money or men to provide the five hundred recruits for Zion's Camp as initially requested by the Lord—see D&C 103:30–34*].

18 **But inasmuch as there are those who have hearkened unto my words** [*since there were many who did obey and march with Zion's Camp*], I have prepared **a blessing and an endowment for them, if they continue faithful**.

19 **I have heard their prayers, and will accept their offering** [*they will receive the blessings despite the failure of the Church as a whole to carry out the commandments of the Lord*]; and it is expedient in me [*it is according to the Lord's wisdom*] **that they** [*the faithful members of Zion's Camp*] **should be brought thus far for a trial of their faith.**

Although it might appear to some that Zion's Camp was a failure, it was not. Many great blessings came to faithful individuals and to the Church as a result of the march of Zion's Camp. For example, nine of the original twelve Apostles of the restored Church were selected from the members of Zion's Camp. All seven presidents of the Seventy's quorum came from this faithful group, and all sixty-three members of that original quorum of the Seventy also came from among those who had marched to Missouri.

Additionally, the members of the "army of Israel," as it was sometimes called, had the privilege of associating closely with and being taught by the Prophet Joseph Smith during the nearly one-thousand-mile journey. Another blessing that came from it was that the members of the Church in Missouri, some of whom had felt neglected by the Prophet and other Church leaders who stayed in the Kirtland area, now felt supported and sustained by the Church at large.

Next, the Lord gives instructions regarding what the members of Zion's Camp should do now they are being disbanded.

20 And now, verily I say unto you, a commandment I give unto you, that **as many as have come up hither** [*to Missouri*]**, that can stay in the region round about, let them stay**;

21 And **those that cannot stay, who have families in the east** [*in the Kirtland area and elsewhere in the eastern United States*]**, let them tarry** [*remain in Missouri*] **for a little season, inasmuch as my servant Joseph shall appoint unto them** [*according to instructions given them by the Prophet*];

22 **For I will counsel him concerning this matter, and all things whatsoever he shall appoint unto them shall be fulfilled.**

Did you notice what is happening in verses 21–22, above? As you can no doubt understand, a few members of the Church, including some members of Zion's Camp, became disgruntled with the Prophet and apostatized from the Church when the "army" was disbanded rather than fighting and restoring the Saints to their lands. In these two verses, the Lord is obviously sustaining and supporting His Prophet in the eyes of the people.

Another issue is addressed in verses 23–24, next. The Saints themselves could do much damage to the prospects of peace in Missouri by boasting and bragging to the local citizens that this land was eventually going to be their land. In these verses, the Lord counsels them to avoid such behavior.

23 And **let all my people who dwell in the regions round about** be very faithful, and prayerful, and humble before me, and **reveal not the things which I have revealed unto them** [*about the future destiny of Zion in Missouri*]**, until it is wisdom in me that they should be revealed** [*in other words, until the timing is right*].

24 **Talk not of judgments, neither boast of faith nor of mighty works, but carefully gather together, as much in one region as can be, consistently with the feelings of the people** [*in other words, don't stir up feelings of the old settlers unnecessarily*];

If the members of the Church in Missouri at this time will be obedient to this counsel, and keep the commandments and instructions the Lord gives next, then they will receive the blessings promised in verses 25–40.

25 And behold, **I will give unto you favor and grace in their eyes, that you may rest in peace and safety**, while you are saying unto the people: Execute judgment and justice for us according to law, and redress us of our wrongs [*while petitioning the government for redress, as instructed in D&C 101:85–89*].

26 Now, behold, I say unto you, my friends, **in this way you may find favor in the eyes of the people, until the army of Israel becomes very great**.

27 And **I will soften the hearts of the people, as I did the heart of Pharaoh, from time to time, until my servant Joseph Smith, Jun., and mine elders**, whom I have appointed, **shall have time to gather up the strength of my house**,

28 **And to have sent wise men, to fulfil that which I have commanded concerning the purchasing of all the lands in Jackson county that can be purchased, and in the adjoining counties** round about [*as instructed in D&C 101:72–74*].

29 For **it is my will that these lands should be purchased**; and after they are purchased **that my saints should possess them according to the laws of consecration** which I have given.

30 And **after these lands are purchased, I will hold the armies of Israel guiltless in taking possession of their own lands**, which they have previously purchased with their moneys [*in other words, this is how the Saints who have been driven from Jackson County can return to their lands*], and of throwing down the towers of mine enemies that may be upon them, and scattering their watchmen, and avenging me of mine enemies unto the third and fourth generation of them that hate me.

31 **But first let my army become very great,** and **let it be sanctified** [*become pure and holy*] before me, that it may become fair as the sun, and clear as the moon, and that her banners may be terrible unto all nations [*may command respect from all nations*];

32 **That the kingdoms of this world may be constrained** [*forced*] **to acknowledge that the kingdom of Zion is in very deed the kingdom of our God and his**

Christ; therefore, **let us become subject unto her laws** [*in other words, by setting a good example, the members of the Church will see people throughout the world desire to join the Church and enjoy the blessings of being subject to the kind and merciful laws of God*].

> Before this can happen, the Kirtland Temple must be completed, as stated in verse 33, next.

33 Verily I say unto you, **it is expedient in me that the first elders** [*the leaders*] **of my church should receive their endowment** [*not endowments, as we know them, rather, the endowment spoken of in verses 11–12, above*] **from on high in my house** [*the Kirtland Temple*], which I have commanded to be built unto my name in the land of Kirtland.

34 And **let those commandments which I have given concerning Zion and her law be executed and fulfilled, after her redemption.**

> You have probably heard the phrase "many are called but few are chosen" (D&C 121:34) several times. In verses 35–37, next, we get some help in understanding what this means.

35 **There has been a day of calling, but the time has come for a day of choosing** [*choosing those who are to receive the promised blessings from the Lord*]; and **let those be chosen that are worthy.**

36 And **it shall be manifest unto my servant, by the voice of the Spirit, those that are chosen**; and **they shall be sanctified** [*made pure and holy, fit to participate in the building up of Zion; the same as being made worthy to dwell in the celestial kingdom*];

37 And **inasmuch as** [*if*] **they follow the counsel which they receive, they shall have power after many days** [*another reminder that it will be some time before Zion is redeemed from her enemies in Missouri*] **to accomplish all things pertaining to Zion** [*symbolic of accomplishing all that is necessary to enter into celestial glory*].

> In summary, from verses 35–37, above, we learn that "many are called but few are chosen" means, in effect, that all are called to receive the highest blessings from God, but relatively few are chosen at this time in the history of the earth to be so blessed because they do not follow the counsels of the Lord.
>
> Finally, as the Lord brings this revelation to a close, He counsels the Saints to be peacemakers.

38 And again I say unto you, **sue**

[*petition the government and the mobbers*] **for peace**, not only to the people that have smitten you, but also to all people;

39 And **lift up an ensign of peace**, and **make a proclamation of peace** unto the ends of the earth;

40 And **make proposals for peace unto those who have smitten you, according to the voice of the Spirit which is in you**, and all things shall work together for your good.

41 Therefore, **be faithful**; and behold, and lo, I am with you even unto the end. Even so. Amen.

SECTION 106

Background

This revelation was given through the Prophet Joseph Smith on November 25, 1834, at Kirtland, Ohio, regarding Warren Cowdery, the oldest brother of Oliver Cowdery (Oliver was the youngest of eight children—see Church History Topics under Oliver Cowdery).

Warren Cowdery had joined the Church through the efforts of his brother, Oliver, and also the influence of Joseph Smith. He was living in Freedom, New York, at the time of this revelation calling him to preside over the small branch of the Church there. About forty converts had been baptized in that area over the past several months.

One of the significant doctrinal contributions of this revelation is the fact that the righteous will not be caught off guard by the Second Coming, whereas the wicked will (verses 4–5).

1 IT is my will that my servant **Warren A. Cowdery should be appointed and ordained a presiding high priest over my church** [*the branch of the Church*], **in the land of Freedom** [*in Freedom, New York*] and the regions round about;

In addition to his duties as presiding high priest over the Freedom Branch of the Church, Brother Cowdery is to serve as a missionary in the area also.

2 **And should preach my everlasting gospel**, and lift up his voice and warn the people, **not only in his own place, but in the adjoining counties**;

3 And devote his whole time to this high and holy calling, which I now give unto him, **seeking diligently the kingdom of heaven and its righteousness, and all things necessary shall be added thereunto**; for the laborer is worthy of his hire [*those who earn the needed blessings are given them*].

Next, in verses 4–5, we are taught that the Second Coming is getting close, that the worldly and the wicked will be caught off guard by it, but the righteous who are acquainted with the word of God will not be.

4 And again, verily I say unto you, **the coming of the Lord draweth nigh**, and **it overtaketh the world** [*the wicked as well as those who do not study the word of God*] **as a thief in the night** [*it will catch them by surprise*]—

Doctrine
The righteous, those who study and live the gospel, will not be caught off guard by the Second Coming of Christ.

5 Therefore, **gird up your loins** [*get prepared*], **that you may be the children of light** [*those who know and live the gospel*], **and that day** [*the Second Coming*] **shall not overtake you as a thief.**

> In verses 6–8, next, Warren Cowdery is cautioned about pride and arrogance and counseled to be humble and faithful in his leadership and missionary responsibilities.

6 And again, verily I say unto you, **there was joy in heaven when my servant Warren bowed to my scepter** [*when he accepted the gospel*], **and separated himself from the crafts of men** [*from the ways of the world*];

7 Therefore, blessed is my servant Warren, for **I will have mercy on him**; and, **notwithstanding the vanity of his heart** [*even though he now has a tendency to be prideful*]**, I will lift him up inasmuch as** [*if*] **he will humble himself before me.**

8 And **I will give him grace** [*the help which the Savior gives us*] **and assurance wherewith he may stand** [*which will give him the strength and ability to live the gospel and carry out his callings*]; and **if he continue to be a faithful witness and a light unto the church I have prepared a crown** [*symbolic of exaltation*] **for him in the mansions of my Father.** Even so. Amen.

> Unfortunately, Warren Cowdery did not heed the counsel to avoid vanity and eventually left the Church, having become critical of its leaders. He left at about the same time his brother, Oliver Cowdery, was excommunicated in 1838. He had moved to Kirtland and continued to live there until his death in 1851 at age sixty-two.

SECTION 107

Background

We will quote the heading to this section as given in the 2013 edition of the Doctrine and Covenants.

Revelation on the priesthood, given through Joseph Smith the Prophet, at Kirtland, Ohio, about April 1835. Although this section was recorded in 1835, the historical records affirm that most of verses 60 through 100 incorporate a revelation given through Joseph Smith on November 11, 1831. This section was associated with the organization of the Quorum of the Twelve in February and March 1835. The Prophet likely delivered it in the presence of those who were preparing to depart May 3, 1835, on their first quorum mission.

As you can see, this revelation is a composite of several revelations given at various times up to and including April 1835. Parts of this section were given as early as November 11, 1831.

This is one of the great revelations on priesthood. In it we are taught about the Aaronic and Melchizedek Priesthoods, the quorums of the First Presidency, the Twelve, and the Seventy, the organization of elders, priests, teachers, and deacons into quorums, and the responsibility of individual priesthood holders to actively learn their duties and responsibilities and carry them out.

Among other things in this section, we are taught the priesthood line of authority from Adam to Noah, and of the meeting held in the valley of Adam-ondi-Ahman three years prior to Adam's death when he was 927 years old.

It is rather exciting to see verse 98, which authorizes Area Seventies. This verse was little noticed until President Gordon B. Hinckley pointed it out several years ago when Area Seventies were first called to serve. It had always been there, placed in this section by the Lord for future use when the time came.

And we live in the marvelous day when additional Quorums of the Seventy are being added as authorized in verses 93–98, to keep up with the leadership needs of the rapidly growing Church.

Before we begin our verse-by-verse study, we will add a bit more background.

The information and instruction in this section paved the way for the restoration and organization of the Quorum of the Twelve Apostles again in our day. During a special conference held on Saturday, February 14, 1835, the

SECTION 107

Three Witnesses to the Book of Mormon (Oliver Cowdery, David Whitmer, and Martin Harris), under the direction of the Prophet Joseph Smith, selected the twelve men who were to become the first Quorum of Twelve Apostles in this dispensation. Earlier, in June 1829, the Book of Mormon witnesses Oliver Cowdery and David Whitmer had been told that they would someday do this (see D&C 18:37). Martin Harris was later called to assist them. Now that day had come. The twelve men they chose, listed according to age at the time they were called, were:

Thomas B. Marsh (35)

David W. Patten (35)

Brigham Young (33)

Heber C. Kimball (33)

Orson Hyde (30)

William E. McLellin (29)

Parley P. Pratt (27)

Luke S. Johnson (27)

William B. Smith (23)

Orson Pratt (23)

John F. Boynton (23)

Lyman E. Johnson (23)

Almost a month later, on March 12, 1835, the newly called Twelve met with the Prophet Joseph Smith. During that meeting, he proposed that they prepare to leave on their first missions through the eastern United States, traveling as far as the Atlantic Ocean. They determined that their departure date should be May 4, 1835.

The *History of the Church* records the feelings and anxieties of these brethren as the weight of their calling as Apostles of Christ began to settle on them. In the minutes of a meeting held by the Twelve, kept by Orson Hyde and William E. McLellin acting as clerks, we read:

"This afternoon [28 March 1835] the Twelve met in council, and had a time of general confession. On reviewing our past course [*spelling in context*] we are satisfied, and feel to confess also, that we have not realized the importance of our calling to that degree that we ought; we have been light-minded and vain, and in many things have done wrong. For all these things we have asked the forgiveness of our heavenly Father; and wherein we have grieved or wounded the feelings of the Presidency, we ask their forgiveness. The time when we are about to separate is near; and when we shall meet again, God only knows; we therefore feel to ask of him whom we have acknowledged to be our Prophet and Seer, that he inquire of God for us, and obtain a revelation, (if consistent) [if appropriate] that we may look upon it when we are separated, that our hearts may be comforted. Our worthiness has not inspired us to make this request, but our unworthiness. We have unitedly asked God our heavenly Father to grant unto us through His Seer, a revelation of His mind and will concerning our duty [during] the coming season, even a great revelation, that will enlarge our hearts, comfort us in adversity, and brighten our hopes amidst the powers of darkness" (*History of the Church,* 2:209–10).

The beginning portion of section 107 was dictated by the Prophet Joseph Smith sometime between March and early May 1835 as the newly called Twelve were preparing to serve their first missions as apostles. This instruction and clarification regarding the priesthood blessed the lives of these early brethren and are invaluable also to us.

We will now proceed with our verse-by-verse study of this section.

In verses 1–6, we are taught that there are two major categories of priesthood in the Church—Aaronic and Melchizedek. In verse 5, further clarification is given, stating that the Aaronic Priesthood is an "appendage" to the Melchizedek Priesthood.

1 **THERE are, in the church, two priesthoods**, namely, the **Melchizedek** and **Aaronic**, including the Levitical Priesthood.

Referring back to verse 1, above, sometimes in gospel conversations, "Aaronic Priesthood" means priests, teachers, and deacons, and "Levitical Priesthood" means teachers and deacons. The terms *Aaronic* and *Levitical* are explained in the Bible Dictionary as follows (**bold** added for teaching emphasis. Note that the quote below picks up about half way through the first paragraph given under "Aaronic Priesthood"):

Aaronic Priesthood

Bible Dictionary under "Aaronic Priesthood"

"**The terms *Aaronic* and *Levitical* are sometimes used synonymously** [*in other words, to mean the same thing*] (D&C 107:1, 6, 10), although there are some specific differences in the offices existing within the Levitical Priesthood. For example, the lesser [*Aaronic*] priesthood was conferred only upon men of the tribe of Levi. However, **within the tribe, only Aaron and his sons could hold the office of priest**. And, still further, from the firstborn of Aaron's sons (after Aaron) was selected the high priest (or president of the priests). Thus Aaron and his sons after him had greater offices in the Levitical Priesthood than did the other Levites.

"**The privileges of the priests were greater than those who functioned in the other Levitical offices**, and a distinction between the two is evident when the scripture speaks of them as 'the priests and the Levites' (1 Kgs. 8:4; Ezra 2:70; John 1:19). **The priests could offer sacrifices for the people, burn incense on the altar, and teach the law, whereas the other Levites were employed in more menial tasks**, such as the housekeeping of the tabernacle, keeping oil in the lamps, transporting the Ark of the Covenant, taking down and setting up the tabernacle when moving, and related tasks in assisting the priests (Num. 3:5–10; 18:1–7; 1 Chr. 23:27–32)."

Next, the Savior teaches us why the higher priesthood is called Melchizedek Priesthood.

Melchizedek Priesthood

2 Why the first [*Melchizedek, the first to be mentioned in verse 1, above*] **is called the Melchizedek Priesthood is because Melchizedek was such a great high priest.** [*He was the high priest and king of Salem or Jerusalem. To learn more about him, see JST Genesis 14:25–40 in the Joseph Smith Translation section at the back of your Latter-day Saint edition of the Bible; Alma 13:14–19; D&C 84:14.*]

3 Before his day [*about 2000 B.C.*] **it was called** *the Holy Priesthood, after the Order of the Son of God.*

4 But out of respect or reverence to the name of the Supreme Being, to avoid the too frequent repetition of his name, they, the church, in ancient days, **called that priesthood after Melchizedek**, or the Melchizedek Priesthood.

5 All other authorities or offices in the church are appendages to this priesthood [*to the Melchizedek Priesthood*].

6 But **there are two divisions** or grand heads—one is the **Melchizedek Priesthood**, and the other is the **Aaronic** or Levitical **Priesthood.**

Next, in verses 7–12, the Master Teacher trains us with more specifics about the Melchizedek Priesthood and the offices within it.

7 The office of an elder comes under the priesthood of Melchizedek.

8 The Melchizedek Priesthood holds the right of presidency, and has power and authority over all the offices in the church in all ages of the world, **to administer in spiritual things.**

The First Presidency

9 The Presidency of the High Priesthood [*the First Presidency—see D&C 81:2; 107:22, 65–66*], after the order of Melchizedek, **have a right to officiate in all the offices in the church.**

Next, in verse 10, we are taught that high priests can officiate in the callings and duties normally filled by elders, priests, teachers, and deacons at the local level. An example of this is when a high priest blesses or passes the sacrament.

Melchizedek Priesthood

10 High priests after the order of the Melchizedek Priesthood have a right to officiate in their own standing [*in their own offices and callings*], **under the direction of the presidency** [*the First Presidency*], in administering spiritual things, **and also in the office of an elder, priest** (of the Levitical order), **teacher, deacon, and member.**

> Next, in verse 12, we see that in the absence of a high priest, an elder may conduct.

11 An elder has a right to officiate in his stead [*in the place of a high priest*] when the high priest is not present.

> In verse 8, above, we were taught that the primary stewardship of the Melchizedek Priesthood is to "administer in spiritual things." Verse 12, next, emphasizes this again and also explains that high priests and elders may preside and function at the local level when no General Authorities are present.

> Perhaps you've noticed that when a General Authority is present, he is designated as the "presiding authority" by the one conducting the meeting. This is often seen at stake conferences.

12 The high priest and elder are to administer in spiritual things, agreeable to the covenants and commandments of the church; and **they have a right to officiate in all these offices of the church when there are no higher authorities present.**

> Next, in verses 13–17, we are given more details about the Aaronic Priesthood.

Aaronic Priesthood

13 The second priesthood [*as mentioned in verse 1, above*] **is called the Priesthood of Aaron, because it was conferred upon Aaron** [*the brother of Moses—see Exodus 7:7*] **and his seed** [*posterity*], **throughout all their generations.**

14 Why it is called the lesser priesthood is because it is an appendage to [*attached to or a lesser part of*] **the greater, or the Melchizedek Priesthood, and has power in administering outward ordinances** [*such as passing the sacrament, collecting fast offerings, preparing the sacrament,* *blessing the sacrament, and baptizing—compare with D&C 20:46–60].*

Next, as the Savior continues giving this great revelation on priesthood, He explains that the bishop is the president of the Aaronic Priesthood. The concept and principle of priesthood keys is also tied in with the bishop.

15 **The bishopric is the presidency of this priesthood** [*Aaronic*], **and holds the keys or authority of the same.**

Verses 16–17, next, must be kept in the context of the presiding bishop of the Church (Bishop Edward Partridge at this time in Church history). It deals only with that office, not with the office of local bishops in the various wards of the Church.

The Presiding Bishop of the Church

16 **No man has a legal right to this office** [*Presiding Bishop of the Church*], **to hold the keys of this priesthood, except he be a literal descendant of Aaron** [*compare with D&C 68:15–21*].

17 But **as a high priest of the Melchizedek Priesthood** has authority to officiate in all the lesser offices, **he may officiate in the office of bishop** [*Presiding Bishop*] **when no literal descendant of Aaron can be found, provided he is called and set apart and ordained unto this power by the hands of the Presidency of the Melchizedek Priesthood** [*the First Presidency*].

We will quote from the teachings of Joseph Fielding Smith for additional explanation of verses 16–17, above.

"It has no reference whatever to bishops of wards. Further, such a one must be designated by the First Presidency of the Church and receive his anointing and ordination under their hands. The revelation comes from the Presidency, not from the patriarch, to establish a claim to the right to preside in this office. In the absence of knowledge concerning such a descendant, any high priest, chosen by the Presidency, may hold the office of Presiding Bishop and serve with counselors" (*Doctrines of Salvation,* 3:92–93).

"The office of Presiding Bishop of the Church is the same as the office which was held by Aaron. . . . It was this office which came to John the Baptist, and it was by virtue of the fact that he held the keys of this power and ministry that he was sent to Joseph Smith and Oliver Cowdery to restore that Priesthood, May 15, 1829. The person who has the legal right to this presiding office has not been discovered; perhaps is not in the Church, but should it be shown by revelation that there is one who is the 'firstborn among the sons of Aaron,' and thus entitled by birthright to this presidency, he could 'claim' his 'anointing' and the right to that office in the Church" (*Church History and Modern Revelation*, 1:259).

Next, in verses 18–19, we are taught more about the role and authority of Melchizedek Priesthood. Yet again, we are reminded that it deals with the spiritual blessings and ordinances that attend the faithful in the true Church of Jesus Christ. Without it, we would not have the gift of the Holy Ghost, administering to the sick, patriarchal blessings, temple ordinances, the privilege of being set apart, fathers' blessings, ongoing revelation, and so forth.

Melchizedek Priesthood

18 The power and authority of the higher, or **Melchizedek Priesthood, is to hold the keys of all the spiritual blessings of the church—**

19 To have the privilege of receiving the mysteries of the kingdom of heaven, [*"spiritual truths known only through revelation"—see Guide to the Scriptures; the basic teachings and truths of the gospel of Jesus Christ—see Bible Dictionary under "Mystery"*] **to have the heavens opened unto them,** to **commune with the general assembly and church of the Firstborn** [*to be taught the doctrines that pertain to exaltation; "church of the Firstborn" refers to those who obtain exaltation in the celestial kingdom—see D&C 76:94–95; 93:21–22*], and to **enjoy the communion and presence of God the Father, and Jesus the mediator of the new covenant.**

Verses 20–21 provide more detail about Aaronic Priesthood.

Aaronic Priesthood

20 The power and authority of the lesser, or Aaronic Priesthood, is to hold the keys of the ministering of angels [*see D&C 13; Moroni 7:29–31*], and **to administer in outward ordinances**, the letter of the gospel, the **baptism** of repentance for the remission of sins, agreeable to the covenants and commandments.

Beginning with verse 21, next, the Savior gives details about the structure and role of General Authority quorums in the Church.

General Authority Quorums

21 Of necessity there are presidents, or presiding officers growing out of, or appointed of or from among those who are ordained to the several offices in these two priesthoods.

The First Presidency

22 Of the Melchizedek Priesthood, three Presiding High Priests, chosen by the body, appointed and ordained to that office, and upheld by the confidence, faith, and prayer of the church, **form a quorum of the Presidency of the Church.**

The Quorum of the Twelve Apostles

23 The twelve traveling councilors are called to be **the Twelve Apostles,** or **special witnesses of the name of Christ in all the world**—thus differing from other officers in the church in the duties of their calling.

24 And they **form a quorum, equal in authority and power to the three presidents** [*the First Presidency*] previously mentioned.

> We must not stop reading at the end of verse 24, above. To do so would leave us with a false concept about the authority of the Quorum of the Twelve with respect to the First Presidency. We might think that the two quorums are absolute equals. This is not the case. To complete this doctrine, we must read verse 33, which states that the Twelve "officiate . . . under the direction of the Presidency of the Church."

What we do learn from verse 24 is that when the President of the Church dies and the Quorum of the First Presidency is thus dissolved, the Quorum of the Twelve Apostles temporarily has full authority to lead the Church until the next president is ordained and set apart to serve as president of the Church.

For example, after the martyrdom of the Prophet Joseph Smith, Brigham Young led the Church for three and a half years as president of the Twelve. The First Presidency was again organized in December 1847 and sustained by the members of the Church on December 27, 1847, during a conference held in Kanesville, Iowa, near Council Bluffs.

The Quorum of the Seventy

25 The Seventy are also called to preach the gospel, and **to be especial witnesses unto the Gentiles and in all the world**—thus differing from other officers in the church in the duties of their calling.

26 And **they form a quorum, equal in authority to that of the Twelve** special witnesses or Apostles just named.

> As was the case with the Twelve (verse 24), we must not stop here with verse 26; rather we must read verse 34, which states that the Seventy "act in the name of the

Lord, under the direction of the Twelve."

President Gordon B. Hinckley explained the "equality" of these quorums as follows: "The question arises, How can they [the three quorums] be equal in authority? Speaking to this question, President Joseph F. Smith (1838–1918) taught: 'I want here to correct an impression that has grown up to some extent among the people, and that is, that the Twelve Apostles possess equal authority with the First Presidency in the Church. This is correct when there is no other Presidency but the Twelve Apostles; but so long as there are three presiding Elders who possess the presiding authority in the Church, the authority of the Twelve Apostles is not equal to theirs. If it were so, there would be two equal authorities and two equal quorums in the Priesthood, running parallel, and that could not be, because there must be a head' (Elders' Journal, Nov. 1, 1906, 43).

"Likewise, the Seventy, who serve under the direction of the Twelve, would become equal in authority only in the event that the First Presidency and the Quorum of the Twelve were somehow destroyed" ("The Quorum of the First Presidency," *Ensign*, Dec. 2005, 47).

Next, the Lord explains that decisions made by these General Authority quorums as they lead and guide the Church should be made unanimously. An exception to this is found in verse 28, below.

27 And **every decision** made by either [*any*] of these quorums **must be by the unanimous voice** of the same; that is, every member in each quorum must be agreed to its decisions, in order to make their decisions of the same power or validity one with the other—

28 **A majority may form a quorum when circumstances render it impossible to be otherwise** [*such as when some are traveling and cannot attend a quorum meeting*]—

In verse 29, we are taught that this structure of a presiding presidency of three high priests was used anciently also.

29 Unless this is the case, their decisions are not entitled to the same blessings which the decisions of **a quorum of three presidents** were **anciently**, who were ordained after the order of Melchizedek, and were righteous and holy men.

The personal qualities of character and integrity listed in verse 30, next, can also apply to any of us as we function in presidencies of priesthood quorums or auxiliaries of the Church on the local and stake level.

30 The decisions of these quorums, or either [*any*] of them, **are to be made in all righteousness, in holiness, and lowliness of heart** [*humility*]**, meekness and long suffering, and in faith, and virtue, and knowledge, temperance, patience, godliness, brotherly kindness and charity;**

31 Because the promise is, if these things abound in them they shall not be unfruitful in the knowledge of the Lord.

> If it were ever necessary, verse 32, next, gives the structure for appealing a decision of any of the General Authority quorums.

32 And in case that any decision of these quorums is made in unrighteousness, it may be brought before a general assembly of the several quorums [*the First Presidency, the Quorum of the Twelve Apostles, and the First Quorum of the Seventy—see* Doctrine and Covenants Student Manual, *1981, 264*]**, which constitute the spiritual authorities of the church;** otherwise there can be no appeal from their decision.

> Next, in verses 33–35, additional duties of the Twelve and the Seventy are given.

The Quorum of the Twelve Apostles

33 The Twelve are a Traveling Presiding High Council, to officiate in the name of the Lord, **under the direction of the Presidency of the Church**, agreeable to the institution of heaven; **to build up the church, and regulate all the affairs of the same in all nations,** first unto the Gentiles and secondly unto the Jews [*in the last days, the "Gentiles" (in this context, meaning all who are not Jews) will get the first chance to accept the gospel, and then the Jews will get another opportunity to accept it—see 1 Nephi 13:42*].

> Elder David A. Bednar of the Quorum of the Twelve Apostles taught about the role of the Quorum of the Twelve. He said "Our commission is to go into all the world and proclaim 'Jesus Christ, and him crucified' (see Mark 16:15; 1 Corinthians 2:2). An Apostle is a missionary and a special witness of the name of Christ. The 'name of Christ' refers to the totality of the Savior's mission, death, and resurrection—His authority, His doctrine, and His unique qualifications as the Son of God to be our Redeemer and our Savior. As special witnesses of the name of Christ, we bear testimony of the reality, divinity, and resurrection of Jesus Christ, His infinite and eternal Atonement, and His gospel"

("Special Witnesses of the Name of Christ," *The Religious Educator: Perspectives on the Restored Gospel*, vol. 12, no. 2 [2011], 1; quoted in the 2018 *Doctrine and Covenants Student Manual*, chapter 42).

The Quorum of the Seventy

34 The Seventy are to act in the name of the Lord, **under the direction of the Twelve** or the traveling high council, in building up the church and regulating all the affairs of the same **in all nations**, first unto the Gentiles and then to the Jews;

35 The Twelve being sent out, **holding the keys**, to open the door by the proclamation of the gospel of Jesus Christ, and first unto the Gentiles and then unto the Jews.

Verses 36–37, next, provide a pattern for local stake presidencies and high councils in the stakes of the Church.

Local Stake Presidencies and High Councils

36 The standing high councils, at the stakes of Zion, form a quorum equal in authority in the affairs of the church, in all their decisions, to the quorum of the presidency [*stake presidencies today*], or to the traveling high council.

37 The high council in Zion form a quorum equal in authority in the affairs of the church, in all their decisions, to the councils of the Twelve at the stakes of Zion.

We will again quote from the *Doctrine and Covenants Student Manual*, 1981, this time for clarification of verses 36–37, above:

"'At the time this Revelation was given, there were two standing High Councils in the Church: One in Kirtland, organized February 17th, 1834, and one in Clay County, Mo., organized July 3rd, the same year.' (Smith and Sjodahl, *Commentary*, p. 702.)

"'This indicates the importance attached to the organization of the High Council in Zion,' wrote Smith and Sjodahl, since the government of the Church would not be in danger of being centralized, but the model of a high council in each stake of Zion had been set. 'The standing High Councils in the various Stakes are presided over by the Stake presidency, and their jurisdiction is confined to the Stakes in which they are located.' (*Commentary*, p. 703.)

"Sperry said: 'The Lord indicates that the High Council in Zion (Missouri) was to form a quorum equal in authority, in the affairs of the Church, to the councils of Twelve (High Councils) at the Stakes of Zion (vs 37). And so today a High Council in any Stake of Zion is as important as that in any other Stake. The authority and power of any Stake High Council is local and confined to the boundaries of the Stake concerned'" (*Compendium*, 565; quoted in *Doctrine and Covenants Student Manual*, 1981, 265).

Additional instructions for the Quorum of the Twelve and the Seventy are given in verses 38–39, next.

The Twelve and the Seventy

38 It is the duty of the traveling high council [*the Twelve*] to call upon the Seventy, when they need assistance, to fill the several calls for preaching and administering the gospel, instead of any others.

Stake Patriarchs

39 It is the duty of the Twelve, in all large branches of the church, **to ordain evangelical ministers** [*patriarchs*], as they shall be designated unto them by revelation—

As you are probably aware, many of the duties originally assigned to the Twelve have now been delegated to stake presidents. This is one of the blessings of ongoing revelation, one of the basic factors that distinguishes our Church from all others. Among these duties is the ordaining of patriarchs. If you will excuse me for being a bit personal, I had the privilege of ordaining a new patriarch for our stake when I was serving as a stake president. I was acting under the direction of the President of the Quorum of the Twelve. Years later, as I was released, our patriarch was called to be the new stake president. Subsequently, he ordained me as the new stake patriarch. Because we are close personal friends, these were extra sweet experiences for both of us.

Next, in verses 40–52, the Savior gives the patriarchal line of priesthood authority from Adam to Noah. This "patriarchal priesthood" will be the order of priesthood in the celestial kingdom, highest degree, where the family unit is preserved. These verses serve to illustrate that the priesthood must be passed from one worthy man to another, by proper authority and by the process of ordination by the laying on of hands.

40 The order of this priesthood was confirmed to be handed down from father to son, and rightly belongs to the literal descendants of the chosen seed [*Israel*], to whom the promises were made.

All who join the Church in these last days are considered to be "Israel" and are a part of the much-prophesied last days gathering of Israel. Priesthood holders today are encouraged to keep a record of their priesthood line of authority and to pass a copy of it on to others they ordain.

41 This order was instituted in the days of Adam, and came down by lineage in the following manner:

42 From Adam to **Seth**, who **was ordained by Adam** at the age of sixty-nine years, and was blessed by him three years previous to his (Adam's) death, and received the promise of God by his father, that his posterity should be the chosen of the Lord, and that they should be preserved unto the end of the earth;

43 Because he (**Seth**) was a perfect man, and his likeness **was the express likeness of his father**, insomuch that **he seemed to be like unto his father in all things**, and could be **distinguished** from him **only by his age**.

44 **Enos was ordained** at the age of one hundred and thirty-four years and four months, **by** the hand of **Adam**.

45 God called upon **Cainan** in the wilderness in the fortieth year of his age; and he **met Adam** in journeying to the place Shedolamak. He was eighty-seven years old when he **received his ordination**.

46 **Mahalaleel** was four hundred and ninety-six years and seven days old when he **was ordained by** the hand of **Adam**, who also blessed him.

47 **Jared** was two hundred years old when he **was ordained under the hand of Adam**, who also blessed him.

48 **Enoch** was twenty-five years old when he **was ordained under the hand of Adam**; and he was sixty-five and Adam blessed him.

49 And **he saw the Lord, and he walked with him, and was before his face continually; and he walked with God three hundred and sixty-five years, making him four hundred and thirty years old when he was translated** [*with the whole City of Enoch—see Moses 7:69*].

> It is interesting to note that President Brigham Young taught that the City of Enoch was taken up with houses, lands, gardens, cattle, and all their possessions. (See *Discourses of Brigham Young*, 105.)

50 **Methuselah** was one hundred years old when he **was ordained under the hand of Adam**.

> Did you notice that all of these men so far were ordained by Adam? This is one of the interesting

evidences that Adam and the inhabitants of the earth before the flood did indeed live hundreds of years. Methuselah (verse 50, above), was Adam's great-great-great-great-great-grandson, and Adam still had fifty-six years to live after ordaining him! Counting Adam and going to Methuselah, we have eight generations.

51 **Lamech** was thirty-two years old when he **was ordained under the hand of Seth.**

52 **Noah** was ten years old when he **was ordained under the hand of Methuselah.**

Adam lived to be 930 years old (see Genesis 5:5). Three years prior to his death, a great council was held in the Valley of Adam-ondi-Ahman (about seventy miles north, northeast of Independence, Missouri), to which the righteous posterity of Adam and Eve were invited. We learn about this in verses 53–57.

53 **Three years previous to the death of Adam**, he called Seth, Enos, Cainan, Mahalaleel, Jared, Enoch, and Methuselah [*all of whom Adam had ordained to the Melchizedek Priesthood—see verses 42–50*], who were all high priests, **with the residue** [*remainder*] **of his posterity who were righteous, into the valley of Adam-ondi-Ahman**, and there bestowed upon them his last blessing.

54 And **the Lord appeared unto them**, and **they rose up and blessed** [*blessed often means praised in this type of context*] **Adam**, and called him Michael, the prince, the archangel.

Adam Presides over This Earth under the Direction of Christ

55 And **the Lord administered comfort unto Adam, and said** unto him: **I have set thee to be at the head**; a multitude of nations shall come of thee, and **thou art a prince over them forever.**

In verse 55, above, we are taught that Adam stands next to Christ as far as authority over this earth is concerned.

56 And **Adam stood up in the midst of the congregation**; and, notwithstanding [*even though*] he was bowed down with age, **being full of the Holy Ghost, predicted whatsoever should befall his posterity unto the latest generation.**

57 **These things were all written in the book of Enoch**, and are to be testified of in due time [*in other words, we will get the Book of Enoch someday in the future*].

Sometime before the Savior's Second Coming, a similar meeting will be held at Adam-ondi-Ahman. It is spoken of in D&C 116 and is described in Daniel 7:9–14, D&C 27:5–14, and *The Millennial Messiah*, by Bruce R. McConkie, pages 578–87, which confirms, along with D&C 27:14, that all of the righteous, living and dead, will attend that glorious meeting.

In verses 58–63, next, additional duties of the Twelve are given. Among other things, we learn that priesthood quorums are to be organized on the local level, with presiding officers over each.

58 **It is the duty of the Twelve, also, to ordain and set in order all the other officers of the church, agreeable to the revelation** [*apparently one of the revelations referred to in the heading of this section, which were "received at sundry (various) times"*] **that says:**

59 To the church of Christ in the land of Zion, **in addition to the church laws respecting church business—**

Presiding Officers for Local Priesthood Quorums

60 **Verily, I say unto you, saith the Lord of Hosts, there must needs be presiding elders to preside over those who are of the office of an elder;**

61 And **also priests to preside over those who are of the office of a priest;**

62 And **also teachers to preside over those who are of the office of a teacher, in like manner, and also the deacons—**

63 Wherefore, **from deacon to teacher**, and from **teacher to priest**, and from **priest to elder,** [*in other words, each quorum is to have local presiding priesthood officers*] severally as they are appointed, according to the covenants and commandments of the church.

The Living Prophet Is the President of the High Priesthood and, as Such, Presides Over All Other Officers in the Church

64 **Then comes the High Priesthood, which is the greatest of all.**

65 Wherefore, **it must needs be that one be appointed of the High Priesthood to preside over the priesthood, and he shall be called President of the High Priesthood of the Church;**

66 Or, in other words, **the Presiding High Priest** over the High Priesthood of the Church.

The Living Prophet Holds All the Priesthood Keys and Thus Directs All Priesthood Functioning in the Church.

67 From the same [*from the President of the Church*] **comes the administering of ordinances and blessings upon the church, by the laying on of the hands.**

Duties of Bishops

68 Wherefore, **the office of a bishop is not equal unto it** [*not equal to the president of the Church*]; for the office of a bishop is in administering all temporal things;

> While we are familiar with the fact that a bishop is not equal in authority to the living prophet (verse 68, above), we do well to keep in mind that to many of the early members of the Church in this last dispensation, it was not obvious. Most of them had come as converts from religious groups in which the local minister or pastor had all the authority. And if there were any central organization and leadership at all associated with that particular religion, it was at best a relatively weak advisory body that could be hearkened to or ignored, depending on the desires of the local minister. Thus, verse 68 required a rather dramatic change in thinking and understanding for many early Saints.
>
> Next, we are taught that a bishop of a ward must be a high priest.

A Local Bishop Must Be a High Priest

69 Nevertheless **a bishop must be chosen from the High Priesthood,** unless he is a literal descendant of Aaron [*see notes associated with verses 16–17 in this section*];

70 For unless he is a literal descendant of Aaron he cannot hold the keys of that priesthood.

71 Nevertheless, **a high priest**, that is, after the order of Melchizedek, **may be set apart unto the ministering of temporal things** [*may be ordained a bishop*], having a knowledge of them by the Spirit of truth;

> In verses 72–74, next, special emphasis is given to the role and responsibility of bishops to serve as judges among the members within their stewardship. This is a great blessing for members, because it allows them to go to someone close by who is authorized by God to assist them in overcoming sin and other difficulties that may arise in their lives. Bishops are often referred to as "common judges in Israel."

72 And also **to be a judge in Israel,** to do the business of the church, **to sit in judgment upon transgressors** upon testimony as it shall be laid before him according to the laws, **by the assistance of his counselors**, whom he has chosen or will choose among the elders of the church.

73 **This is the duty of a bishop who** is not a literal descendant of Aaron, but **has been ordained to the High Priesthood after the order of Melchizedek.**

74 **Thus shall he be a judge**, even **a common judge** among the inhabitants of Zion, or in a stake of Zion, or in any branch of the church where he shall be set apart unto this ministry, until the borders of Zion are enlarged and it becomes necessary to have other bishops or judges in Zion or elsewhere.

Verse 75, next, alerts these members in 1835 that the Church will continue to grow and that as it does so, additional bishops will be needed, and they will have the same responsibilities and duties as listed above.

75 And **inasmuch as there are other bishops appointed they shall act in the same office.**

You have seen the term "literal descendant of Aaron" (as in verse 76, next) a number of times now. This may be one of those things that will be put to use someday in the future, at which time we will be delighted to finally understand what it means and how it is implemented. We will have to wait and see.

Looking ahead to verses 81 and 84, we see that no one is exempt from accountability in this Church, including members of the First Presidency. The last part of verse 76, next, explains that if a member of the First Presidency were to exercise his agency to commit serious transgression, the Presiding Bishop, with two counselors, would preside at the disciplinary council for him.

76 But **a literal descendant of Aaron has a legal right to the presidency of this priesthood** [*the office of Presiding Bishop—see notes and commentary for verses 16–17*], **to the keys of this ministry, to act** in the office of bishop independently, **without counselors, except in a case where a President of the High Priesthood** [*a member of the First Presidency*], after the order of Melchizedek, **is tried, to sit as a judge in Israel** [*in other words, to preside at that membership council, formerly called "disciplinary council"*].

We will include two quotes here that give additional clarification for verse 76, above. The first is by Joseph Fielding Smith; the second is by John A. Widtsoe (**bold** added for emphasis):

"The bishop is a common judge in Israel, and members are amenable to his jurisdiction. **In case of** an accusation made against one of the First Presidency, the case would be tried before the presiding bishop and a council of high priests" (*Church History and Modern Revelation*, 2:21).

"**The Presiding Bishop's Court** [*membership council*] **consists of the Presiding Bishop with his two counselors, and twelve High Priests especially chosen for the purpose**. It is a tribunal extraordinary, from which there is no appeal, **to be convened if it should be necessary to try a member of the First Presidency** for crime or neglect of duty" (*Priesthood and Church Government*, 212).

Next, beginning with verse 77, the Lord explains that extra difficult local issues, including the results of local membership councils, may be appealed to the First Presidency (compare with D&C 102:27).

The Decisions of Local "Judges," Including Those in Wards and Stakes, Regarding Extra Difficult Matters May Be Appealed to the First Presidency

77 And **the decision of either of these councils** [*any of these local councils*], agreeable to the commandment which says:

78 Again, verily, I say unto you, the most important business of the church, and **the most difficult cases** of the church [*at the local level*], **inasmuch as there is not satisfaction upon the decision of the bishop or judges, it shall be handed over and carried up** [*appealed*] unto the council of the church, **before the Presidency of the High Priesthood** [*the First Presidency*].

79 And **the Presidency of the council of the High Priesthood shall have power to call other high priests, even twelve, to assist as counselors**; and thus **the Presidency of the High Priesthood and its counselors shall have power to decide** upon testimony according to the laws of the church.

80 And after this decision it shall be had in remembrance no more before the Lord; for **this is the highest council of the church of God, and a final decision** upon controversies in spiritual matters.

81 **There is not any person belonging to the church who is exempt from this council of the church** [*see also verse 84*].

82 And **inasmuch as** [*if*] **a President of the High Priesthood** [*a member of the First Presidency*] **shall transgress**, he shall be had in remembrance before [*he shall*

be brought before] the common council of the church [*a membership council presided over by the Presiding Bishop of the Church—see verse 76*], who shall be assisted by twelve counselors of the High Priesthood [*by twelve high priests especially assembled for this membership council*];

83 And **their decision upon his head shall be an end of controversy concerning him**.

84 Thus, **none shall be exempted from the justice and the laws of God**, that all things may be done in order and in solemnity before him, according to truth and righteousness.

> Next, in verses 85–89, the numbers of priesthood holders making up full quorums at the local level are given.

Deacons Quorum

85 And again, verily I say unto you, **the duty of a president over the office of a deacon is to preside over twelve deacons, to sit in council with them, and to teach them their duty, edifying one another**, as it is given according to the covenants.

Teachers Quorum

86 And also the duty of **the president over the office of the teachers is to preside over twenty-four** of the teachers, and to sit in council with them, teaching them the duties of their office, as given in the covenants.

Priests Quorum

87 Also the duty of **the president over the Priesthood of Aaron is to preside over forty-eight priests**, and sit in council with them, to teach them the duties of their office, as is given in the covenants—

The Bishop Is the President of the Priests Quorum in His Ward

88 **This president is to be a bishop**; for this is one of the duties of this priesthood.

Elders Quorum

89 Again, **the duty of the president** over the office of elders **is to preside over ninety-six** elders, and to sit in council with them, and to teach them according to the covenants.

> By the way, it is significant that a deacons quorum is the smallest in terms of members. In this way, in a general sense, those who are newest in the priesthood can be given the most individual attention by quorum leaders.
>
> In our day, we have witnessed a significant revelation regarding the membership of elders quorums.

As you may recall, as of the April 2018 general conference (the Saturday evening priesthood session on March 31), all high priests and elders in a given ward are now members of the elders quorum of their ward. President Russell M. Nelson announced the following in that priesthood session: "Tonight we announce a significant restructuring of our Melchizedek Priesthood quorums to accomplish the work of the Lord more effectively. In each ward, the high priests and the elders will now be combined into one elders quorum."

This is a marvelous example of continuing revelation. It is a very real example of the fact that the words of the living Prophet take precedence over the words in the scriptures.

Next, in verse 90, emphasis is given to the fact that elders quorums serve locally in their wards and are not expected to travel as is the case with General Authority Seventies.

90 **This presidency** [*the elders quorum presidency—verse 89*] **is a distinct one from that of the seventy, and is designed for those who do not travel into all the world.**

The President of the Church Presides over the Whole Church and Possesses All the Gifts of God

91 **And again, the duty of the President of the office of the High Priesthood is to preside over the whole church, and to be like unto Moses—**

92 Behold, here is wisdom; yea, **to be a seer, a revelator, a translator, and a prophet, having all the gifts of God** which he bestows upon the head of the church.

As you know, we live in an exciting time in the growth of the Church. In verses 93–98, next, we see the organization of the Seventy, put in place by the Savior in the early 1830s and being used to handle the expanding General Authority leadership needs of the Church in our day.

The General Authority Seventy Quorums Have Seven Presidents

93 **And it is according to the vision showing the order of the Seventy, that they should have seven presidents to preside over them, chosen out of the number of the seventy;**

94 And **the seventh president of these presidents is to preside over the six;**

Verses 95–97, next, point out that General Authority Seventies and Quorums of Seventy can be added as needed to keep up with the growth of the Church.

95 And **these seven presidents**

are to choose other seventy besides the first seventy to whom they belong, **and are to preside over them**;

96 **And also other seventy**, until seven times seventy, **if the labor in the vineyard of necessity requires it.**

97 And **these seventy are to be traveling ministers**, unto the Gentiles first and also unto the Jews.

> President Gordon B. Hinckley pointed out verse 98, next, at the time area authority Seventies were called. They are now referred to as "Area Seventies." This verse allows for these brethren to continue working in their occupations and live in their own homes while holding "as high and responsible offices in the church" (end of verse 98) as the Seventy who are called upon to travel constantly throughout the world.

98 Whereas **other officers** [*Area Seventies*] of the church, who belong not unto the Twelve, neither to the Seventy, **are not under the responsibility to travel among all nations, but are to travel as their circumstances shall allow, notwithstanding** [*even though*] **they may hold as high and responsible offices in the church.**

You may recall from the background notes given at the beginning of this section in this study guide that the twelve men who were called to serve in the first Quorum of the Twelve Apostles in this dispensation felt the heavy weight of responsibility settling in upon them. As a result, they asked the Prophet Joseph Smith to seek a revelation from the Lord for them "that we may look upon it when we are separated [*serving missions throughout the Church*], that our hearts may be comforted."

The Savior has granted their request and taught them much about priesthood and the offices within it in this section. Now, in conclusion, He invites them to "learn [their] duty, and to act in the office in which [they] are appointed, in all diligence" (verse 99, next). This council applies to all of us who accept callings in the Church. We have the revelations of the Lord to study, through which we too can learn our duty.

99 Wherefore, now **let every man learn his duty, and to act in the office in which he is appointed, in all diligence.**

100 **He that is slothful shall not be counted worthy to stand, and he that learns not his duty and shows himself not approved shall not be counted worthy to stand.** Even so. Amen.

SECTION 108

Background

This revelation was given through the Prophet Joseph Smith to Lyman Sherman, a personal friend of the Prophet, on December 26, 1835, in Kirtland, Ohio. Brother Sherman and his wife, Delcena, had joined the Church in January 1832 in New York and subsequently moved to Kirtland.

Brother Sherman had been a faithful member of Zion's Camp and was called to serve as one of the Seven Presidents of the First Quorum of the Seventy (see D&C 107:93). He'd had concerns about his worthiness for some time and came to the Prophet on the day after Christmas, seeking the word of the Lord in his behalf. Joseph Smith gave some background to this revelation. He said:

"Brother Lyman Sherman came in, and requested to have the word of the Lord through me; 'for,' said he, 'I have been wrought upon to make known to you my feelings and desires, and was promised that I should have a revelation which should make known my duty'" (*History of the Church*, 2:345).

Having been concerned about his worthiness before the Lord, the first three verses of this revelation were no doubt sweet indeed to him. The Savior told him that his sins were forgiven and confirmed the fact that he had been prompted by the Spirit to come to the Prophet. Furthermore, he was given a gentle warning to avoid resisting the promptings of the Lord in the future and to be more strict in keeping his covenants with the Lord.

1 VERILY thus saith the Lord unto you, my servant Lyman: **Your sins are forgiven you, because you have obeyed my voice in coming up hither this morning to receive counsel of him whom I have appointed** [*Joseph Smith*].

2 Therefore, **let your soul be at rest concerning your spiritual standing**, and **resist no more my voice**.

3 And arise up and **be more careful henceforth in observing your vows, which you have made and do make, and you shall be blessed with exceeding great blessings**.

The "solemn assembly" spoken of in verse 4, next, could well be the upcoming dedication of the Kirtland Temple, or one of the meetings associated with it. Also, the Saints held additional solemn assemblies after the Kirtland Temple dedication. A quote from the 2018 *Doctrine and Covenants Student Manual* is helpful here:

"A solemn assembly was held three days after the dedication of the

Kirtland Temple on March 27, 1836, and may have been a fulfillment of the command to 'call a solemn assembly . . . of those who are the first laborers in this last kingdom' (D&C 88:70; see also D&C 88:117; 95:7; 108:4; 109:6, 10). The Prophet Joseph Smith recorded that on March 30, 1836, a congregation of about three hundred Church leaders and members met in the Kirtland Temple and participated in the ordinances of the washing of feet and the sacrament. The Prophet gave instruction, and Church leaders pronounced blessings and prophesied. Joseph Smith recorded that he left the meeting 'at about 9 o'clock in the evening,' and the members of the Quorum of the Twelve Apostles continued the meeting, during which there was 'exhorting, prophesying and speaking in tongues until 5 o'clock in the morning—the Savior made His appearance to some, while angels ministered unto others, and it was a Pentecost and [an] endowment indeed, long to be remembered' (in *The Joseph Smith Papers, Journals, Volume 1: 1832–1839*, 215–16; spelling, punctuation, and capitalization standardized)."

"Solemn assemblies continue to be held in modern times, as explained by Elder David B. Haight (1906–2004) of the Quorum of the Twelve Apostles: 'A solemn assembly, as the name implies, denotes a sacred, sober, and reverent occasion when the Saints assemble under the direction of the First Presidency. Solemn assemblies are used for three purposes: the dedication of temples, special instruction to priesthood leaders, and sustaining a new President of the Church' ("Solemn Assemblies," *Ensign*, Nov. 1994, 14)."

4 Wait patiently until the solemn assembly shall be called of my servants [*by the leaders of the Church*], then you shall be remembered with the first of mine elders [*apparently a reference to the leaders of the Church, including the Seventies—compare D&C 88:85, 105:7*], and receive right by ordination with the rest of mine elders whom I have chosen.

President Spencer W. Kimball taught the following about solemn assemblies:

Solemn assemblies "have been known among the Saints since the days of Israel. They have been of various kinds but generally have been associated with the dedication of a temple or a special meeting appointed for the sustaining of a new First Presidency or a meeting for the priesthood to sustain a revelation, such as the tithing revelation to President Lorenzo Snow. . . .

"Joseph Smith and Brigham Young were first sustained by a congregation, including a fully organized priesthood. Brigham Young was sustained on March 27, 1846, and was 'unanimously elected president over the whole Camp of Israel' by the council. (B. H. Roberts, *A Comprehensive History of the Church,* vol. 3, p. 52.) Later he was sustained, and the Hosanna Shout was given.

"Each of the presidents of the Church has been sustained by the priesthood of the Church in solemn assembly down to and including President Harold B. Lee, who was sustained October 6, 1972" (in Conference Report, April 1974, 64–65; or "What Do We Hear?" *Ensign,* May 1974, 45).

In verse 5, next, Brother Sherman is promised that the blessings mentioned in verse 4, above, will come to him if he remains faithful.

5 Behold, this is the promise of the Father unto you **if you continue faithful.**

6 And it shall be fulfilled upon you in that day that **you shall have right to preach my gospel wheresoever I shall send you**, from henceforth from that time.

Using hindsight, the "wheresoever" in verse 6, above, may have been a foreshadowing of a mission in the spirit world (D&C 138:57) for Brother Lyman since he died faithful to the Church on January 27, 1839, in Far West, Missouri, at the age of thirty-four.

The counsel given by the Savior in verse 7, next, certainly applies to all of us.

7 Therefore, **strengthen your brethren in all your conversation, in all your prayers, in all your exhortations, and in all your doings.**

8 And behold, and lo, **I am with you to bless you and deliver you forever.** Amen.

SECTION 109

Background

This section consists of the dedicatory prayer given by the Prophet Joseph Smith at the dedication of the Kirtland Temple on March 27, 1836. As you can see in the heading to section 109 in your Doctrine and Covenants, the Prophet confirmed that this prayer was given to him by revelation.

At the end of December 1832 and on January 3, 1833, the Saints were given what is now known as section 88 (see heading to section 88 in your Doctrine and Covenants) in which they were commanded by the Lord to build a temple in Kirtland (D&C 88:119). By June 1833, they had still not begun. Consequently, the Savior chastised them rather severely (D&C 95:2–3) and said, "Let the house [*the Kirtland Temple*] be built" (D&C 95:13). Four days later, they began digging foundation trenches and hauling stones for the temple construction (see the gospel doctrine teacher's manual, *Doctrine and Covenants and Church History,* 100).

The temple was constructed at a cost estimated to be between $40,000 and $60,000 during a time of extreme poverty and hardship for the members of the Church. Nevertheless, after almost three years, it was completed and ready for this dedicatory prayer on Sunday, March 27, 1836.

Some people have wondered why the Lord would have the members go through such extreme hardship and sacrifice to build a temple that would soon be abandoned. In D&C 64:21, the Saints were clearly told that Kirtland would be a stronghold of the Church for only five years, and at the time of the dedication of the temple, about four and a half of the five years was up. Perhaps there is some important symbolism in this. A chart has been included (at right) to illustrate some possible symbolism.

When we stop to think about it, as illustrated in the chart, the temporary nature of the Kirtland Temple was not a problem at all in the eternal nature of things, just as the temporary nature of mortality is not a problem when viewed from the perspective of eternity. We come to mortality, accomplish its purposes by keeping the commandments if we so choose, and then leave, having been better prepared for the highest blessings of eternity. The Saints built the Kirtland Temple, benefited beyond words from its eternal purposes, and then left it having been better prepared for the future.

Mortality	Kirtland Temple	Mortality	Kirtland Temple
Is temporary	Was for temporary use.	Designed to bring us back into God's presence through our obedience to God's commandments.	Designed to bring God's presence to the Saints (D&C 110:1–8) upon their obedience to the commandment to build a temple.
Requires sacrifice and prioritizing in order to keep God's commandments.	Required sacrifice and prioritizing in order to keep God's commandment to build a temple.		
Requires that we put our best into serving God and keeping His commandments in order to progress toward our exaltation.	Required that the Saints put their best into building the temple in order to qualify for the promised blessings that would enable them to progress toward exaltation. These blessings included the appearance of the Savior and the coming of Moses, Elias, and Elijah who restored priesthood keys necessary for sealing families together forever (D&C 110).	Designed to develop in us the power to become like God (in other words, to attain exaltation), through gaining physical bodies and learning obedience to God's commandments, during our temporary mortal state.	Built for the purpose (during its temporary service as a holy temple) of giving revelation, instruction (D&C 95:4, 8; 109:14–15, etc.), and restoring priesthood keys (D&C 110) which empower the righteous to become like God (in other words, to attain exaltation).

It is interesting to note that the day of the dedication of the Kirtland Temple was Palm Sunday, the Sunday before Easter, on which day many celebrate the Savior's triumphal entry into Jerusalem. The Master's entry into Jerusalem was accompanied by the spreading of palm branches along His path (John 12:13; Matthew 21:1–9), thus the name Palm Sunday. In biblical culture, palm branches symbolize triumph and victory.

In *History of the Church,* volume 2, beginning on page 416, we find an account of the dedication of the Kirtland Temple. We will include a brief summary of the day and the dedicatory services:

- Hundreds of people gathered early in the morning, hoping to get a seat in the temple for the services.

- The doors of the Kirtland Temple were opened at 8:00 A.M.

- About a thousand members were seated inside, but hundreds remained who could not get in. They were eventually seated in the schoolhouse, and the services were repeated for them the following Thursday.

- At 9:00 A.M., President Sidney Rigdon began the seven-hour-long services by reading Psalms 24 and 96.

- The choir sang.

- Sidney Rigdon offered an opening prayer.

- A hymn was sung.

- Sidney Rigdon spoke for two and a half hours.

- Joseph Smith was sustained as the Prophet and Seer of the Church.

- The hymn "Now Let Us Rejoice" was sung.

- A twenty-minute intermission followed.

- Services were resumed by singing "Adam-ondi-Ahman."

- Joseph Smith spoke briefly.

- The First Presidency and Twelve were then sustained as prophets, seers, and revelators, followed by the sustaining of other officers and leaders.

- The Prophet then "prophesied to all, that inasmuch as they would uphold these men in their several stations, (alluding to the different quorums in the Church), the Lord would bless them; yea, in the name of Christ, the blessings of heaven should be theirs; and when the Lord's anointed go forth to proclaim the word, bearing testimony to this generation, if they receive it they shall be blessed; but if not, the judgments of God will follow close upon them, until that city or that house which rejects

SECTION 109

them, shall be left desolate" (*History of the Church*, 2:418–19).

- A hymn was sung.

- The dedicatory prayer was offered by the Prophet Joseph Smith (as recorded in section 109).

- Following the dedicatory prayer, the choir sang "The Spirit of God," composed especially for the occasion by W. W. Phelps.

- The Prophet "then asked the several quorums separately, and then the congregation, if they accepted the dedication prayer, and acknowledged the house dedicated. The vote was unanimous in the affirmative, in every instance" (*History of the Church*, 2:427).

- The sacrament was then administered and passed to the congregation.

- Various testimonies were given, including the witness that several angels had been seen during the services thus far.

- Sidney Rigdon gave some closing remarks.

- Sidney Rigdon gave a closing prayer.

- The congregation stood and participated in the Hosanna Shout.

Thus, the first temple in this dispensation was dedicated. Of the final portion of the dedicatory service, beginning with the administration of the sacrament, the Prophet recorded:

"The Lord's Supper was then administered; President Don Carlos Smith blessed the bread and the wine, which was distributed by several Elders to the Church; after which I bore record of my mission, and of the ministration of angels.

"President Don Carlos Smith also bore testimony of the truth of the work of the Lord in which we were engaged.

"President Oliver Cowdery testified of the truth of the Book of Mormon, and of the work of the Lord in these last days.

"President Frederick G. Williams arose and testified that while President Rigdon was making his first prayer, an angel entered the window and took his seat between Father Smith and himself, and remained there during the prayer.

"President David Whitmer also saw angels in the house.

"President Hyrum Smith made some appropriate remarks congratulating those who had endured so many toils and privations to build the house" (*History of the Church*, 2:427).

The Prophet continued by describing the Hosanna Shout (**bold** added for emphasis):

Hosanna Shout

"President Rigdon then made a few appropriate closing remarks, and a short prayer, at the close of which we sealed the proceedings of the day by shouting **hosanna, hosanna, hosanna to God and the Lamb**, three times, sealing it each time with **amen, amen, and amen**.

"President Brigham Young gave a short address in tongues, and David W. Patten interpreted, and gave a short exhortation in tongues himself, after which I blessed the congregation in the name of the Lord, and the assembly dispersed a little past four o'clock, having manifested the most quiet demeanor during the whole exercise" (*History of the Church,* 2:428).

That evening, a special priesthood meeting was held in the temple. Joseph Smith recorded special manifestations during that meeting. He said:

"Brother George A. Smith arose and began to prophesy, when a noise was heard like the sound of a rushing mighty wind, which filled the Temple, and all the congregation simultaneously arose, being moved upon by an invisible power; many began to speak in tongues and prophesy; others saw glorious visions; and I beheld the Temple was filled with angels, which fact I declared to the congregation. The people of the neighborhood came running together (hearing an unusual sound within, and seeing a bright light like a pillar of fire resting upon the Temple), and were astonished at what was taking place. This continued until the meeting closed at eleven p. m." (*History of the Church,* 2:428).

Before we study the dedicatory prayer for the Kirtland Temple as given in this section, we will pause to say a bit more about the Hosanna Shout.

The basic meaning of the word *Hosanna* is "save now" (see Bible Dictionary under "Hosanna"). You may wish to turn to Psalm 118:25, where you will see a beautiful context demonstrating its meaning. It is essentially a plea to the Lord to "save us now, please."

In biblical times, the waving of palm branches (palm fronds) was symbolic of triumph and victory. The hoped-for victory over enemies was demonstrated with palm fronds during the triumphal entry of the Savior into Jerusalem (Matthew 21:9). Spiritually, palm branches are used to symbolize triumph and victory over sin and imperfection because of the Savior's Atonement. An example of this is seen in Revelation 7:9.

White handkerchiefs used in the Hosanna Shout at temple dedications today are symbolic of the waving of palm fronds and represent our humble and enthusiastic plea that the Savior and His

SECTION 109

Atonement give us victory over sin and save us in His Father's kingdom forever.

Keep in mind that in just seven days following this dedicatory prayer, in a series of glorious manifestations, Christ, Moses, Elias, and Elijah will appear to the Prophet and Oliver Cowdery in the Kirtland Temple (D&C 110).

As we proceed with our study of this section, our primary focus will be the blessings of the temple, along with our responsibilities to prepare for temple worship. We will use **bold** exclusively in this section to point these things out and make less than usual use of notes and commentary, thus letting the scripture speak for itself. We will use *Our Responsibilities* to point out some things we should do in order to gain the blessings of the temple, and *Blessings of Temple Attendance* to indicate what some of the precious benefits of temple attendance are. In cases where both responsibilities and blessings occur in the same verse, we will repeat the verse. You will no doubt find additional blessings and responsibilities beyond what we have listed.

1 THANKS be to thy name, O Lord God of Israel, who keepest covenant and showest mercy unto thy servants who walk uprightly before thee, with all their hearts—

2 Thou who hast commanded thy servants to build a house to thy name in this place [*Kirtland*].

Our Responsibilities

3 And now thou beholdest, O Lord, that **thy servants have done according to thy commandment**.

4 And now we ask thee, Holy Father, in the name of Jesus Christ, the Son of thy bosom, in whose name alone salvation can be administered to the children of men, we ask thee, O Lord, to accept of this house, the workmanship of the hands of us, thy servants, which thou didst command us to build [*the Savior will accept it in one week, as recorded in D&C 110:7*].

Blessings of Temple Attendance

5 For thou knowest that we have done this work through great tribulation; and out of our poverty we have given of our substance to build a house to thy name, that **the Son of Man** might have a place to **manifest** himself **to his people**.

6 And as thou hast said in a revelation, given to us, calling us thy friends, saying—Call your solemn assembly, as I have commanded you;

Our Responsibilities

7 And as all have not faith, **seek ye diligently** and **teach**

one another words of wisdom; yea, **seek ye out of the best books words of wisdom, seek learning even by study and also by faith;**

Our Responsibilities

8 **Organize** yourselves; **prepare** every needful thing, and **establish** a house, even **a house of prayer**, a house of **fasting**, a house of **faith**, a house of **learning**, a house of **glory**, a house of **order**, **a house of God;**

Our Responsibilities

> One of the things we learn from verse 9, next, is that we need to have a constant awareness of who we are and of the covenants we make in the name of Jesus Christ. Also, while in the temple, everything we do is in the name of the Lord. We are in a celestial environment and gain firsthand knowledge and feelings of what heaven is like.

9 **That your incomings** may be **in the name of the Lord,** that your **outgoings** may be **in the name of the Lord, that all your salutations may be in the name of the Lord,** with uplifted hands unto the Most High—

Blessings of Temple Attendance

10 And now, Holy Father, we ask thee to **assist us,** thy people, **with thy grace,** in calling our solemn assembly, that it may be done to thine honor and to thy divine acceptance;

Blessings of Temple Attendance

11 And in a manner that we may be found worthy, in thy sight, to **secure a fulfilment of the promises** which thou hast made unto us, thy people, **in the revelations given unto us;**

Blessings of Temple Attendance

12 **That thy glory may rest down upon thy people,** and upon this thy house, which we now dedicate to thee, that it may be sanctified and consecrated to be holy, and **that thy holy presence may be continually in this house;**

Blessings of Temple Attendance

13 And **that all people who shall enter** upon the threshold of the Lord's house **may feel thy power,** and feel constrained to acknowledge that thou hast sanctified it, and that it is thy house, a place of thy holiness.

Blessings of Temple Attendance

14 And do thou grant, Holy Father, **that all those who shall**

worship in this house may be **taught words of wisdom** out of the best books, and that they may seek learning even by study, and also by faith, as thou hast said [*in D&C 88:118*];

Blessings of Temple Attendance

15 And **that they may grow up in thee**, and **receive a fulness of the Holy Ghost**, and **be organized according to thy laws, and be prepared to obtain every needful thing**;

16 And **that this house may be a house of prayer, a house of fasting, a house of faith, a house of glory and of God**, even thy house;

17 **That all** the incomings of thy people, into this house, **may be in the name of the Lord**;

18 **That all** their outgoings from this house **may be in the name of the Lord**;

19 And **that all** their salutations **may be in the name of the Lord**, with holy hands, uplifted to the Most High;

Our Responsibilities

20 And **that no unclean thing shall be permitted to come into thy house to pollute it**;

Blessings of Temple Attendance

21 And **when thy people transgress**, any of them, **they may speedily repent and return unto thee, and find favor in thy sight, and be restored to the blessings which thou hast ordained to be poured out upon those who shall reverence thee in thy house**.

Our Responsibilities

(Verse 21, repeated)

21 And **when thy people transgress**, any of them, they may **speedily repent and return unto thee**, and find favor in thy sight, and be restored to the blessings which thou hast ordained to be poured out upon those who shall **reverence thee in thy house**.

Blessings of Temple Attendance

22 And we ask thee, Holy Father, **that thy servants may go forth from this house armed with thy power**, and **that thy name may be upon them**, and **thy glory be round about them**, and **thine angels have charge over them**;

Blessings of Temple Attendance

23 And from this place they may bear exceedingly great and glorious tidings, in truth, unto the ends of the earth, that **they may know that this is thy work**, and that thou hast put forth thy hand, to fulfil that which thou hast spoken by the mouths of the prophets, concerning the last days.

Blessings of Temple Attendance

24 We ask thee, Holy Father, to **establish the people that shall worship**, and honorably hold a name and standing in this thy house, **to all generations and for eternity**;

Our Responsibilities

(Verse 24, repeated)

24 We ask thee, Holy Father, to establish the people that shall worship, and **honorably hold a name and standing in this thy house**, to all generations and for eternity;

Blessings of Temple Attendance

25 That **no weapon formed against them shall prosper**; that he who diggeth a pit for them shall fall into the same himself [*the wicked who attempt to snare and destroy the righteous will ultimately fall into their own trap, meaning the buffetings of Satan and answering to God for their wickedness*];

> The fulfilling of verses 25–26 is best seen in an eternal, spiritual context since many righteous throughout history have gone through misery and even death because of their faithfulness to God. But in the eternal scheme of things, no wicked ever triumph over the righteous who endure to the end.

Blessings of Temple Attendance

26 **That no combination of wickedness shall have power to rise up and prevail** [*ultimately win*] **over thy people upon whom thy name shall be put in this house**;

27 And **if any people shall rise against this people**, that **thine anger be kindled against them**;

Blessings of Temple Attendance

28 And **if they shall smite this people thou wilt smite them; thou wilt fight for thy people** as thou didst in the day of battle, **that they may be delivered from the hands of all their enemies** [*especially the enemies of their spirituality*].

29 We ask thee, Holy Father, to **confound, and astonish, and to bring to shame and confusion, all those who have spread lying reports abroad, over the world, against thy servant or servants, if they will not repent**, when the everlasting gospel shall be proclaimed in their ears;

30 And **that all their works may be brought to naught**, and be swept away by the hail, and by the judgments which thou wilt send upon them in thine anger, that there may be an end to lyings and slanders against thy people.

31 For thou knowest, O Lord, that thy servants have been innocent before thee in bearing record of thy name, for which they have suffered these things.

32 Therefore we plead before thee for **a full and complete deliverance** from under this yoke;

Blessings of Temple Attendance

33 Break it off, O Lord; break it off from the necks of thy servants, by thy power, **that we may rise up in the midst of this generation and do thy work.**

Blessings of Temple Attendance

34 O Jehovah, have **mercy** upon this people, and as all men sin **forgive the transgressions of thy people, and let them be blotted out forever.**

Blessings of Temple Attendance

35 **Let the anointing** of thy ministers **be sealed upon them** with power from on high.

36 Let it be fulfilled upon them, as upon those on the day of Pentecost; let the gift of tongues be poured out upon thy people, even cloven tongues as of fire, and the interpretation thereof.

37 And let thy house be filled, as with a rushing mighty wind, with thy glory.

Blessings of Temple Attendance

38 Put upon thy servants the testimony of the covenant, that when they go out and proclaim thy word they may seal up the law, and **prepare the hearts of thy saints for all those judgments thou art about to send**, in thy wrath, **upon the inhabitants of the earth**, because of their transgressions, **that thy people may not faint** [*give up;*

lose hope; get caught up in despair, gloom and doom] **in the day of trouble.**

Blessings of Temple Attendance

39 And whatsoever city thy servants shall enter, and the people of that city receive their testimony, let thy peace and thy salvation be upon that city; that they may gather out of that city **the righteous, that they may come forth to Zion, or to her stakes**, the places of thine appointment, with songs of everlasting joy;

> Verse 40, next, is an inspired plea for mercy upon the wicked, requesting that they be given a chance to repent (verse 39, above). This is a major insight into how God works with all of us and a doctrinal reminder that everyone must have a perfect opportunity to hear and understand the gospel before the final judgment. Verse 43 reminds us that all souls are precious.

40 And until this be accomplished, let not thy judgments fall upon that city.

41 And whatsoever city thy servants shall enter, and the people of that city receive not the testimony of thy servants, and thy servants warn them to save themselves from this untoward [*wicked*] generation, let it be upon that city according to that which thou hast spoken by the mouths of thy prophets.

42 But **deliver thou**, O Jehovah, we beseech thee, **thy servants from their hands**, and cleanse them from their blood [*the sins and abominations of the wicked*].

43 O Lord, we delight not in the destruction of our fellow men; their souls are precious before thee;

44 But thy word must be fulfilled. Help thy servants to say, with thy grace assisting them: Thy will be done, O Lord, and not ours.

45 We know that thou hast spoken by the mouth of thy prophets terrible things concerning the wicked, in the last days—that thou wilt pour out thy judgments, without measure;

Blessings of Temple Attendance

46 Therefore, O Lord, **deliver thy people from the calamity of the wicked**; enable thy servants to seal up the law, and bind up the testimony, **that they may be prepared against the day of burning.**

47 We ask thee, Holy Father, to remember those who have been driven by the inhabitants of Jackson county, Missouri, from the lands of their inheritance, and break off, O Lord, this yoke of affliction that has been put upon them.

48 Thou knowest, O Lord, that they have been greatly oppressed and afflicted by wicked men; and our hearts flow out with sorrow because of their grievous burdens.

49 O Lord, how long wilt thou suffer this people to bear this affliction, and the cries of their innocent ones to ascend up in thine ears, and their blood come up in testimony before thee, and not make a display of thy testimony in their behalf?

> Verses 50 and 53–55 contain yet another inspired reminder of the Christlike mercy that must be developed in the hearts of those who strive to become gods.

50 Have mercy, O Lord, upon the wicked mob, who have driven thy people, that they may cease to spoil, that they may repent of their sins if repentance is to be found;

51 But if they will not, make bare thine arm, O Lord, and redeem that which thou didst appoint a Zion unto thy people.

52 And if it cannot be otherwise, that the cause of thy people may not fail before thee may thine anger be kindled, and thine indignation fall upon them, that they may be wasted away, both root and branch, from under heaven;

53 But inasmuch as they will repent, thou art gracious and merciful, and wilt turn away thy wrath when thou lookest upon the face of thine Anointed.

54 Have mercy, O Lord, upon all the nations of the earth; have mercy upon the rulers of our land; may those principles, which were so honorably and nobly defended, namely, the Constitution of our land, by our fathers, be established forever.

55 **Remember the kings, the princes, the nobles, and the great ones of the earth, and all people**, and the churches, all the poor, the needy, and afflicted ones of the earth;

56 **That their hearts may be softened** when thy servants shall go out from thy house, O Jehovah, to bear testimony of thy name; **that their prejudices may give way before the truth, and thy people may obtain favor in the sight of all**;

On occasion, a student will ask why Joseph Smith addresses Jehovah (as in verse 56, above), since we know that we are to pray only to the Father (as in verse 47, above). One possible answer appears to be rather simple and straightforward. The Prophet is praying to the Father, as evidenced in the prayer, but occasionally speaks directly to the Savior who is present at the dedicatory services.

Blessings of Temple Attendance

57 That all the ends of the earth may know that we, thy servants, have heard thy voice, and that thou hast sent us;

58 That from among all these, thy servants, the sons of Jacob [*the literal and spiritual descendants of Abraham, Isaac, and Jacob*], may gather out the righteous to build a holy city to thy name, as thou hast commanded them.

Blessings of Temple Attendance

59 We ask thee to appoint unto Zion other stakes besides this one which thou hast appointed, **that the gathering of thy people may roll on in great power and majesty,** that thy work may be cut short in righteousness.

60 Now these words, O Lord, we have spoken before thee, concerning the revelations and commandments which thou hast given unto us, who are identified with the Gentiles.

61 But thou knowest that thou hast a great love for the children of Jacob, who have been scattered upon the mountains for a long time, in a cloudy and dark day.

Beginning with verse 62, we see that the collective righteousness of the Saints, endowed with power from on high in temples (see D&C 95:8), can have a beneficial effect on the rest of the world.

The Potential Effects of Our Temple Attendance Upon Others

62 We therefore ask thee to have mercy upon the children of Jacob [*the house of Israel*], **that Jerusalem, from this hour, may begin to be redeemed**;

63 **And the yoke of bondage may begin to be broken off from the house of David** [*the Jews*];

64 **And the children of Judah may begin to return to the lands which thou didst give to Abraham,** their father [*their ancestor*].

65 And cause that **the remnants of Jacob** [*Israel*], who have been cursed and smitten because of their transgression, be **converted**

from their wild and savage condition to the fulness of the everlasting gospel;

66 **That they may lay down their weapons of bloodshed, and cease their rebellions.**

67 And may all the scattered remnants of Israel, who have been driven to the ends of the earth, come to a knowledge of the truth, believe in the Messiah, and be redeemed from oppression, and rejoice before thee.

68 O Lord, remember thy servant, Joseph Smith, Jun., and all his afflictions and persecutions—how he has covenanted with Jehovah, and vowed to thee, O Mighty God of Jacob—and the commandments which thou hast given unto him, and that he hath sincerely striven to do thy will.

69 **Have mercy, O Lord, upon his wife and children**, that they may be exalted in thy presence, and preserved by thy fostering hand.

70 **Have mercy upon all their immediate connections, that their prejudices may be broken up and swept away as with a flood**; that they may be converted and redeemed with Israel, and know that thou art God.

71 Remember, O Lord, the presidents, even all the presidents of thy church, that thy right hand may exalt them, with all their families, and their immediate connections, that their names may be perpetuated and had in everlasting remembrance from generation to generation.

72 Remember all thy church, O Lord, with all their families, and all their immediate connections, with all their sick and afflicted ones, with all the poor and meek of the earth; **that the kingdom, which thou hast set up without hands, may become a great mountain and fill the whole earth**;

73 **That thy church may come forth out of the wilderness** of darkness [*of apostasy and spiritual darkness*], **and shine forth fair as the moon, clear as the sun, and terrible as an army with banners**;

74 **And be adorned as a bride for that day** [*be prepared for the Second Coming*] when thou shalt unveil the heavens, and cause the mountains to flow down at thy presence, and the valleys to be exalted, the rough places made smooth; that thy glory may fill the earth;

Blessings of Temple Attendance

75 That when the trump shall sound for the dead, we shall be caught up in the cloud to meet thee, that we may ever be with the Lord;

Blessings of Temple Attendance

76 That our garments [*symbolic of our lives*] **may be pure, that we may be clothed upon with robes of righteousness, with palms in our hands** [*symbolic of triumph and victory over all things that could keep us from celestial glory*]**, and crowns of glory upon our heads** [*crowns symbolize being kings and queens (see* Mormon Doctrine, *pages 173 and 613) and ruling as gods (see D&C 132:20) in exaltation*]**, and reap eternal joy for all our sufferings.**

77 O Lord God Almighty, hear us in these our petitions, and answer us from heaven, thy holy habitation, where thou sittest enthroned, with glory, honor, power, majesty, might, dominion, truth, justice, judgment, mercy, and an infinity of fulness, from everlasting to everlasting.

78 O hear, O hear, O hear us, O Lord! And answer these petitions, and accept the dedication of this house unto thee, the work of our hands, which we have built unto thy name;

Blessings of Temple Attendance

79 And also this church, to put upon it thy name. And help us by the power of thy Spirit, **that we may mingle our voices with those bright, shining seraphs around thy throne, with acclamations of praise, singing Hosanna to God and the Lamb!**

Blessings of Temple Attendance

80 And let these, thine anointed ones, be clothed with salvation, and thy saints shout aloud for joy. Amen, and Amen.

SECTION 110

Background

This section records four visions in which the Savior, Moses, Elias, and Elijah appeared to the Prophet Joseph Smith and Oliver Cowdery in the Kirtland Temple on Easter Sunday, April 3, 1836, just one week after the temple dedication. The Prophet recorded these visions in his Journal and it was later published as section 110.

On that very special Sunday morning, about 1,000 Saints had gathered in the temple to worship.

Remember that the Kirtland Temple was not like the temples we attend to perform ordinance work for the living and the dead. Rather, it was more like a tabernacle or large meeting house where meetings and conferences were held. However, it served its function as a temple magnificently as these four visions took place in it.

The Prophet Joseph Smith gave the following background to the events of that day:

"*Sunday, 3 [April 3, 1836].*—Attended meeting in the Lord's House, and assisted the other Presidents of the Church in seating the congregation, and then became an attentive listener to the preaching from the stand. Thomas B. Marsh and David W. Patten [*the senior members of the Quorum of the Twelve* Apostles] spoke in the forenoon to an attentive audience of about one thousand persons. In the afternoon, I assisted the other Presidents in distributing the Lord's Supper [*the sacrament*] to the Church, receiving it from the Twelve, whose privilege it was to officiate at the sacred desk this day. After having performed this service to my brethren, I retired to the pulpit, the veils [*the canvas curtains that were used to divide the large meeting room into classrooms*] being dropped, and bowed myself, with Oliver Cowdery, in solemn and silent prayer. After rising from prayer, the following vision was opened to both of us [section 110]—" (*History of the Church,* 2:434–35).

It is interesting to note, based on D&C 67:11 and Moses 1:11, that in order to see the Savior while in a mortal body, a person would have to be "transfigured," or, in other words, "quickened," changed temporarily by the Spirit of God to a higher spiritual state in order to not be destroyed in the flesh by the intense glory of God. Thus, we understand that Joseph and Oliver were quickened during this vision of the Savior.

The appearance of Christ on Easter Sunday, the yearly anniversary and celebration of His coming forth from the tomb, was certainly a special reconfirmation of His literal resurrection.

It is also of special significance that Elijah came on April 3, 1836, which was Easter Sunday that year. As you may recall, the Jews celebrate Passover at the time of year during which we celebrate Easter. They faithfully believe that Elijah will come as promised in Malachi 4:5–6 and that he will come during Passover. Furthermore, as part of their Passover observance, a vacant seat is reserved for Elijah and the door is opened to invite him in, in the hope that this may be the year of his coming (see Bible Dictionary under "Elijah").

Elijah did indeed come on Easter Sunday during the time that faithful

Jews around the world were celebrating Passover! He came to the Kirtland Temple where he restored the keys of work for the dead, including sealing families together. Our belief in the coming of Elijah can be a strong bond between us and our Jewish friends.

This series of glorious visions certainly made all the sacrifice and trials of the Saints in building the temple worthwhile.

We will now proceed with our verse-by-verse study. As mentioned above, there were four marvelous visions.

Vision #1
The Savior

1 THE veil was taken from our [*Joseph Smith and Oliver Cowdery*] **minds, and the eyes of our understanding were opened** [*by the power of the Holy Ghost*].

> Next, in verses 2–3, we are given a description of the Savior, which includes much biblical symbolism.

2 We saw the Lord [*Jesus Christ*] **standing upon the breastwork of the pulpit** [*the small wall that extends out from both sides of the pulpit*], **before us; and under his feet was a paved work of pure gold** [*in biblical symbolism, gold represents the very best, celestial glory, God*]**, in color like amber** [*symbolic of divine glory—compare with Ezekiel 1:3–4*].

3 His eyes were as a flame of fire [*symbolic of celestial glory*]**; the hair of his head was white** [*symbolic of purity; celestial glory*] **like the pure snow** [*symbolic of the Savior's ability to cleanse—compare with Isaiah 1:18*]**; his countenance shone above the brightness of the sun; and his voice was as the sound of the rushing of great waters**, even the voice of Jehovah, saying:

> Next, in verse 4, the Savior specifically identifies Himself and personally introduces Himself to the Prophet and Oliver Cowdery.

4 I am the first and the last [*Jesus Christ is involved in all things for our potential exaltation under the direction of the Father*]**; I am he who liveth** [*He is resurrected*]**, I am he who was slain** [*crucified*]**; I am your advocate with the Father.** [*He is constantly working with us to save us.*]

> All of us worry somewhat about whether we will be found worthy to meet the Savior. Next, we see the Lord's kindness and mercy as He quickly puts Joseph and Oliver at ease on this matter.

5 Behold, **your sins are forgiven you; you are clean before me;**

therefore, **lift up your heads and rejoice** [compare with Mosiah 3:3–9, where King Benjamin is told that he may rejoice and that he can tell his people that they, too, may have joy because of the Atonement and their efforts to live worthy of it].

6 Let the hearts of your brethren rejoice, and let the hearts of all my people rejoice, who have, with their might, **built this house to my name.**

In verse 7, next, the Savior answers the Prophet's plea, given one week previously in the dedicatory prayer of the Kirtland Temple, wherein he said, "We ask thee, O Lord, to accept of this house, the workmanship of the hands of us, thy servants, which thou didst command us to build" (D&C 109:4).

7 For behold, I have accepted this house, and my name shall be here; and **I will manifest myself to my people in mercy in this house.**

As you probably know, the Savior can be represented by the Holy Ghost, as well as by angels as if it were the Savior Himself speaking (as was the case with the angel in Revelation 1:1; 19:9–10). This is sometimes referred to as "divine investiture." In verse 8, next, however, the Savior says that He, personally, will appear and speak to them with His own voice if they will remain worthy.

8 Yea, I will appear unto my servants, and speak unto them with mine own voice, if my people will keep my commandments, and do not pollute this holy house [by unworthiness].

Next, in verses 9–10, the Savior prophesies concerning the Kirtland Temple. The "endowment" spoken of in verse 9 is not what we do in temples today when we "receive our endowment." Rather, it involves the endowment (gift) of power and priesthood keys that will be bestowed upon Joseph Smith and Oliver Cowdery by Moses, Elias, and Elijah on this day, as well as revelations, inspiration, and instruction that will be given during the remaining time of the Kirtland Temple's authorized use.

Next, the Savior prophesies about the Kirtland Temple:

9 Yea the hearts of thousands and tens of thousands shall greatly rejoice in consequence of the blessings which shall be poured out, and the endowment with which my servants have been endowed in this house.

10 And the fame of this house shall spread to foreign lands; and **this is the beginning of the blessing which shall be poured out upon the heads of my people.** Even so. Amen.

Next, in verse 11, the appearance of Moses is recorded. He will restore the keys of the gathering of Israel throughout the earth and the leading of the ten tribes from the north.

Vision #2
Moses

11 After this vision closed, the heavens were again opened unto us; and Moses appeared before us, **and committed unto us the keys of the gathering of Israel** from the four parts of the earth, **and the leading of the ten tribes from the land of the north.**

> The work of gathering Israel in the last days is one of the most often-prophesied events in the scriptures and is a prominent sign of the times being fulfilled in our day. Our modern prophets speak of it very often and of gathering Israel on both sides of the veil. Also, you can read more about the "leading of the ten tribes from the land of the north" in D&C 133:26–33.
>
> Regarding the gathering of Israel, President Russell M. Nelson, then an Apostle, taught: "The choice to come unto Christ is not a matter of physical location; it is a matter of individual commitment. People can be "brought to the knowledge of the Lord" without leaving their homelands. True, in the early days of the Church, conversion often meant emigration as well. But now the gathering takes place in each nation. The Lord has decreed the establishment of Zion in each realm where He has given His Saints their birth and nationality. Scripture foretells that the people "shall be gathered home to the lands of their inheritance, and shall be established in all their lands of promise." "Every nation is the gathering place for its own people." The place of gathering for Brazilian Saints is in Brazil; the place of gathering for Nigerian Saints is in Nigeria; the place of gathering for Korean Saints is in Korea; and so forth. Zion is "the pure in heart." Zion is wherever righteous Saints are. Publications, communications, and congregations are now such that nearly all members have access to the doctrines, keys, ordinances, and blessings of the gospel, regardless of their location" (October 2006 general conference, Sunday morning session).
>
> Elder Bruce R. McConkie spoke of the keys restored by Moses. He said (**bold** added for emphasis):
>
> "Israel's great lawgiver, the prophet whose life was in similitude of the Messiah himself, the one who delivered Israel from Egyptian bondage and led them to their land of promise, came to Joseph Smith and Oliver Cowdery on 3 April 1836, in the Kirtland Temple. **He gave them: (1) 'the keys of the gathering of Israel** from the four parts of the earth,' and **(2)**

the keys of 'the leading of the ten tribes from the land of the north' (D&C 110:11).

"Since then, with increasing power and in great glory, **we have gathered**, from their Egyptian bondage as it were, the dispersed of Ephraim and few others, initially to the mountains of America, but now **into the stakes of Zion in the various nations** of the earth. The gathering of Israel is a reality. **When the ten tribes return they will come at the direction of the President of The Church of Jesus Christ of Latter-day Saints**, for he now holds and will then hold the keys of presidency and direction for this mighty work" ("This Final Glorious Gospel Dispensation," *Ensign,* April 1980, 22; quoted in *Doctrine and Covenants Student Manual,* 1981, 275).

Many people wonder and speculate as to where the lost ten tribes are. Joseph Fielding Smith gave the following advice on this matter:

"Whether these tribes are in the north or not, I am not prepared to say. As I said before, they are 'lost' and until the Lord wishes it, they will not be found. All that I know about it is what the Lord has revealed, and He declares that they will come from the North. He has also made it very clear and definite that these lost people are separate and apart from the scattered Israelites now being gathered out" (*Signs of the Times,* 186; quoted in *Doctrine and Covenants Student Manual,* 1981, 275).

Next, in verse 12, Elias appears and restores the keys and blessings related to the Abrahamic Covenant (see Genesis 12:1–3, 17:1–8, 22:17–18, Abraham 2:9–11). These blessings relate to attaining exaltation ourselves and taking the gospel to all people so they likewise have the opportunity to do so.

According to the Bible Dictionary, we do not know who this Elias was, other than that he lived during the days of Abraham (see Bible Dictionary under "Elias," definition number 4). It will be interesting someday to meet him and find out more about his life and mission.

Vision #3
Elias

12 After this, Elias appeared, and committed the dispensation of the gospel of Abraham, saying that **in us and our seed all generations after us should be blessed.**

We will say just a bit more about the "dispensation of the gospel of Abraham," spoken of in verse 12, above. The covenants that the Lord made with Abraham figure prominently in our lives, too, if we seek them and live worthy of them. The last phrase of verse 12 reminds us of Abraham 2:9–11, which is a summary of the blessings and responsibilities of the descendants of Abraham, Isaac, and Jacob if they desire to receive exaltation. The "blessings of Abraham, Isaac, and Jacob" (as often mentioned in patriarchal blessings) definitely have reference to exaltation, since all three of these ancient prophets have already become gods (see D&C 132:37).

We will quote Abraham 2:9–11 and add notes and commentary in order to gain additional insights as to the keys restored by Elias in this appearance in the Kirtland Temple. As you read through these three verses, which provide a summary of the Abrahamic Covenant, keep in mind that we are seeking instruction as to what the "dispensation of the gospel of Abraham" is. You will find that it involves promises and covenants of exaltation as well as responsibilities of those who desire to attain it. It also deals with blessings needed along the way. We will use **bold** for emphasis.

The Abrahamic Covenant

Abraham 2:9–11

9 And I will make of thee a great nation [*symbolically, a reference to having innumerable spirit children of our own as gods (compare with "a continuation of the seeds forever and ever"—D&C 132:19*], and I will bless thee above measure [*exaltation*], and make thy name great among all nations [*symbolic of exaltation, becoming gods*], and thou shalt be a blessing unto thy seed [*posterity*] after thee, that in their hands they shall bear this ministry and Priesthood unto all nations [*missionary work; part of our responsibility as members of the Church*];

10 And I will bless them through thy name; **for as many as receive this Gospel shall be called after thy name** [*will be called the descendants of Abraham*], and **shall be accounted thy seed** [*will be given the same blessings and promises of exaltation that Abraham was given; they will be considered to be of Abraham, Isaac, and Jacob (Israel), or, in other words, will be called Israel and will be gathered home to God*], and shall rise up and bless thee, as their father [*ancestor*];

11 And **I will bless them that bless thee, and curse them that curse thee** [*the Lord's blessings and spiritual protection will be poured out upon righteous Israel*]; **and in thee** [*that is, in thy priesthood*] **and in thy seed** [*that is, thy Priesthood*], for I give unto thee a promise that this right shall continue in thee,

and in thy seed after thee [*that is to say, the literal seed, or the seed of the body*] **shall all the families of the earth be blessed, even with the blessings of the Gospel, which are the blessings of salvation, even of life eternal** [*exaltation; life eternal is another scriptural term for exaltation*].

Next, in verses 13–15, Elijah appears. You may wish to read a summary of his life and mission in the Bible Dictionary under "Elijah." Imagine how humbled and pleased he must have been to be the one chosen to restore these priesthood keys as prophesied in Malachi 4:5–6.

Vision #4
Elijah

13 After this vision had closed, another great and glorious vision burst upon us; for **Elijah** the prophet, who was taken to heaven without tasting death [*2 Kings 2:11*], **stood before us, and said:**

14 Behold, **the time has fully come, which was spoken of by the mouth of Malachi** [*Malachi 4:5–6*]—**testifying that he** [*Elijah*] **should be sent, before the great and dreadful day of the Lord come** [*the Second Coming*]—

Next, in verse 15, we learn that a major function of the priesthood keys restored by Elijah was to get the work of family history and work for the dead going upon the earth before the Second Coming of Christ.

15 **To turn the hearts of the fathers to the children, and the children to the fathers**, lest the whole earth be smitten with a curse [*in other words, if families are not sealed together in exaltation by the power of the priesthood for time and all eternity, then a major purpose of the earth and its creation would not have been fulfilled*]—

Joseph Fielding Smith explained the importance of family history work and the keys restored by Elijah as follows:

"What was the nature of this restoration? It was the conferring upon men in this dispensation of the sealing power of the priesthood, by which all things are bound in heaven as well as on earth. It gave the authority to Joseph Smith to perform in the temple of God all the ordinances essential to salvation for both the living and the dead.

"Through the power of this priesthood which Elijah bestowed, husband and wife may be sealed, or married for eternity; children may be sealed to their parents for eternity; thus the family is made eternal, and death does not separate the members. This is the great principle that will save the world from utter destruction.

"Vicariously the dead may obtain the blessings of the gospel—baptism, confirmation, ordination, and the higher blessings, which are sealed upon them in the temples of the Lord, by virtue of the authority restored by Elijah. Through the restoration of these keys, the work of the Lord is fully inaugurated before the coming of Jesus Christ in glory.

"These keys of the binding, or sealing power, which were given to Peter, James, and John in their dispensation, are keys which make valid all the ordinances of the gospel. They pertain more especially to the work in the temples, both for the living and for the dead. They are the authorities which prepare men to enter the celestial kingdom and to be crowned as sons and heirs of God.

"These keys hold the power to seal husbands and wives for eternity as well as for time. They hold the power to seal children to parents, the key of adoption, by which the family organization is made intact forever. This is the power that will save the obedient from the curse in the coming of the great and dreadful day of the Lord. Through these keys the hearts of the children have turned to their fathers" (*Doctrines of Salvation,* 2:118–19; quoted in *Doctrine and Covenants Student Manual,* 277).

It could be that in verse 16, next, Elijah is referring to the keys that he restored to Joseph Smith and Oliver Cowdery. However, it may also be that he is summarizing the restoration of priesthood keys in the Kirtland Temple on that day by Moses, Elias, and himself. This restitution of keys is a sign of the times (one of many prophecies that will be fulfilled in the last days prior to the Savior's coming), indicating that the Second Coming of the Lord is getting relatively close.

16 Therefore, **the keys of this dispensation are committed into your hands**; and **by this ye may know that the great and dreadful day of the Lord** [*the Second Coming of Christ*] **is near, even at the doors.**

In conclusion, the marvelous manifestations and revelations, including the restoration of vital priesthood keys, which took place on Easter Sunday, April 3, 1836, in the Kirtland Temple, continue to bless the lives of faithful Saints throughout the world, as well as millions who have passed beyond the veil. The work of sealing families, living and dead, accelerates, accompanied by the blessings of heaven and advances in technology.

These blessings alone, which came on this special Easter Sunday, more than justify every effort to build the Kirtland Temple in spite of being forced to abandon it relatively soon thereafter such as these early Saints were compelled to do. The blessings of eternity, conferred by those having these restored priesthood keys and accepted by individuals through the gift of moral agency under temporary mortal conditions, are part of the perspective and schooling designed by a loving Father for His children as they follow the Savior back home.

SECTION 111

Background

This revelation was given through the Prophet Joseph Smith on August 6, 1836, at Salem, Massachusetts.

The Church was still deeply in debt at this time due to the building of the Kirtland Temple as well as expenses incurred in funding Zion's Camp and providing for the Saints who had been driven from their homes in Missouri. Many of them had been left destitute and relied on the generosity of impoverished members in Kirtland and elsewhere.

In the midst of this financial difficulty came news from Brother William Burgess that he knew of a large amount of money hidden in the basement of a deceased widow's house in Salem, Massachusetts, which was available for the taking. Upon hearing of this, Joseph Smith, Sidney Rigdon, Hyrum Smith, and Oliver Cowdery departed for Salem. B. H. Roberts, a prominent early historian of the Church, explained what happened.

"Ebenezer Robinson, for many years a faithful and prominent elder in the church, and at Nauvoo associated with Don Carlos Smith—brother of the Prophet—in editing and publishing the *Times and Seasons,* states that the journey to Salem arose from these circumstances. There came to Kirtland a brother by the name of Burgess who stated that he had knowledge of a large amount of money secreted in the cellar of a certain house in Salem, Massachusetts, which had belonged to a widow (then deceased), and thought he was the only person who had knowledge of it, or of the location of the house. The brethren accepting the representations of Burgess as true made the journey to Salem to secure, if possible, the treasure. Burgess, according to Robinson, met the brethren in Salem, but claimed that time had wrought such changes in the town that he could not for a certainty point out the house 'and soon left'" (*Comprehensive History of the Church,* 1:411).

Imagine the feelings in the minds and hearts of these brethren after Burgess acknowledged that he could not remember which house it was and left them. The Lord's kindness and mercy, in response to this venture, is encouraging to all of us who have likewise been involved in "follies" (verse 1).

In fact, when we understand the background, this section becomes one of the great sections in the Doctrine and Covenants because it reveals so clearly the tenderness of the Master as He continues to patiently school His little flock. Watch as He picks them up and looks at the bright side of things in verses 1–4 while acknowledging to them that their main motivation for coming here was folly.

1 **I, THE Lord your God, am not displeased** with your coming this journey, **notwithstanding your follies** [*likely referring to their coming here to find treasure*].

2 **I have much treasure** [*souls*] **in this city** for you, for the benefit of Zion, **and many people in this city, whom I will gather out in due time** for the benefit of Zion, through your instrumentality.

3 Therefore, it is expedient that you should **form acquaintance with men in this city, as you shall be led, and as it shall be given you.**

4 And it shall come to pass **in due time** [*according to the Lord's schedule*] that **I will give this city into your hands**, that you shall have power over it, insomuch that they shall not discover your secret parts [*embarrass you or put you to shame—compare with Isaiah 3:17*]; and its wealth pertaining to gold and silver shall be yours [*obviously a prophecy of the future; possibly referring to the many converts in the Salem area who joined the Church within the next few years, many of whom moved to Nauvoo and then on west. Their financial resources would be a "treasure" indeed to the Church's financial needs*].

By 1842, there were ninety members in the Salem Branch of the Church, and on April 11, 1843, Elder Erastus Snow recorded in his journal that he had baptized more than one hundred converts from Salem (quoted in *Doctrine and Covenants Student Manual,* 1981, 278).

As you no doubt know, the Lord could easily point out to our Church leaders today the location of oil, gold, precious minerals, and so forth, which could free the members of the Church from the necessity of sacrificing and making financial contributions. But this would not bless us. Rather, it would curse us, because we would be denied the blessings of personal, voluntary sacrifice, which leads us to focus on eternal priorities.

As this section continues, the Savior counsels these brethren concerning the debts of the Church.

5 **Concern not yourselves about your debts,** for **I will give you power to pay them.**

6 Concern not yourselves about Zion [*the Church and its members in Missouri*]**, for I will deal mercifully with her.**

> Next, in verses 7–9, the Savior instructs them to stay for a while in the Salem area and tells them that the Spirit will point out a place that they can rent. One of the lessons we learn here is that the Holy Ghost communicates with us and approves our decisions by giving us peace.

7 Tarry in this place, and in the regions round about;

8 And **the place** [*housing accommodations*] where it is my will that you should tarry, for the main, **shall be signalized unto you by the peace and power of my Spirit, that shall flow unto you.**

9 This place you may obtain by hire [*rent*]. And **inquire diligently concerning the more ancient inhabitants and founders of this city** [*learn what you can about the original inhabitants of Salem*];

10 For **there are more treasures than one for you in this city.**

> A quote from the 2018 *Doctrine and Covenants Student Manual*, chapter 44, sheds additional light on verses 9 and 10, above.
>
> "In obedience to the Lord's command to 'inquire diligently concerning the more ancient inhabitants and founders of this city' (D&C 111:9), during their stay in Salem, Massachusetts, the Prophet Joseph Smith and his companions traveled throughout Salem and its surrounding areas visiting museums, historical sites, and libraries (see *The Joseph Smith Papers, Documents, Volume 5: October 1835–January 1838*, 278, note 248). They learned more about the city's founding by the Puritan pilgrims in the early 1600s and about the American Revolutionary War and the establishment of the United States (see *Manuscript History of the Church*, vol. B-1, page 749, josephsmithpapers.org).
>
> "Some of the brethren spent time learning about the Salem witch trials (see Oliver Cowdery, 'Prospectus,' *Latter Day Saints' Messenger and Advocate*, Oct. 1836, 388–91). In addition, the Prophet Joseph Smith and his companions visited the remains of the Charlestown Ursuline Convent, which had been destroyed by an anti-Catholic mob motivated by religious intolerance. Referring to this experience, the Prophet wrote: 'When will man cease to war with man, and wrest from him his sacred right, of worshiping his God according as his conscience dic-

tates? Holy Father, hasten the day' (in *Manuscript History of the Church*, vol. B-1, page 749, josephsmithpapers.org)."

Finally, from verse 1, above, we get the impression that the initial motivation for the trip to Salem was not thought through very well. As the Savior concludes this merciful and encouraging revelation, He appears to be gently counseling these leaders to be wiser in the future and assures them that He will continue helping and guiding them as they grow.

11 Therefore, **be ye as wise** as serpents and yet without sin; **and I will order all things for your good, as fast as ye are able to receive them.** Amen.

SECTION 112

Background

This revelation was given through the Prophet Joseph Smith to Thomas B. Marsh, one of the original Twelve Apostles in this dispensation, on July 23, 1837, at Kirtland, Ohio.

At this time, Brother Marsh was the president of the Quorum of the Twelve. Verses 1–12 are mainly to him personally. Verses 13–34 are primarily instructions for him to give to the Twelve.

Thomas Baldwin Marsh was six years older than Joseph Smith, having been born on November 1, 1799, in Massachusetts. He was baptized on September 3, 1830, by David Whitmer and became a member of the Quorum of the Twelve Apostles when it was organized in 1835.

As mentioned above, verses 1–12 were given as personal counsel and instruction to Thomas Marsh. When we study these verses, we will see advice to control the feelings of the heart (verse 2) and warnings to avoid pride and be humble (verses 3 and 10). Sadly, Brother Marsh failed to heed these specific words of the Lord to him. His life provides a disappointing lesson about the results of failure to follow the Lord's counsel.

Perhaps you have heard of the case involving milk strippings, which led to his apostasy and excommunication from the Church. Briefly put, Brother Marsh's wife, Elizabeth, and Lucinda Harris, wife of George Harris, wanted to make cheese, but neither had enough cows to do it alone. Therefore, they agreed to exchange milk, including the strippings (the last of the milking, which is extra rich with cream). Sister Harris kept her part of the bargain, but when it was Sister Marsh's turn to provide milk, she cheated, keeping back a pint of strippings from each cow. George A. Smith spoke of this in a talk delivered some years later in Salt Lake City. He was warning about how small matters can lead to big troubles if not quickly resolved. He said:

"For instance, while the Saints were living in Far West, there were two sisters wishing to make cheese, and, neither of them possessing the requisite number of cows, they agreed to exchange milk.

"The wife of Thomas B. Marsh, who was then President of the Twelve Apostles, and sister Harris concluded they would exchange milk, in order to make a little larger cheese than they otherwise could. To be sure to have justice done, it was agreed that they should not save the strippings, but that the milk and strippings should all go together. Small matters to talk about here, to be sure, two women's exchanging milk to make cheese.

"Mrs. Harris, it appeared, was faithful to the agreement and carried to Mrs. Marsh the milk and strippings, but Mrs. Marsh, wishing to make some extra good cheese, saved a pint of strippings from each cow and sent Mrs. Harris the milk without the strippings.

"Finally it leaked out that Mrs. Marsh had saved strippings, and it became a matter to be settled by the Teachers. They began to examine the matter, and it was proved that Mrs. Marsh had saved the strippings, and consequently had wronged Mrs. Harris out of that amount.

"An appeal was taken from the Teacher to the Bishop, and a regular Church trial was had. President Marsh did not consider that the Bishop had done him and his lady justice, for they decided that the strippings were wrongfully saved, and that the woman had violated her covenant.

"Marsh immediately took an appeal to the High Council, who investigated the question with much patience, and I assure you they were a grave body. Marsh being extremely anxious to maintain the character of his wife, as he was the President of the Twelve Apostles, and a great man in Israel, made a desperate defence, but the High Council finally confirmed the Bishop's decision.

"Marsh, not being satisfied, took an appeal to the First Presidency of the Church, and Joseph and his Counsellors had to sit upon the case, and they approved the decision of the High Council.

"This little affair, you will observe, kicked up a considerable breeze, and Thomas B. Marsh then declared that he would sustain the character of his wife, even if he had to go to hell for it.

"The then President of the Twelve Apostles, the man who should have been the first to do justice and cause reparation to be made for wrong, committed by any member of his family, took that position, and what next? He went before a magistrate and swore that the 'Mormons' were hostile towards the State of Missouri.

"That affidavit brought from the government of Missouri an exterminating order, which drove some fifteen thousand Saints from their homes and habitations, and some thousands perished through suffering the exposure consequent on this state of affairs" (George A. Smith, in *Journal of Discourses*, 3:284).

Thomas B. Marsh was excommunicated on March 17, 1839, and was out of the Church for eighteen years. He was rebaptized on July 16, 1857, in Florence, Nebraska, a weak and emaciated shadow of what he once was. He came to Salt Lake City and then moved to Ogden, Utah, where he died penniless and in poor health in January 1866.

We will now proceed with our study of section 112. Remember, as stated above, that verses 1–12 are personal counsel to Thomas B. Marsh.

1 VERILY thus saith the Lord unto you my servant Thomas: I have heard thy prayers; and thine alms [*offerings and personal sacrifices*] have come up as a memorial before me, in behalf of those, thy brethren [*the other members of the Twelve*], who were chosen to bear testimony of my name and to send it abroad among all nations, kindreds, tongues, and people, and ordained through the instrumentality of my servants,

Next, in verses 2–12, Thomas is given direct, gentle counsel, which, if followed, could have saved him much anguish. He is also given the encouragement of having his sins forgiven (verse 3), which gives him a whole new start.

2 Verily I say unto you, **there have been some few things in thine heart and with thee with which I, the Lord, was not well pleased.**

3 **Nevertheless,** inasmuch as thou hast abased [*humbled*] thyself thou shalt be exalted; therefore, **all thy sins are forgiven thee.**

4 **Let thy heart be of good cheer** [*be positive and upbeat*] before my face; and **thou shalt bear record of my name, not only unto the Gentiles, but also unto the Jews; and thou shalt send forth my word unto the ends of the earth.**

In the next verses, Brother Marsh is told of the good he can do in spreading the gospel, locally and among the nations of the earth.

5 Contend thou, therefore, morning by morning; and day after day **let thy warning voice go forth;** and when the night cometh let not

the inhabitants of the earth slumber, because of thy speech.

6 Let thy habitation be known in Zion, and **remove not thy house** [*don't leave the Church*]; for I, the Lord, have a great work for thee to do, in publishing my name among the children of men [*people*].

7 Therefore, **gird up thy loins** [*prepare*] **for the work**. Let thy feet be shod also, for thou art chosen, and thy path lieth **among the mountains, and among many nations**.

8 And by thy word many high ones shall be brought low [*humbled*], and by thy word many low ones [*humble people*] shall be exalted.

9 Thy voice shall be a rebuke unto the transgressor; and at thy rebuke let the tongue of the slanderer cease its perverseness.

> Verse 10, next, is one of the often-quoted verses in the Doctrine and Covenants. You may wish to mark it in your own Doctrine and Covenants.

10 **Be thou humble; and the Lord thy God shall lead thee by the hand, and give thee answer to thy prayers**.

11 **I know thy heart, and have heard thy prayers** concerning thy brethren. **Be not partial towards them in love above many others** [*don't show more love toward your colleagues in the Quorum of the Twelve and other Church leaders than to others*], but **let thy love be for them as for thyself**; and **let thy love abound unto all men, and unto all who love my name**.

> As we read verse 12, next, it is helpful to remember that all members, including the leaders, are basically new in the Church at this time in the Restoration. None of them are seasoned veterans, because the Church has been organized for only a little more than seven years. Many are still working on making the transitions from other belief systems and lifestyles to those of the true gospel. In order to help the Twelve continue to change into the understanding and worthiness needed to serve as Apostles, and to accelerate these changes, Brother Marsh is counseled by the Lord to be very direct in teaching and correcting these brethren as needed.
>
> Also, be aware that in many settings, it is common for men and women of position and power to believe that they can do no wrong and are not subject to the same rules that apply to those over whom they preside. The Lord makes it clear that such is not the case in the true Church.

12 And **pray for thy brethren**

of the Twelve. **Admonish them sharply** [*be very direct with them as you warn them about unworthiness*] for my name's sake, and **let them be admonished for all their sins** [*the Twelve must repent if they sin; there is no privileged class in the Church, who are exempt from the penalties of sin*], and **be ye faithful before me unto my name** [*can include being faithful to covenants made in the name of Jesus Christ*].

As mentioned above, in serving as the President of the Quorum of the Twelve Apostles, Thomas B. Marsh had the responsibility of instructing and teaching the other members of the Twelve. Verses 13–34 instruct him as to his duties as president and teach him things he is to pass on to the other members of the Quorum.

First, in verse 13, next, we see that some of these quorum members are still in the process of being thoroughly converted to the restored gospel of Jesus Christ. This should not surprise us, since we, ourselves, are still going through the conversion process when it comes to living some aspects of the gospel. A beautiful message is given to these men and to all of us. It is that as we go through trials and tribulations, if we will humble ourselves and remain teachable instead of getting angry at the Lord because of hardships, we will be converted more deeply, and He will heal us.

13 And **after their temptations**, and **much tribulation**, behold, **I, the Lord, will feel after them** [*the Lord's tender heart will reach out to them*], and **if they harden not their hearts, and stiffen not their necks** [*if they do not become prideful*] **against me, they shall be converted, and I will heal them.**

Much sacrifice is required on the part of the Twelve Apostles and their families in our day. These Brethren travel throughout the world to preach the gospel and to keep the Church in order (see D&C 107:33). In verse 14, next, the Lord tells Thomas and the rest of the Twelve at the time of this revelation to "take up your cross." This is biblical terminology meaning to sacrifice whatever is necessary in order to fulfill their callings. The taking up of one's cross implies that there will be very difficult times. As you know, crucifixion was common in the days of the Bible. Thus, cross implies severe trial and tribulation.

14 Now, I say unto you, and what I say unto you, I say unto all the Twelve: Arise and **gird up your loins** [*prepare for action*], **take up your cross** [*give whatever is required in order to fulfill your calling*], **follow me, and feed my sheep**.

In verse 15, next, the Savior gives a special warning not to rebel against the Prophet Joseph

Smith. At this time, there was much of dissension and rebellion in Kirtland and elsewhere against the Prophet. One of the big factors was the failing Kirtland Safety Society (a banking system owned by the Prophet and others) that, along with hundreds of other banks throughout the nation, was failing during what was called "the Panic of 1837." Even some members of the Quorum of the Twelve Apostles were rebelling against Joseph Smith and calling him a fallen prophet.

In fact, back in February 1837, several who considered Joseph to be a fallen Prophet had called a meeting in the temple for the purpose of installing David Whitmer as the leader of the Church (see *Church History in the Fulness of Times,* 2003, 173–74). Their attempt met with failure but serves as a reminder of the spirit of apostasy that was prominent at the time section 112 was given. And in August 1837, while Joseph Smith and most of the Apostles were away on missions, John F. Boynton (one of the Apostles) joined other apostates in attempting to take over the Kirtland Temple by storming it, armed with pistols and bowie knives. They, too, failed (see *Church History in the Fulness of Times,* 2003, 176–77).

This next verse serves as a strong warning to all of us to avoid rebelling against the Prophet Joseph Smith and also against our living prophet.

15 **Exalt not yourselves** [*don't get caught up in pride and thinking you should lead the Church*]; **rebel not against my servant Joseph; for verily I say unto you, I am with him**, and my hand shall be over him; and **the keys which I have given unto him**, and also to you-ward [*to the Twelve*], **shall not be taken from him till I come.** [*We understand that all the prophets, living and dead, will turn their priesthood keys back over to the Savior prior to the Second Coming. This is to be done at the council in Adam-ondi-Ahman. We will say more about this when we get to section 116.*]

There is perhaps another message we should get by implication from verse 15, above. It is that the Lord will not let the living prophet lead us astray. This is found also in D&C 28:2 and 43:3–5.

Next, in verse 16, Brother Marsh is taught that he holds the keys of directing the Twelve in their ministry to all the world. And, in verse 17, he is taught his role in using his "keys" to "unlock doors" in places where the First Presidency does not have the time to travel and serve directly.

16 Verily I say unto you, **my servant Thomas, thou art the man whom I have chosen to hold the keys of my kingdom, as**

pertaining to the Twelve [*just as the President of the Quorum of the Twelve does today*], abroad among all nations—

17 **That thou mayest be my servant to unlock the door of the kingdom in all places where my servant Joseph, and my servant Sidney, and my servant Hyrum** [*the First Presidency at this time*], **cannot come**;

> We will quote from the 1981 Institute of Religion *Doctrine and Covenants Student Manual* in order to get a brief background as to why Hyrum Smith is serving in the First Presidency at the time of this revelation.
>
> "The passage in verse 17 about Joseph, Hyrum, and Sidney refers to the First Presidency as it was constituted when the revelation was given. When the First Presidency of the Church was originally organized, Jesse Gause and Sidney Rigdon were called to be counselors to the Prophet. After Jesse Gause's apostasy (see Historical Background for D&C 81 [*in the 1981* Doctrine and Covenants Student Manual]), the Presidency was reorganized in 1833 with Frederick G. Williams as Second Counselor. At a conference held at Far West, Missouri, on 7 November 1837, Frederick G. Williams was replaced by Hyrum Smith (see *History of the Church*, 2:522–23)" (*Doctrine and Covenants Student Manual*, 1981, 282).

Next, in verses 18–22, we see a short course on authority and delegation as it pertains to the leading quorums of the Church. It is a reminder that the Twelve function under the direction of the First Presidency (as stated in D&C 107:33) and that many others function under the authority and direction of the Twelve.

18 For **on them** [*the First Presidency*] **have I laid the burden of all the churches** [*the branches, wards, and stakes*] for a little season.

19 Wherefore, **whithersoever they** [*the First Presidency*] **shall send you, go ye**, and **I will be with you**; and in whatsoever place ye shall proclaim my name an effectual door shall be opened unto you, that they may receive my word.

> Verse 20, next, is a simple, straightforward reminder that you cannot be a member of this Church in good standing with the Lord unless you support and sustain the First Presidency in your words and actions.

20 **Whosoever receiveth my word receiveth me**, and **whosoever receiveth me, receiveth** those, **the First Presidency**, whom I have sent, whom I have made counselors [*advisors and*

supervisors] for my name's sake unto you [*the Twelve*].

21 And again, I say unto you, that **whosoever ye shall send** in my name, **by the voice of your brethren, the Twelve**, duly recommended and authorized by you, **shall have power to open the door of my kingdom unto any nation whithersoever ye shall send them**—

22 **Inasmuch as they shall humble themselves** before me, and **abide in my word** [*stick with the scriptures and the words of the living prophets*], and **hearken to the voice of my Spirit**.

> Next, beginning with verse 23, Brother Marsh is told that spiritual darkness is covering the earth, that wickedness is taking over, and that the need for repentance will be preached by calamities and troubles upon the earth.

23 Verily, verily, I say unto you, **darkness covereth the earth**, and **gross darkness the minds of the people**, and **all flesh** [*everyone*] **has become corrupt** before my face.

24 Behold, **vengeance cometh speedily upon the inhabitants of the earth, a day of wrath**, a day of **burning**, a day of **desolation**, of **weeping**, of **mourning**, and of **lamentation**; and **as a whirlwind** [*which spares none in its path*] **it shall come upon all the face of the earth, saith the Lord.**

> As mentioned in previous notes, there was already much of apostasy in Kirtland at the time of this revelation. Verses 25–28 point this out. First, the Lord points out that the Church must be cleansed (a major purpose of trials and tribulation of the Saints) before it can fulfill its role in taking the gospel to others.

25 And **upon my house** [*the Church*] **shall it** [*the troubles spoken of in verses 23–24*] **begin, and from my house shall it go forth**, saith the Lord;

26 **First among those among you**, saith the Lord, **who have professed to know my name** [*who have claimed to be faithful members of the Church*] **and have not known me** [*but are not*], **and have blasphemed against me in the midst of my house** [*likely meaning the Kirtland Temple; see notes following verse 14, above*], saith the Lord.

> In verses 27–29, next, the Twelve, including Thomas B. Marsh, are told to get their own lives in order before they try to direct and teach others in living the gospel. In verse 27, they are told not to worry about the apostasy taking place at that time in Kirtland.

27 Therefore, **see to it that ye trouble not yourselves concerning the affairs of my church in this place** [*Kirtland*], saith the Lord.

28 **But purify your hearts before me; and then go ye into all the world**, and preach my gospel unto every creature who has not received it;

29 And **he that believeth and is baptized shall be saved, and he that believeth not, and is not baptized, shall be damned** [*stopped in their progression*].

> Next, the Savior gives a brief review concerning the priesthood keys that have been given to the Twelve and the First Presidency in this last dispensation, which is known as "the dispensation of the fullness of times" (the last time the gospel will be restored before the Second Coming and the dispensation in which all the priesthood keys and authority from previous dispensations have been restored).

30 For **unto you, the Twelve, and** those, **the First Presidency**, who are appointed with you to be your counselors [*advisors*] and your leaders, **is the power of this priesthood given**, for the last days and **for the last time**, in the which is the dispensation of the fulness of times.

31 **Which power you hold, in connection with all those who have received a dispensation at any time from the beginning of the creation;**

32 For verily I say unto you, **the keys of the dispensation, which ye have received, have come down from the fathers** [*ancient prophets*], **and last of all, being sent down from heaven unto you.**

33 Verily I say unto you, behold **how great is your calling. Cleanse your hearts and your garments** [*garments in this context symbolize our lives*], **lest the blood of this generation be required at your hands** [*in other words, if you don't get your lives in order so you can teach the gospel to the world, you will bear a responsibility for their sins*].

34 **Be faithful until I come**, for I come quickly; and **my reward is with me to recompense** [*reward*] **every man according as his work shall be.** I am Alpha and Omega [*"the beginning and the end," Jesus Christ*]. Amen.

SECTION 113

Background

This section consists of questions and answers about Isaiah, chapters 11 and 52, given by the Prophet Joseph Smith in March 1838. From the context of *History of the Church,* volume 3, pages 9–10, in which this section is recorded, it appears likely that these questions and answers were given in the last half of March in Far West, Missouri.

Isaiah uses much symbolism, and, as a result, his writings and imagery can be difficult to understand without help. The inspired teachings of the Prophet Joseph Smith, here and elsewhere, provide us with significant help in understanding Isaiah.

We will first go through section 113, using **bold** to point out the questions and answers. Then we will quote the referenced Isaiah verses, adding Joseph Smith's helps by way of notes.

Question

1 **WHO is the Stem of Jesse** [*Jesse was King David's father—see 1 Samuel 16:19, and thus, an ancestor of Christ—see Matthew 1:5–6, 16–17*] **spoken of in the 1st, 2d, 3d, 4th, and 5th verses of the Isaiah?**

Answer

2 Verily thus saith the Lord: **It is Christ.**

Question

3 **What is the rod spoken of in the first verse of the 11th chapter of Isaiah, that should come of the Stem of Jesse?**

Answer

4 Behold, thus saith the Lord: **It is a servant in the hands of Christ, who is partly a descendant of Jesse as well as of Ephraim, or of the house of Joseph, on whom there is laid much power.**

Question

5 **What is the root of Jesse** spoken of in the 10th verse of the 11th chapter?

Answer

6 Behold, thus saith the Lord, **it is a descendant of Jesse, as well as of Joseph, unto whom rightly belongs the priesthood, and the keys of the kingdom, for an ensign, and for the gathering of my people in the last days.**

Question

7 Questions by Elias Higbee: **What is meant by the command in Isaiah, 52d chapter, 1st verse,**

which saith: **Put on thy strength, O Zion—and what people had Isaiah reference to?**

Answer

8 He had reference to those whom God should call in the last days, who should hold the power of priesthood to bring again Zion, and the redemption of Israel; and **to put on her strength is to put on the authority of the priesthood,** which she, Zion, has a right to by lineage; **also to return to that power which she had lost.**

Question

9 What are we to understand by Zion loosing herself from the bands of her neck; 2d verse?

Answer

10 We are to understand that the scattered remnants [*of Israel*] **are exhorted to return to the Lord** from whence they have fallen; which **if they do, the promise of the Lord is that he will speak to them,** or **give them revelation.** See the 6th, 7th, and 8th verses. **The bands of her neck are the curses of God upon her, or the remnants of Israel in their scattered condition among the Gentiles.**

As you can see, verses 1–5 in this section deal with Isaiah 11:1–5, 10. When Moroni appeared to Joseph Smith on September 21, 1823, he quoted Isaiah, chapter 11, "saying that it was about to be fulfilled" (Joseph Smith—History 1:40). Thus, we understand that Isaiah 11 has directly to do with Joseph Smith and the restoration of the gospel in the last days. We will now quote these Isaiah verses, adding the helps from Joseph Smith as we go.

Isaiah 11:1–5

1 AND there shall come forth a rod [*a servant of Christ (see D&C 113:3–4) who will serve in the last days (according to Moroni—Joseph History 1:40)*] out of **the stem of Jesse** [*Christ—see D&C 113:1–2*]**, and a Branch shall grow out of his roots:**

Verses 2–3 appear to list a number of leadership qualities, which apply to the Savior and could also apply to faithful leaders, including Joseph Smith.

2 And the spirit of the LORD shall rest upon him, the spirit of wisdom and **understanding,** the spirit of **counsel** and **might,** the spirit of **knowledge** and of the **fear of the LORD** [*respect for God*]**;**

3 And shall make him of quick understanding in the fear of the LORD: and **he shall not judge after the sight of his eyes, neither reprove after the hearing of his ears**:

Verse 4, next, appears to apply to Christ (the "stem of Jesse," verse 1).

4 But **with righteousness shall he judge** the poor, **and reprove with equity** [*fairness*] for the meek of the earth: and **he shall smite the earth with the rod of his mouth, and with the breath of his lips shall he slay the wicked.**

Verse 5, next, certainly applies to Christ and could also apply to any great leader who is humble and has respect for God. In effect, it says that such leaders would be clothed with personal righteousness and would be deeply faithful to God.

5 And **righteousness shall be the girdle of his loins** [*clothed with righteousness*], and **faithfulness the girdle of his reins** [*deepest thoughts and desires*].

Isaiah 11:10

10 And in that day there shall be **a root of Jesse** [*a mighty leader in the kingdom of God in the last days (see D&C 113:5–6); this could easily be Joseph Smith*], which shall stand for an ensign of the people; to it shall the Gentiles seek: and **his rest** [*exaltation—see D&C 84:24*] **shall be glorious.**

Verses 7–10 of section 113 refer to Isaiah 52:1–2, 6–8. We will quote them here and then add Joseph Smith's explanations as notes.

Isaiah 52:1–2, 6–8

1 **AWAKE, awake; put on thy strength** [*From D&C 113:8 "put on the authority of the priesthood"*], **O Zion** [*"those whom God should call in the last days, who should hold the power of priesthood to bring again Zion, and the redemption of Israel"—see D&C 113:8*]; **put on thy beautiful garments, O Jerusalem**, the holy city: for henceforth there shall no more come into thee the uncircumcised and the unclean.

2 Shake thyself from the dust; arise, *and* sit down, O Jerusalem: **loose thyself from the bands of thy neck** [*from D&C 113:10; "the curses of God upon her, or the remnants of Israel in their scattered condition among the Gentiles"—see D&C 113:10*], O captive daughter of Zion.

6 [*From D&C 113:10; "The scattered remnants are exhorted to return to the Lord from whence they have fallen; which if they do,*

the promise of the Lord is that he will speak to them, or give them revelation. See the 6th, 7th, and 8th verses"—see D&C 113:10] **Therefore my people shall know my name: therefore** *they shall know* **in that day that I** *am* **he that doth speak: behold,** *it is* **I.**

7 **How beautiful upon the mountains are the feet of him that bringeth good tidings, that publisheth peace; that bringeth good tidings of good, that publisheth salvation; that saith unto Zion, Thy God reigneth!**

8 **Thy watchmen shall lift up the voice; with the voice together shall they sing: for they shall see eye to eye, when the LORD shall bring again Zion.**

SECTION 114

Background

This revelation was given through the Prophet Joseph Smith on April 11, 1838, in Far West, Missouri.

In verse 1, David W. Patten is addressed. Brother Patten was a faithful member of the original Quorum of the Twelve Apostles called in this last dispensation. At the time of this revelation, he had been living with the Saints in Missouri for some time, and was a stabilizing influence there. It was a difficult time in Missouri, with much dissension and apostasy among the members, including some of the leaders of the Church there. In fact, the members of the stake presidency in Missouri, David Whitmer, William W. Phelps, and John Whitmer, were themselves in a state of apostasy at this time. This is helpful background for verse 2.

We will provide a bit more background on David Patten. He was born on November 14, 1799, in New York and was thus a little over six years older than Joseph Smith. He was a bit over six feet, one inch tall and weighed over two hundred pounds when he was baptized in the early 1830s. He was ordained an Apostle and member of the Twelve on February 15, 1835.

As we look back through the eyes of history, the mission call given to him in verse 1, next, may well have foreshadowed his martyrdom, and the mission was to the spirit world mission field.

He was fatally shot in Missouri in the abdomen by a member of a Missouri mob during the Battle of Crooked River on October 25, 1838. He was thirty-eight years of age.

We know through revelation that he returned to the presence of God, as stated by the Savior as follows:

D&C 124:130

130 David Patten I have taken unto myself; behold, his priesthood no man taketh from him; but, verily I say unto you, another may be appointed unto the same calling.

We will now read the two verses of section 114.

1 VERILY thus saith the Lord: It is wisdom in my servant David W. Patten, that he **settle up all his business as soon as he possibly can**, and make a disposition of his merchandise, **that he may perform a mission unto me** next spring, in company with others, even twelve including himself, to testify of my name and bear glad tidings unto all the world.

In verse 2, next, the Savior gives instruction regarding replacing those leaders who have gone into apostasy.

2 For verily thus saith the Lord, that **inasmuch as there are those among you who deny my name** [*who have apostatized and left the Church*], **others shall be planted in their stead and receive their bishopric** [*their leadership positions*]. Amen.

As implied in verse 2, above, this was indeed a difficult time in Missouri and an especially trying time as far as apostasy was concerned. Among the prominent members of the Church who left during this period were the following:

The Stake Presidency in Missouri

- David Whitmer—excommunicated on April 13, 1838.

- John Whitmer (also one of the Eight Witnesses of the Book of Mormon)—excommunicated on March 10, 1838.

- William W. Phelps—excommunicated on February 10, 1838.

Apostles

- Luke S. Johnson—excommunicated spring 1837.

- Lyman E. Johnson—excommunicated on April 13, 1838.

- John F. Boynton—excommunicated on April 12, 1838.

- William E. McLellin—excommunicated spring 1837.

Other

- Oliver Cowdery (one of the Three Witness)—excommunicated on April 12, 1838.

- Hiram Page (one of the Eight Witnesses)—excommunicated during this period in Far West, Missouri.

- Martin Harris (one of the Three Witnesses)—left the Church near the end of 1837.

SECTION 115

Background

This revelation was given through the Prophet Joseph Smith on April 26, 1838, at Far West, Missouri.

By the time of this revelation, Far West, Missouri, had become the main gathering place for members of the Church. It is located in Caldwell County, some fifty miles northeast of Independence.

In January 1838, the Prophet and other leaders of the Church left Kirtland, Ohio, forced to leave because of the apostasy there. The exodus continued, with most other faithful members following.

By this time, the citizens of Clay County, Missouri (to which the majority of the Missouri Saints had fled upon their expulsion from Jackson County), had requested that the Mormons move on. These citizens had been kind and generous to the impoverished Saints in the meantime, but the time had come when it was becoming a serious difficulty for Clay County to have the Latter-day Saints continue in their communities.

As a result, the state legislature of Missouri had exclusively established Caldwell County as a gathering place for the Saints. Far West, in Caldwell County, became the central gathering place. The Prophet and others joined the members of the Church there.

This revelation is addressed to the officers and members of the Church, and particularly to the First Presidency and the Presiding Bishopric.

1 VERILY **thus saith the Lord unto you**, my servant **Joseph Smith, Jun.**, and also my servant **Sidney Rigdon,** and also my servant **Hyrum Smith** [*the First Presidency*], **and your counselors** who are and shall be appointed hereafter;

It appears from the wording in verse 1, above, that President Joseph Smith had more than two counselors at this time. Indeed, this was the case. We will quote from the 1981 *Doctrine and Covenants Student Manual* in order to explain this (**bold** added for emphasis):

"At a conference held at Kirtland, Ohio, on 3 September 1837, Oliver Cowdery, Joseph Smith, Sr., Hyrum Smith, and John Smith were sustained as **assistant counselors**.

"At the time the revelation in Doctrine and Covenants 115 was given, however, only Joseph Smith, Sr., and John Smith were serving as assistant counselors (26 April 1838). Hyrum Smith had taken the place of Frederick G. Williams in the First Presidency, and Oliver Cowdery had lost his membership in the Church (see *History of the*

Church, 2:509; Smith, *Essentials in Church History,* 569).

"Later, in Nauvoo, others served as counselors to the Prophet: John C. Bennett (who served a short time because Sidney Rigdon was ill), William Law, and Amasa Lyman (see *History of the Church,* 4:255, 264, 282–86, 341)" (*Doctrine and Covenants Student Manual,* 1981, 286).

2 **And also unto you, my servant Edward Partridge, and his counselors** [*the Presiding Bishopric*]*;*

Perhaps you have noticed in your reading of Church history that it was not until this time that the name of the Church was firmly established. Until this revelation was given, it was referred to by various names, including The Church of Christ, The Church of Jesus Christ, The Church of the Latter Day Saints, The Church of Christ of Latter Day Saints, and the Church of God. In verses 3 and 4, the Lord instructs as to the exact name of His Church in the last days.

The Official Name of the Church

3 **And also unto my faithful servants who are of the high council of my church in Zion, for thus it shall be called, and unto all the elders and people of my Church of Jesus Christ of Latter-day Saints,** scattered abroad **in all the world;**

4 For **thus shall my church be called in the last days, even The Church of Jesus Christ of Latter-day Saints.**

In summing up a landmark address regarding our using the correct, revealed name of the Church (verse 4, above), the Prophet, President Russell M. Nelson, taught the following in the Sunday morning session of the October 2018 session of general conference:

"My dear brothers and sisters, I promise you that if we will do our best to restore the correct name of the Lord's Church, He whose Church this is will pour down His power and blessings upon the heads of the Latter-day Saints, the likes of which we have never seen. We will have the knowledge and power of God to help us take the blessings of the restored gospel of Jesus Christ to every nation, kindred, tongue, and people and to prepare the world for the Second Coming of the Lord.

"So, what's in a name? When it comes to the name of the Lord's Church, the answer is 'Everything!' Jesus Christ directed us to call the Church by His name because it is His Church, filled with His power."

Verse 5, next, is given to all members (see verse 3, above).

5 Verily I say unto you all: **Arise and shine forth, that thy light may be a standard for the nations;**

Verse 6, next, is quite often quoted in sermons and classes in the Church. It clearly states that a major purpose of stakes throughout the world is to serve as a "defense, and for a refuge" for the Saints. Wherever stakes exist, members have the full program of the Church available to them, including patriarchs who can give them their patriarchal blessings. They can associate with others who have similar beliefs and commitments to God. In our day, we are watching the continuing organization of stakes throughout the world.

6 And **that the gathering together upon the land of Zion, and upon her stakes, may be for a defense, and for a refuge from the storm**, and from wrath when it shall be poured out without mixture [*without being diluted*] upon the whole earth.

One other note about stakes, as mentioned in verse 6, above. In scriptural imagery and symbolism, stakes hold up the Church, just as stakes are used to hold up a tent. Isaiah uses this imagery to prophesy the last days' growth of the Church:

Isaiah 54:2

2 **Enlarge the place of thy tent** [*keep building new chapels, temples, and so forth to accommodate the growth of the Church*], and let them stretch forth the curtains of thine habitations: spare not, **lengthen thy cords**, and **strengthen thy stakes;**

Next, beginning with verse 7, the Lord teaches these members that they are on holy ground and that a temple is to be built in Far West. If you have ever been to Far West, you can testify that it is indeed holy ground because of the Spirit that abides there. The Lord commands them to begin laying the foundation on July 4, 1838.

7 **Let the city, Far West, be a holy and consecrated land unto me**; and it shall be called most holy, for **the ground upon which thou standest is holy.**

8 Therefore, **I command you to build a house** [*a temple*] **unto me**, for the gathering together of my saints, that they may worship me.

9 And **let there be a beginning of this work, and a foundation, and a preparatory work,** this following summer;

10 And **let the beginning be made on the fourth day of July next**; and from that time forth let

my people labor diligently to build a house unto my name;

> In obedience to this commandment, more than five hundred men gathered on July 4, 1838, and dug a five-foot-deep foundation, 120 feet by 80 feet, in less than half a day. They also laid the four corner stones of the Far West Temple that day.
>
> Beginning with verse 11, additional instructions are given regarding the building of the Far West Temple, including that this time the brethren are not to go into debt to build the temple, as was the case with the Kirtland Temple.
>
> Looking at the difference in instructions for the Kirtland Temple and the Far West Temple, we are reminded that the leaders of the Church are guided by the Lord through ongoing revelation. And, when things are changed in the Church, we should rejoice in continuous revelation to the brethren, rather than wonder why they don't do things the same as in times past.

11 And **in one year from this day let them re-commence laying the foundation of my house.**

12 Thus **let them from that time forth labor diligently until it shall be finished**, from the corner stone thereof unto the top thereof, until there shall not anything remain that is not finished.

13 Verily I say unto you, **let not my servant Joseph, neither my servant Sidney, neither my servant Hyrum, get in debt any more for the building of a house unto my name**;

14 But **let a house be built unto my name according to the pattern which I will show unto them**.

15 And **if my people build it not according to the pattern which I shall show unto their presidency, I will not accept it** at their hands.

16 But **if my people do build it according to the pattern which I shall show unto their presidency**, even my servant Joseph and his counselors, **then I will accept it** at the hands of my people.

> Beginning with verse 17, next, we see another example of a change in how things are to be done (in other words, an example of ongoing revelation). In D&C 58:56, the Saints were instructed not to gather "in haste, nor by flight." Again, in D&C 63:24, they were told to gather to Zion, in Missouri, "not in haste." Yet, here, they are told to gather "speedily" to Far West.

17 And again, verily I say unto you, it is my will that the city of **Far West should be built up speedily by the gathering of my saints**;

Have you noticed that the Lord specifically shows support for His prophet in the eyes of the people? He has done this a number of times already (see D&C 28:2; 43:3–5; 112:15) and does it again in verses 18–19, next. This is yet another reminder to us that the Lord sustains His living prophet and that we are completely safe following him.

It is also particularly significant considering the apostasy taking place in Ohio and Missouri at the time of this revelation, as pointed out in the notes accompanying section 114 in this study guide.

18 And **also that other places should be appointed for stakes in the regions round about, as they shall be manifested unto my servant Joseph,** from time to time.

19 For behold, **I will be with him, and I will sanctify him before the people; for unto him have I given the keys of this kingdom and ministry.** Even so. Amen.

SECTION 116

Background

This revelation was given to the Prophet Joseph Smith on May 19, 1838, at a place called Spring Hill in the area the Lord refers to as Adam-ondi-Ahman in Missouri.

The Prophet recorded the following (**bold** added for emphasis):

"In the afternoon I went up the river [*the Grand River*] about half a mile to Wight's Ferry, accompanied by President Rigdon, and my clerk, George W. Robinson, for the purpose of selecting and laying claim to a city plat near said ferry in Daviess County, township 60, ranges 27 and 28, and sections 25, 36, 31, and 30, **which the brethren called 'Spring Hill,' but by the mouth of the Lord it was named Adam-ondi-Ahman**" (*History of the Church,* 3:35).

Adam-ondi-Ahman is located in Missouri roughly seventy miles north, northeast of Independence. While we do not know the exact meaning of the name Adam-ondi-Ahman, Bruce R. McConkie explains that we do have some clues. He said:

"Adam was the first man of all men; Ahman is one of the names by which God was known to Adam [D&C 78:20, 95:17]. Adam-ondi-Ahman, a name carried over from the pure Adamic language into English, is one for which we have not been given a revealed, literal translation. As near as we can judge—and this view comes down from the early brethren who associated with the Prophet Joseph Smith, who was the first one to use the name in this dispensation—Adam-ondi-Ahman means the place or land of God where Adam dwelt" (*Mormon Doctrine,* 19).

We will first go through the verse and then add additional commentary.

1 Spring Hill is named by the Lord **Adam-ondi-Ahman**, because, said he, it **is the place where Adam shall come to visit his people**, or the Ancient of Days [*Adam*] shall sit, as spoken of by Daniel the prophet [*in Daniel 7:9–14*].

In the Doctrine and Covenants we are taught that a great conference of Adam and Eve's righteous posterity was held in Adam-ondi-Ahman, three years prior to Adam's death. We read:

D&C 107:53–56

53 **Three years previous to the death of Adam, he called Seth, Enos, Cainan, Mahalaleel, Jared, Enoch, and Methuselah**, who were all high priests, **with the residue of his posterity who were righteous, into the valley of Adam-ondi-Ahman**, and there bestowed upon them his last blessing.

54 And **the Lord appeared unto them**, and **they rose up and blessed Adam**, and called him Michael, the prince, the archangel.

55 And **the Lord administered comfort unto Adam**, and said unto him: I have set thee to be at the head; a multitude of nations shall come of thee, and thou art a prince over them forever.

56 **And Adam stood up** in the midst of the congregation; **and**, notwithstanding he was bowed down with age, **being full of the Holy Ghost, predicted whatsoever should befall his posterity unto the latest generation**.

Shortly before the Second Coming of Christ, another great council will be held at Adam-ondi-Ahman. We read of this in the book of Daniel in the Old Testament. He had a vision in which he saw that millions of righteous people will attend this great meeting.

Daniel 7:9–10, 13–14

9 **I beheld till the thrones were cast down** [*Daniel saw the future, including the downfall of governments in the last days, as spoken of in D&C 87:6*], and **the Ancient of days** [*Adam*] **did sit** [*compare with the last part of this section*], whose garment *was* white as snow, and the hair of his head like the pure wool: his throne [*Adam is in a position of great power and authority*] *was like* the fiery flame, *and* his wheels *as* burning fire.

10 A fiery stream issued and came forth from before him: **thousand thousands** [*millions*] **ministered unto him, and ten thousand times ten thousand** [*a hundred million*] **stood before him**: the judgment was set, and the books were opened.

13 **I** [*Daniel*] **saw in the night visions,** and, behold, ***one*** **like the Son of man** [*a biblically respectful way of saying Jehovah, or in other words, Christ*] came with the clouds of heaven, and **came to the Ancient of days**, and they brought him near before him.

Next, we see, in Daniel's vision that the keys of leadership are given back to Christ during this grand council in preparation for His ruling and reigning as "Lord of lords, and King of kings" (Revelation 17:14) during the Millennium.

14 And **there was given him** [*Christ*] **dominion**, and **glory**, and **a kingdom, that all people, nations, and languages, should serve him** [*during the Millennium*]: his dominion *is* an everlasting dominion, which shall not pass away, and his kingdom *that* which shall not be destroyed.

Joseph Fielding Smith taught about this meeting at Adam-ondi-Ahman before the Second Coming. He said that "all who have held keys will make their reports and deliver their stewardships, as they shall be required. Adam will . . . then . . . make his report, as the one holding the keys for this earth, to his Superior Officer, Jesus Christ. Our Lord will then assume the reins of government; directions will be given to the Priesthood; and He, whose right it is to rule, will be installed officially by the voice of the Priesthood there assembled. This grand council of Priesthood will be composed, not only of those who are faithful who now dwell on this earth, but also of the prophets and apostles of old, who have had directing authority. Others may also be there, but if so they will be there by appointment, for this is to be an official council called to attend to the most momentous matters concerning the destiny of this earth" (*Way to Perfection,* 1984 hardcover edition, 290–91).

Among other things, Bruce R. McConkie taught the following about this council at Adam-ondi-Ahman (**bold** added for emphasis):

"But Daniel has yet more to say about the great events soon to transpire at Adam-ondi-Ahman. And we need not suppose that all these things shall happen in one single meeting or at one single hour in time. It is proper to hold numerous meetings at a general conference, some for the instruction of leaders, others for edification of all the saints. In some, business is transacted; others are for worship and spiritual refreshment. And so Daniel says: 'I saw in the night visions, and, behold, one like the Son of man came with the clouds of heaven, and came to the Ancient of days, and they brought him near before him.' **Christ comes to Adam**, who is sitting in glory. He comes to conform to his own priestal order. He comes to hear the report of Adam for his stewardship. **He comes to take back the keys of the earthly kingdom**. He comes to be invested with glory and dominion so that he can reign personally upon the earth" (*Millennial Messiah,* 585).

You may wish to read more about this meeting at Adam-ondi-Ahman in *The Millennial Messiah* (quoted above), 578–88.

Brother McConkie also taught:

"At this council, all who have held keys of authority will give an accounting of their stewardship to Adam. Christ will then come, receive back the keys, and thus take one of the final steps preparatory to reigning personally upon the earth. (Dan. 7:9–14; *Teachings*, p. 157.)" (*Mormon Doctrine,* 21).

Before we leave section 116, we will consider one other insight. It is interesting to note that the Garden of Eden was located in what is now Jackson County, Missouri.

Joseph Fielding Smith taught this as follows:

"In accord with the revelations given to the Prophet Joseph Smith, we teach that the Garden of Eden was on the American continent located where the City Zion [in Jackson County, Missouri], or the New Jerusalem, will be built.... When Adam and Eve were driven out of the Garden, they eventually dwelt at a place called Adam-ondi-Ahman, situated in what is now Daviess County, Missouri" (*Doctrines of Salvation,* 3:74).

Thus, when Adam and Eve were cast out from the Garden of Eden, they went to the area of Adam-ondi-Ahman to dwell. In other words, things got started in Missouri in the Garden of Eden as far as mortal life on this earth is concerned. It will have gone full-circle back to Missouri with the council at Adam-ondi-Ahman as the time for the Millennium approaches.

SECTION 117

Background

This revelation was given through the Prophet Joseph Smith to William Marks, Newel K. Whitney, and Oliver Granger on July 8, 1838, at Far West, Missouri. It is the first of five given on this date and recorded in the Prophet's journal. Sections 118, 119, 120, and an unpublished one to

Frederick G. Williams and William W. Phelps are the other four.

Because of the apostasy and dangerous conditions that had developed in Kirtland, Joseph Smith and Sidney Rigdon had fled to Far West in January 1838. William Marks had been assigned to remain in Kirtland and take care of the Church's temporal concerns there. Newell Whitney was the bishop in Kirtland. Oliver Granger was a member of the Kirtland high council as well as a financial agent for the Church there. He traveled to Far West, arriving by July 8, 1838.

In section 115, verse 17, the Lord commanded the Saints in Kirtland to come "speedily" to Far West. That commandment was given April 26, 1838. On July 6, 1838, a company of 515, known as the "Kirtland Camp," left Kirtland for Far West. However, some of the members of the Church in Kirtland who owned property had a hard time parting with it. Among these were William Marks and Bishop Newel K. Whitney. They were not with this company.

Two days later, in this revelation, the Lord revealed to the Prophet that Brother Marks and Bishop Whitney were not coming with the company from Kirtland. Their hearts were set on their temporal properties and concerns to the point that they would not comply with the command to come quickly to Far West. The fact that the Prophet Joseph Smith knew their situation just two days after the Kirtland Camp left is a testimony of his calling as the Prophet.

In verses 1–9, the Savior teaches a short course in perspective to William Marks (*a member of the Kirtland high council and an "agent" called to assist Bishop Whitney*) and Newel K. Whitney (*the Bishop in Kirtland*) regarding the relative worth of "property" (verse 4) compared to eternal blessings and the worth of the "drop" compared to "the more weighty matters" (verse 8). This is an important course for all of us.

1 VERILY **thus saith the Lord unto** my servant **William Marks, and also** unto my servant **Newel K. Whitney**, let them **settle up their business speedily and journey from the land of Kirtland**, before I, the Lord, send again the snows upon the earth.

2 **Let them awake, and arise, and come forth, and not tarry, for I, the Lord, command it.**

3 Therefore, **if they tarry it shall not be well with them.**

4 **Let them repent of all their sins, and of all their covetous desires** [*including coveting their own property and finances over and above the value of obedience to the Lord's commands to quickly relocate*

to Far West], before me, saith the Lord; **for what is property unto me? saith the Lord.**

> Next, in verse 5, the Lord instructs these men to sell their property and Church property to pay the debts of the Church, and if any is left over after that, they may keep it.

5 Let the properties of Kirtland be turned out for debts, saith the Lord. **Let them go** [*let go of your holdings*], saith the Lord, and **whatsoever remaineth, let it remain in your hands**, saith the Lord.

> Next, in verses 6–7, the Savior reminds them who it is who is giving them this command, with special emphasis on the fact that He has the power to keep His promises to them if they obey Him and come quickly to Far West.

6 For have I not the fowls of heaven, and also the fish of the sea, and the beasts of the mountains? Have I not made the earth? Do I not hold the destinies of all the armies of the nations of the earth?

7 Therefore, will I not make solitary places to bud and to blossom, and to bring forth in abundance? saith the Lord.

8 Is there not room enough on the mountains of Adam-ondi-Ahman, and on the plains of Olaha Shinehah [*perhaps a part of Adam-ondi-Ahman; Shinehah means "sun" according to Abraham 3:13*], or the land where Adam dwelt, **that you should covet that which is but the drop, and neglect the more weighty matters?**

9 Therefore, come up hither unto the land of my people, even Zion.

> Verse 10, next, is given to Brother Marks. He will accept the counsel and will come to Far West. But he will not be completely successful in overcoming the tendencies that caused him to hesitate in the first place. Eventually, he will apostatize, join the conspirators against Joseph Smith, and after the Martyrdom, he will join one break-off group from the Church after another, finally settling in the Reorganized Church of Jesus Christ of Latter-Day Saints where he stayed until his death at age seventy-nine on May 22, 1872.

10 Let my servant William Marks be faithful over a few things, and he shall be a ruler over many [*a formula for obtaining exaltation*]. **Let him preside in the midst of my people in the city of Far West**, and **let him be blessed with the blessings of my people.**

> As you can see, verse 11, next, is a rather stinging rebuke to Bishop

Whitney. The "Nicolaitane band" is a reference to Revelation 2:6 and refers to people who want to be in the world and in the Church at the same time. In other words, they want to be loyal to the Church, but they also want to be loyal to their worldly pursuits and selfish interests. It can't be done.

11 **Let my servant Newel K. Whitney be ashamed of the Nicolaitane band** and of all their secret abominations, **and of all his littleness of soul** before me, saith the Lord, **and come up to the land of Adam-ondi-Ahman, and be a bishop** unto my people, saith the Lord, **not in name but in deed** [*you must carry out your duties as bishop, not just have the title*], saith the Lord.

Bishop Whitney accepted this counsel and rebuke and came to Far West. He humbly worked on overcoming the weaknesses spoken of by the Lord in verse 11, above, and grew in wisdom and ability to serve faithfully. He remained a dear friend of the Prophet, and after the Martyrdom, he was called as the Presiding Bishop of the Church.

He and his family came west with the Saints, arriving in the Salt Lake Valley in 1848. He passed away, faithful to the end, on Monday, September 23, 1850.

Next, the Lord compliments Oliver Granger, who had already come to Far West from Kirtland. He was a humble man of faith who had great business skills. He personally carried a copy of this revelation to his associates William Marks and Newel K. Whitney in Kirtland after the Prophet received it.

12 And again, I say unto you, **I remember my servant Oliver Granger**; behold, verily I say unto him that **his name shall be had in sacred remembrance from generation to generation**, forever and ever, saith the Lord.

Next, in verse 13, Brother Granger is appointed to help settle the debts of the Church in Kirtland. He was so successful and demonstrated such high integrity in accomplishing this that he became highly respected in the Kirtland area.

13 Therefore, **let him contend earnestly for the redemption of the First Presidency** of my Church [*among other things, help them pay off their debts and the debts of the Church incurred at Kirtland*], saith the Lord; and when he falls he shall rise again, for **his sacrifice shall be more sacred unto me than his increase** [*his personal profits from business ventures*], saith the Lord.

14 Therefore, **let him come up hither speedily** [*return quickly from*

Kirtland back to Far West], **unto the land of Zion**; and in the due time he shall be made a merchant unto my name, saith the Lord, for the benefit of my people.

15 Therefore **let no man despise my servant Oliver Granger, but let the blessings of my people be on him forever and ever.**

> Oliver Granger moved with the Saints to Commerce (Nauvoo), Illinois, and became a land agent for the First Presidency. He was again sent to Kirtland in 1840, representing the Prophet to settle remaining financial matters of the Church. He died faithful in Kirtland in 1841 at age forty-seven.
>
> Verse 16, next, is addressed to all members of the Church in the Kirtland area. The phrase "in mine own due time" is a reminder that the Lord's timetable is often different than ours.

16 And again, verily I say unto you, **let all my servants in the land of Kirtland remember the Lord their God, and mine house** [*the Kirtland Temple*] **also, to keep and preserve it holy**, and to overthrow the moneychangers [*probably a reference to those who are taking dishonest advantage of the Saints as they move out to go to Far West*] **in mine own due time**, saith the Lord. Even so. Amen.

SECTION 118

Background

This revelation was given through the Prophet Joseph Smith on July 8, 1838, at Far West, Missouri. It is one of five given on the same day (as explained in the background notes to section 117 in this study guide).

As you can see in the heading to section 118 in your Doctrine and Covenants, this revelation came in response to the request, "Show us thy will, O Lord, concerning the Twelve."

By way of background, by now Apostles John F. Boynton, Luke Johnson, Lyman Johnson, and William E. McLellin had apostatized and been excommunicated.

In verse 1, the Savior instructs that the Quorum of the Twelve should be reorganized with new Apostles called to replace those who apostatized. In verse 6, He will give the names of those who are to be called as Apostles in order for this reorganization to take place.

1 VERILY, thus saith the Lord: **Let a conference be held immediately; let the Twelve be organized**; and **let men be appointed to supply the place of those who are fallen.**

Next, in verse 2, Thomas B. Marsh is told to stay in Missouri and preach the gospel there for the time being.

2 Let my servant Thomas remain for a season in the land of Zion, to publish my word.

Brother Marsh was publishing the *Elders' Journal* in Far West at this time, which he had already been publishing in Kirtland. It ran from October 1837 to August 1838.

Next, the remaining faithful Apostles are given a conditional promise regarding their families.

3 Let the residue [*the rest of the Twelve*] **continue to preach** from that hour, **and *if* they will do this in all lowliness of heart, in meekness and humility, and long-suffering, I, the Lord, give unto them a promise that I will provide for their families; and an effectual door shall be opened for them, from henceforth** [*from now on*].

Perhaps you've noticed that temporal blessings are conditional upon our faithfulness and sometimes upon the faithfulness of others.

Ultimately, however, our exaltation is based upon our own use of moral agency, coupled with the Savior's Atonement. We cannot blame anyone else if we fail. In other words, each person is ultimately responsible for whether he or she is saved. Brigham Young taught this. He said (**bold** added for emphasis):

"Who has influence over any one of you, to cause you to miss salvation in the celestial kingdom of God? I will answer these questions for myself. If brother Brigham and I shall take a wrong track, and be shut out of the kingdom of heaven, no person will be to blame but brother Brigham and I. **I am the only being in heaven, earth, or hell, that can be blamed.**

"This will equally apply to every Latter-day Saint. **Salvation is an individual operation. I am the only person that can possibly save myself.** When salvation is sent to me, I can reject or receive it" (*Journal of Discourses,* 1:312).

Next, in verses 4–5, the members of the Twelve, including the new ones to be called, are commanded to go on an overseas mission, leaving from Far West on April 26, 1839. The specifying of such an exact date by the Lord sets the groundwork for a marvelous miracle.

4 And next spring let them depart to go over the great waters, and there promulgate [*spread, preach*] **my gospel,** the fulness thereof, **and bear record of my name.**

5 Let them take **leave** of my saints **in the city of Far West, on the twenty-sixth day of April**

next, on the building-spot of my house [*from the Far West Temple site*], saith the Lord.

We will explain the "marvelous miracle" mentioned above. By the time April 26, 1839, arrived, the Saints had been completely driven from Missouri and into Illinois. Not only that, but also some of the Missourians knew of the plan of the Twelve to leave from Far West on that date. They were determined to prevent it so that Joseph Smith would become a false prophet, at least as far as this prophecy was concerned. Any members of the Church who entered Missouri were "fair game."

Nevertheless, the prophecy was fulfilled. Just after midnight on April 26, 1839, Apostles Brigham Young, Heber C. Kimball, Orson Pratt, John E. Page, John Taylor, Wilford Woodruff, and George A. Smith, along with about twenty other members of the Church, gathered at the Far West Temple site as a preliminary to the mission of several of the Twelve to England. They sang part of a hymn, and Elder Alpheus Cutler, the master workman of the house, then recommenced laying the foundation of the Lord's House by rolling a large stone near the southeast corner. All seven of the Apostles present offered prayers, and the group sang the hymn "Adam-ondi-Ahman." We will quote from *History of the Church* for what happened after this:

"Thus was fulfilled a revelation of July 8, 1838, which our enemies had said could not be fulfilled, as no 'Mormon' would be permitted to be in the state.

"As the Saints were passing away from the meeting, Brother Turley said to Elders Page and Woodruff, 'Stop a bit, while I bid Isaac Russell [*an apostate and enemy to the Church*] good bye;' and knocking at the door, called Brother Russell. His wife answered, 'Come in, it is Brother Turley.' Russell replied, 'It is not; he left here two weeks ago;' and appeared quite alarmed; but on finding it was Brother Turley, asked him to sit down; but the latter replied, 'I cannot, I shall lose my company.' 'Who is your company?' enquired Russell. 'The Twelve.' '*The Twelve!*' 'Yes, don't you know that this is the twenty-sixth, and the day the Twelve were to take leave of their friends on the foundation of the Lord's House, to go to the islands of the sea? The revelation is now fulfilled, and I am going with them.' Russell was speechless, and Turley bid him farewell.

"The brethren immediately returned to Quincy, taking with them the families from Tenney's Grove" (*History of the Church,* 3:340).

Wilford Woodruff recorded what happened:

"When the revelation was given [in 1838], all was peace and quietude in Far West, Missouri, the city where most of the Latter-day Saints dwelt; but before the time came for its fulfillment, the Saints of God had been driven out of the State of Missouri into the State of Illinois, under the edict of Governor Boggs; and the Missourians had sworn that if all the other revelations of Joseph Smith were fulfilled, that [one] should not be. It stated the day and the place where the Twelve Apostles should take leave of the Saints, to go on their mission across the great waters, and the mobocrats of Missouri had declared that they would see that it should not be fulfilled. . . .

"Having determined to carry out the requirement of the revelation, . . . we started for Far West. . . .

"On the morning of the 26th of April, 1839, notwithstanding the threats of our enemies that the revelation which was to be fulfilled this day should not be, and notwithstanding that ten thousand of the Saints had been driven out of the State by the edict of the governor, . . . we moved on to the temple ground in the city of Far West, and held a council, and fulfilled the revelation and commandment given unto us, and we performed many other things at this council. . . .

"Bidding good-by to the small remnant of Saints who remained on the temple ground to see us fulfill the revelation and commandments of God, we turned our back on Far West and Missouri, and returned to Illinois. We had accomplished the mission without a dog moving his tongue at us [see Exodus 11:7], or any man saying, 'Why do you so?'" (*Teachings: Wilford Woodruff*, 139–41).

As mentioned previously, verse 6, next, names four men to replace the four Apostles who had apostatized.

6 Let my servant **John Taylor**, and also my servant **John E. Page**, and also my servant **Wilford Woodruff**, and also my servant **Willard Richards**, be appointed to fill the places of those who have fallen, and be officially notified of their appointment.

Of the four men called to be Apostles in verse 6, above, all but John E. Page will remain faithful, and as you can see, two of them, John Taylor and Wilford Woodruff, will eventually serve as presidents of the Church.

Elder Page was called in April 1840 to accompany Orson Hyde to dedicate Palestine for the return of the Jews. He started out on the journey but would not leave the United States, thus forcing Elder Hyde to go alone. After the martyrdom of Joseph Smith, Page affiliated with apostate James Strang and was excommunicated on June 26, 1846. He left the Strangites in 1849 and joined the Brewsterites (another break-off from the Church). He left them in 1850 and joined another faction.

Finally, he joined the Hedrikites and became an apostle in that break-off organization. He helped them secure ownership of the temple site in Independence, Missouri, which they still own today. He died on October 14, 1867, at age sixty-eight.

SECTION 119

Background

This revelation was one of five given through the Prophet Joseph Smith on the same day—July 8, 1838—in Far West, Missouri. See the background for section 117 in this study guide for more information.

This section and section 120 go together since they both involve the law of tithing. This is the section in which we are instructed that tithing is ten percent of our income annually. For additional background, we will quote the heading to section 119 as given in your Doctrine and Covenants.

"*Revelation given through Joseph Smith the Prophet, at Far West, Missouri, July 8, 1838, in answer to his supplication: 'O Lord, show unto thy servants how much thou requirest of the properties of thy people for a tithing.' HC 3:44. The law of tithing, as understood today, had not been given to the Church previous to this revelation. The term 'tithing' in the prayer just quoted and in previous revelations (64:23; 85:3; 97:11) had meant not just one-tenth, but all free-will offerings, or contributions, to the Church funds. The Lord had previously given to the Church the law of consecration and stewardship of property, which members (chiefly the leading elders) entered into by a covenant that was to be everlasting. Because of failure on the part of many to abide by this covenant, the Lord withdrew it for a time, and gave instead the law of tithing to the whole Church. The Prophet asked the Lord how much of their property he required for sacred purposes. The answer was this revelation."*

Joseph Fielding Smith also explained the background to this section. He said:

"The Lord had given to the Church the law of consecration and had called upon the members, principally the official members, to enter into a covenant that could not be broken and to be everlasting in which they were to consecrate their properties and receive stewardships, for this is the law of the celestial kingdom. Many of those who entered into this solemn covenant broke it and by so doing brought upon their heads, and the heads of their brethren and sisters, dire punishment and persecution. This celestial law of necessity was thereupon withdrawn for the time, or until the time of the redemption of Zion. While suffering intensely because of their debts and lack of means to meet their obligations Joseph Smith and Oliver Cowdery, November 29, 1834, in solemn prayer promised the Lord that they would give one tenth of all that the Lord should give unto them, as an offering to be bestowed upon the poor; they also prayed that their children, and the children's children after them should obey this law. (*History of the Church,* 2:174–75.) Now, however, it became necessary for the law to be given to the whole Church so the Prophet prayed for instruction. The answer they received [came] in the revelation [D&C 119]" (*Church History and Modern Revelation,* 2:90–91).

The "covenant" made by Joseph Smith and Oliver Cowdery in 1834, referenced by Joseph Fielding Smith in the above quote, was recorded by the Prophet as follows:

"On the evening of the 29th of November, I united in prayer with Brother Oliver for the continuance of blessings. After giving thanks for the relief which the Lord had lately sent us by opening the hearts of the brethren from the east, to loan us $430; after commencing and rejoicing before the Lord on this occasion, we agreed to enter into the following covenant with the Lord, viz.:

"That if the Lord will prosper us in our business and open the way before us that we may obtain means to pay our debts; that we be not troubled nor brought into disrepute before the world, nor His people; after that, of all that He shall give unto us, we will give a tenth to be bestowed upon the poor in His Church, or as He shall command; and that we will be faithful over that which He has entrusted to our care, that we may obtain much; and that our children after us shall remember to observe this sacred and holy covenant; and that our children, and our children's children, may know of the same, we have subscribed our names with our own hands.

"(Signed)

Joseph Smith, Jun.

Oliver Cowdery"

(*History of the Church,* 2:174–75).

Tithing is an established principle in the Bible and is required of worthy temple recommend holders today. It was paid by Abraham to Melchizedek (see Genesis 14:20), is taught strongly in Malachi 3:8–12, and was commonly paid in New Testament times (see Matthew 23:23, Luke 18:12).

As noted in the background given above, at the time of this revelation the Church and its leaders were deeply in debt. In answer to the Prophet's question that led up to this revelation, the Lord spelled out what was to be done. First, as stated in verses 1–3, all members of the Church were to donate their "surplus property" (verse 1) to the

Church, for several purposes as given in verse 2. In this context, surplus meant all that they could spare, above and beyond their basic needs.

1 VERILY, thus saith the Lord, **I require all their surplus property to be put into the hands of the bishop** of my church in Zion,

2 **For the building of mine house** [*the temple in Far West*], and **for the laying of the foundation of Zion** [*establishing the Church in Missouri*] and **for the priesthood, and for the debts of the Presidency of my Church.**

3 And **this shall be the beginning of the tithing of my people**.

In other words, this will set the stage for beginning to practice the law of tithing, meaning that, from this time on, members will pay ten percent of their annual income as tithing to the Church, through the bishop, as stated in verse 4, next.

4 And **after that**, those who have thus been tithed [*who have given all their surplus, as commanded in verses 1–3, above*] shall **pay one-tenth of all their interest annually**; and this shall be a standing law unto them forever, for my holy priesthood, saith the Lord.

The word "interest," in verse 4, above, needs to be defined as commonly used at the time of this revelation. Otherwise, there could be many different definitions, which would affect how much tithing we pay. The word "interest" means income as used in D&C 124:89.

Also, an entry in John Taylor's *Nauvoo Journal,* dated Saturday, January 11, 1845, defines the term. Regarding the payment of tithing, he wrote (**bold** added for emphasis):

"One tenth of their interest, or **income** yearly afterward" (*BYU Studies,* Vol. 23 [Summer 1983]: 20).

Even if we didn't have Elder Taylor's definition of "interest" as being "income," we have the words of our modern prophets and Apostles instructing us on this matter. For example, Apostle John A. Widtsoe taught (**bold** added for emphasis):

"Tithing means one-tenth. Those who give less do not really pay tithing; they are lesser contributors to the Latter-day cause of the Lord. **Tithing means one-tenth of a person's income**, interest, or increase. The merchant should pay tithing upon the net income of his business, the farmer upon the net income of his farming operations; the wage earner or salaried man upon the wage or salary earned by him. Out of the remaining nine-tenths he pays his current expenses, taxes, savings, etc. To deduct living costs, taxes, and similar expenses from the income and pay tithing upon the remainder does not conform to the Lord's commandment. Under such a system most people would show nothing on which to pay tithing. There is really no place for quibbling on this point. **Tithing should be given upon the basis of our full earned income**. If the nature of a business requires special interpretation, the tithepayer should consult the father of his ward, the bishop" (*Evidences and Reconciliations,* 86).

In general conference, President Spencer W. Kimball taught (**bold** used for emphasis):

"Inquiries are received at the office of the First Presidency from time to time from officers and members of the Church asking for information as to what is considered a proper tithe.

"We have uniformly replied that the simplest statement we know of is the statement of the Lord himself, namely, that the members of the Church should pay '**one-tenth of all their interest annually**' which **is understood to mean income** (see D&C 119:4)" ("The Law of Tithing," *Ensign,* November 1980, 77).

Verse 5, next, summarizes verses 1–4, above, stating that all members at the time who are gathering to Missouri are to donate all their surplus to the Church and then pay tithing (as defined in verse 4) thereafter.

5 Verily I say unto you, it shall come to pass that **all those who gather unto the land of Zion shall be tithed of their surplus properties, and shall observe this law** [*pay ten percent of their income annually*], or they shall not be found worthy to abide among you.

Verse 6, next, contains a warning about what will happen if the Saints do not keep these commandments.

6 And I say unto you, **if my people observe not this law**, to keep it holy, and by this law sanctify the land of Zion unto me, that my statutes and my judgments may be kept thereon, that it may be most holy, behold, verily I say unto you, **it shall not be a land of Zion unto you**.

The same lesson (end of verse 6, above) could be applied to members of the Church today who have tithing to pay but don't. In effect, the Church will not be Zion to them because they are not qualifying for the blessings of faithful membership.

Next, in verse 7, the Savior applies the law of tithing to all members of the Church, not just those emigrating to Missouri at the time of this revelation. Thus, worthy members pay an honest tithe today.

7 And **this shall be an ensample** [*example*] **unto all the stakes of Zion**. Even so. Amen.

Elder David A. Bednar taught what the payment of tithing does for each of us:

"The honest payment of tithing is much more than a duty; it is an important step in the process of personal sanctification" ("The Windows of Heaven," Ensign, Nov. 2013, 20).

By the way, "sanctification" means made pure and holy and fit to be in the presence of God.

SECTION 120

Background

This revelation was given through the Prophet Joseph Smith on July 8, 1838, at Far West, Missouri.

According to *The Joseph Smith Papers,* from the time of the organization of the Church on April 6, 1830, the funds of the Church were managed and distributed by various leaders, including bishops and members of the United Firm, the First Presidency, stake presidencies, and the high council (see *The Joseph Smith Papers, Documents, Volume 6: February 1838–August 1839,* 189).

This revelation specifically specifies and defines the committee that oversees the use and spending of the tithing funds of the Church. As you will see, the Savior is a member of this committee. There are nineteen members who serve on this council. We will use **bold** to point them out.

1 VERILY, thus saith the Lord, the time is now come, that **it** [*tithing—see section 119*] **shall be disposed of** [*spent*] **by a council**, composed of **the First Presidency** [*who are three members serving on this Council on the Disposition of the Tithes*] of my Church, and of **the bishop and his council** [*the Presiding Bishopric—three more members*], and by **my high council** [*the Quorum of the Twelve Apostles—twelve more members*]; and by **mine own voice** [*the Savior, making 19 members in all who serve on this council that oversees the spending of the tithing funds of the Church*] **unto them**, saith the Lord. Even so. Amen.

As you can see from the above revelation, we have absolutely no concerns or worries about the use and spending of the tithing we pay.

SECTION 121

Background

This section, as well as sections 122 and 123, are taken from two letters written between March 20–25, 1839 (see footnote in *History of the* Church, 3:289), by the

Prophet Joseph Smith from Liberty Jail in Liberty, Missouri. They were addressed to Bishop Edward Partridge and the Saints who had now taken refuge in Quincy, Illinois, and surrounding locations. We will include the complete text of these letters at the end of section 123 in this study guide, with sections 121, 122, and 123 in **bold**.

As the Saints continued to gather to Missouri, tensions continued to rise. Even though the Missouri state legislature had established two new counties, Caldwell and Daviess in northwestern Missouri, with the express purpose of providing a place for members to gather, many old settlers opposed this gathering. They formed mobs and began persecuting the Saints anew in the summer of 1838. Parley P. Pratt described the situation as follows:

"Soon after these things the war clouds began again to lower with dark and threatening aspect. Those who had combined against the laws in the adjoining counties [especially Jackson County], had long watched our increasing power and prosperity with jealousy, and with greedy and avaricious eyes. It was a common boast that, as soon as we had completed our extensive improvements, and made a plentiful crop, they would drive us from the State, and once more enrich themselves with the spoils" (*Autobiography of Parley P. Pratt,* 150).

Persecution of the Saints continued through the rest of the summer and into the fall. Mobs burned houses and crops, stole domestic animals, took prisoners, beat men, and ravished Mormon women.

On October 27, 1838, Gov. Lilburn W. Boggs of Missouri, believing false reports about the Saints and refusing to investigate the reports himself, issued the infamous "extermination order" that stated: "The Mormons must be treated as enemies and must be exterminated or driven from the state, if necessary for the public good. Their outrages are beyond all description" (*History of the Church,* 3:175).

Among the atrocities committed against the Saints was the Haun's Mill Massacre. On Tuesday afternoon, October 30, 1838, about 240 mobbers approached the small LDS settlement of Haun's Mill (sometimes spelled "Hawn's Mill") about twelve miles east of Far West. As the women and children fled into the surrounding woods, most of the men ran into the blacksmith shop. The mob shot without mercy at women and children, as well as men, and with devilish glee, hacked one of the men to death with a corn knife. In all, at least seventeen settlers of Haun's Mill were killed and about thirteen were wounded. It is sad to note that Jacob Haun, the leader of this settlement, had disregarded the counsel of the

SECTION 121

Prophet in which he counseled all of the Saints in nearby settlements to gather immediately to Far West where they could take a stand together against the mobs.

By October 31, 1838, more than two thousand Missourians surrounded Far West, threatening to carry out the governor's orders to drive the Mormons from the state or exterminate them. On the same day, Joseph Smith and other Church leaders were betrayed into the hands of General Samuel D. Lucas, leader of the Missouri state militia. They were mistreated, imprisoned, and tried. By the end of November, the Prophet and five others, including his brother Hyrum and Sidney Rigdon, were placed in Liberty Jail, where they languished in the most miserable winter conditions from November 30, 1838, to the first part of April 1839.

Liberty Jail was a cold, poorly ventilated stone dungeon, with four-foot-thick walls and two small barred windows. The outside measured twenty-two and a half feet long, twenty-two feet wide, with twelve-foot-high walls, making the interior measurements about fourteen by fourteen by twelve feet. It had an upper level and a lower level, with access to the lower level through a hole in the upper floor. Joseph Smith was six feet tall and could not stand up straight in the lower level. They were forced to sleep on filthy straw on the hard floor or on split logs. They were served filthy food and suffered terribly from the winter cold.

And perhaps worst of all, they were helpless to assist their families and the rest of the Saints who were at the same time being driven completely from the state. Imagine the feelings of the Prophet Joseph Smith, who had seen the Father and the Son, Moroni, John the Baptist, Peter, James, and John, Moses, Elias, Elijah, and many others, and whose prayers had been answered countless times, who had been saved and protected on so many occasions. He now found himself in such a miserable prison, with the days turning to weeks and then to months. Imagine the anguish in his heart that caused him, after almost four months in this vile prison, to cry out:

1 **O GOD, where art thou?** And where is the pavilion [*in biblical imagery, the place where Jehovah dwells in His majesty—compare with Psalm 27:4–5*] that covereth thy hiding place?

2 **How long shall thy hand be stayed**, and thine eye, yea thy pure eye, behold from the eternal heavens the wrongs of thy people and of thy servants, and thine ear be penetrated with their cries?

3 Yea, O Lord, **how long shall they suffer these wrongs and**

unlawful oppressions, before thine heart shall be softened toward them, and thy bowels be moved with compassion toward them?

4 **O Lord God Almighty**, maker of heaven, earth, and seas, and of all things that in them are, and who controllest and subjectest the devil, and the dark and benighted dominion of Sheol—**stretch forth thy hand** [*exercise Thy power*]; **let thine eye pierce**; let thy pavilion be taken up; **let thy hiding place no longer be covered; let thine ear be inclined**; let **thine heart be softened,** and **thy bowels** [*a biblical term for deepest feelings and emotions*] **moved with compassion toward us.**

5 **Let thine anger be kindled against our enemies**; and, in the fury of thine heart, **with thy sword avenge us of our wrongs**.

6 **Remember thy suffering saints, O our God; and thy servants will rejoice in thy name forever.**

> We will pause here to point out one of the many great lessons to be learned from sections 121, 122, and 123. As mentioned in the background notes to this section, all three sections are taken from the same two letters written by the Prophet from Liberty Jail.

Now that you have felt the pain and anguish of the Prophet's heart and his desperate plea for God's intervention in verses 1–6, above, please go to the last verse of section 123, and read it (verse 17).

Did you notice the difference in the Prophet's feelings and emotions? He is still in the same prison, under the same circumstances. The Lord has not said anything about getting him and the others out of prison. Yet the words cheerfully describe his feelings and accurately represent the tone at the end of section 123. What has happened in such a short time, from the first of section 121 to the end of section 123? Watch carefully for the answer as we continue with the Lord's response to the Prophet's humble and desperate plea in the first six verses of section 121. You will see that it has to do with perspective, confidence in your standing with the Lord, and seeing things the way the Lord sees them.

We will continue using **bold** to emphasize things, letting these precious words of the Savior speak mainly for themselves.

Perspective

7 **My son, peace be unto thy soul; thine adversity and thine afflictions shall be but a small moment;**

Perspective

8 And then, **if thou endure it well, God shall exalt thee on high; thou shalt triumph over all thy foes.**

Perspective

9 **Thy friends do stand by thee, and they shall hail thee again with warm hearts and friendly hands** [*a very comforting prophecy for Joseph at this moment*].

Perspective

10 **Thou art not yet as Job**; thy friends do not contend against thee, neither charge thee with transgression, as they did Job.

Perspective

11 And **they who do charge thee with transgression, their hope shall be blasted, and their prospects shall melt away as the hoar frost** [*the frost on things just before the sun comes up and melts it*] **melteth before the burning rays of the rising sun;**

12 And also that **God hath set his hand** and seal **to change the times and seasons** [*to disrupt their plans*]**, and to blind their minds,** that they may not understand his marvelous workings; **that he may prove them also and take them in their own craftiness;**

13 Also **because their hearts are corrupted**, and **the things which they are willing to bring upon others, and love to have others suffer, may come upon themselves to the very uttermost;**

14 **That they may be disappointed** [*among other things, in the fact that they will not stop the work of the Lord and the growth and spread of the Church*] **also, and their hopes may be cut off;**

As you read verse 15 about the fate of these persecutors of the Saints and their posterity, you would do well to read Ezekiel 18, which explains that if the children of wicked people choose not to follow in the footsteps of their wayward parents but rather turn to God, the chain of wickedness will not continue with them. Among other things, verse 15 could be a reference to the destruction of the wicked at the Second Coming.

15 And **not many years hence**, that **they and their posterity shall be swept from under heaven**, saith God, that not one of them is left to stand by the wall.

Perspective

16 **Cursed are all those that shall lift up the heel against mine anointed** [*a term that usually means the leaders of the Church*], saith the Lord, **and cry they**

have sinned when they have not sinned before me, saith the Lord, but have done that which was meet [*required*] in mine eyes, and which I commanded them.

17 But **those who cry transgression do it because they are the servants of sin** [*they are the ones who are caught up in sin*]**, and are the children of disobedience themselves.**

18 And **those who swear falsely against my servants**, that they might bring them into bondage and death—

19 Wo unto them; because they have offended my little ones they **shall be severed from the ordinances of mine house** [*they will be cut off from the Church and from the temple blessings of exaltation*].

20 Their basket shall not be full, their houses and their barns shall perish, and **they themselves shall be despised by those that flattered them** [*those who encouraged them to betray and mob the Saints and their leaders*].

21 **They shall not have right to the priesthood, nor their posterity after them from generation to generation.**

22 **It had been better for them that a millstone had been hanged about their necks, and they drowned in the depth of the sea.**

23 **Wo unto all those that discomfort my people, and drive, and murder, and testify against them**, saith the Lord of Hosts; **a generation of vipers shall not escape the damnation of hell** [*there is no ultimate escape for the wicked except repentance*].

Verse 24, next, appears to be a direct response to Joseph's plea in verse 2, above.

24 Behold, **mine eyes see and know all their works, and I have in reserve a swift judgment in the season thereof** [*when the time is right, after they have had a fair opportunity to repent*]**, for them all;**

Sometimes it is difficult for the righteous to be patient with the Lord while He gives the wicked more time to repent. Verse 25, next, is a reminder that everyone's time to face the consequences of their evil will come if they do not repent.

25 For **there is a time appointed for every man, according as his works shall be** [*everyone gets a completely fair opportunity and then will ultimately be judged according to agency choices*].

In verses 26–32, the Lord takes

the Prophet's mind far away from Liberty Jail and gives him a perspective of great knowledge and blessings that await him, including the fact that through his faithfulness, he will eventually understand the universe, the gods, the orbits and revolutions of the stars and planets, and so forth. Abraham, who was also persecuted (see Abraham 1), was given similar perspective (see Abraham 3) as preparation for him to continue his great mission as a prophet.

Perspective

26 God shall give unto you knowledge by his Holy Spirit, yea**, by the unspeakable gift of the Holy Ghost, that has not been revealed since the world was until now** [*Joseph will be given knowledge that has not been revealed on earth before—for example, details of the resurrection found in D&C 88, compared with Alma 40:19–21; details about the three degrees of glory, D&C 76, compared with 1 Corinthians 15:39–42*];

27 **Which our forefathers have awaited with anxious expectation to be revealed in the last times** [*the last days*], which their minds were pointed to by the angels, as held in reserve **for the fulness of their glory** [*for their exaltation*];

28 **A time to come in the which nothing shall be withheld, whether there be one God or many gods** [*Joseph Smith was later privileged to reveal to us that there are many gods—see, for example, D&C 132:20, which tells that righteous, temple-married husbands and wives will become gods; see also the Prophet's explanation of 1 Corinthians 8:5 in* Teachings of the Prophet Joseph Smith*, 370–71*]**, they shall be manifest.**

29 **All thrones and dominions, principalities and powers, shall be revealed** and set forth upon [*given to*] all who have endured valiantly for the gospel of Jesus Christ [*in other words, all those who are worthy of exaltation*].

30 **And also, if there be bounds set to the heavens** or to the **seas**, or to the dry **land**, or to the **sun, moon,** or **stars**—

31 **All the times of their revolutions**, all the appointed days, months, and years, and all the days of their days, months, and years, and **all their glories, laws,** and **set times**, shall be revealed in the days of the dispensation of the fulness of times [*chiefly through the Prophet Joseph Smith; compare with D&C 35:17*]—

32 **According to that which was ordained in the midst of the Council of the Eternal God of**

all other gods before this world was, that should be reserved unto the finishing and the end thereof, when every man [*every worthy person*] shall enter into his eternal presence and into his immortal rest.

Perspective

33 How long can rolling waters remain impure? What power shall stay the heavens [*what can stop the power of heaven? Nothing!*] **As well might man stretch forth his puny arm to stop the Missouri river in its decreed course, or to turn it up stream, as to hinder the Almighty from pouring down knowledge from heaven upon the heads of the Latter-day Saints.**

> Next, in verses 34–44, all of us are given a brief lesson in the prerequisites for using the priesthood effectively and how to use it properly. It is also a warning about the effects of uncontrolled negative personality traits upon our relationships with others.
>
> This is one of the greatest sermons ever given on proper use of the priesthood.

Perspective

34 Behold, there are many called [*to serve God and keep His commandments*] **but few are chosen** [*to use the priesthood effectively and, ultimately, receive all the blessings of the gospel, including exaltation*]. **And why are they not chosen?**

35 Because their hearts are set so much upon the things of this world, and aspire to the honors of men [*they desire praise of man more than approval from God*], **that they do not learn this one lesson—**

Perspective

36 That the rights of the priesthood are inseparably connected with the powers of heaven, and that the powers of heaven cannot be controlled nor handled only [*except*] **upon the principles of righteousness.**

37 That they may be conferred upon us, it is true; but when we undertake to cover our sins, or to gratify our pride, our vain ambition, or to exercise control or dominion or compulsion upon the souls of the children of men, in any degree of unrighteousness, behold, the heavens withdraw themselves; the Spirit of the Lord is grieved; and when it is withdrawn, Amen to the priesthood or the authority of that man.

38 Behold, **ere he is aware, he is left unto himself, to kick against the pricks** [*sharp, pointed sticks used in olden times to drive cattle; symbolic of conscience; the promptings of the Spirit*], **to persecute the saints, and to fight against God.**

> Verse 39, next, is a short course in human nature, a word to the wise to those who will humbly listen.

39 **We have learned by sad experience that it is the nature and disposition of almost all men, as soon as they get a little authority, as they suppose, they will immediately begin to exercise unrighteous dominion.**

40 **Hence** [*this is why*] **many are called, but few are chosen** [*as stated in verse 34, above*].

> Next, in verses 41–45, the Savior explains how priesthood holders should use the priesthood as they lead others. The principles taught apply to anyone in leadership positions, man or woman.

41 **No power or influence can or ought to be maintained by virtue of the priesthood** [*because one holds the priesthood*], **only** [*except*] **by persuasion, by long-suffering** [*patience, pure love*], **by gentleness and meekness, and by love unfeigned** [*genuine love*];

42 By **kindness, and pure knowledge** [*including knowledge of gospel doctrines and principles, knowledge of the people's needs and backgrounds within one's stewardship, and so forth*], which shall greatly enlarge the soul [*including the ability to be compassionate*] **without hypocrisy, and without guile** [*without ulterior motives*]—

> Many people misunderstand the word "betimes" in verse 43, next, and think it means "occasionally." Instead, it means "soon, right away, early on in the situation" (see any good dictionary of the English language).

43 **Reproving** [*offering correction; scolding*] **betimes** [*right away, immediately, while the situation is still in focus*] **with sharpness** [*with directness; can also mean with clarity, explaining what the problem or concern is*], **when moved upon by the Holy Ghost; and then showing forth afterwards an increase of love toward him whom thou hast reproved, lest he esteem thee to be his enemy;**

44 **That he may know that thy faithfulness is stronger than the cords of death.**

> The last part of verse 43, above, beginning with "showing forth afterwards an increase of love," is a

vital part of leading others in righteousness. There is a tendency on the part of many leaders who exercise "unrighteous dominion" (verse 39, above) to ostracize, cut off, ignore, or avoid those whom they have reproved. The Savior "stretches forth his hands unto them all the day long" (Jacob 6:4), inviting them to repent and return to the fold.

So it is that parents, teachers, priesthood and auxiliary leaders, and all who have influence on others should show "forth afterwards an increase of love," helping those who have been scolded or disciplined to return to confident fellowship in the fold, knowing that your correcting him or her was done out of love as explained in verse 43–44.

As we move on to verse 45, next, don't forget the "classroom" (the dungeon) that Joseph finds himself in as he is being taught these lessons in Christlike leadership and care for others. It is a setting in which it would be most difficult to have "charity towards all men" as instructed in verse 45. It is a great credit to the Prophet and an insight into his great strength of character that he becomes genuinely cheerful at the end of section 123 (see 123:17). Of course, these lessons apply to us also.

45 Let thy bowels [*your whole being*] **also be full of charity towards all men** [*including those who influenced your being placed in Liberty Jail*], **and to the household of faith** [*to the faithful members of the Church*], and **let virtue garnish** [*adorn, decorate, give beauty to*] **thy thoughts unceasingly; then shall thy confidence wax** [*grow*] **strong in the presence of God** [*then you will feel more and more comfortable with God, including praying for help from Him*]; **and the doctrine of the priesthood** [*proper understanding and use of the priesthood*] **shall distil upon** [*gently come upon*] **thy soul as the dews from heaven** [*symbolic of pure truth coming down from above*].

46 The Holy Ghost shall be thy constant companion, and thy scepter [*symbolic of power and priesthood authority; exaltation; becoming gods*] **an unchanging scepter of righteousness and truth** [*just as is the case with God*]; **and thy dominion shall be an everlasting dominion** [*as a god*], **and without compulsory means it** [*perhaps referring back to dominion; it could also refer back to "righteousness and truth"*] **shall flow unto thee forever and ever.**

One possible meaning of the phrase "without compulsory means," in verse 46, above, is that all things in the universe voluntarily honor and obey God because of the righteousness and truth that is in Him (compare with D&C 29:36, where we see that God's honor is the source of His power). This principle would naturally apply to any who become gods.

SECTION 122

Background

As stated in the background notes for section 121 in this study guide, sections 121 through 123 go together, being excerpts from two letters written by the Prophet Joseph Smith from the jail in Liberty, Missouri. One is dated March 20, 1839, and the other about two days later. The full text of these letters is included at the end of section 123 in this study guide.

Section 122 is much quoted. It contains poignant feelings and a sweet reminder that the Savior is acquainted with any and all of our griefs and sorrows, because He suffered far beyond what any of us can. He understands our troubles and suffering better than we possibly can. Thus, He is in a position to strengthen and bless us according to our real needs and what is best for us, no matter what our condition or grief.

An amazing prophecy is given in this section, which echoes what Moroni told young Joseph in 1823 when he said that Joseph's "name should be had for good and evil among all nations" (Joseph Smith–History 1:33). It is verses 1–2 in which the Lord prophecies that all the world will know of Joseph Smith. Some will seek after his work and teachings as a prophet of God and come to salvation. Others will mock and ridicule.

Any time you see or hear anti-Latter-day Saint rhetoric belittling Joseph Smith, you can, in a significant way, say in your heart, "There is another proof that Joseph Smith was indeed a true prophet! They know about him! This is prophecy being fulfilled! The Church is true!"

Likewise, whenever you hear a conversion story or read about the Prophet Joseph Smith being honored in faraway places as well as close by, you can rejoice, knowing that this prophecy, given when he was but an obscure farm boy in upstate New York (when Moroni told him he would be known throughout the earth) and repeated here in section 122 when he was still relatively unknown, is being fulfilled.

We will now proceed with our study of section 122. Among other things, we will continue to point out perspectives given the Prophet by the Lord that enable him to understand and become cheerful by the end of the letters from Liberty Jail (see D&C 123:17) in spite of the oppressive and terribly difficult conditions and suffering he has been forced to endure over the past almost four months.

Perspective

1 THE ends of the earth shall inquire after thy name [*will want to know more about you*], **and fools shall have thee in derision, and hell shall rage against thee**;

2 While the pure in heart, and **the wise,** and the **noble,** and the **virtuous, shall seek counsel, and authority, and blessings constantly from under thy hand** [*those things restored by the Lord through the Prophet Joseph will constantly bless countless lives*].

Perspective

3 And thy people shall never be turned against thee by the testimony of traitors.

Perspective

4 And **although their** [*traitors and enemies*] **influence shall cast thee into trouble,** and into bars and walls [*jails and prisons*], **thou shalt be had in honor; and but for a small moment** [*just a little while longer*] and **thy voice shall be** more **terrible in the midst of thine enemies** than the fierce lion, **because of thy righteousness** [*an affirmation of his good standing with the Lord, no doubt a great comfort to Joseph*]; and **thy God shall stand by thee forever and ever.**

Did you notice an important lesson for all of us at the end of verse 4, above? It has to do with the Lord's statement "thy God shall stand by thee forever and ever." Sometimes we may tend to believe that "stand by" means "not allow anything bad to happen to us." Such is obviously not the case. In fact, that would not be good for us eternally. Rather, it means that He will support us and help us "in every time of trouble" (see D&C 3:8).

Virtually every trial and tribulation mentioned in verses 5–7 happened to the Prophet Joseph Smith. Feel the power of these lines as they lead up to two of the most powerful quotes in all of the scriptures. We will **bold** these well-known lines at the end of verse 7 and in verse 8.

5 If thou art called to pass through tribulation; if thou art in perils among false brethren [*traitors, betrayers*]; if thou art in perils among robbers; if thou art in perils by land or by sea;

6 If thou art accused with all manner of false accusations; if thine enemies fall upon thee; if they tear thee from the society of thy father and mother and brethren and sisters; and if with a drawn sword thine enemies tear thee from the bosom of thy wife, and of thine offspring, and thine elder

son, although but six years of age, shall cling to thy garments, and shall say, My father, my father, why can't you stay with us? O, my father, what are the men going to do with you? and if then he shall be thrust from thee by the sword, and thou be dragged to prison, and thine enemies prowl around thee like wolves for the blood of the lamb [*no doubt symbolic of the evil people who persecuted the Savior*];

7 And if thou shouldst be cast into the pit, or into the hands of murderers, and the sentence of death passed upon thee; if thou be cast into the deep; if the billowing surge conspire against thee; if fierce winds become thine enemy; if the heavens gather blackness, and all the elements combine to hedge up the way; and above all, if the very jaws of hell shall gape open the mouth wide after thee, **know thou, my son, that all these things shall give thee experience, and shall be for thy good.**

8 **The Son of Man** [*the Savior; the Son of Man of Holiness; in other words, the Son of Heavenly Father—see Moses 6:57*] **hath descended below them all. Art thou greater than he?**

One of the important lessons we learn from verse 9, next, is that Satan and his evil followers have limits set by God.

Perspective

9 Therefore, hold on thy way, and **the priesthood shall remain with thee**; for **their bounds are set, they cannot pass**. Thy days are known, and thy years shall not be numbered less; therefore, **fear not what man can do, for God shall be with you forever and ever.**

A question that sometimes comes up regarding verse 9, above, is whether there was a set time for Joseph Smith to die. From what we know about agency and that predestination is a false doctrine, we may probably conclude that there was not a set time for the Prophet to die. Rather, the Lord may have been telling him that, in spite of his enemies, he would accomplish his mission successfully.

During the last seven months of his life, Joseph seemed to feel that his life was drawing to a close. Consequently, he met with the Quorum of the Twelve almost every day, preparing them for his departure. "In an extraordinary council meeting in late March 1844, he solemnly told the Twelve that he could now leave them, because his work was done and the foundation was laid so the kingdom of God could be reared" (*Church History in the Fulness of Times,* 2003, 293–94).

SECTION 123

Background

This section goes together with sections 121 and 122. All three are excerpts from two letters written by Joseph Smith to Bishop Edward Partridge and members of the Church who had taken refuge in Quincy, Illinois. Joseph wrote the letters while in Liberty Jail, just a few days apart, starting on March 20, 1839. The complete text of the two letters is included at the end of this section.

You may wish to read the background notes for section 121 in this study guide if you haven't already done so. In them, the question is asked as to what happened to the Prophet between the first six verses of section 121 and the last verse of section 123? What was it that led to such an upbeat approach to things at the end of the second letter as opposed to the desperate cry for help at the first of section 121?

The answer, in part, is that the Lord gave the Prophet perspective. He allowed Joseph to see things as He sees them in the perspective of eternity. He assured him that he was in good standing with God and that his work was acceptable and would eternally benefit countless souls. This perspective and assurance, coupled no doubt with blessings and strengthening from the Lord, led to a tremendous change in the thirty-three-year-old Prophet's feelings and outlook. The Lord spoke to him in sections 121 and 122, and Joseph speaks to the Saints and teaches them as their prophet in this section.

The first topic addressed here by Joseph Smith and his fellow prisoners is that the members of the Church should keep records and gather evidence of the persecutions and illegal acts against them to be presented to government officials (verse 6). This is in harmony with the Lord's counsel in D&C 101:86–89.

1 AND again, **we** [*the Prophet and the others in Liberty Jail*] **would suggest for your consideration the propriety of** [*the importance of*] **all the saints gathering up a knowledge of all the facts, and sufferings and abuses put upon them by the people of this State;**

2 **And also of all the property and amount of damages which they have sustained, both of character and personal injuries, as well as real property** [*homes, farms, livestock, and so forth*];

3 And **also the names of all persons that have had a hand in their oppressions,** as far as they

can get hold of them and find them out.

4 And perhaps a committee can be appointed to find out these things, and to **take statements and affidavits; and also to gather up the libelous** [*lies and slander that break the law*] **publications that are afloat**;

> As you perhaps are aware, many of the Prophet Joseph Smith's enemies have characterized him as an unlearned and illiterate farm boy. They forget that he was tutored by the Lord and His angels, as well as constantly being taught by the Holy Ghost. In light of the thinking and attitude of his critics, it is almost humorous to see the vocabulary words he used in verse 5, next. We will **bold** them to point them out. In fact, you may want to see how many of them you can define yourself.

5 And all that are in the magazines, and in the encyclopedias, and all the **libelous** histories that are published, and are writing, and by whom, and present the whole **concatenation** of **diabolical rascality** and **nefarious** and murderous **impositions** that have been practised upon this people—

> As you can see, the Prophet was indeed highly educated. We will repeat verse 5 and provide definitions for the words in **bold**.

Verse 5 repeated

5 And all that are in the magazines, and in the encyclopedias, and all the **libelous** [*slanderous*] histories that are published, and are writing, and by whom, and present the whole **concatenation** [*series of related items*] of **diabolical** [*devilish*] **rascality** [*trouble causing*] and **nefarious** [*wicked, evil*] and murderous **impositions** [*trouble; persecutions; disruptions of normal life and liberty*] that have been practised upon this people—

> We will now continue, moving ahead to verse 6, where the Prophet explains why he is asking the Saints to gather evidence against their persecutors.

6 **That we may not only publish to all the world, but present them to the heads of government in all their dark and hellish hue**, as the last effort which is enjoined on [*required from*] us by our Heavenly Father, **before we can fully and completely claim that promise which shall call him forth from his hiding place** [*as explained in D&C 101:86–90*]; **and also that the whole nation may be left without excuse before he can send forth the power of his mighty arm.**

> Many students of the Doctrine and Covenants miss one of the major

messages contained in verses 7–10, next. **It is that false creeds and beliefs hold an iron grip on the hearts and behaviors of most of mankind. Satan has been highly successful in accomplishing this.** Note the power words such as *riveted, iron yoke, strong band, handcuffs, chains, shackles,* and *fetters* used by the Prophet to describe the "inherited lies" (verse 7) that bind people to false doctrine, unrighteous behaviors, and bitter prejudice against the Lord's true Church and its members.

We will **bold** a number of these power words and phrases that describe the terrible damage caused by false creeds passed down from generation to generation.

7 It is an imperative duty that we owe to God, to angels, with whom we shall be brought to stand, and also to ourselves, to our wives and children, who have been made to bow down with grief, sorrow, and care, under the most damning hand of **murder, tyranny, and oppression**, supported and urged on and upheld by the influence of that spirit which hath so **strongly riveted** the **creeds of the fathers**, who have inherited lies, **upon the hearts of the children**, and **filled the world with confusion**, and has been growing stronger and stronger, and is now **the very mainspring of all corruption**, and the whole earth groans under the weight of its iniquity.

8 **It is an iron yoke**, it is **a strong band**; they are the very **handcuffs**, and **chains**, and **shackles**, and **fetters of hell** [*the chains and shackles of hell*].

9 Therefore it is an imperative duty that we owe, not only to our own wives and children, but to the widows and fatherless, whose husbands and fathers have been murdered under **its iron hand**;

10 **Which dark and blackening deeds are enough to make hell itself shudder**, and to stand aghast and pale, **and the hands of the very devil to tremble and palsy**.

11 And **also it** [*the work of recording and exposing the atrocities against the Saints*] **is an imperative duty that we owe to all the rising generation, and to all the pure in heart—**

Note the merciful teaching that many "are only kept from the truth because they know not where to find it" in verse 12, next.

Perspective

12 **For there are many yet on the earth** among all sects, parties, and denominations, who are blinded by the subtle craftiness of

men, whereby they lie in wait to deceive, and **who are only kept from the truth because they know not where to find it—**

13 **Therefore**, that **we should waste** [*use up our energies*] **and wear out our lives in bringing to light all the hidden things of darkness, wherein we know them**; and they are truly manifest from heaven—

14 **These** [*the instructions to collect evidence of persecution*] **should then be attended to with great earnestness.**

Verse 15, next, is prophetic, and we are seeing some of its fulfillment today as government entities and public figures apologize to the Church and its people for persecutions of the past.

15 **Let no man count them** [*the evidences of persecution*] as small things; for **there is much which lieth in futurity** [*there is much in the future*], pertaining to the saints, **which depends upon these things.**

Next, the Prophet emphasizes how seemingly small things can profoundly influence much larger matters.

16 You know, brethren, that **a very large ship is benefited very much by a very small helm** [*tiller; steering wheel of a ship*] **in the time of a storm**, by being kept workways [*at the proper angle*] with the wind and the waves.

Finally, in verse 17, next, we see and feel the effects of the blessings and counsels of the Lord upon the Prophet Joseph Smith since the opening six verses of section 121. He has been given perspective, knowledge, and understanding that have strengthened and cheered him, even though his physical circumstances have not been altered. He is still in Liberty Jail and at the mercy of bigotry and hatred. This verse holds a powerful lesson for all of us.

17 Therefore, dearly beloved brethren, **let us cheerfully do all things that lie in our power; and then may we stand still, with the utmost assurance, to see the salvation of God, and for his arm to be revealed** [*as taught by the Lord in D&C 101:85–93*].

The Prophet and his fellow inmates were kept in Liberty Jail until early April 1839. In the meantime, public opinion in Missouri had turned against Governor Boggs, the mobs, and the corrupt legal system because of their treatment of the Latter-day Saints. Some government officials and people in law enforcement quietly began trying to figure a way to let the prisoners "escape." Finally, they were granted a change of venue and transferred to Gallatin, Missouri, for trial where a drunken jury made a mockery of the judicial system.

Joseph and his brethren were then given a change of venue to Boone County. About mid-April, the company, consisting of the prisoners, a sheriff, and four guards, left Gallatin for the new court venue. The sheriff had been privately instructed to let the prisoners escape. Hyrum Smith relates what happened next (**bold** added for emphasis):

"We went down that day as far as Judge Morin's—a distance of some four or five miles. There we stayed until the next morning, when we started on our journey to Boone county, and traveled on the road about twenty miles distance. There we bought a jug of whisky, with which we treated the company; and while there the sheriff showed us the mittimus before referred to, without date or signature, and said that Judge Birch told him never to carry us to Boone county, and never to show the mittimus; and, said he, **I shall take a good drink of grog and go to bed, and you may do as you have a mind to.**

"Three others of the guard drank pretty freely of whisky, sweetened with honey. They also went to bed, and were soon asleep, and **the other guard went along with us, and helped to saddle the horses.**

"Two of us mounted the horses, and the other three started on foot, and we took our change of venue for the state of Illinois, and in the course of nine or ten days arrived safe at Quincy, Adams county [*April 22, 1839*], where we found our families in a state of poverty, although in good health, they having been driven out of the state previously by the murderous militia, under the exterminating order of the executive of Missouri" (*History of the Church,* 3:423).

As mentioned in the background notes for section 121, we will here include the complete text of the letters written from Liberty Jail by the Prophet Joseph Smith, which contain sections 121, 122, and 123. We will **bold** the verses of the three sections as they appear in the text of the letters. We are quoting from *History of the Church,* 3:289–303.

"Liberty Jail, Clay County, Missouri,

"March 25, 1839.

(Note that more recent research dates these letters as starting on March 20, 1839. Quoting from the 2018 *Doctrine and Covenants Student Manual*, we read: "On March 20, 1839, the Prophet dictated a letter to Bishop Edward Partridge and Church members in Quincy, Illinois, and in other locations. It was followed approximately two days later by another letter to Bishop Partridge and the Saints, in which the Prophet offered comfort and provided counsel. (See *The Joseph Smith Papers, Documents, Volume 6: February 1838–August 1839*, 357, 389.) Portions of these letters are recorded in Doctrine and Covenants 121–23.")

"To the Church of Latter-day Saints at Quincy, Illinois, and Scattered Abroad, and to Bishop Partridge in Particular:

"Your humble servant, Joseph Smith, Jun., prisoner for the Lord Jesus Christ's sake, and for the Saints, taken and held by the power of mobocracy, under the exterminating reign of his excellency, the governor, Lilburn W. Boggs, in company with his fellow prisoners and beloved brethren, Caleb Baldwin, Lyman Wight, Hyrum Smith, and Alexander McRae, send unto you all greeting. May the grace of God the Father, and of our Lord and Savior Jesus Christ, rest upon you all, and abide with you forever. May knowledge be multiplied unto you by the mercy of God. And may faith and virtue, and knowledge and temperance, and patience and godliness, and brotherly kindness and charity be in you and abound, that you may not be barren in anything, nor unfruitful.

"For inasmuch as we know that the most of you are well acquainted with the wrongs and the high-handed injustice and cruelty that are practiced upon us; whereas we have been taken prisoners charged falsely with every kind of evil, and thrown into prison, enclosed with strong walls, surrounded with a strong guard, who continually watch day and night as indefatigable as the devil does in tempting and laying snares for the people of God:

"Therefore, dearly beloved brethren, we are the more ready and willing to lay claim to your fellowship and love. For our circumstances are calculated to awaken our spirits to a sacred remembrance of everything, and we think that yours are also, and that nothing therefore can separate us from the love of God and fellowship one with another; and that every species of wickedness and cruelty practiced upon us will only tend to bind our hearts together and seal them together in love. We have no need to say to you that we are held in bonds without cause, neither is it needful that you say unto us, We are driven from our homes and smitten without cause. We mutually understand that if the inhabitants of the state of Missouri had let the Saints alone, and had been as desirable of peace as they were, there would have been nothing but peace and quietude in the state unto this day; we should not have been in this hell, surrounded with demons (if not those who are damned, they are those who shall be damned) and where we are compelled to hear nothing but blasphemous oaths, and witness a scene of blasphemy, and drunkenness and hypocrisy, and debaucheries of every description.

"And again, the cries of orphans and widows would not have ascended up to God against them. Nor would innocent blood have stained the soil of Missouri. But oh! the unrelenting hand! The inhumanity and murderous disposition of this people! It shocks all nature; it beggars and defies all description; it is a tale of woe; a lamentable tale; yea a sorrowful tale; too much to tell; too much for contemplation; too much for human beings; it cannot be found among the heathens; it cannot be found among the nations where kings and tyrants are enthroned; it cannot be found among the savages of the wilderness; yea, and I think it cannot be found among the wild and ferocious beasts of the forest—that a man should be mangled for sport! women be robbed of all that they have—their last morsel for subsistence, and then be violated to gratify the hellish desires of the mob, and finally left to perish with their helpless offspring clinging around their necks.

"But this is not all. After a man is dead, he must be dug up from his grave and mangled to pieces, for no other purpose than to gratify their spleen against the religion of God.

"They practice these things upon the Saints, who have done them no wrong, who are innocent and virtuous; who loved the Lord their God, and were willing to forsake all things for Christ's sake. These things are awful to relate, but they are verily true. It must needs be that offenses come, but woe unto them by whom they come.

"**[*Section 121:1–6*] Oh God! where art Thou? And where is the pavilion that covereth Thy hiding place? How long shall Thy hand be stayed, and Thine eye, yea Thy pure eye, behold from the eternal heavens, the wrongs of Thy people, and of Thy servants, and Thy ear be penetrated with their cries? Yea, O Lord, how long shall they suffer these wrongs and unlawful oppressions, before Thine heart shall be softened towards them, and Thy bowels be moved with compassion towards them?**

"**O Lord God Almighty, Maker of Heaven, Earth and Seas, and of all things that in them are, and who controllest and subjectest the devil, and the dark and benighted dominion of Sheol! Stretch forth Thy hand, let Thine eye pierce; let Thy pavilion be taken up; let Thy hiding place no longer be covered; let Thine ear be inclined; let Thine heart be softened, and Thy bowels moved with compassion towards us, Let Thine anger be kindled against our enemies; and in the fury of Thine heart, with Thy sword avenge us of**

our wrongs; remember Thy suffering Saints, O our God! and Thy servants will rejoice in Thy name forever.

"Dearly and beloved brethren, we see that perilous times have come, as was testified of. We may look, then, with most perfect assurance, for the fulfillment of all those things that have been written, and with more confidence than ever before, lift up our eyes to the luminary of day, and say in our hearts, Soon thou wilt veil thy blushing face. He that said "Let there be light," and there was light, hath spoken this word. And again, Thou moon, thou dimmer light, thou luminary of night, shalt turn to blood.

"We see that everything is being fulfilled; and that the time shall soon come when the Son of Man shall descend in the clouds of heaven. Our hearts do not shrink, neither are our spirits altogether broken by the grievous yoke which is put upon us. We know that God will have our oppressors in derision; that He will laugh at their calamity, and mock when their fear cometh.

"O that we could be with you, brethren, and unbosom our feelings to you! We would tell, that we should have been liberated at the time Elder Rigdon was, on the writ of habeas corpus, had not our own lawyers interpreted the law, contrary to what it reads, against us; which prevented us from introducing our evidence before the mock court.

"They have done us much harm from the beginning. They have of late acknowledged that the law was misconstrued, and tantalized our feelings with it, and have entirely forsaken us, and have forfeited their oaths and their bonds; and we have a come-back on them, for they are co-workers with the mob.

"As nigh as we can learn, the public mind has been for a long time turning in our favor, and the majority is now friendly; and the lawyers can no longer browbeat us by saying that this or that is a matter of public opinion, for public opinion is not willing to brook it; for it is beginning to look with feelings of indignation against our oppressors, and to say that the "Mormons" were not in the fault in the least. We think that truth, honor, virtue and innocence will eventually come out triumphant. We should have taken a habeas corpus before the high judge and escaped the mob in a summary way; but unfortunately for us, the timber of the wall being very hard, our auger handles gave out, and hindered us longer than we expected; we applied to a friend, and a very slight incautious act gave rise to some suspicions, and before we could fully succeed, our plan was discovered; we had everything in readiness, but the last stone, and we could have made our escape in one minute, and should have succeeded admirably, had it not been for a little imprudence or over-anxiety on the part of our friend.

"The sheriff and jailer did not blame us for our attempt; it was a fine breach, and cost the county a round sum; but public opinion says that we ought to have been permitted to have made our escape; that then the disgrace would have been on us, but now it must come on the state; that there cannot be any charge sustained against us; and that the conduct of the mob, the murders committed at Haun's Mills, and the exterminating order of the governor, and the one-sided, rascally proceedings of the legislature, have damned the state of Missouri to all eternity. I would just name also that General Atchison has proved himself as contemptible as any of them.

"We have tried for a long time to get our lawyers to draw us some petitions to the supreme judges of this state, but they utterly refused. We have examined the law, and drawn the petitions ourselves, and have obtained abundance of proof to counteract all the testimony that was against us, so that if the supreme judge does not grant us our liberty, he has to act without cause, contrary to honor, evidence, law or justice, sheerly to please the devil, but we hope better things and trust before many days God will so order our case, that we shall be set at liberty and take up our habitation with the Saints.

"We received some letters last evening—one from Emma, one from Don C. Smith, and one from Bishop Partridge—all breathing a kind and consoling spirit. We were much gratified with their contents. We had been a long time without information; and when we read those letters they were to our souls as the gentle air is refreshing, but our joy was mingled with grief, because of the sufferings of the poor and much injured Saints. And we need not say to you that the floodgates of our hearts were lifted and our eyes were a fountain of tears, but those who have not been enclosed in the walls of prison without cause or provocation, can have but little idea how sweet the voice of a friend is; one token of friendship from any source whatever awakens and calls into action every sympathetic feeling; it brings up in an instant everything that is passed; it seizes the present with the avidity of lightning; it grasps after the future with the fierceness of a tiger; it moves the mind backward and forward, from one thing to another, until finally all enmity, malice and hatred, and past differences, misunderstandings and mismanagements are slain victorious at the feet of hope; and when the heart is sufficiently contrite, then the voice of inspiration steals along and whispers, [*section 121:7–25*] **My son, peace be unto** thy soul; thine adversity and thine afflictions shall be but a small moment; and then if thou endure it well, God shall exalt thee on high; thou shalt triumph over all thy foes; thy friends do stand by thee, and they shall hail thee again, with warm hearts and friendly hands; thou art not yet as Job; thy friends do not contend against thee, neither charge thee with transgression, as they did Job; and they who do charge thee with transgression, their hope shall be blasted and their prospects shall melt away as the hoar frost melteth before the burning rays of the rising sun; and also that God hath set His hand and seal to change the times and seasons, and to blind their minds, that they may not understand His marvelous workings, that He may prove them also and take them in their own craftiness; also because their hearts are corrupted, and the things which they are willing to bring upon others, and love to have others suffer, may come upon themselves to the very uttermost; that they may be disappointed also, and their hopes may be cut off; and not many years hence, that they and their posterity shall be swept from under heaven, saith God, that not one of them is left to stand by the wall. Cursed are all those that shall lift up the heel against mine anointed, saith the Lord, and cry they have sinned when they have not sinned before me, saith the Lord, but have done that which was meet in mine eyes, and which I commanded them; but those who cry transgression do it because they are the servants of sin and are the children of disobedience themselves; and those who swear falsely against my servants, that they might bring them into bondage and death; wo unto them; because they have offended my little ones; they shall be severed from the ordinances of mine house; their basket shall not be full, and their houses and their barns shall perish, and they themselves shall be despised by those that flattered them; they shall not have right to the Priesthood, nor their posterity after them, from generation to generation; it had been better for them that a millstone had been hanged about their necks, and they drowned in the depth of the sea.

"Wo unto all those that discomfort my people, and drive and murder, and testify against them, saith the Lord of Hosts; a generation of vipers shall not escape the damnation of hell. Behold mine eyes see and know all their works, and I have in reserve a swift judgment in the season thereof, for them all; for there is a time appointed for every man according as his work shall be.

"And now, beloved brethren, we say unto you, that inasmuch as God hath said that He would have a tried people, that He would purge them as gold, now we think that this time He has chosen His own crucible, wherein we have been tried; and we think if we get through with any degree of safety, and shall have kept the faith, that it will be a sign to this generation, altogether sufficient to leave them without excuse; and we think also, it will be a trial of our faith equal to that of Abraham, and that the ancients will not have whereof to boast over us in the day of judgment, as being called to pass through heavier afflictions; that we may hold an even weight in the balance with them; but now, after having suffered so great sacrifice and having passed through so great a season of sorrow, we trust that a ram may be caught in the thicket speedily, to relieve the sons and daughters of Abraham from their great anxiety, and to light up the lamp of salvation upon their countenances, that they may hold on now, after having gone so far unto everlasting life.

"Now, brethren, concerning the places for the location of the Saints, we cannot counsel you as we could if we were present with you; and as to the things that were written heretofore, we did not consider them anything very binding, therefore we now say once for all, that we think it most proper that the general affairs of the Church, which are necessary to be considered, while your humble servant remains in bondage, should be transacted by a general conference of the most faithful and the most respectable of the authorities of the Church, and a minute of those transactions may be kept, and forwarded from time to time, to your humble servant; and if there should be any corrections by the word of the Lord, they shall be freely transmitted, and your humble servant will approve all things whatsoever is acceptable unto God. If anything should have been suggested by us, or any names mentioned, except by commandment, or thus saith the Lord, we do not consider it binding; therefore our hearts shall not be grieved if different arrangements should be entered into. Nevertheless we would suggest the propriety of being aware of an aspiring spirit, which spirit has often times urged men forward to make foul speeches, and influence the Church to reject milder counsels, and has eventually been the means of bringing much death and sorrow upon the Church.

"We would say, beware of pride also; for well and truly hath the wise man said, that pride goeth before destruction, and a haughty spirit before a fall. And again, outward appearance is not always a criterion by which to judge our fellow man; but the lips betray the haughty and overbearing imaginations of the heart; by his words

SECTION 123

and his deeds let him be judged. Flattery also is a deadly poison. A frank and open rebuke provoketh a good man to emulation; and in the hour of trouble he will be your best friend; but on the other hand, it will draw out all the corruptions of corrupt hearts, and lying and the poison of asps is under their tongues; and they do cause the pure in heart to be cast into prison, because they want them out of their way.

"A fanciful and flowery and heated imagination beware of; because the things of God are of deep import; and time, and experience, and careful and ponderous and solemn thoughts can only find them out. Thy mind, O man! if thou wilt lead a soul unto salvation, must stretch as high as the utmost heavens, and search into and contemplate the darkest abyss, and the broad expanse of eternity—thou must commune with God. How much more dignified and noble are the thoughts of God, than the vain imaginations of the human heart! None but fools will trifle with the souls of men.

"How vain and trifling have been our spirits, our conferences, our councils, our meetings, our private as well as public conversations—too low, too mean, too vulgar, too condescending for the dignified characters of the called and chosen of God, according to the purposes of His will, from before the foundation of the world! We are called to hold the keys of the mysteries of those things that have been kept hid from the foundation of the world until now. Some have tasted a little of these things, many of which are to be poured down from heaven upon the heads of babes; yea, upon the weak, obscure and despised ones of the earth. Therefore we beseech of you, brethren, that you bear with those who do not feel themselves more worthy than yourselves, while we exhort one another to a reformation with one and all, both old and young, teachers and taught, both high and low, rich and poor, bond and free, male and female; let honesty, and sobriety, and candor, and solemnity, and virtue, and pureness, and meekness, and simplicity crown our heads in every place; and in fine, become as little children, without malice, guile or hypocrisy.

"And now, brethren, after your tribulations, if you do these things, and exercise fervent prayer and faith in the sight of God always, [*section 121:26–32*] **He shall give unto you knowledge by His Holy Spirit, yea by the unspeakable gift of the Holy Ghost, that has not been revealed since the world was until now; which our forefathers have waited with anxious expectation to be revealed in the last times, which their minds were pointed to by the angels, as held in reserve for the fullness of their glory; a time to come in the which** nothing shall be withheld, whether there be one God or many Gods, they shall be manifest; all thrones and dominions, principalities and powers, shall be revealed and set forth upon all who have endured valiantly for the Gospel of Jesus Christ; and also if there be bounds set to the heavens, or to the seas; or to the dry land, or to the sun, moon or stars; all the times of their revolutions; all the appointed days, months and years, and all the days of their days, months and years, and all their glories, laws, and set times, shall be revealed, in the days of the dispensation of the fullness of times, according to that which was ordained in the midst of the Council of the Eternal God of all other Gods, before this world was, that should be reserved unto the finishing and the end thereof, when every man shall enter into His eternal presence, and into His immortal rest.**

"But I beg leave to say unto you, brethren, that ignorance, superstition and bigotry placing itself where it ought not, is oftentimes in the way of the prosperity of this Church; like the torrent of rain from the mountains, that floods the most pure and crystal stream with mire, and dirt, and filthiness, and obscures everything that was clear before, and all rushes along in one general deluge; but time weathers tide; and notwithstanding we are rolled in the mire of the flood for the time being, the next surge peradventure, as time rolls on, may bring to us the fountain as clear as crystal, and as pure as snow; while the filthiness, floodwood and rubbish is left and purged out by the way.

"[*Section 121:33*] **How long can rolling water remain impure? What power shall stay the heavens? As well might man stretch forth his puny arm to stop the Missouri river in its decreed course, or to turn it up stream, as to hinder the Almighty from pouring down knowledge from heaven, upon the heads of the Latter-day Saints**.

"What is Boggs or his murderous party, but wimbling willows upon the shore to catch the flood-wood? As well might we argue that water is not water, because the mountain torrents send down mire and roil the crystal stream, although afterwards render it more pure than before; or that fire is not fire, because it is of a quenchable nature, by pouring on the flood; as to say that our cause is down because renegades, liars, priests, thieves and murderers, who are all alike tenacious of their crafts and creeds, have poured down, from their spiritual wickedness in high places, and from their strongholds of the devil, a flood of dirt and mire and filthiness and vomit upon our heads.

"No! God forbid. Hell may pour forth its rage like the burning lava of mount Vesuvius, or of Etna, or of the most terrible of the burning mountains; and yet shall "Mormonism" stand. Water, fire, truth and God are all realities. Truth is "Mormonism." God is the author of it. He is our shield. It is by Him we received our birth. It was by His voice that we were called to a dispensation of His Gospel in the beginning of the fullness of times. It was by Him we received the Book of Mormon; and it is by Him that we remain unto this day; and by Him we shall remain, if it shall be for our glory; and in His Almighty name we are determined to endure tribulation as good soldiers unto the end.

"But, brethren, we shall continue to offer further reflections in our next epistle. You will learn by the time you have read this, and if you do not learn it, you may learn it, that walls and irons, doors and creaking hinges, and half-scared-to-death guards and jailers, grinning like some damned spirits, lest an innocent man should make his escape to bring to light the damnable deeds of a murderous mob, are calculated in their very nature to make the soul of an honest man feel stronger than the powers of hell.

"But we must bring our epistle to a close. We send our respects to fathers, mothers, wives and children, brothers and sisters; we hold them in the most sacred remembrance.

"We feel to inquire after Elder Rigdon; if he has not forgotten us, it has not been signified to us by his writing. Brother George W. Robinson also; and Elder Cahoon, we remember him, but would like to jog his memory a little on the fable of the bear and the two friends who mutually agreed to stand by each other. And perhaps it would not be amiss to mention uncle John [Smith], and various others. A word of consolation and a blessing would not come amiss from anybody, while we are being so closely whispered by the bear. But we feel to excuse everybody and everything, yea the more readily when we contemplate that we are in the hands of persons worse that a bear, for the bear would not prey upon a dead carcass.

"Our respects and love and fellowship to all the virtuous Saints. We are your brethren and fellow-sufferers, and prisoners of Jesus Christ for the Gospel's sake, and for the hope of glory which is in us. Amen.

"We continue to offer further reflections to Bishop Partridge, and to the Church of Jesus Christ of Latter-day Saints, whom we love with a fervent love, and do always bear them in mind in all our prayers to the throne of God.

"It still seems to bear heavily on our minds that the Church would do well to secure to themselves the contract of the land which is proposed to them by Mr. Isaac

Galland, and to cultivate the friendly feelings of that gentleman, inasmuch as he shall prove himself to be a man of honor and a friend to humanity; also Isaac Van Allen, Esq., the attorney-general of Iowa Territory, and Governor Lucas, that peradventure such men may be wrought upon by the providence of God, to do good unto His people. We really think that Mr. Galland's letter breathes that kind of a spirit, if we may judge correctly. Governor Lucas also. We suggest the idea of praying fervently for all men who manifest any degree of sympathy for the suffering children of God.

"We think that the United States Surveyor of the Iowa Territory may be of great benefit to the Church, if it be the will of God to this end; and righteousness should be manifested as the girdle of our loins.

"It seems to be deeply impressed upon our minds that the Saints ought to lay hold of every door that shall seem to be opened unto them, to obtain foothold on the earth, and be making all the preparation that is within their power for the terrible storms that are now gathering in the heavens, "a day of clouds, with darkness and gloominess, and of thick darkness," as spoken of by the Prophets, which cannot be now of a long time lingering, for there seems to be a whispering that the angels of heaven who have been entrusted with the counsel of these matters for the last days, have taken counsel together; and among the rest of the general affairs that have to be transacted in their honorable council, they have taken cognizance of the testimony of those who were murdered at Haun's Mills, and also those who were martyred with David W. Patten, and elsewhere, and have passed some decisions peradventure in favor of the Saints, and those who were called to suffer without cause.

"These decisions will be made known in their time; and the council will take into consideration all those things that offend.

"We have a fervent desire that in your general conferences everything should be discussed with a great deal of care and propriety, lest you grieve the Holy Spirit, which shall be poured out at all times upon your heads, when you are exercised with those principles of righteousness that are agreeable to the mind of God, and are properly affected one toward another, and are careful by all means to remember, those who are in bondage, and in heaviness, and in deep affliction for your sakes. And if there are any among you who aspire after their own aggrandizement, and seek their own opulence, while their brethren are groaning in poverty, and are under sore trials and temptations, they cannot be benefited by the intercession of the Holy Spirit, which maketh intercession for us day and night with groanings that cannot be uttered.

"We ought at all times to be very careful that such high-mindedness shall never have place in our hearts; but condescend to men of low estate, and with all long-suffering bear the infirmities of the weak.

"[*Section 121:34–46*] Behold, there are many called, but few are chosen. And why are they not chosen? Because their hearts are set so much upon the things of this world, and aspire to the honors of men, that they do not learn this one lesson—that the rights of the Priesthood are inseparably connected with the powers of heaven, and that the powers of heaven cannot be controlled nor handed only upon the principles of righteousness. That they may be conferred upon us, it is true; but when we undertake to cover our sins, or to gratify our pride, our vain ambition, or to exercise control, or dominion, or compulsion, upon the souls of the children of men, in any degree of unrighteousness, behold, the heavens withdraw themselves; the Spirit of the Lord is grieved; and when it is withdrawn, *Amen to the Priesthood,* or the authority of that man. Behold! ere he is aware, he is left unto himself, to kick against the pricks; to persecute the Saints, and to fight against God.

"We have learned by sad experience that it is the nature and disposition of almost all men, as soon as they get a little authority, as they suppose, they will immediately begin to exercise unrighteous dominion. Hence many are called, but few are chosen.

"No power or influence can or ought to be maintained by virtue of the Priesthood, only by persuasion, by long-suffering, by gentleness, and meekness, and by love unfeigned; by kindness, and pure knowledge, which shall greatly enlarge the soul without hypocrisy, and without guile, reproving betimes with sharpness, when moved upon by the Holy Ghost, and then showing forth afterwards an increase of love toward him whom thou hast reproved, lest he esteem thee to be his enemy; that he may know that thy faithfulness is stronger than the cords of death; let thy bowels also be full of charity towards all men, and to the household of faith, and virtue garnish thy thoughts unceasingly, then shall thy confidence wax strong in the presence of God, and the doctrine of the Priesthood shall distill upon thy soul as the dews from heaven. The Holy Ghost shall be thy constant companion, and thy sceptre an unchanging sceptre of righteousness and truth, and thy dominion shall be an everlasting dominion, and without compulsory means it shall flow unto thee forever and ever.

"[*Section 122:1–9*] The ends of the earth shall inquire after thy name, and fools shall have thee in derision, and hell shall rage against thee, while the pure in heart, and the wise, and the noble, and the virtuous, shall seek counsel, and authority and blessings constantly from under thy hand, and thy people shall never be turned against thee by the testimony of traitors; and although their influence shall cast thee into trouble, and into bars and walls, thou shalt be had in honor, and but for a small moment and thy voice shall be more terrible in the midst of thine enemies, than the fierce lion, because of thy righteousness; and thy God shall stand by thee forever and ever.

"If thou art called to pass through tribulations; if thou art in perils among false brethren; if thou art in perils among robbers; if thou art in perils by land or by sea; if thou art accused with all manner of false accusations; if thine enemies fall upon thee; if they tear thee from the society of thy father and mother and brethren and sisters, and if with a drawn sword thine enemies tear thee from the bosom of thy wife, and of thine offspring, and thine elder son, although but six years of age, shall cling to thy garment, and shall say, My father, my father, why can't you stay with us? O, my father, what are the men going to do with you? and if then he shall be thrust from thee by the sword, and thou be dragged to prison, and thine enemies prowl around thee like wolves for the blood of the lamb; and if thou shouldst be cast into the pit, or into the hands of murderers, and the sentence of death passed upon thee; if thou be cast into the deep; if the billowing surge conspire against thee; if fierce winds become thine enemy; if the heavens gather blackness, and all the elements combine to hedge up the way; and above all, if the very jaws of hell shall gape open the mouth wide after thee, know thou, my son, that all these things shall give thee experience, and shall be for thy good. The Son of Man hath descended below them all; art thou greater than he?

"Therefore, hold on thy way, and the Priesthood shall remain with thee, for their bounds are set, they cannot pass. Thy days are known, and thy years shall not be numbered less; therefore, fear not what man can do, for God shall be with you forever and ever.

"Now, brethren, I would suggest for the consideration of the conference, its being carefully and wisely understood by the council or conferences that our brethren scattered abroad, who understand the spirit of the gathering, that they fall into the places and refuge of safety that God shall open unto them, between Kirtland and Far West. Those from the east and from the west, and from far countries, let them fall in somewhere between those two boundaries, in the most safe and quiet places they can find; and let this be the present understanding, until God shall open a more effectual door for us for further considerations.

"And again, we further suggest for the considerations of the Council, that there be no organization of large bodies upon common stock principles, in property, or of large companies of firms, until the Lord shall signify it in a proper manner, as it opens such a dreadful field for the avaricious, the indolent, and the corrupt hearted to prey upon the innocent and virtuous, and honest.

"We have reason to believe that many things were introduced among the Saints before God had signified the times; and notwithstanding the principles and plans may have been good, yet aspiring men, or in other words, men who had not the substance of godliness about them, perhaps undertook to handle edged tools. Children, you know, are fond of tools, while they are not yet able to use them.

"Time and experience, however, are the only safe remedies against such evils. There are many teachers, but, perhaps, not many fathers. There are times coming when God will signify many things which are expedient for the well-being of the Saints; but the times have not yet come, but will come, as fast as there can be found place and reception for them.

"[*Section 123:1–17*] **And again, we would suggest for your consideration the propriety of all the Saints gathering up a knowledge of all the facts and sufferings and abuses put upon them by the people of this state; and also of all the property and amount of damages which they have sustained, both of character and personal injuries, as well as real property; and also the names of all persons that have had a hand in their oppressions, as far as they can get hold of them and find them out; and perhaps a committee can be appointed to find out these things, and to take statements, and affidavits, and also to gather up the libelous publications that are afloat, and all that are in the magazines, and in the encyclopaedias, and all the libelous histories that are published, and are writing, and by whom, and present** the whole concatenation of diabolical rascality, and nefarious and murderous impositions that have been practiced upon this people, that we may not only publish to all the world, but present them to the heads of government in all their dark and hellish hue, as the last effort which is enjoined on us by our Heavenly Father, before we can fully and completely claim that promise which shall call Him forth from His hiding place, and also that the whole nation may be left without excuse before He can send forth the power of His mighty arm.

"It is an imperative duty that we owe to God, to angels, with whom we shall be brought to stand, and also to ourselves, to our wives and children, who have been made to bow down with grief, sorrow, and care, under the most damning hand of murder, tyranny, and oppression, supported and urged on and upheld by the influence of that spirit which hath so strongly riveted the creeds of the fathers, who have inherited lies, upon the hearts of the children, and filled the world with confusion, and has been growing stronger and stronger, and is now the very mainspring of all corruption, and the whole earth groans under the weight of its iniquity.

"It is an iron yoke, it is a strong band; they are the very handcuffs, and chains, and shackles, and fetters of hell.

"Therefore it is an imperative duty that we owe, not only to our own wives and children, but to the widows and fatherless, whose husbands and fathers have been murdered under its iron hand; which dark and blackening deeds are enough to make hell itself shudder, and to stand aghast and pale, and the hands of the very devil to tremble and palsy. And also it is an imperative duty that we owe to all the rising generation, and to all the pure in heart, (for there are many yet on the earth among all sects, parties, denominations, who are blinded by the subtle craftiness of men, whereby they lie in wait to deceive, and who are only kept from the truth because they know not where to find it); therefore, that we should waste and wear out our lives in bringing to light all the hidden things of darkness, wherein we know them; and they are truly manifest from heaven.

"These should then be attended to with great earnestness. Let no man count them as small things; for there is much which lieth in futurity, pertaining to the Saints, which depends upon these things. You know, brethren, that a very large ship is benefited very much by a

very small helm in the time of a storm, by being kept workways with the wind and the waves.

"Therefore, dearly beloved brethren, let us cheerfully do all things that lie in our power, and then may we stand still with the utmost assurance, to see the salvation of God, and for His arm to be revealed.

"And again, I would further suggest the impropriety of the organization of bands or companies, by covenant or oaths, by penalties or secrecies; but let the time past of our experience and sufferings by the wickedness of Doctor Avard suffice and let our covenant be that of the Everlasting Covenant, as is contained in the Holy Writ and the things that God hath revealed unto us. Pure friendship always becomes weakened the very moment you undertake to make it stronger by penal oaths and secrecy.

"Your humble servant or servants, intend from henceforth to disapprobate everything that is not in accordance with the fullness of the Gospel of Jesus Christ, and is not of a bold, and frank, and upright nature. They will not hold their peace—as in times past when they see iniquity beginning to rear its head—for fear of traitors, or the consequences that shall follow by reproving those who creep in unawares, that they may get something with which to destroy the flock. We believe that the experience of the Saints in times past has been sufficient, that they will from henceforth be always ready to obey the truth without having men's persons in admiration because of advantage. It is expedient that we should be aware of such things; and we ought always to be aware of those prejudices which sometimes so strangely present themselves, and are so congenial to human nature, against our friends, neighbors, and brethren of the world, who choose to differ from us in opinion and in matters of faith. Our religion is between us and our God. Their religion is between them and their God.

"There is a love from God that should be exercised toward those of our faith, who walk uprightly, which is peculiar to itself, but it is without prejudice; it also gives scope to the mind, which enables us to conduct ourselves with greater liberality towards all that are not of our faith, than what they exercise towards one another. These principles approximate nearer to the mind of God, because it is like God, or Godlike.

"Here is a principle also, which we are bound to be exercised with, that is, in common with all men, such as governments, and laws, and regulations in the civil concerns of life. This principle guarantees to all parties, sects, and denominations, and classes of religion, equal, coherent, and indefeasible rights; they are things that pertain to this life; therefore all are alike interested; they make our responsibilities one towards another in matters of corruptible things, while the former principles do not destroy the latter, but bind us stronger, and make our responsibilities not only one to another, but unto God also. Hence we say, that the Constitution of the United States is a glorious standard; it is founded in the wisdom of God. It is a heavenly banner; it is to all those who are privileged with the sweets of its liberty, like the cooling shades and refreshing waters of a great rock in a thirsty and weary land. It is like a great tree under whose branches men from every clime can be shielded from the burning rays of the sun.

"We, brethren, are deprived of the protection of its glorious principles, by the cruelty of the cruel, by those who only look for the time being, for pasturage like the beasts of the field, only to fill themselves; and forget that the "Mormons," as well as the Presbyterians, and those of every other class and description, have equal rights to partake of the fruits of the great tree of our national liberty. But notwithstanding we see what we see, and feel what we feel, and know what we know, yet that fruit is no less precious and delicious to our taste; we cannot be weaned from the milk, neither can we be driven from the breast; neither will we deny our religion because of the hand of oppression; but we will hold on until death.

"We say that God is true; that the Constitution of the United States is true; that the Bible is true; that the Book of Mormon is true; that the Book of Covenants is true; that Christ is true; that the ministering angels sent forth from God are true, and that we know that we have an house not made with hands eternal in the heavens, whose builder and maker is God; a consolation which our oppressors cannot feel, when fortune, or fate, shall lay its iron hand on them as it has on us. Now, we ask, what is man? Remember, brethren, that time and chance happen to all men.

"We shall continue our reflections in our next.

"We subscribe ourselves, your sincere friends and brethren in the bonds of the everlasting Gospel, prisoners of Jesus Christ, for the sake of the Gospel and the Saints.

"We pronounce the blessings of heaven upon the heads of the Saints who seek to serve God with undivided hearts, in the name of Jesus Christ. Amen.

"Joseph Smith, Jun.,
Hyrum Smith,
Lyman Wight,
Caleb Baldwin,
Alexander McRae."

SECTION 124

Background

This revelation was given to the Prophet Joseph Smith on January 19, 1841, in Nauvoo, Illinois. It is the longest section in the Doctrine and Covenants and deals with several topics, including the following:

- Reassurance to the Prophet Joseph Smith that his work is acceptable to the Lord (verse 1)

- A command to make a proclamation to all the world (verses 2–14)

- Specific instructions and assignments to several brethren (verses 15–21)

- An assignment to build a hotel for guests and visitors in Nauvoo, to be called the "Nauvoo House" (verses 22–24, 56–83, 119–22)

- A commandment to build the Nauvoo Temple (verses 25–28, 40–48, 55)

- Instructions that baptisms for the dead are normally to be performed in temples and that permission to perform them temporarily in the Mississippi River will soon be withdrawn (verses 29–36)

- Additional instructions on the purposes of temples throughout the ages (verses 37–39)

- Doctrine concerning faithful members who try with all their hearts to keep God's commandments but are prevented by circumstances beyond their control (verses 49–54)

- Instructions to individuals to settle in Nauvoo and remain there (verses 84–86)

- Instructions for William Law to serve as a counselor to Joseph Smith (verses 87–91)

- Hyrum Smith is called to be patriarch to the Church and replace Oliver Cowdery in several functions in the Church (verses 91–96)

- Instructions to several individuals, including warnings to some (verses 97–118)

- Additional instructions regarding Hyrum Smith's call to serve as patriarch and a review of priesthood keys, quorums, and presidencies, including several callings of brethren to serve in quorum presidencies (verses 123–45)

As we proceed, we will make considerable use of **bold**, letting the scriptures speak for themselves, and point out some important lessons along the way with notes and commentary.

Reassurance to the Prophet Joseph Smith that his work is acceptable to the Lord (verse 1)

1 VERILY, thus saith the Lord unto you, my servant Joseph Smith, I am well pleased with your offering and acknowledgments, which you have made; for unto this end have I raised you up, that I might show forth my wisdom through the weak things of the earth.

A command to make a proclamation to all the world (verses 2–14)

> The Proclamation to All the World, spoken of here, was completed in 1845 by the Quorum of the Twelve after the martyrdom of the Prophet Joseph Smith and his brother, Hyrum. You can read a summary of the main content of this proclamation in an article by President Ezra Taft Benson ("A Message to the World," *Ensign*, November 1975, 32–34).

2 Your prayers are acceptable before me; and in answer to them I say unto you, that **you are now called immediately to make a solemn proclamation** of my gospel, and of this stake which I have planted to be a cornerstone of Zion, which shall be polished with the refinement which is after the similitude of a palace.

3 This proclamation shall be made to all the kings of the world, to the four corners thereof, to the honorable president-elect, and the high-minded governors of the nation in which you live, and **to all the nations of the earth** scattered abroad.

4 Let it be **written in the spirit of meekness and by the power of the Holy Ghost, which shall be in you at the time of the writing** of the same;

5 For **it shall be given you by the Holy Ghost** to know my will concerning those kings and authorities, even what shall befall them in a time to come.

6 For, behold, I am about **to call upon them to give heed to the light and glory of Zion**, for the set time has come to favor her.

7 **Call ye, therefore, upon them** with loud proclamation, and **with your testimony**, fearing them not, for they are as grass [*they are only temporarily in power*], and all their glory as the flower thereof which soon falleth, **that they may be left also without excuse—**

8 And **that I may visit them** in the day of visitation [*the day of punishment—see Isaiah 10, footnote 3a*]**, when I shall unveil the face**

of my covering, to appoint the portion [*the just reward*] of the oppressor among hypocrites, where there is gnashing of teeth, **if they reject my servants and my testimony** which I have revealed unto them.

> The "if" in the last part of verse 8, above, is an important reminder that they will have a fair chance to understand and accept the gospel before the day of final judgment. And verse 9, next, reminds us that the Lord will continue to work with them.

9 And again, **I will visit and soften their hearts**, many of them for your good, that ye may find grace in their eyes, **that they may come to the light of truth,** and the Gentiles to the exaltation or lifting up of Zion.

10 For **the day of my visitation cometh speedily, in an hour when ye think not** of; and where shall be the safety of my people, and refuge for those who shall be left of them?

11 **Awake, O kings of the earth! Come ye, O, come ye, with your gold and your silver, to the help of my people**, to the house of the daughters of Zion.

12 And again, verily I say unto you, **let my servant Robert B. Thompson help you to write this proclamation**, for I am well pleased with him, and that he should be with you;

13 **Let him, therefore, hearken to your counsel**, and I will bless him with a multiplicity of blessings; let him be faithful and true in all things from henceforth, and he shall be great in mine eyes;

> Verse 14, next, is a quick reminder that accountability goes along with responsibility.

14 But **let him remember that his stewardship will I require at his hands.**

Specific instructions and assignments to several brethren (verses 15–21)

> Verse 15, next, is quite often quoted in church classes and discussions. You may wish to mark it in your scriptures.

15 And again, verily I say unto you, **blessed is my servant Hyrum Smith; for I, the Lord, love him because of the integrity of his heart, and because he loveth that which is right before me**, saith the Lord.

> Next, in verses 16–17, John C. Bennett, who will eventually have his membership withdrawn (the terminology now requested by the leaders of the Church in place of

"excommunication"), is instructed to help write the proclamation and to stand by the Prophet in times of trouble. Notice the "ifs" in these verses, which I have pointed out.

16 Again, **let my servant John C. Bennett help you in your labor in sending my word to the kings and people of the earth, and stand by you,** even you my servant Joseph Smith, **in the hour of affliction**; and his reward shall not fail *if* he receive counsel.

17 And for his love he shall be great, for he shall be mine *if* he do this, saith the Lord. I have seen the work which he hath done, which I accept *if* he continue, and will crown him with blessings and great glory.

> Unfortunately, Bennett apostatized from the Church and became one of Joseph's most bitter and destructive enemies.
>
> Over my years of teaching, students occasionally asked why the Lord would call such people as John C. Bennett to high and trusted positions in the Church when he would apostatize later and cause much trouble. The 1981 *Doctrine and Covenants Student Manual* has an excellent answer (**bold** added for emphasis):
>
> "Smith and Sjodahl summarized John C. Bennett's introduction to the Church and his eventual apostasy to explain why the Lord commended him:
>
> "'[John C. Bennett] was well educated and possessed many gifts and accomplishments. He was a physician, a university professor, and a brigadier-general. On the 27th of July, 1840, he offered his services to the Church. The Prophet Joseph replied, inviting him to come to Commerce [*Nauvoo*], if he felt so disposed, but warned him at the same time not to expect exaltation "in this generation," from devotion to the cause of truth and a suffering people; nor worldly riches; only the approval of God. The outcome of the correspondence was that he joined the Church and rose to prominent positions among the Saints. His fellowship with the people of God did not last long, however. On the 25th of May, 1842, he was notified that the leaders of the Church did no longer recognize him as a member, because of his impure life, and shortly afterwards the Church took action against him. Then he became one of the most bitter enemies of the Church. His slanders, his falsehoods and unscrupulous attacks, which included perjury and attempted assassination were the means of inflaming public opinion to such an extent that the tragedy at Carthage became possible.
>
> "'Why, then, did his name appear, in this Revelation, as that of a trusted assistant of Joseph?

John Taylor furnishes the answer to that question. He says, "Respecting John C. Bennett: I was well acquainted with him. At one time he was a good man, but fell into adultery, and was cut off from the Church for his iniquity" (*History of the Church,* Vol. V, p. 81). **At the time of the revelation he was a good man**. But he was overcome by the adversary and made the slave of his carnal desires. The Lord knew him and warned him. "His reward shall not fail if he receive counsel." "He shall be great . . . if he do this," etc. **Bennett did not heed these warning "ifs"** from Him who knew what was in his heart.' (Commentary, pp. 770–71.)

"**The Lord does not withhold present blessings because of future sinful behavior**. He blessed King David as long as he was faithful and did not withhold opportunity, although he had foreknowledge of David's future transgressions with Bathsheba. As long as one obeys, the blessings come. With the perspective of history one may be tempted to ask why the Lord chose men who would eventually falter to be leaders in the Church, but one should remember that at the time of their calling they were faithful and true" (*Doctrine and Covenants Student Manual,* 1981, 306).

18 And again, I say unto you that it is my will that my servant **Lyman Wight should continue in preaching for Zion**, in the spirit of meekness, confessing me before the world; and I will bear him up as on eagles' wings; and he shall beget glory and honor to himself and unto my name.

> Next, in verse 19, we are told that three faithful men, including the Prophet's father, who have died by the date of this revelation, are with the Lord in heaven.

19 That when he shall finish his work I may receive him unto myself, even as I did my servant **David Patten**, who **is with me at this time, and also my servant Edward Partridge, and also my aged servant Joseph Smith, Sen., who sitteth with Abraham** [*symbolic of exaltation*] at his right hand, and blessed and holy is he, for he is mine.

> You may wish to make a cross-reference in your scriptures from Abraham, in verse 19, above, to D&C 132:29 and 37, wherein we are informed that Abraham has now become a god.

20 And again, verily I say unto you, my servant **George Miller** is without guile [*without ulterior motives; has a pure heart*]; he **may be trusted** because of the integrity of his heart; and for the love which he has to my testimony I, the Lord, love him.

21 I therefore say unto you, **I seal upon his head the office of a bishopric** [*Brother Miller is to be called and ordained a bishop*], like unto my servant Edward Partridge, that he may receive the consecrations [*donations to the Church*] of mine house, that he may administer blessings upon the heads of the poor of my people, saith the Lord. Let no man despise my servant George, for he shall honor me.

An assignment to build a hotel for guests and visitors in Nauvoo, to be called the "Nauvoo House" (verses 22–24, 56–83, 119–22)

22 **Let** my servant **George** [*Miller*], and my servant **Lyman** [*Wight*], **and** my servant **John Snider, and others, build a house** [*a hotel, the Nauvoo House—see verse 60—which still exists today on the banks of the Mississippi River*] unto my name, such a one as my servant Joseph shall show unto them, upon the place which he shall show unto them also.

23 And it shall be for **a house for boarding**, a house **that strangers may come from afar to lodge therein**; therefore let it be a good house, worthy of all acceptation, **that the weary traveler may find health and safety while he shall contemplate the word of the Lord**; and the corner-stone I have appointed for Zion.

24 **This house shall be a healthful habitation** if it be built unto my name, and if the governor which shall be appointed unto it shall not suffer any pollution [*crude or evil activities*] to come upon it. It shall be holy, or the Lord your God will not dwell therein.

A commandment to build the Nauvoo Temple (verses 25–28, 40–48, 55)

25 And again, verily I say unto you, **let all my saints come from afar.**

26 And send ye swift messengers, yea, chosen messengers, and say unto them: **Come ye, with all your gold, and your silver, and your precious stones**, and with all your antiquities [*perhaps including knowledge of ancient temples and construction materials, as described in the Bible for the Tabernacle, Solomon's Temple, and so forth*]; **and with all who have knowledge of antiquities** [*possibly meaning building skills for constructing such things*], that will come, may come, and bring the box-tree [*used in building the Tabernacle used by the Children of Israel—see Exodus 26:15*], and the fir-tree, and the pine-tree, together with all the precious trees of the earth;

27 And **with iron**, with **copper**, and with **brass**, and with **zinc**, and with **all your precious things** of the earth; **and build a house to my name**, for the Most High to dwell therein.

28 For **there is not a place** [*temple*] found on earth **that he may come to and restore again that which was lost unto you, or which he hath taken away, even the fulness of the priesthood.**

Instructions that baptisms for the dead are normally to be performed in temples and that permission to perform them temporarily in the Mississippi River will soon be withdrawn (verses 29–36)

29 For **a baptismal font there is not upon the earth, that they, my saints, may be baptized for those who are dead**—

> At this time, the Saints were performing baptisms for the dead in the Mississippi River near Nauvoo.

30 For **this ordinance belongeth to my house** [*should be done in a temple*], **and cannot be acceptable to me, only** [*except*] **in the days of your poverty, wherein ye are not able to build a house unto me.**

31 **But I command you**, all ye my saints, **to build a house unto me** [*the Nauvoo Temple*]; and **I grant unto you a sufficient time to build a house** unto me; and **during this time your baptisms** [*for the dead in the Mississippi River*] **shall be acceptable unto me.**

32 **But** behold, **at the end of this appointment** [*the time granted by the Lord for the building of the Nauvoo Temple*] **your baptisms for your dead shall not be acceptable unto me**; and if you do not these things at the end of the appointment ye shall be rejected as a church, with your dead, saith the Lord your God.

> In verse 33, next, we are told, in effect, that we were taught about the purpose of temples in the premortal councils. Thus, we understood that if we were sent to earth during a time when the gospel was not available to us, our work would be done by proxies in temples and we would have a completely fair opportunity to attain exaltation also.

33 For verily I say unto you, that **after you have had sufficient time to build a house to me, wherein the ordinance of baptizing for the dead belongeth**, and for which **the same** [*the plan to have temples on earth*] **was instituted from before the foundation of the world** [*was a part of the plan of salvation, instituted and taught by the Father in premortality*], **your**

baptisms for your dead cannot be acceptable unto me;

34 For **therein** [*in temples*] **are the keys of the holy priesthood ordained**, that you may receive honor and glory.

35 And **after this time** [*after the time allotted by the Lord for the building of the Nauvoo Temple*], **your baptisms for the dead**, by those who are scattered abroad, **are not acceptable** unto me, saith the Lord.

> Next, in verse 36, these Saints are told that there are to be many temples built, including one in Jerusalem in the last days.

36 For **it is ordained** [*it is part of the Father's plan*] **that in Zion**, and **in her stakes**, and **in Jerusalem**, those places which I have appointed for refuge [*a major purpose of stakes—see D&C 115:6*], **shall be the places** [*the temples—compare with the first phrase of verse 30, above*] **for your baptisms for your dead**.

Additional instructions on the purposes of temples throughout the ages (verses 37–39)

37 And again, verily I say unto you, how shall your washings be acceptable unto me, except ye perform them in a house [*temple*] which you have built to my name?

38 For, for this cause I commanded Moses that he should build a tabernacle, that they should bear it with them in the wilderness, and to build a house [*temple*] in the land of promise, that those ordinances might be revealed which had been hid from before the world was.

39 Therefore, verily I say unto you, that your **anointings**, and your **washings**, and your **baptisms for the dead**, and your **solemn assemblies**, and your memorials for your **sacrifices by the sons of Levi**, and for **your oracles** [*revelations from God—see D&C 90, footnote 4a*] in your most holy places wherein you receive **conversations**, and your **statutes and judgments**, for the beginning of the revelations and foundation of Zion, and for the glory, honor, and endowment of all her municipals [*citizens*], are ordained [*authorized*] by the ordinance of **my holy house, which my people are always commanded to build unto my holy name.**

More instructions regarding the building of the Nauvoo Temple (verses 40–48)

40 And verily I say unto you, **let this house be built** unto my

name, **that I may reveal mine ordinances therein unto my people**;

> Remember, although Moses, Elias, and Elijah came to the Kirtland Temple and restored priesthood keys, the endowment as we know it, as well as celestial marriage, had not been available to the Saints yet. Therefore, "mine ordinances" (verse 40, above) would not be made available until the construction of the Nauvoo Temple.

41 For **I deign** [*plan*] **to reveal unto my church things which have been kept hid from before the foundation of the world**, things **that pertain to the dispensation of the fulness of times** [*our dispensation, meaning the time from the Restoration of the gospel to the earth through the Prophet Joseph Smith to the time of the Savior's Second Coming*].

42 And **I will show unto my servant Joseph all things pertaining to this house, and the priesthood thereof, and the place whereon it shall be built.**

43 And **ye shall build it on the place where you have contemplated building it**, for that is the spot which I have chosen for you to build it.

44 **If ye labor with all your might, I will consecrate that spot that it shall be made holy.**

45 And **if my people will hearken unto my voice, and unto the voice of my servants whom I have appointed to lead my people, behold, verily I say unto you, they shall not be moved out of their place.**

46 **But** *if* **they will not hearken to my voice, nor unto the voice of these men whom I have appointed, they shall not be blest**, because they pollute mine holy grounds, and mine holy ordinances, and charters, and my holy words which I give unto them.

> Verses 47–48, next, contain a clear explanation of the principle found in D&C 82:10, which declares, "I, the Lord, am bound when ye do what I say; but when ye do not what I say, ye have no promise."

47 And it shall come to pass **that if you build a house unto my name, and do not do the things that I say, I will not perform the oath which I make unto you, neither fulfil the promises which ye expect at my hands**, saith the Lord.

48 **For instead of blessings, ye, by your own works, bring cursings** [*troubles*]**, wrath, indignation,**

and judgments upon your own heads, by your follies, and by all your abominations, which you practise before me, saith the Lord.

Doctrine concerning faithful members who try with all their hearts to keep God's commandments but are prevented by circumstances beyond their control (verses 49–54)

49 Verily, verily, I say unto you, that when I give a commandment to any of the sons of men to do a work unto my name, and those sons of men go with all their might and with all they have to perform that work, and cease not their diligence, and their enemies come upon them and hinder them from performing that work, behold, **it behooveth me** [*I am obligated*] **to require that work no more** at the hands of those sons of men, **but to accept of their offerings** [*their efforts to perform the work required by the Lord*].

> Next, in verse 50, the Savior explains that the responsibility for the required work not being done will be transferred from the person who tried to do it, to those who prevented it from being done.

50 And **the iniquity and transgression of my holy laws and commandments I will visit upon the heads of those who hindered my work**, unto the third and fourth generation, **so long as they repent not**, and hate me, saith the Lord God.

> The principle explained in verses 49–50, above, applies to the faithful Saints who tried to build Zion, including the temple, in Jackson County, Missouri.

51 Therefore, **for this cause** [*because of this principle*] **have I accepted the offerings of those whom I commanded to build up a city and a house unto my name, in Jackson county, Missouri, and were hindered by their enemies**, saith the Lord your God.

52 And **I will answer** judgment, wrath, and indignation, wailing, and anguish, and gnashing of teeth **upon their heads** [*they will be held accountable*], unto the third and fourth generation, **so long as they repent not**, and hate me, saith the Lord your God.

> People are sometimes bothered by the scriptural phrase "unto the third and fourth generation" (verse 52, above) when it comes to the sins of the parents being passed to their children, grandchildren, and so forth. It seems unfair that children get punished for the sins of their parents.

This can easily be misunderstood as an unfair "curse." But did you notice the answer to this concern at the end of verse 52, above? It is quite natural in most cases for children to learn from their parents, including from their sins and wickedness. However, if people repent, no matter how they became acquainted with sin, the wickedness is gone and the chain is broken. Read Ezekiel 18 for a more thorough explanation of this principle.

53 And **this** [*the principles taught in verses 49–52, above*] **I make an example unto you, for your consolation** [*comfort; relief*] **concerning all those who have been commanded to do a work and have been hindered by the hands of their enemies, and by oppression**, saith the Lord your God.

> As summarized in verse 54, next, being pure in heart is the important factor in eventually receiving exaltation.

54 For **I am the Lord your God, and will save all those of your brethren who have been pure in heart, and have been slain in the land of Missouri**, saith the Lord.

More instruction regarding the building of the Nauvoo Temple (verse 55)

55 And again, verily I say unto you, **I command you again to build a house to my name, even in this place** [*Nauvoo*]**, that you may prove yourselves unto me that ye are faithful in all things** whatsoever I command you, **that I may bless you, and crown you with honor, immortality, and eternal life** [*exaltation*].

More about building the Nauvoo House (verses 56–83)

56 And now I say unto you, **as pertaining to my boarding house** [*the Nauvoo House*] which I have commanded you to build [*see verses 22–24*] **for the boarding of strangers, let it be built** unto my name, and **let my name be named upon it** [*let it be a pleasant, righteous environment—see verse 60*]**, and let my servant Joseph and his house have place therein**, from generation to generation.

57 **For this anointing** [*blessing*] **have I put upon his head**, that his blessing shall also be put upon the head of his posterity after him.

58 And **as I said unto Abraham** concerning the kindreds of the earth, **even so I say unto my servant Joseph: In thee and in thy seed shall the kindred of the earth be blessed.**

59 Therefore, **let my servant Joseph and his seed** [*posterity*] **after him have place in that house,** from generation to generation, forever and ever, saith the Lord.

60 And **let the name of that house be called Nauvoo House;** and **let it be a delightful habitation for man, and a resting-place for the weary traveler, that he may contemplate the glory of Zion** [*the beauties of the gospel*], and the glory of this, the corner-stone thereof;

61 **That he may receive also the counsel from those whom I have set to be** as plants of renown, and as **watchmen** upon her walls [*in other words, from the leaders of the Church*].

> Next, in verse 62, the Lord organizes a building committee for the purpose of building the Nauvoo House.

62 Behold, verily I say unto you, let my servant **George Miller,** and my servant **Lyman Wight,** and my servant **John Snider,** and my servant **Peter Haws, organize themselves, and appoint one of them to be a** president over their quorum [*their committee*] **for the purpose of building that house.**

> Beginning with verse 63, next, and coming into play in many more verses, we see that these brethren were authorized to sell stock to finance the construction of the Nauvoo House. Rules and regulations concerning the selling of this stock are spelled out. Stock is to be issued in minimum amounts of fifty dollars and maximum amounts of fifteen thousand dollars for one individual stockholder.

63 And **they shall form a constitution** [*draw up an agreement*], **whereby they may receive stock for the building of that house.**

64 And **they shall not receive less than fifty dollars for a share of stock** in that house, and they shall be permitted to receive **fifteen thousand** dollars from any one man for stock in that house.

65 But **they shall not be permitted to receive over fifteen thousand dollars stock from any one man.**

66 And **they shall not be permitted to receive under fifty dollars for a share of stock** from any one man in that house.

67 And **they shall not be permitted to receive any man, as a stockholder** in this house, **except the same shall pay** his stock into their hands **at the time he receives stock;**

SECTION 124

68 And **in proportion to the amount of stock he pays into their hands he shall receive stock** in that house; but **if he pays nothing into their hands he shall not receive any stock** in that house.

> This stock is to be transferable to descendants of the stockholders.

69 And if any pay stock into their hands **it shall be for stock in that house, for himself, and for his generation after him, from generation to generation**, so long as he and his heirs shall hold that stock, and do not sell or convey the stock away out of their hands by their own free will and act, if you will do my will, saith the Lord your God.

> No monies received for stock in the Nauvoo House are to be used for any other purposes.

70 And again, verily I say unto you, if my servant George Miller, and my servant Lyman Wight, and my servant John Snider, and my servant Peter Haws, receive any stock into their hands, in moneys, or in properties wherein they receive the real value of moneys, **they shall not appropriate any portion of that stock to any other purpose**, only in that house.

> The penalty for violating the rule given in verse 70, above, is severe.

71 And **if they do appropriate any portion of that stock anywhere else**, only in that house, **without the consent of the stockholder, and do not repay fourfold** for the stock which they appropriate anywhere else, only in that house, **they shall be accursed, and shall be moved out of their place**, saith the Lord God; for I, the Lord, am God, and cannot be mocked in any of these things.

> One of the major messages from the Lord that we are seeing as we go along here is that it is a sacred trust and responsibility to handle the funds of the Church. Anyone who mishandles or misappropriates them is in serious trouble with Him.
>
> Next, in verse 72, we are reminded that the prophet of the Church is subject to the same rules and commandments to which the members are held.

72 Verily I say unto you, let my servant Joseph pay stock into their hands for the building of that house, as seemeth him good; but **my servant Joseph cannot pay over fifteen thousand dollars stock in that house, nor under fifty dollars; neither can any other man**, saith the Lord.

73 And there are **others also** who **wish to know my will concerning them**, for they have asked it at my hands.

74 Therefore, I say unto you concerning my servant **Vinson Knight**, if he will do my will **let him put stock into that house** for himself, and for his generation after him, from generation to generation.

75 And **let him lift up his voice long and loud, in the midst of the people, to plead the cause of the poor and the needy**; and let him not fail, neither let his heart faint [*give up*]; **and I will accept of his offerings**, for they shall not be unto me as the offerings of Cain [*which were rejected by the Lord—see Moses 5:19–21*], for he shall be mine, saith the Lord.

76 Let his family rejoice and turn away their hearts from affliction; for I have chosen him and anointed him, and he shall be honored in the midst of his house, for **I will forgive all his sins**, saith the Lord. Amen.

77 Verily I say unto you, **let my servant Hyrum** [*Smith*] **put stock into that house** [*buy stock in the Nauvoo House*] as seemeth him good, for himself and his generation after him, from generation to generation.

78 **Let** my servant **Isaac Galland put stock into that house**; for **I, the Lord, love him for the work he hath done, and will forgive all his sins**; therefore, let him be remembered for an interest in that house from generation to generation.

> Have you noticed how often the Savior tells people in this section that He forgives them of their sins? They get a new start! This applies to us too as we honestly strive to live the gospel and improve. In fact, each time we honestly and sincerely partake of the sacrament, thus renewing our covenants, it is as if we had been rebaptized!

> Perhaps you've noticed that on many occasions the Lord has told members to follow the instructions given them by His Prophet. We see this next in verse 79. This carries the strong message that the Lord supports His Prophet, and we would be very wise to follow his counsel.

79 Let my servant Isaac Galland be appointed among you, and be ordained by my servant William Marks, and be blessed of him, to go with my servant Hyrum [*Smith*] **to accomplish the work that my servant Joseph shall point out to them, and they shall be greatly blessed.**

80 **Let** my servant **William Marks pay stock into that house**, as seemeth him good, for himself and his generation, from generation to generation.

81 **Let** my servant **Henry G. Sherwood pay stock into that house**, as seemeth him good, for himself and his seed after him, from generation to generation.

82 **Let** my servant **William Law pay stock into that house**, for himself and his seed after him, from generation to generation.

> William Law had planned to take his family back to Kirtland but is counseled by the Lord to remain in Nauvoo. He is told here that hard times are coming to residents of Kirtland. He stayed and became second counselor to Joseph in the First Presidency.

83 **If he will do my will let him not take his family unto the eastern lands, even unto Kirtland**; nevertheless, I, the Lord, will build up Kirtland, but I, the Lord, have a scourge prepared for the inhabitants thereof.

Instructions to individuals to settle in Nauvoo and remain there (verses 84–86)

> The counsel of the Prophet and the First Presidency at this time was for the Saints to gather in the Nauvoo area and build it up. Apparently, Almon W. Babbitt was counseling members to leave Nauvoo to settle elsewhere, including Kirtland. The imagery of the golden calf in verse 84, next, is symbolic of someone who attempts to lead the people away from the Prophet's counsel, as was the case with Moses's brother, Aaron, when he set up the golden calf for the Children of Israel to worship while Moses was on the mountain communing with the Lord (see Exodus 32:1–4).

84 And **with** my servant **Almon Babbitt, there are many things with which I am not pleased**; behold, **he aspireth to establish his counsel instead of the counsel which I have ordained** [*authorized, approved*], **even that of the Presidency of my Church**; and **he setteth up a golden calf** for the worship of my people [*he is attempting to lead the Saints astray*].

85 **Let no man go from this place** [*Nauvoo*] **who has come here essaying** [*attempting; planning*] **to keep my commandments.**

> We learn an important and comforting doctrine in verse 86, next. It is that if we die faithful to God, we are allowed to continue working toward our exaltation in the next life.

86 If they live here let them live

unto me [*be faithful and loyal to God*]; and **if they die let them die unto me; for they shall rest from all their labors here, and shall continue their works** [*in the next life*].

Instructions for William Law to serve as a counselor to Joseph Smith (verses 87–91)

87 Therefore, **let my servant William** [*Law*] **put his trust in me,** and cease to fear concerning his family, because of the sickness of the land [*perhaps a reference to the malaria and sickness suffered initially by the Saints before they successfully drained the swampy lands of Nauvoo*]. **If ye love me, keep my commandments; and the sickness of the land shall redound to your glory** [*will end up being a blessing to you*].

88 **Let my servant William** go and **proclaim my everlasting gospel** with a loud voice, and with great joy, as he shall be moved upon by my Spirit, **unto the inhabitants of Warsaw** [*Illinois, a few miles south of Nauvoo*], and also unto the inhabitants of **Carthage**, and also unto the inhabitants of **Burlington**, and also unto the inhabitants of **Madison**, and await patiently and diligently for further instructions at my general conference, saith the Lord.

89 **If he will do my will** [*if he really wants to do the will of the Lord*] **let him from henceforth** [*from now on*] **hearken to the counsel of my servant Joseph, and with his interest** [*financial means; income—see D&C 119:4*] **support the cause of the poor, and publish the new translation of my holy word** [*the Joseph Smith Translation of the Bible*] **unto the inhabitants of the earth.**

90 And **if he will do this I will bless him with a multiplicity of blessings, that he shall not be forsaken, nor his seed be found begging bread.**

91 And again, verily I say unto you, **let** my servant **William** [*Law*] **be appointed, ordained, and anointed, as counselor unto my servant Joseph** [*as second counselor in the First Presidency*], **in the room of** [*in place of*] **my servant Hyrum** [*Smith*], **that my servant Hyrum may take the office of** Priesthood and **Patriarch**, which was appointed unto him by his father, by blessing and also by right;

Hyrum Smith is called to be patriarch to the Church and replace Oliver Cowdery in several functions in the Church (verse 91, above, and verses 92–96)

The Prophet's father, Joseph Smith Sr., had been serving as the patriarch to the Church prior to his death on September 14, 1840, in Nauvoo. Now Hyrum was called to fill that position, serving the general population of the Church as needed.

92 That **from henceforth he shall hold the keys of the patriarchal blessings upon the heads of all my people,**

93 That **whoever he blesses shall be blessed**, and **whoever he curses shall be cursed**; that **whatsoever he shall bind on earth shall be bound in heaven**; and **whatsoever he shall loose on earth shall be loosed in heaven.**

94 And from this time forth I appoint unto him **that he may be a prophet, and a seer, and a revelator unto my church, as well as my servant Joseph;**

95 **That he may act in concert also with my servant Joseph;** and **that he shall receive counsel from my servant Joseph** [*in other words, he is to work under the direction of Joseph, the Prophet*], who shall show unto him the keys whereby he may ask and receive, **and be crowned with the same blessing, and glory, and honor, and priesthood, and gifts of the priesthood, that once were put upon him that was my servant Oliver Cowdery;**

Remember that Oliver Cowdery had apostatized and had been excommunicated in April 1838. At this time, he is still out of the Church but will return and request rebaptism during a conference of the Church held at Kanesville, Iowa, in October 1848. His request will be approved, and he will be rebaptized in November 1848.

96 That my servant Hyrum may bear record of the things which I shall show unto him, **that his name may be had in honorable remembrance from generation to generation, forever and ever** [*as you know, this prophecy has been thoroughly and marvelously fulfilled*].

Instructions to several individuals, including warnings to some (verses 97–118)

97 **Let my servant William Law** also receive the keys by which he may ask and receive blessings; let him **be humble before me, and be without guile, and he shall receive of my Spirit, even the Comforter** [*the Holy Ghost*], **which shall manifest unto him the truth of all things, and shall give him, in the very hour, what he shall say.**

As you can see, William Law is

given marvelous promises if he will "be humble before me" (verse 97, above). Unfortunately, he will not follow this counsel, and will apostatize, becoming one of the Prophet's most bitter enemies.

One of the lessons we can learn from this is that blessings, including patriarchal blessings, can point out to us what our potential is. But we still have agency and can lose the blessings by poor agency choices.

98 And **these signs shall follow him—he shall heal the sick,** he shall **cast out devils,** and shall **be delivered** from those who would administer unto him deadly poison;

99 And **he shall be led in paths where the poisonous serpent** [*can be symbolic of Satan and his temptations and poisonous false doctrines and philosophies*] **cannot lay hold upon his heel, and he shall mount up in the imagination of his thoughts as upon eagles' wings.**

100 And **what if I will that he should raise the dead, let him not withhold his voice.**

101 Therefore, **let my servant William cry aloud and spare not, with joy and rejoicing,** and with hosannas to him [*God*] that sitteth upon the throne forever and ever, saith the Lord your God.

Next, in verse 102, we see that both William Law and Hyrum Smith are to take pressure off the Prophet Joseph.

102 Behold, I say unto you, **I have a mission in store for my servant William, and my servant Hyrum, and for them alone; and let my servant Joseph tarry at home, for he is needed.** The remainder I will show unto you hereafter. Even so. Amen.

103 And again, verily I say unto you, **if** my **servant Sidney** [*Rigdon*] **will serve me and be counselor unto my servant Joseph, let him arise and come up and stand in the office of his calling, and humble himself before me.**

104 And **if he will offer unto me an acceptable offering, and acknowledgments** [*perhaps meaning that Sidney must confess his tendencies toward apostasy that were in his heart at this time*], **and remain with my people** [*in Nauvoo*], behold, **I, the Lord your God, will heal him** [*he was suffering from poor health at this time*] that he shall be healed; **and he shall lift up his voice again** on the mountains, **and be a spokesman** before my face.

105 **Let him come and locate**

his family in the neighborhood in which my servant Joseph resides.

106 And in all his journeyings **let him lift up his voice** [*preach the gospel*] as with the sound of a trump, and warn the inhabitants of the earth to flee the wrath to come.

> Next, both Sidney Rigdon and William Law, counselors in the First Presidency, are instructed to help the Prophet write the proclamation spoken of in verses 2–3, at the beginning of this section.

107 **Let him assist my servant Joseph, and also let my servant William Law assist my servant Joseph, in making a solemn proclamation** unto the kings of the earth, even as I have before said unto you.

108 **If my servant Sidney will do my will** [*if Sidney Rigdon truly desires to be obedient*], **let him not remove his family unto the eastern lands** [*probably meaning Kirtland—see verse 83*], but let him change their habitation, even as I have said [*in other words, they need to relocate to live near the Prophet as stated in verse 105*].

109 Behold, **it is not my will that he shall seek to find safety and refuge out of** the city which I have appointed unto you, even the city of **Nauvoo**.

110 Verily I say unto you, even now, **if he will hearken unto my voice, it shall be well with him**. Even so. Amen.

> Have you noticed that there are a lot of "ifs" to many of these individuals? It is certainly a reminder that we do indeed have agency.

111 And again, verily I say unto you, **let my servant Amos Davies pay stock** into the hands of those whom I have appointed **to build** a house for boarding, even **the Nauvoo House**.

112 This let him do if he will have an interest [*if he wants to be a stockholder*]; and **let him hearken unto the counsel of my servant Joseph**, and labor with his own hands that he may obtain the confidence of men.

> A principle that applies to all of us is taught to Brother Amos Davies in verse 112, next.

113 And **when he shall prove himself faithful in** all things that shall be entrusted unto his care, yea, even **a few things, he shall be made ruler over many** [*this usually refers to exaltation—see verse 114—when we become gods*];

114 **Let him therefore abase**

[*humble*] **himself that he may be exalted**. Even so. Amen.

> Robert Foster, spoken of in verse 115, next, became one of the most bitter and dangerous apostates, bringing false charges against the Prophet and conspiring with others to bring about his death.

115 And again, verily I say unto you, **if** my servant **Robert D. Foster will** [*truly desires to*] **obey my voice**, let him build a house for my servant Joseph, according to the contract which he has made with him, as the door shall be open to him from time to time.

116 And **let him repent of all his folly, and clothe himself with charity; and cease to do evil, and lay aside all his hard** [*mean, bitter*] **speeches**;

117 And pay stock also into the hands of the quorum [*building committee*] of the Nauvoo House, for himself and for his generation after him, from generation to generation;

> There is much more to the picture here than merely donating money for the building of the Nauvoo House by buying stock in it (verse 117, above). It is the principle of joining with others in supporting and sustaining the work of the Lord and unselfishly doing whatever it takes to be obedient and follow the Prophet.

118 **And hearken unto the counsel of my servants Joseph, and Hyrum, and William Law, and unto the authorities** which I have called to lay the foundation of Zion; and **it shall be well with him forever and ever**. Even so. Amen.

More instructions regarding the Nauvoo House (verses 119–22)

119 And again, verily I say unto you, **let no man pay stock to the quorum** [*the building committee—see verse 62*] **of the Nauvoo House unless he shall be a believer in the Book of Mormon, and the revelations I have given unto you**, saith the Lord your God;

> The policy that no one could buy stock in the Nauvoo House unless they believed in the scriptures (verse 119, above) is similar to the policy today, that no one may pay tithing unless he or she is a member of the Church. Verse 120 is a stern warning not to change that rule.

120 For **that which is more or less than this cometh of evil, and shall be attended with cursings** [*trouble*] **and not blessings**, saith the Lord your God. Even so. Amen.

> Next, in verse 121, the Lord shows a high degree of trust in the honesty

and integrity of those serving on the Nauvoo House building committee by allowing them to set their own wages.

121 And again, verily I say unto you, **let the quorum of the Nauvoo House** [*the building committee*] **have a just recompense of wages** [*be paid a fair salary*] **for all their labors** which they do in building the Nauvoo House; and let their wages be **as shall be agreed among themselves**, as pertaining to the price thereof.

122 **And let every man who pays stock bear his proportion of their wages,** if it must needs be, for their support, saith the Lord; otherwise, their labors shall be accounted [*credited*] unto them for stock in that house [*otherwise, they can be credited with stock in the Nauvoo House as wages*]. Even so. Amen.

Additional instructions regarding Hyrum Smith's call to serve as patriarch and a review of priesthood keys, quorums, and presidencies, including several callings of brethren to serve in quorum presidencies (verses 123–45)

In these next verses, the Savior gives a brief review and overview of the priesthood organization of the Church. The Nauvoo Stake will be organized with a presidency and a high council, and several priesthood quorums will be organized.

In verse 123, next, we are reminded that the Savior, Himself, holds the Melchizedek Priesthood and is a high priest, as was Melchizedek.

123 Verily I say unto you, **I now give unto you the officers belonging to my Priesthood**, that ye may hold the keys thereof, even **the Priesthood** which is **after the order of Melchizedek** [*the priesthood that Melchizedek held*], **which is after the order of** [*which is the same as that held by*] **mine Only Begotten Son**.

Did you notice what just happened at the end of verse 123, above? The Savior spoke for the Father without alerting us first that He was going to do so. This is often referred to as "Divine Investiture" and means that the Savior speaks directly for the Father, as if the Father were doing the talking. You can see other examples of this in D&C 29:1, 42, and 46, as well as in Moses 1:6 as explained in *Doctrines of Salvation,* 1:27.

124 First, **I give unto you Hyrum Smith to be a patriarch unto you, to hold the sealing blessings of my church,** even the Holy Spirit of promise [*the sealing power exercised by the Holy Ghost—see*

D&C 132:7, 19], whereby ye are sealed up unto the day of redemption, that ye may not fall notwithstanding the hour of temptation that may come upon you.

125 I give unto you my servant **Joseph** [*the Prophet*] to be a **presiding elder over all my church**, to be **a translator, a revelator, a seer, and prophet**.

126 I give unto him for **counselors** my servant **Sidney Rigdon** and my servant **William Law**, that these may **constitute a quorum and First Presidency**, to receive the oracles [*revelations*] for the whole church.

127 I give unto you my servant **Brigham Young** to be a **president over the Twelve** traveling council [*the Twelve Apostles*];

128 **Which Twelve hold the keys to open up the authority of my kingdom upon the four corners of the earth** [*the whole world*], **and after that to send my word to every creature**.

129 They are **Heber C. Kimball, Parley P. Pratt, Orson Pratt, Orson Hyde, William Smith, John Taylor, John E. Page, Wilford Woodruff, Willard Richards, George A. Smith**;

130 David Patten [*who was killed in the Battle of the Big Blue during mob violence in Missouri*] I have taken unto myself; behold, **his priesthood no man taketh from him**; but, verily I say unto you, **another may be appointed unto the same calling** [*to replace him as an Apostle in the Quorum of the Twelve Apostles*].

131 And again, I say unto you, **I give unto you a high council, for the corner-stone of Zion** [*for the Nauvoo Stake*]—

132 Namely, **Samuel Bent, Henry G. Sherwood, George W. Harris, Charles C. Rich, Thomas Grover, Newel Knight, David Dort, Dunbar Wilson**—Seymour Brunson I have taken unto myself; no man taketh his priesthood, but another may be appointed unto the same priesthood in his stead; and verily I say unto you, let my servant **Aaron Johnson** be ordained unto this calling in his stead—**David Fullmer, Alpheus Cutler, William Huntington**.

133 And again, **I give unto you Don C. Smith** [*Joseph Smith's younger brother*] **to be a president over a quorum of high priests**;

134 Which ordinance [*procedure*] is instituted for the purpose of qualifying those who shall be appointed **standing presidents**

[*presidents of local quorums as opposed to General Authorities*] or servants **over different stakes scattered abroad**;

> Can you see that this is a sweeping panorama of how the priesthood is organized to handle the expansion of the Church? While it is quite familiar to us in our day, it was new and vital instruction for these early Saints.

135 And they may travel also if they choose, but rather be **ordained for standing presidents** [*to serve as local quorum presidencies*]; this is the office of their calling, saith the Lord your God.

136 **I give unto him** [*Don Carlos Smith*] **Amasa Lyman and Noah Packard for counselors**, that they may **preside over the quorum of high priests** of my church, saith the Lord.

137 And again, I say unto you, **I give unto you John A. Hicks, Samuel Williams, and Jesse Baker, which priesthood is to preside over the quorum of elders**, which quorum is instituted for **standing ministers** [*priesthood leaders who preside over local quorums and are not required to travel throughout the world as is the case with General Authorities*]; nevertheless **they may travel, yet they are ordained to be standing ministers** to my church, saith the Lord.

138 And again, **I give unto you Joseph Young, Josiah Butterfield, Daniel Miles, Henry Herriman, Zera Pulsipher, Levi Hancock, James Foster, to preside over the quorum of seventies** [*to serve as the seven presidents of the General Authority Seventies*];

> Verse 139, next, instructs that the General Authority Seventies are presided over by the Quorum of the Twelve Apostles (see D&C 107:34).

139 Which quorum is instituted for **traveling elders to bear record of my name in all the world, wherever the traveling high council, mine apostles, shall send them** to prepare a way before my face.

140 The difference between this quorum and the quorum of elders is that one is to travel continually [*the Apostles*], and the other [*the Seventies*] is to preside over the churches from time to time; the one has the responsibility of presiding from time to time, and the other has no responsibility of presiding [*at this time in the development of the Church*], saith the Lord your God.

141 And again, I say unto you, **I**

give unto you **Vinson Knight, Samuel H. Smith, and Shadrach Roundy,** if he will receive it, **to preside over the bishopric**; a knowledge of said bishopric is given unto you in the book of Doctrine and Covenants.

142 And again, I say unto you, **Samuel Rolfe and his counselors for priests** [*a priests quorum presidency*], and **the president of the teachers and his counselors** [*a teachers quorum presidency*], and also **the president of the deacons and his counselors** [*a deacons quorum presidency*], and also **the president of the stake and his counselors** [*the stake presidency for the Nauvoo Stake*].

> Next, the Savior summarizes the above instructions for expanding the priesthood organization of the Church. It will be essential for the continued growth of the Church to have these quorum presidencies function properly in the new stakes and wards as they are formed.

143 **The above offices I have given unto you, and the keys thereof, for helps and for governments, for the work of the ministry and the perfecting of my saints.**

> The sustaining of officers in conference is addressed in verse 144, next, and is based on the law of common consent as given in D&C 26:2.

144 And a commandment I give unto you, that you should fill all these offices and **approve of those names which I have mentioned, or else disapprove of them at my general conference**;

145 And that **ye should prepare rooms** [*offices*] **for all these offices** [*priesthood leaders*] **in my house** [*the Nauvoo Temple—see footnote 145a*] **when you build it unto my name, saith the Lord your God. Even so. Amen.**

SECTION 125

Background

This revelation was given through the Prophet Joseph Smith in March 1841 at Nauvoo, Illinois.

When the Saints were driven from Missouri and began settling in what became Nauvoo, Illinois, some of them settled across the Mississippi River in the territory of Iowa to the west of Nauvoo and began establishing settlements there. Church leaders had arranged to buy 700 acres in Illinois in what became Nauvoo, and around 18,000 acres of land in Lee County, Iowa Territory.

With the large numbers of Saints fleeing persecution elsewhere, having these large tracts of land available for settlement was most helpful. It obviously allowed the members to find homesites and begin building without overcrowding certain locations. Branches of the Church were established in Iowa Territory in Zarahemla (see verse 3) and Nashville (near Montrose), as well as in small settlements near the existing settlement of Montrose.

By October 5, 1839, the Iowa Stake was created. About a year and a half later, as mentioned above, in March 1841, the Prophet Joseph Smith received this revelation after asking the Lord about the settlements across the Mississippi River in Iowa Territory.

Question

1 WHAT is the will of the Lord concerning the saints in the Territory of Iowa?

Answer

2 Verily, thus saith the Lord, I say unto you, **if those who call themselves by my name** [*members of the Church who have taken upon themselves the name of Jesus Christ through baptism*] **and are essaying** [*attempting, endeavoring, striving*] **to be my saints,** if they **will do my will and keep my commandments** concerning them [*in other words, if they truly want to be obedient*], **let them gather** themselves together **unto the places which I shall appoint unto them by my servant Joseph, and build up cities unto my name**, that they may be prepared for that which is in store for a time to come.

One of the important messages in the scriptures is that the Lord supports His prophets. In verse 2, above, we see yet another example of this in which the Lord points the people to the Prophet Joseph for inspired instructions concerning the settlements in the Territory of Iowa.

3 **Let them build** up a city unto my name upon the land **opposite the city of Nauvoo,** and let the name of **Zarahemla** be named upon it.

Zarahemla was near Montrose, Iowa, and at one time had over three hundred members living in it.

Next, in verse 4, the Lord tells the Saints that they are free to choose any of the named locations or to live in any stakes that were established.

4 And **let all those** who come from the east, and the west, and the north, and the south, **that have desires to dwell therein, take up their inheritance in the same** [*in other words, those who desire to live in Zarahemla are welcome to do so*], **as well as in** the city of **Nashville** [*in Lee County, Iowa*], **or in the city**

of Nauvoo, and in all the stakes which I have appointed, saith the Lord.

In August 1841, the Iowa Stake name was changed to the Zarahemla Stake. Some months later, in January 1842, the Iowa Territory settlements had served their temporary purpose and the Zarahemla Stake was dissolved because so many members had moved to Nauvoo to help build the temple and assist in other construction projects.

SECTION 126

Background

This revelation was given through the Prophet Joseph Smith to Brigham Young (the president of the Quorum of the Twelve Apostles at the time—see D&C 124:127) on July 9, 1841, in Nauvoo, Illinois.

Brigham Young had studied the Book of Mormon extensively for two years before being baptized in his own millpond by Eleazar Miller on April 15, 1832. After his baptism, he traveled extensively on missions in Upper Canada and several eastern states, including New York. He faithfully participated in the march of Zion's Camp from Ohio to Missouri in 1834. He became a member of the Quorum of the Twelve Apostles on February 14, 1835. He left Montrose, Iowa, on September 14, 1839, to serve a mission in England. On July 1, 1841, having completed his mission to England, he rejoined his wife Mary Ann and his children who were living in Nauvoo. Now, in this revelation, the Lord tells him to send other missionaries abroad (verse 3) and to stay home with his family from now on.

One of the things we see here is the fact that the Lord is keeping Brigham closer to the Prophet, no doubt, to train him to become the next prophet. He spent twenty-eight of the last thirty-six months of the Prophet's life in close contact with him. On July 9, 1841, Joseph visited Brigham in his home and dictated this revelation to him.

Brigham Young gave his all in whatever he was called to do by the Lord, and in verse 1, we hear the Lord compliment him and accept his work.

1 **DEAR and well-beloved brother, Brigham Young**, verily thus saith the Lord unto you: My servant Brigham, **it is no more required at your hand to leave your family as in times past, for your offering is acceptable to me.**

2 **I have seen your labor and toil** in journeyings for my name.

3 I therefore command you to **send my word abroad** [*as President of the Twelve, direct others in*

missionary work], and **take especial care of your family from this time, henceforth** and forever. Amen.

SECTION 127

Background

This is a letter written by the Prophet Joseph Smith to the Saints in Nauvoo, Illinois, dated September 1, 1842.

At the time Joseph Smith wrote this letter, he was in hiding in the home of John Taylor's father in Nauvoo (see *Doctrine and Covenants Student Manual,* 1981, 314). Persecution against him had increased in Illinois, and repeated attempts by Missourians to trap him and take him to Missouri had forced him into hiding.

In the first two verses of this letter, we get insights into the indomitable and cheerful personality of the Prophet of the Restoration.

1 **FORASMUCH** as the Lord has revealed unto me **that my enemies, both in Missouri and this State, were again in the pursuit of me**; and inasmuch as **they pursue me without a cause, and have not the least shadow or coloring of justice or right on their side** in the getting up of their prosecutions against me; and inasmuch as their pretensions are all founded in falsehood of the blackest dye, **I have thought it expedient** [*necessary*] **and wisdom in me to leave the place for a short season, for my own safety and the safety of this people**. I would say to all those with whom I have business, that I have left my affairs with agents and clerks who will transact all business in a prompt and proper manner, and will see that all my debts are canceled [*paid off*] in due time, by turning out property, or otherwise, as the case may require, or as the circumstances may admit of. **When I learn that the storm is fully blown over, then I will return to you again.**

2 And **as for the perils which I am called to pass through, they seem but a small thing to me**, as the envy and wrath of man have been my common lot all the days of my life; and for what cause it seems mysterious, unless I was ordained from before the foundation of the world for some good end, or bad, as you may choose to call it. Judge ye for yourselves. God knoweth all these things, whether it be good or bad. But nevertheless, **deep water is what I am wont** [*accustomed*] **to swim in. It all has become a second nature to me**; and I feel, like Paul, to glory in tribulation; for to this day has the God of my fathers

delivered me out of them all, and will deliver me from henceforth; for behold, and lo, **I shall triumph over all my enemies, for the Lord God hath spoken it.**

3 **Let all the saints rejoice, therefore, and be exceedingly glad**; for Israel's God is their God, and he will mete out a just recompense of reward upon the heads of all their oppressors.

> Next, in verse 4, the Prophet urges the Saints to continue work on building the Nauvoo Temple, as well as other projects.

4 And again, verily thus saith the Lord: **Let the work of my temple, and all the works which I have appointed unto you, be continued on and not cease**; and let your diligence, and your perseverance, and patience, and your works be redoubled [*increased*], and you shall in nowise lose your reward, saith the Lord of Hosts. And **if they persecute you, so persecuted they the prophets and righteous men that were before you.** For all this there is a reward in heaven.

> Perhaps one of the important messages we gain from the last part of verse 4, above, is that the righteous are always persecuted by the wicked. And if the Church is not being persecuted on occasion, it may be that we are not living our religion as we should.

> Next, the Prophet writes and instructs about baptism for the dead. He had introduced the topic as early as August 15, 1840, in a funeral sermon for Brother Seymore Brunson, after which baptisms for the dead were conducted in the Mississippi River. In section 124, verses 29–33, given January 19, 1841, the Saints were warned that the time would soon come in which their baptisms for the dead would no longer be valid unless they built the Nauvoo Temple and performed them in it.

> The first baptisms for the dead in the Nauvoo Temple baptismal font (the rest of the building was not yet completed) were performed on Sunday, November 21, 1841 (see *Doctrine and Covenants Student Manual,* 1981, 314).

5 And again, **I give unto you a word in relation to the baptism for your dead.**

> Any of you who have had the privilege of being baptized for the dead know that there is a recorder present who makes sure that the baptisms are officially and accurately recorded in the records of the temple. The instruction for this is seen in verse 6, next. The reasons for it are given in verses 7 and 9.

6 Verily, thus saith the Lord unto you concerning your dead: When

SECTION 128

any of you are baptized for your dead, **let there be a recorder**, and let him be eye-witness of your baptisms; let him hear with his ears, that he may testify of a truth, saith the Lord;

7 **That in all your recordings it may be recorded in heaven; whatsoever you bind on earth, may be bound in heaven; whatsoever you loose on earth, may be loosed in heaven;**

8 For I am about to restore many things to the earth, pertaining to the priesthood, saith the Lord of Hosts.

9 And again, **let all the records be had in order, that they may be put in the archives of my holy temple**, to be held in remembrance from generation to generation, saith the Lord of Hosts.

In verses 10–12, next, we feel the loneliness and yearning of the Prophet to again be able to openly associate with the Saints.

10 I will say to all the saints, that **I desired, with exceedingly great desire, to have addressed them from the stand** [*the pulpit; in other words, in public meetings of the Church*] on the subject of baptism for the dead, on the following Sabbath. **But inasmuch as it is out of my power to do so, I will write the word of the Lord from time to time**, on that subject, and send it to you by mail, as well as many other things.

11 **I now close my letter for the present, for the want of more time; for the enemy is on the alert**, and as the Savior said, **the prince of this world cometh** [*a quote from John 14:30, meaning the devil is much involved in the persecutions*], **but he hath nothing in me** [*he will not take me*].

12 Behold, **my prayer to God is that you all may be saved**. And **I subscribe myself** [*I present myself to you as*] **your servant in the Lord** [*in the work of the Lord*], **prophet and seer of the Church of Jesus Christ of Latter-day Saints.**

JOSEPH SMITH.

SECTION 128

Background

As was the case with section 127, this letter from the Prophet was also written while he was in hiding. This time he was hiding in the attic of Edward Hunter's home, which was accessed by a trap door. There was not enough room for Joseph to stand up. We read (**bold** added for emphasis), "President Smith, accompanied by

Brother Erastus Derby, left Brother Whitney's about nine o'clock, and went to Brother Edward Hunter's, where he was welcomed, and made comfortable by the family, and **where he can be kept safe from the hands of his enemies**" (*History of the Church,* 5:146).

The letter was dated September 6, 1842, in Nauvoo, Illinois. In it the Prophet gives additional instruction on work for the dead.

1 AS I stated to you in my letter [*section 127*] before I left my place, that I would write to you from time to time and give you information in relation to many subjects, **I now resume the subject of the baptism for the dead,** as that subject seems to occupy my mind, and **press itself upon my feelings** the strongest, since I have been pursued by my enemies.

In verse 1, above, we gain an important insight as to one of the ways the Spirit of the Lord communicates with us. The Holy Ghost "presses" things upon our minds and feelings.

Next, in verses 2–5, Joseph Smith gives instruction regarding the role of temple recorders. The importance of record-keeping is strongly emphasized.

2 I wrote a few words of revelation to you **concerning a recorder** [*a person who witnesses and officially records baptisms for the dead—see D&C 127:6*]. **I have had a few additional views in relation to this matter, which I now certify.** That is, it was declared in my former letter that **there should be a recorder, who should be eye-witness, and also to hear with his ears, that he might make a record of a truth before the Lord.**

3 Now, in relation to this matter, **it would be very difficult for one recorder to be present at all times, and to do all the business.** To obviate [*eliminate*] this difficulty, **there can be a recorder appointed in each ward of the city, who is well qualified for taking accurate minutes;** and **let him be very particular and precise** in taking the whole proceedings, certifying in his record that he saw with his eyes, and heard with his ears, giving the date, and names, and so forth, and the history of the whole transaction; **naming also some three individuals that are present,** if there be any present, who can at any time when called upon certify to the same, **that in the mouth of two or three witnesses every word may be established.**

4 Then, **let there be a general recorder,** to whom these other

records can be handed, being attended with certificates over their own signatures, certifying that the record they have made is true. **Then the general church recorder can enter the record on the general church book**, with the certificates and all the attending witnesses, with his own statement that he verily believes the above statement and records to be true, from his knowledge of the general character and appointment of those men by the church. And when this is done on the general church book, the record shall be just as holy, and shall answer the ordinance just the same as if he had seen with his eyes and heard with his ears, and made a record of the same on the general church book.

5 **You may think this order of things to be very particular; but let me tell you that it is only to answer the will of God**, by conforming to the ordinance and preparation that the Lord ordained and prepared before the foundation of the world, **for the salvation of the dead who should die without a knowledge of the gospel.**

> Next, the Prophet emphasizes the importance of keeping accurate records by quoting the Apostle John, who recorded his vision in the Book of Revelation.

6 And further, I want you to remember that **John the Revelator** was contemplating this very subject in relation to the dead, when he declared, as you will find recorded in **Revelation 20:12**—*And I saw the dead, small and great* [relatively unknown as well as famous], *stand before God; and the books were opened; and another book was opened, which is the book of life* [the record of our lives, which is kept in heaven—see verse 7, next]; *and* ***the dead were judged out of those things which were written in the books***, *according to their works.*

7 **You will discover in this quotation that the books were opened; and another book was opened, which was the book of life; but the dead were judged out of those things which were written in the books**, according to their works; consequently, **the books spoken of must be the books which contained the record of their works, and refer to the records which are kept on the earth**. And the book which was **the book of life is the record which is kept in heaven**; the principle agreeing precisely with the doctrine which is commanded

you in the revelation contained in the letter which I wrote to you previous to my leaving my place—that in all your recordings it may be recorded in heaven.

> Next, in verse 8, the Prophet teaches of the power of the priesthood to bind and loose in heaven and earth and continues to emphasize the importance of records. Perhaps you know of someone whose records were lost or whose ordinance, such as baptism or a priesthood ordination, was not recorded. In such cases, the ordinance must be performed again, and a proper record kept and submitted to the Church.
>
> Also, the Prophet Joseph Smith explains that the work done for the dead by proxy counts just the same as if the dead had received the ordinances themselves.

8 Now, the nature of this ordinance consists in the power of the priesthood, by the revelation of Jesus Christ, wherein it is granted that **whatsoever you bind on earth shall be bound in heaven, and whatsoever you loose on earth shall be loosed in heaven.** Or, in other words, taking a different view of the translation, **whatsoever you record on earth shall be recorded in heaven, and whatsoever you do not record on earth shall not be recorded in heaven; for out of the books** shall your dead be judged, according to their own works, whether they themselves have attended to the ordinances in their own *propria persona* [*in person*], or by the means of their own agents [*proxies*], according to the ordinance which God has prepared for their salvation from before the foundation of the world, according to the records which they have kept concerning their dead.

9 **It may seem to some to be a very bold doctrine that we talk of—a power which records or binds on earth and binds in heaven. Nevertheless, in all ages of the world, whenever the Lord has given a dispensation of the priesthood to any man by actual revelation, or any set of men, this power has always been given.** Hence, whatsoever those men did in authority, in the name of the Lord, and did it truly and faithfully, **and kept a proper and faithful record of the same, it became a law on earth and in heaven,** and could not be annulled, according to the decrees of the great Jehovah. This is a faithful saying. Who can hear it?

> Beginning with verse 10, next, the Prophet explains to the Saints that the doctrine of sealing and loosing

on earth and heaven through the power of the priesthood delegated to man is not a new doctrine. Rather, it is clearly taught in the Bible.

10 **And again, for the precedent, Matthew 16:18, 19**: *And I say also unto thee, That thou art Peter, and upon this rock I will build my church; and the gates of hell shall not prevail against it. And I will give unto thee the keys of the kingdom of heaven: and* **whatsoever thou shalt bind on earth shall be bound in heaven; and whatsoever thou shalt loose on earth shall be loosed in heaven**.

11 Now the great and grand secret of the whole matter, and **the *summum bonum*** [*the main point*] **of the whole subject** that is lying before us, **consists in obtaining the powers of the Holy Priesthood. For him to whom these keys are given there is no difficulty in obtaining a knowledge of facts in relation to the salvation of the children of men, both as well for the dead as for the living.**

Next, we are instructed about the necessity for baptism and the symbolism of baptism.

12 **Herein is** glory and honor, and immortality and **eternal life** [*exaltation*]—The ordinance of **baptism by water** [*in other words, baptism is required for exaltation unless an individual dies before age eight—see D&C 137:10*]**, to be immersed therein in order to answer to the likeness of** [*symbolic of*] **the dead** [*in being baptized, our old self is buried, like the dead—compare with Romans 6:4–6*]**, that one principle might accord with** [*work in harmony with*] **the other; to be immersed in the water and come forth out of the water is in the likeness of the resurrection of the dead in coming forth out of their graves; hence, this ordinance** [*baptism by immersion—see first of this verse*] **was instituted to form a relationship with the ordinance of baptism for the dead**, being in likeness of the dead.

Perhaps you have noticed that, wherever possible, our baptismal fonts are constructed so that they are below ground level. The symbolism behind this is explained in verse 13, next.

13 Consequently, **the baptismal font was instituted as a similitude of** [*to symbolize*] **the grave, and was commanded to be in a place underneath** [*below ground level*] where the living are wont to assemble, **to show forth the living and the dead, and that all things may have their likeness**, and that they may accord [*agree;*

harmonize] one with another—**that which is earthly conforming to that which is heavenly, as Paul hath declared**, 1 Corinthians 15:46, 47, and 48:

14 Howbeit [*however*] **that was not first which is spiritual, but that which is natural; and afterward that which is spiritual** [*in other words, first we get our mortal bodies; next, we get our immortal, resurrected bodies*]. **The first man** [*Adam*] **is of the earth, earthy** [*Adam received a mortal body first, made of earthly elements*]; **the second man** [*Christ*] **is the Lord from heaven. As is the earthy** [*just like Adam*], **such are they also that are earthy** [*all of us get a mortal body subject to death*]; **and as is the heavenly** [*just as Christ received a resurrected celestial body*], **such are they also that are heavenly** [*so also will all the righteous get a celestial, resurrected body*]. **And as are the records on the earth in relation to your dead, which are truly** [*accurately*] **made out, so also are the records in heaven. This, therefore, is the sealing and binding power**, and, in one sense of the word, the keys of the kingdom, which consist in the key of knowledge.

Joseph Fielding Smith explained the reason for having baptismal fonts in our temples below ground level, as follows:

"The Lord has placed the baptismal font in our temples below the foundation, or the surface of the earth. This is symbolical, since the dead are in their graves, and we are working for the dead when we are baptized for them. Moreover, baptism is also symbolical of death and the resurrection, in fact, is virtually a resurrection from the life of sin, or from spiritual death, to the life of spiritual life. (See D. & C. 29:41–45.) Therefore when the dead have had this ordinance performed in their behalf they are considered to have been brought back into the presence of God, just as this doctrine is applied to the living" (*Church History and Modern Revelation*, 2:332).

Verse 15, next, teaches vital doctrine about our own salvation and doing the work for our dead.

Doctrine
When we can do the work for our dead, doing it is essential for our own salvation.

15 **And now, my dearly beloved brethren and sisters, let me assure you that these are principles in relation to the dead and the living that cannot be lightly passed over, as pertaining to our salvation. For their salvation is necessary and essential to our salvation**, as Paul

says concerning the fathers—that **they without us cannot be made perfect—neither can we without our dead be made perfect** [*you may wish to cross-reference this phrase with the similar phrase in verse 18*].

> Remember that this concept of doing work for the dead is a new, even startling doctrine for these early Saints. Next, the Prophet helps them understand that it is not new; rather, it was taught by the Apostle Paul in the Bible, as well as being a part of Elijah's mission as prophesied in Malachi.

16 And now, **in relation to the baptism for the dead, I will give you another quotation of Paul**, 1 Corinthians 15:29: *Else what shall they do which are baptized for the dead, if the dead rise not at all? Why are they then baptized for the dead?*

17 And again, in connection with this quotation I will give you a quotation from one of the prophets, who had his eye fixed on the restoration of the priesthood, the glories to be revealed in the last days, and in an especial manner this most glorious of all subjects belonging to the everlasting gospel, namely, the **baptism for the dead**; for **Malachi says**, last chapter, verses 5th and 6th: *Behold, I will send you Elijah the prophet before the coming of the great and dreadful day of the Lord: And* **he shall turn the heart of the fathers to the children, and the heart of the children to their fathers**, *lest I come and smite the earth with a curse.*

> Sometimes we find ourselves wishing that the Prophet Joseph Smith had clarified and rewritten almost every verse in the Bible. In verse 18, next, we see that he could have done much in that regard, but it was not necessary in many cases.

18 **I might have rendered a plainer translation to this, but it is sufficiently plain to suit my purpose as it stands.** It is sufficient to know, in this case, that **the earth will be smitten with a curse** [*won't fulfill its ultimate purpose of providing the opportunity for exaltation in family units for all who qualify*] **unless there is a welding link of some kind or other between the fathers and the children**, upon some subject or other—and **behold what is that subject? It is the baptism for the dead.** For **we without them cannot be made perfect; neither can they without us be made perfect.** Neither can they nor we be made perfect without those who have died in the gospel also; **for it is necessary** in the ushering in of the dispensation

of the fulness of times, which dispensation is now beginning to usher in, **that a whole and complete and perfect union, and welding together of dispensations, and keys, and powers, and glories should take place, and be revealed from the days of Adam even to the present time**. And not only this, but those things which never have been revealed from the foundation of the world, but have been kept hid from the wise and prudent, shall be revealed unto babes and sucklings in this, the dispensation of the fulness of times.

> Having mentioned how important and special the dispensation of the fullness of times is (verse 18, above), the Prophet will now summarize several aspects of the restoration, including appearances of past prophets who have come to restore things pertaining to their dispensations to our dispensation, which is the last dispensation before the Second Coming. As you can see, we do indeed have the restored gospel, restored from the past.

19 Now, **what do we hear** in the gospel which we have received? **A voice of gladness! A voice of mercy from heaven;** and **a voice of truth out of the earth** [*the Book of Mormon*]; **glad tidings for the dead; a voice of gladness for the living and the dead** [*because work for the dead has been restored*]; glad tidings of great joy. How beautiful upon the mountains are the feet of those that bring glad tidings of good things, and that say unto Zion: Behold, thy God reigneth! As the dews of Carmel, so shall the knowledge of God descend upon them!

20 And again, what do we hear? Glad tidings from Cumorah! **Moroni**, an angel from heaven, declaring the fulfilment of the prophets—the book to be revealed. **A voice of the Lord** in the wilderness of Fayette, Seneca county, declaring the three witnesses to bear record of the book! The voice of **Michael** [*Adam*] on the banks of the Susquehanna, detecting the devil when he appeared as an angel of light [*this is all we know about this appearance*]! The voice of **Peter, James, and John** in the wilderness between Harmony, Susquehanna county, and Colesville, Broome county, on the Susquehanna river, declaring themselves as possessing the keys of the kingdom, and of the dispensation of the fulness of times!

21 And again, **the voice of God** in the chamber of old Father Whitmer, in Fayette, Seneca county, and at sundry times, and

in divers [various] places through all the travels and tribulations of this Church of Jesus Christ of Latter-day Saints! And the voice of **Michael, the archangel** [*Adam*]; the voice of Gabriel, and of **Raphael** [*we don't know who this is*], and of **divers** [*various*] **angels**, from Michael or Adam down to the present time, **all declaring their dispensation, their rights, their keys, their honors, their majesty and glory, and the power of their priesthood; giving line upon line, precept upon precept**; here a little, and there a little; giving us consolation by holding forth that which is to come, confirming our hope!

As indicated in the above verses, the Prophet Joseph Smith was taught by many who came from beyond the veil. We will include a partial list here, quoting from President John Taylor:

"When God selected Joseph Smith to open up the last dispensation . . . the **Father** and the **Son** appeared to him . . . **Moroni** came to Joseph . . . Then comes another personage, whose name is **John the Baptist** . . . Afterwards came **Peter, James and John** . . . Then we read again of **Elias or Elijah**, . . . who committed to him the powers and authority associated with his position. Then **Abraham**, who had the Gospel, the Priesthood and Patriarchal powers in his day; and **Moses** who stood at the head of the gathering dispensation in his day. . . . We are informed that **Noah**, who was a Patriarch, and all in the line of the Priesthood, in every generation back to **Adam**, who was the first man, possessed the same. Why was it that all these people could communicate with Joseph Smith? Because he stood at the head of the dispensation of the fullness of times. . . . If you were to ask Joseph what sort of a looking man **Adam** was, he would tell you at once; he would tell you his size and appearance and all about him. You might have asked him what sort of men **Peter, James, and John** were, and he could have told you. Why? Because he had seen them" (in *Journal of Discourses,* 18:325–26).

"And when Joseph Smith was raised up as a Prophet of God, **Mormon, Moroni, Nephi and others of the ancient Prophets who formerly lived on this Continent, and Peter and John and others who lived on the Asiatic Continent**, came to him and communicated to him certain principles pertaining to the gospel of the Son of God" (in *Journal of Discourses,* 17:374).

"I know of what I speak for I was very well acquainted with him (Joseph Smith) and was with him a great deal during his life, and was with him when he died. The principles which he had, placed him in communication with the Lord, and not only with the Lord, but with the ancient apostles and prophets, such men, for instance, as **Abraham, Isaac, Jacob, Noah, Adam, Seth, Enoch, and Jesus and the Father, and the apostles that lived on this continent as well as those who lived on the Asiatic Continent**. He seemed to be as familiar with these people as we are with one another" (in *Journal of Discourses*, 21:94).

Also, the Prophet Joseph Smith gave the following description of the **Apostle Paul**: "He is about five feet high; very dark hair; dark complexion; dark skin; large Roman nose; sharp face; small black eyes, penetrating as eternity; round shoulders; a whining voice, except when elevated, and then it almost resembled the roaring of a lion. He was a good orator, active and diligent, always employing himself in doing good to his fellow man" (*Teachings of the Prophet Joseph Smith,* 180).

We feel the enthusiasm and great spirit of the Prophet Joseph Smith as he brings this letter to a close. Remember, he himself is in relatively miserable circumstances again at the time he wrote this epistle to the Saints.

22 **Brethren, shall we not go on in so great a cause? Go forward and not backward. Courage, brethren; and on, on to the victory!** Let your hearts rejoice, and be exceedingly glad. Let the earth break forth into singing. **Let the dead speak forth anthems of eternal praise to the King Immanuel, who hath ordained, before the world was, that which would enable us to redeem them out of their prison; for the prisoners shall go free.**

23 Let the mountains shout for joy, and all ye valleys cry aloud; and all ye seas and dry lands tell the wonders of your Eternal King! And ye rivers, and brooks, and rills, flow down with gladness. Let the woods and all the trees of the field praise the Lord; and ye solid rocks weep for joy! And let the sun, moon, and the morning stars sing together, and let all the sons of God shout for joy! And let the eternal creations declare his name forever and ever! **And again I say, how glorious is the voice we hear from heaven, proclaiming in our ears, glory, and salvation, and honor, and immortality, and eternal life; kingdoms, principalities, and powers!**

Verse 24, next, is a cross-reference for the phrase "until the sons of Levi do offer again an offering unto the Lord in righteousness," as found in section

13. Upon close examination, we see that one possible interpretation of this phrase is that we are, in effect, the sons of Levi.

They held the priesthood and performed ordinances among the children of Israel. In our day, we hold the priesthood and perform ordinances, including saving ordinances for the dead. Therefore, symbolically, we can be considered to be the "sons of Levi." And, because of the restoration of the priesthood, including the keys of sealing by Elijah (D&C 110:13–16), we can "offer again an offering unto the Lord in righteousness." In other words, we can once again perform valid saving priesthood ordinances upon the earth.

24 Behold, **the great day of the Lord is at hand** [*the Second Coming of Christ is getting close*]; and who can abide [*survive*] the day of his coming, and who can stand when he appeareth? For he is like a refiner's fire, and like fuller's soap; and he shall sit as a refiner and purifier of silver, and **he shall purify the sons of Levi**, and purge them as gold and silver, **that they may offer unto the Lord an offering in righteousness. Let us, therefore**, as a church and a people, and as Latter-day Saints, **offer unto the Lord an offering in righteousness**; and let us present in his holy temple, when it is finished, a book containing the records of our dead, which shall be worthy of all acceptation.

25 Brethren, **I have many things to say to you on the subject; but shall now close for the present**, and continue the subject another time. I am, as ever, your humble servant and never deviating friend,

JOSEPH SMITH.

SECTION 129

Background

This section consists of instructions by the Prophet Joseph Smith given on February 9, 1843, in Nauvoo, Illinois, regarding how to tell the difference between angels with resurrected bodies, righteous spirits, and evil spirits attempting to make people believe they are from God.

Most members of the Church have probably heard about "offering to shake hands" (verse 4) with messengers from the other side as a means of detecting impostors. This was an important issue in the early days of the Church, because Satan and his evil spirits were using every possible ploy to deceive the Saints with false revelations.

As you will see, three kinds of beings beyond the veil are mentioned by the Prophet in this instruction:

1. Resurrected beings with bodies of flesh and bone.

2. Righteous spirits who have only a spirit body and either have been to earth already but are not yet resurrected, or who have not yet been born on earth.

3. Evil spirits who have only their spirit bodies, which they obtained in premortality.

Before we study this section verse by verse, there is an additional major message implied here that we will just mention. It is the wonderful assurance that Satan and his evil hosts are bound by God and His laws. They are limited by Him. He has power to command, and they must obey!

Otherwise, any of Satan and his evil spirits could simply read section 129 of the Doctrine and Covenants and fool us by refusing to shake hands (verses 6–7). Thus, we would think him to be from God and would listen to his message with obedience in mind. As it is, however, Satan, or any other evil spirit, must offer his hand (because God requires it of them) when requested to do so (verse 8), and thus can be detected as evil by the righteous and informed.

Parley P. Pratt and others were present on February 9, 1843, when the Prophet gave this instruction. We will use **bold**, as usual, for teaching purposes.

1 **THERE are two kinds of beings in heaven**, namely: **Angels**, who are **resurrected personages, having bodies of flesh and bones**—

2 For instance, Jesus said: *Handle me and see, for a spirit hath not flesh and bones, as ye see me have.*

3 **Secondly**: the **spirits of just** [*righteous men who faithfully obey the laws and ordinances of the gospel*] **made perfect**, they **who are not resurrected**, but inherit the same glory [*meaning righteous "spirits who have once had a mortal body and are awaiting resurrection"—see Guide to the Scriptures under "Angels," churchofjesuschrist.org*].

4 **When a messenger comes saying he has a message from God, offer him your hand** and request him to shake hands with you.

5 **If he be an angel** [*a resurrected being—see verse 1*] **he will do so, and you will feel his hand.**

6 **If he be the spirit of a just man made perfect** he will come in his glory; for that is the only way he can appear—

7 Ask him to shake hands with you, but he will not move, because it is contrary to the order of heaven for a just man to deceive; but he will still deliver his message.

8 If it be the devil as an angel of light [*trying to masquerade as a messenger from God*], **when you ask him to shake hands he will offer you his hand, and you will not feel anything**; you may therefore detect him.

9 These are three grand keys whereby you may know whether any administration is from God.

> We receive further clarification on this topic from the 2018 *Doctrine and Covenants Student Manual* as follows:
>
> "While the Prophet Joseph Smith referred only to resurrected beings as angels, President George Q. Cannon (1827–1901) of the First Presidency explained, 'In the broadest sense, any being who acts as a messenger for our Heavenly Father is an angel, be he a God, a resurrected man, or the spirit of a just man" ("Editorial Thoughts," *The Juvenile Instructor*, Jan. 15, 1891, 53). Thus, in addition to the heavenly messengers described in Doctrine and Covenants 129, God's angels also include spirits who 'have not yet obtained a body of flesh and bone' (*Guide to the Scriptures,* "Angels," scriptures.lds.org; see also Ether 3:6–16; Moses 5:6) as well as translated beings—individuals whose mortal bodies are changed so that they do not experience pain or death (see 3 Nephi 28:6–9; Mormon 8:10–11; D&C 7:1–3)."

Over the years, some of my students have asked why we don't hear more of this now. One possible reason is that we have the gift of the Holy Ghost and thus can be warned by Him when evil approaches. Also, the Church is well-established now and the leadership is solidly in place as opposed to the frequent apostasy of Church leaders in the early days of the Restoration.

Whatever the case, the counsel and guidance in this section is still in force should it be needed by the righteous.

SECTION 130

Background

This section consists of items of instruction given by the Prophet Joseph Smith on Sunday, April 2, 1843, while accompanied by some of the brethren for dinner and visiting at his sister's home (Sophronia; see Joseph Smith–History 1:4 for a listing of his siblings) in Ramus, Illinois, about twenty miles southeast of Nauvoo.

The Prophet gave a little background for this Sunday as follows:

"*Sunday, 2.*—Wind N.E. Snow fell several inches, but melted more or less.

"At ten a.m. went to meeting. Heard Elder Orson Hyde preach. . . . Alluding to the coming of the Savior, he said, 'When He shall appear, we shall be like Him, &c. He will appear on a white horse as a warrior, and maybe we shall have some of the same spirit. Our God is a warrior (John 14:23). It is our privilege to have the Father and Son dwelling in our hearts, &c.'

"We dined with my sister Sophronia McCleary, when I told Elder Hyde that I was going to offer some corrections to his sermon this morning. He replied, 'They shall be thankfully received'" (*History of the Church*, 5:323).

The Prophet recorded these teachings in his journal and they became the instruction on a variety of topics given here in section 130.

Doctrine

The Savior is a glorified man, with a glorified resurrected body of flesh and bones—see also verse 22)

1 WHEN **the Savior shall appear we shall see him as he is. We shall see that he is a man like ourselves.**

Doctrine

We will enjoy socializing in the next life but will have the capacity to enjoy it even more.

2 And **that same sociality which exists among us here will exist among us there**, only it will be coupled with eternal glory, which glory we do not now enjoy.

Doctrine

The Father and the Son do not dwell in our heart.

3 John 14:23—The appearing of the Father and the Son in that verse is a personal appearance; and **the idea that the Father and the Son dwell in a man's heart is an old sectarian** [*coming from other religions*] **notion, and is false**.

Doctrine

Time systems are controlled by the planets upon which beings live. No angels minister to us other than those who belong to this earth.

4 In answer to the question—**Is not the reckoning of God's time, angel's time, prophet's time, and man's time, according to the planet on which they reside?**

5 I answer, **Yes**. But there are **no angels** who **minister to this**

earth but those who do belong or have belonged to it.

Doctrine

The planet upon which the Father resides serves as a Urim and Thummim.

6 The angels do not reside on a planet like this earth;

7 But they reside in the presence of God, on a globe like a sea of glass and fire, where all things for their glory are manifest, past, present, and future, and are continually before the Lord.

8 The place where God resides is a great [*huge*] **Urim and Thummim.**

Doctrine

This earth will become a Urim and Thummim for those who belong to it and attain celestial glory.

Christ will live on this earth when it is celestialized.

9 This earth, in its sanctified and immortal state [*in its glorified, celestial state*], will be made like unto crystal and **will be a Urim and Thummim to the inhabitants who dwell thereon**, whereby all things pertaining to an inferior kingdom, or **all kingdoms of a lower order, will be manifest to those who dwell on it**; and **this earth will be Christ's.**

Joseph Smith taught that this earth will be moved back into the presence of God when it finishes up. He said:

"This earth will be rolled back into the presence of God, and crowned with celestial glory" (*Teachings of the Prophet Joseph Smith,* 181).

Brigham Young taught about the earth when it is celestialized. He said:

"When it [the earth] becomes celestialized, it will be like the sun, and be prepared for the habitation of the saints, and be brought back into the presence of the Father and the Son [near Kolob], it will not then be an opaque body as it now is, but it will be like the stars of the firmament, full of light and glory; it will be a body of light. John compared it, in its celestial state, to a sea of glass" (in *Journal of Discourses,* 7:163).

He also taught: "This earth, when it becomes purified and sanctified, or celestialized, will become like a sea of glass; and a person, by looking into it, can know things past, present, and to come; though none but celestialized beings can enjoy this privilege. They will look into the earth, and the things they desire to know will be exhibited to them, the same as the face is seen by looking into a mirror" (in *Journal of Discourses*, 9:87).

Orson Pratt taught that other worlds will also become celestial kingdoms for their worthy inhabitants. Speaking of the celestialization of other worlds and their inhabitants, he said (**bold** added for emphasis):

"By and by, when each of these creations has fulfilled the measure and bounds set and the times given for this continuance in a temporal state [*their mortal time period*], **it and its inhabitants who are worthy will be made celestial and glorified together**. Then, from that time henceforth and for ever, there will be no intervening veil between God and his people who are sanctified and glorified, and he will not be under the necessity of withdrawing from one to go and visit another, because **they will all be in his presence**" (in *Journal of Discourses,* 17:332–33; quoted also in *Doctrine and Covenants Student Manual*, 1981, 201).

Doctrine

Everyone who attains the celestial kingdom will be given a white stone that will serve as a Urim and Thummim for them.

10 Then the **white stone** mentioned in Revelation 2:17, **will become a Urim and Thummim** to each individual who receives one, **whereby things pertaining to a higher order of kingdoms will be made known**;

11 And **a white stone is given to each of those who come into the celestial kingdom,** whereon is a new name written, which no man knoweth save he that receiveth it. The new name is the key word [*those who have received their endowments know about the "new name"*].

Doctrine

The Civil War would start in South Carolina (of course, this prophecy has already been fulfilled).

This prophecy, given 18 years before the beginning of the Civil War, in verses 12–13, next, is a strong reminder that Joseph Smith was indeed a prophet of God. Shortly before the Civil War began, popular opinion was that the Northern States, with their superior power and financial capability, would start the war. It appeared unlikely that South Carolina would start it.

However, on April 12, 1861, South Carolina fired on Union Troops at Fort Sumter, and thus the Civil War was underway. This exacting prophecy was given eighteen years before its precise fulfillment.

12 I prophesy, in the name of the

Lord God, that **the commencement of the difficulties** which will cause much bloodshed previous to the coming of the Son of Man **will be in South Carolina.**

13 It may probably arise through the slave question. This a voice declared to me, while I was praying earnestly on the subject, December 25th, 1832.

Doctrine

No one knows the exact timing of the Second Coming.

14 **I was once praying very earnestly to know the time of the coming of the Son of Man**, when I heard a voice repeat the following:

15 Joseph, my son, if thou livest until thou art eighty-five years old, thou shalt see the face of the Son of Man; therefore let this suffice, and **trouble me no more on this matter.**

16 **I was left thus, without being able to decide whether this coming referred to the beginning of the millennium or to some previous appearing, or whether I should die and thus see his face.**

17 I believe the coming of the Son of Man will not be any sooner than that time.

Doctrine

The knowledge and intelligence we gain in this life will continue with us in the resurrection and be advantageous for us.

18 **Whatever principle of intelligence we attain unto in this life, it will rise with us in the resurrection.**

19 And **if a person gains more knowledge and intelligence in this life** through his diligence and obedience than another, **he will have so much the advantage in the world to come.**

I was once chatting with an elderly sister in her early eighties when she expressed her concern about continuing to study the scriptures. Her problem was that the next day, she couldn't even remember what she had been reading the day before. She was somewhat comforted when I reminded her that verses 18–19 say nothing about when we rise in the "morning," rather, in the "resurrection."

Thus, we understand it to be worthwhile to continue studying and learning, because we are filing it away now to come forth with us in the resurrection, whether or not we can retrieve it from our memories now. There, it will become an advantage to us.

Doctrine

All blessings received are based on laws.

20 There is a law, irrevocably decreed [*cannot be revoked*] in heaven before the foundations of this world [*in premortality*], **upon which all blessings are predicated** [*based*]—

21 And **when we obtain any blessing from God, it is by obedience to that law upon which it is predicated.**

Doctrine

The Father and Son have glorified, resurrected bodies of flesh and bones. The Holy Ghost is a spirit and must be a spirit in order to fulfill His calling.

22 The Father has a body of flesh and bones as tangible [*as touchable*] as man's; **the Son also;** but **the Holy Ghost** has not a body of flesh and bones, but **is a personage of Spirit. Were it not so, the Holy Ghost could not dwell in us.**

Doctrine

A person can receive temporary help from the Holy Ghost but must join the Church in order to have the constant companionship of the Holy Ghost.

23 A man may receive the Holy Ghost, and it may descend upon him and not tarry [*remain*] **with him.**

One of the common applications of verse 23, above, is when a prospective convert is being taught the gospel. The Holy Ghost can bear strong witness that what he or she is hearing is the truth. However, unless the person acts upon that witness and joins the Church, the Holy Ghost withdraws and the testimony often fades.

A common question asked by my students over the years has been whether the Holy Ghost will ever get a body. While there are many things we do not know about Him, we can read a quote from the *Ensign* which informs us that Joseph Smith taught that He will someday get a body (**bold** added for emphasis):

"**The Holy Ghost**. The Bible gives little detail about the personage of the Holy Ghost. The Prophet, however, gave us a number of insights about that spirit being and his office. On several occasions, especially in Nauvoo in 1842–43, the Prophet spoke of the Holy Ghost as a being 'in the form of a personage,' as a 'spirit without tabernacle,' separate and distinct from the personages of the Father and the Son. According to the George Laub journal, on another occasion Joseph taught that "**the Holy Ghost is yet a spiritual body and waiting to take to himself a body**" (Donald Q. Cannon, Larry E. Dahl, and John W. Welch, "The Restoration of Major Doctrines through Joseph Smith: The Godhead, Mankind, and the Creation," *Ensign,* January 1989, 29).

SECTION 131

Background

This section consists of instructions given by the Prophet Joseph Smith on May 16–17, 1843, at Ramus, Illinois, a settlement about twenty miles southeast of Nauvoo.

Verses 1–4 were given to William Clayton that evening (May 16). Verses 5 and 6 were given the next morning (May 17) in a meeting, and verses 7–8 were given in the evening (May 17).

Four important doctrines are taught here.

Doctrine

The celestial kingdom has three degrees of glory in it. Celestial marriage is required for entrance into the highest. The family unit exists only in the highest of the three.

1 In the celestial glory there are three heavens or degrees;

2 And **in order to obtain the highest, a man must enter into this order of the priesthood** [*meaning the new and everlasting covenant of marriage*];

Apostle Parley P. Pratt described how wonderful the Prophet Joseph's teachings were to him regarding celestial marriage.

"It was from [Joseph Smith] that I learned that the wife of my bosom might be secured to me for time and all eternity. . . . It was from him that I learned that we might cultivate these affections, and grow and increase in the same to all eternity; while the result of our endless union would be an offspring as numerous as the stars of heaven, or the sands of the sea shore. . . .

"I had loved before, but I knew not why. But now I loved—with a pureness—an intensity of elevated, exalted feeling" (*The Autobiography of Parley Parker Pratt,* 297).

3 And **if he does not, he cannot obtain it.**

4 **He may enter into the other, but that is the end of his kingdom; he cannot have an increase** [*he cannot become a God and have children eternally—compare with what he and his wife can have as stated in D&C 132:19–20*].

The Prophet gave background for what is included as the next two verses of this section (**Bold** added for emphasis):

"*Wednesday, 17.*—Partook of breakfast at Brother Perkins'; after which we took a pleasure ride through Fountain Green.

"At ten A.M. **preached from 2nd Peter, 1st chapter** and showed that knowledge is power; and the man who has the most knowledge has the greatest power.

"Salvation means a man's being placed beyond the power of all his enemies.

"The more sure word of prophecy means a man's knowing that he is sealed up into eternal life by revelation and the spirit of prophecy, through the power of the holy priesthood. It is impossible for a man to be saved in ignorance.

"Paul saw the third heavens, **and I more**. Peter penned the most sublime language of any of the apostles" (*History of the Church*, 5:392).

As you can see, verses 5 and 6 were taken from the second to last paragraph of the quote, above.

You may wish to read all of 2 Peter 1 as a background for the Prophets statements in these verses.

Doctrine

It is possible to know that you have qualified for exaltation.

5 (May 17th, 1843.) The more sure word of prophecy [2 *Peter 1:19*] **means a man's knowing that he is sealed up unto eternal life** [*exaltation*]**, by revelation and the spirit of prophecy, through the power of the Holy Priesthood.**

We understand from D&C 132:49 that the Prophet Joseph Smith was "sealed up unto eternal life"; in other words, his calling and election were made sure. We will quote it here and add **bold** for teaching purposes.

D&C 132:49

49 For I am the Lord thy God, and will be with thee even unto the end of the world, and through all eternity; for verily **I seal upon you your exaltation,** and prepare a throne for you in the kingdom of my Father, with Abraham your father.

Elder Bruce R. McConkie taught the following (**bold** added for emphasis):

"Those members of the Church who devote themselves wholly to righteousness, living by every word that proceedeth forth from the mouth of God, **make their calling and election sure**. That is, they **receive the more sure word of prophecy, which means that the Lord seals their exaltation upon them while they are yet in this life**. Peter summarized the course of righteousness which the saints must pursue to make their calling and election sure and then (referring to his experience on the Mount of Transfiguration with James and John) said that those three had received this more sure word of prophecy (2 Pet. 1.)" (*Mormon Doctrine,* 109).

Having one's "calling and election made sure" does not have to happen in mortality. No doubt, for most Saints, it will happen in the next life. This will be true of those who died after age eight without having had the opportunity to accept the gospel and who accept the gospel fully in the spirit world mission field.

Doctrine

It is impossible to be saved without knowing the gospel.

6 It is impossible for a man to be saved in ignorance [*of the gospel*].

President Marion G. Romney of the First Presidency years ago explained what type of knowledge is meant in verse 6, above. He taught:

"By receiving the Savior's message and accepting him for what he was and is, the Apostles obtained eternal life [see John 17:1–2, 6–8].

"This knowledge of 'the only true God, and Jesus Christ' (John 17:3) is the most important knowledge in the universe; it is the knowledge without which the Prophet Joseph Smith said no man could be saved. The lack of it is the ignorance referred to in the revelation wherein it is written: 'It is impossible for a man to be saved in ignorance.' (D&C 131:6.)" ("Except a Man Be Born Again," *Ensign,* Nov. 1981, 14).

The Prophet recorded some background for verses 7–8, next, as follows:

"In the evening went to hear a Methodist preacher lecture. After he got through, offered some corrections as follows:

"The 7th verse of 2nd chapter of Genesis ought to read—God breathed into Adam his spirit [*i.e. Adam's spirit*] or breath of life; but when the word "rauch" applies to Eve, it should be translated lives.

"Speaking of eternal duration of matter, I said:

"There is no such thing as immaterial matter. All spirit is matter, but is more fine or pure, and can only be discerned by purer eyes. We cannot see it, but when our bodies are purified, we shall see that it is all matter.

"The priest seemed pleased with the correction, and stated his intention to visit Nauvoo" (*History of the Church,* 5:393).

Doctrine

Spirit is matter. Our spirit bodies are made out of actual matter.

7 There is no such thing as immaterial matter. All spirit is matter, but it is more fine or pure, and can only be discerned by purer eyes;

8 We cannot see it; but when our bodies are purified we shall see that it is all matter.

One of the things the beautiful and simple doctrine given by the Prophet in verses 7–8, above, helps us understand is that we were "real" people in our premortal existence as spirit children of our Heavenly Parents ("The Family—A Proclamation to the World," *Ensign,* November 1995, 102). "Spirit is matter," and thus, we were made out of actual matter, rather than being in some strange, wispy, indefinable state of existence.

Another lesson we learn here is that some things cannot be discovered by scientific methods; rather, it must be given to us through pure revelation from God.

SECTION 132

Background

This great revelation on eternal marriage was dictated by the Prophet Joseph Smith on July 12, 1843, in Nauvoo, Illinois. As you can see in the heading to section 132 in your Doctrine and Covenants, we understand that the doctrines and principles taught in this section were given to the Prophet as early as 1831.

Generally speaking, as indicated in the *Doctrine and Covenants Student Manual,* 2018, chapters 51–52, this revelation can be divided into two main sections:

1. Verses 3–33 deal mainly with the doctrine of celestial marriage, meaning eternal marriage, often referred to as the "new and everlasting covenant of marriage" (D&C 131:2). This is the beautiful, eternal marriage covenant that we enter into together as husband and wife when we are sealed in the temple.

2. Having explained the law of celestial marriage in verses 3–33, the Lord then returns to Joseph's original question about plural marriage (verse 1) and answers it in verses 34–66.

If we fail to note the above two general divisions within this revelation, we can get caught up in some false doctrines and serious misunderstandings, including believing that plural marriage should still be actively practiced among members of the Church today. In other words, if you interpret the phrase "this law," in verse 3, to mean plural marriage, you will be off track and could easily be led astray.

However, if you correctly interpret "this law" in verse 3 to mean the law of celestial marriage itself and how you can make yours last eternally, you will have a correct understanding of verses 3–33 specifically, and section 132 generally.

First, we see in verse one that Joseph Smith had asked the Lord why plural marriage was allowed in Old Testament times. This question may well have come into his mind while he was working on the Joseph Smith Translation of the Bible in 1831. He would have been working on the Old Testament at that time and would have encountered plural marriage practiced by Abraham, Isaac, Jacob, and others in ancient times.

As you can see, the Lord expresses His willingness to answer Joseph's question (verses 1 and 2) but first He will teach His Prophet about the foundational principle of eternal marriage before returning to the topic of plural marriage.

1 VERILY, thus saith the Lord unto you my servant Joseph, that **inasmuch as you have inquired** of my hand **to know and understand wherein I, the Lord, justified my servants Abraham, Isaac, and Jacob, as also Moses, David and Solomon, my servants, as touching the principle and doctrine of their having many wives and concubines** [*legally married, second class wives, according to the social and cultural system of the day*]—

2 Behold, and lo, **I am the Lord thy God, and will answer thee** as touching this matter.

By the way, "polygamy" is often used to mean plural marriage in discussions about the subject, but if you want to be accurate, "polygamy" means having more than one wife or more than one husband, whereas "plural marriage" means having more than one wife.

As we continue, verses 3–33 will teach us the law of celestial marriage, not to be confused with the explanation of plural marriage in verses 34–66.

Verses 3–33

The Law of Celestial Marriage

As stated above, the law of celestial marriage is that law that must be complied with by a husband and wife who desire to be sealed for time and eternity, to live in the family unit forever. In order to emphasize that verses 3–33 are dealing with this law, we will first go through these verses without commentary, using **bold** to point out various forms of the phrase "**this law**." Our purpose is to further point out the fact that these verses are explaining the law of eternal, celestial marriage, not plural marriage. After we have done this, we will repeat the verses, adding notes and commentary.

You may wish to mark or highlight what we **bold** in these verses in your own Doctrine and Covenants as a simple way of pointing out in your own scriptures that verses 3–33 are given in reference to the law and principle of celestial marriage.

3 Therefore, prepare thy heart to receive and obey the instructions which I am about to give unto you; for all those who have **this law** revealed unto them must obey the same.

4 For behold, I reveal unto you a new and an everlasting covenant; and if ye abide not that covenant, then are ye damned; for no one can reject this covenant and be permitted to enter into my glory.

5 For all who will have a blessing at my hands shall abide **the law** which was appointed for that blessing, and the conditions thereof, as were instituted from before the foundation of the world.

6 And as pertaining to the new and everlasting covenant, it was instituted for the fulness of my glory; and he that receiveth a fulness thereof must and shall abide **the law**, or he shall be damned, saith the Lord God.

7 And verily I say unto you, that the conditions of **this law** are these: All covenants, contracts, bonds, obligations, oaths, vows, performances, connections, associations, or expectations, that are not made and entered into and sealed by the Holy Spirit of promise, of him who is anointed, both as well for time and for all eternity, and that too most holy, by revelation and commandment through the medium of mine anointed, whom I have appointed on the earth to hold this power (and I have appointed unto my servant Joseph to hold this power in the last days, and there is never but one on the earth at a time on whom this power and the keys of this priesthood are conferred), are of no efficacy, virtue, or force in and after the resurrection from the dead; for all contracts that are not made unto this end have an end when men are dead.

8 Behold, mine house is a house of order, saith the Lord God, and not a house of confusion.

9 Will I accept of an offering, saith the Lord, that is not made in my name?

10 Or will I receive at your hands that which I have not appointed?

11 And will I appoint unto you, saith the Lord, except it be by **law**, even as I and my Father ordained unto you, before the world was?

12 I am the Lord thy God; and I give unto you this commandment—that no man shall come unto the Father but by me or by my word, which is **my law**, saith the Lord.

13 And everything that is in the world, whether it be ordained of men, by thrones, or principalities, or powers, or things of name, whatsoever they may be, that are not by me or by my word, saith the Lord, shall be thrown down, and shall not remain after men are dead, neither in nor after the resurrection, saith the Lord your God.

14 For whatsoever things remain are by me; and whatsoever things are not by me shall be shaken and destroyed.

15 Therefore, if a man marry him a wife in the world, and he marry her not by me nor by my word, and he covenant with her so long as he is in the world and she with him, their covenant and marriage are not of force when they are dead, and when they are out of the world; therefore, they are not bound by any law when they are out of the world.

16 Therefore, when they are out of the world they neither marry nor are given in marriage; but are appointed angels in heaven, which angels are ministering servants, to minister for those who are worthy of a far more, and an exceeding, and an eternal weight of glory.

17 For these angels did not abide **my law**; therefore, they cannot be enlarged, but remain separately and singly, without exaltation, in their saved condition, to all eternity; and from henceforth are not gods, but are angels of God forever and ever.

18 And again, verily I say unto you, if a man marry a wife, and make a covenant with her for time and for all eternity, if that covenant is not by me or by my word, which is **my law**, and is not sealed by the Holy Spirit of promise, through him whom I have anointed and appointed unto this power, then it is not valid neither of force when they are out of the world, because they are not joined by me, saith the Lord, neither by my word; when they are out of the world it cannot be received there,

because the angels and the gods are appointed there, by whom they cannot pass; they cannot, therefore, inherit my glory; for my house is a house of order, saith the Lord God.

19 And again, verily I say unto you, if a man marry a wife by my word, which is **my law**, and by the new and everlasting covenant, and it is sealed unto them by the Holy Spirit of promise, by him who is anointed, unto whom I have appointed this power and the keys of this priesthood; and it shall be said unto them—Ye shall come forth in the first resurrection; and if it be after the first resurrection, in the next resurrection; and shall inherit thrones, kingdoms, principalities, and powers, dominions, all heights and depths—then shall it be written in the Lamb's Book of Life, that he shall commit no murder whereby to shed innocent blood, and if ye abide in **my covenant**, and commit no murder whereby to shed innocent blood, it shall be done unto them in all things whatsoever my servant hath put upon them, in time, and through all eternity; and shall be of full force when they are out of the world; and they shall pass by the angels, and the gods, which are set there, to their exaltation and glory in all things, as hath been sealed upon their heads, which glory shall be a fulness and a continuation of the seeds forever and ever.

20 Then shall they be gods, because they have no end; therefore shall they be from everlasting to everlasting, because they continue; then shall they be above all, because all things are subject unto them. Then shall they be gods, because they have all power, and the angels are subject unto them.

21 Verily, verily, I say unto you, except ye abide **my law** ye cannot attain to this glory.

22 For strait is the gate, and narrow the way that leadeth unto the exaltation and continuation of the lives, and few there be that find it, because ye receive me not in the world neither do ye know me.

23 But if ye receive me in the world, then shall ye know me, and shall receive your exaltation; that where I am ye shall be also.

24 This is eternal lives—to know the only wise and true God, and Jesus Christ, whom he hath sent. I am he. Receive ye, therefore, **my law**.

25 Broad is the gate, and wide the way that leadeth to the deaths; and many there are that go in thereat,

because they receive me not, neither do they abide in **my law**.

26 Verily, verily, I say unto you, if a man marry a wife according to my word, and they are sealed by the Holy Spirit of promise, according to mine appointment, and he or she shall commit any sin or transgression of the new and everlasting covenant whatever, and all manner of blasphemies, and if they commit no murder wherein they shed innocent blood, yet they shall come forth in the first resurrection, and enter into their exaltation; but they shall be destroyed in the flesh, and shall be delivered unto the buffetings of Satan unto the day of redemption, saith the Lord God.

27 The blasphemy against the Holy Ghost, which shall not be forgiven in the world nor out of the world, is in that ye commit murder wherein ye shed innocent blood, and assent unto my death, after ye have received my new and everlasting covenant, saith the Lord God; and he that abideth not **this law** can in nowise enter into my glory, but shall be damned, saith the Lord.

28 I am the Lord thy God, and will give unto thee **the law of my Holy Priesthood**, as was ordained by me and my Father before the world was.

29 Abraham received all things, whatsoever he received, by revelation and commandment, by my word, saith the Lord, and hath entered into his exaltation and sitteth upon his throne.

30 Abraham received promises concerning his seed, and of the fruit of his loins—from whose loins ye are, namely, my servant Joseph—which were to continue so long as they were in the world; and as touching Abraham and his seed, out of the world they should continue; both in the world and out of the world should they continue as innumerable as the stars; or, if ye were to count the sand upon the seashore ye could not number them.

31 This promise is yours also, because ye are of Abraham, and the promise was made unto Abraham; and by **this law** is the continuation of the works of my Father, wherein he glorifieth himself.

32 Go ye, therefore, and do the works of Abraham; enter ye into **my law** and ye shall be saved.

33 But if ye enter not into **my law** ye cannot receive the promise of my Father, which he made unto Abraham.

As you can see from the above **bolding**, verses 3–33 clearly refer to the law of celestial marriage, which applies to all who wish to qualify for exaltation, meaning to have their own eternal family unit as gods. After we have repeated verses 3–33 in order to add commentary, we will then deal with the topic of plural marriage, as explained in verses 34–66.

Now, a repeat of verses 3–33.

In verse 3, Joseph is told that once he becomes aware of the law of celestial marriage, he will be held accountable to obey it.

3 Therefore, **prepare thy heart to receive and obey the instructions which I am about to give unto you**; for **all those who have this law** [*the law of celestial marriage*] **revealed unto them must obey the same**.

4 For behold, I reveal unto you **a new and an everlasting covenant**; and **if ye abide not** [*do not enter into and obey*] **that covenant, then are ye damned** [*stopped in progression as far as exaltation is concerned*]; for no one can reject this covenant and be permitted to enter into my glory.

President Spencer W. Kimball defined the phrase "new and everlasting covenant" **as used in verse 4**, above, **as celestial marriage**. He said (**bold** added for emphasis):

"Though relatively few people in this world understand it, **the new and everlasting covenant is the marriage ordinance in the holy temple** by the properly constituted leaders who hold the genuine, authoritative keys. This glorious blessing is available to men and women on this earth" ("Temples and Eternal Marriage," *Ensign*, August 1974, 5).

Elder Marcus B. Nash of the Seventy further expanded our knowledge of the meaning of "**the new and everlasting covenant**" to include marriage and all other ordinances of the restored gospel.

"The new and everlasting covenant 'is the sum total of all gospel covenants and obligations' [Joseph Fielding Smith, *Doctrines of Salvation*, comp. Bruce R. McConkie (1955), 1:156] given anciently [see Jeremiah 32:40; D&C 22:1] and again restored to the earth in these latter days. . . . Because the covenant has been restored in the last dispensation of time, it is 'new,' and because it spans all eternity [see D&C 132:7], it is 'everlasting.'

"In the scriptures the Lord speaks of both 'the' new and everlasting covenant and 'a' new and everlasting covenant. For example, in Doctrine and Covenants 22:1, He refers to baptism as 'a new and an everlasting covenant, even that which was from the beginning.' In Doctrine and Covenants 132:4, He likewise refers to eternal marriage as 'a new and an everlasting covenant.' When He speaks of 'a' new and everlasting covenant, He is speaking of one of the many covenants encompassed by His gospel.

"When the Lord speaks generally of 'the' new and everlasting covenant, He is speaking of the fulness of the gospel of Jesus Christ, which embraces all ordinances and covenants necessary for the salvation and exaltation of mankind. Neither baptism nor eternal marriage is 'the' new and everlasting covenant; rather, they are each parts of the whole" ("The New and Everlasting Covenant," *Ensign*, Dec. 2015, 42–43).

5 For **all who will have a blessing at my hands shall abide the law which was appointed** [*established*] **for that blessing** [*as stated in D&C 130:20–21*], and the conditions thereof, as were instituted from before the foundation of the world [*before the world was created; in other words, in premortality*].

Doctrine
Celestial marriage is required for exaltation.

6 **And as pertaining to the new and everlasting covenant**, it **was instituted for the fulness of my glory** [*in other words, for exaltation*]; and **he that receiveth a fulness thereof must and shall abide the law** [*of celestial marriage*], **or he shall be damned** [*stopped, held back from the highest blessings*], **saith the Lord God.**

Doctrine
All ordinances must be ratified and sealed by the Holy Ghost (the Holy Spirit of promise) in order to be valid in the next life.

7 And verily I say unto you, that **the conditions of this law** [*the rules that apply to the law of celestial marriage*] **are these: All covenants, contracts, bonds, obligations, oaths, vows, performances, connections, associations, or expectations**, that are **not made and entered into and sealed by the Holy Spirit of promise** [*the Holy Ghost, who was promised by the Savior to come upon His Apostles*], **of him who is anointed** [*by authorized priesthood holders*], **both as well for time and for all eternity, and that too most holy, by revelation and commandment through the medium of mine anointed** [*under the direction of the living Prophet who holds and exercises all the priesthood keys*], **whom I have appointed on the earth to hold this power (and I have appointed unto my servant Joseph to hold this power in the last days, and there is never but one on the earth at a time on whom this power and the keys of

this priesthood are conferred), **are of no efficacy, virtue, or force in and after the resurrection from the dead;** for **all contracts that are not made unto this end** [*not performed by proper authority and not sealed by the Holy Ghost*] **have an end when men are dead.**

> The phrase "there is never but one on the earth at a time on whom this power and the keys of this priesthood are conferred," in verse 7, above, bears added explanation.
>
> At the present time, we have fifteen Apostles. They are the three members of the First Presidency and the twelve members of the Quorum of the Twelve Apostles. Each of them was given all the priesthood keys at the time he was ordained an Apostle and set apart as a member of the Twelve.
>
> However, only the prophet himself is authorized to exercise all of these priesthood keys (as stated in one of the temple recommend interview questions). The others hold them, but they are, in effect, latent, until if and when he becomes the Prophet, the President of the Church.
>
> The Prophet, in his position of holding and exercising all the priesthood keys, may delegate to any other member of the First Presidency or the Twelve, as well as to any other man who holds the proper priesthood, the privilege and responsibility of performing specific priesthood ordinances. Thus, temple sealers are authorized to perform celestial marriages and sealings in holy temples.
>
> In verses 8–14, the Savior explains that there is to be no confusion on this and other issues because His "house is a house of order." In other words, He operates according to laws and rules; therefore, we can trust Him completely and can rely on salvation if we follow the rules.

8 Behold, **mine house is a house of order**, saith the Lord God, and not a house of confusion.

9 Will I accept of an offering, saith the Lord, that is not made in my name?

10 Or will I receive at your hands that which I have not appointed?

11 And will I appoint unto you, saith the Lord, except it be by law, even as I and my Father ordained unto you, before the world was?

12 **I am the Lord thy God; and I give unto you this commandment—that no man shall come unto the Father but by me or by my word, which is my law, saith the Lord.**

Doctrine

All ordinances not authorized by God or His authorized

servants, regardless of who authorized or performed them, are not valid in the next life.

13 And **everything that is in the world**, whether it be ordained [*authorized*] of men, by thrones, or principalities, or powers, or things of name, whatsoever they may be, that are **not by me or by my word**, saith the Lord, shall be thrown down, and **shall not remain after men are dead**, neither in nor after the resurrection, saith the Lord your God.

14 For **whatsoever things remain** [*are valid in eternity*] **are by me** [*are those things done by proper priesthood authority*]; and whatsoever things are not by me shall be shaken and destroyed.

Doctrine

All marriages not performed by proper priesthood authority for time and all eternity are not valid in eternity.

15 Therefore, **if a man marry him a wife in the world** [*during this mortal life*], and he marry her **not by me nor by my word**, and he covenant with her so long as he is in the world and she with him, **their covenant and marriage are not of force when they are dead**, and when they are out of the world; therefore, **they are not bound** [*together as husband and wife*] **by any law when they are out of the world**.

16 **Therefore**, when they are out of the world **they** neither marry nor are given in marriage; but **are appointed angels in heaven** [*the celestial kingdom*], which angels are ministering servants, **to minister for those who are worthy of a far more, and an exceeding, and an eternal weight of glory** [*as gods in family units forever*].

Did you notice the great difference between exaltation and even the other two categories in the celestial kingdom, as pointed out in verse 16, above? This is certainly another reminder that it is more than worth every effort to attain celestial exaltation.

17 **For these angels did not abide my law** [*did not keep the law of celestial marriage*]; **therefore, they cannot be enlarged** [*procreate, have children; have the power and privilege of increasing power and dominion as gods eternally*], **but remain separately and singly, without exaltation**, in their saved condition, **to all eternity**; and from henceforth [*from then on*] **are not gods, but are angels of God forever and ever.**

Question

What if a faithful person wanted to marry in the temple but did not have a valid opportunity to do so during mortality?

Also, what if a faithful member did marry in the temple, but due to circumstances beyond the individual's control, the marriage did not work out?

Answer

In the postmortal spirit world, such individuals will be given a completely fair opportunity to meet and choose an eternal companion whom they can love and respect. Then, mortal proxies will perform the sealing for them in a temple during the Millennium. Thus, by the time of the final judgment, they will have kept the law of celestial marriage and can be judged worthy of exaltation.

President Spencer W. Kimball addressed this concern as follows:

"To you we say this: You are making a great contribution to the world as you serve your families and the Church and the world. You must remember that the Lord loves you and the Church loves you. To you women, we can only say we have no control over the heartbeats or the affections of men, but pray that you may find fulfillment. And in the meantime, we promise you that insofar as eternity is concerned, no soul will be deprived of rich and high and eternal blessings for anything which that person could not help, that the Lord never fails in his promises, and that every righteous person will receive eventually all to which the person is entitled and which he or she has not forfeited through any fault of his or her own. We encourage both men and women to keep themselves well-groomed, well-dressed, abreast of the times, attractive mentally, spiritually, physically, and especially morally, and then they can lean heavily upon the Lord's promises for these heavenly blessings" ("The Importance of Celestial Marriage," *Ensign*, October 1979, 5).

In verse 18, next, the Savior repeats what He has said above, emphasizing that even if the wording of a ceremony says "for time and for all eternity," it is still not valid unless performed by proper priesthood authority and then sealed by the Holy Ghost. He also explains that it cannot be received after the world is finished up, meaning after the earth has become a celestial planet (see D&C 130:9), and there are no more mortals upon it who can serve as proxies for work for the dead.

18 And **again**, verily I say unto you, **if a man marry a wife, and make a covenant with her for time and for all eternity,** if that covenant is **not by me or by my word** [*not according to the laws of*

the gospel], which is **my law, and is not sealed by the Holy Spirit of promise, through him whom I have anointed and appointed unto this power** [*under the direction of the keys held by the living Prophet*], **then it is not valid** neither of force **when they are out of the world**, because they are not joined by me, saith the Lord, neither by my word; **when they are out of the world** [*after the final Judgment Day; after this world has become a celestial planet*] **it cannot be received there**, because the angels and the gods are appointed there, by whom they cannot pass; **they cannot, therefore, inherit my glory** [*exaltation*]; for my house is a house of order, saith the Lord God.

> After quoting D&C 132:13, President Spencer W. Kimball taught about the above verses as follows:
>
> "How final! How frightening! Since we know well that mortal death does not terminate our existence, since we know that we live on and on, how devastating to realize that marriage and family life, so sweet and happy in so many homes, will end with death because we fail to follow God's instructions or because we reject his word when we understand it.
>
> "It is clear in the Lord's announcement that righteous men and women will receive the due rewards of their deeds. They will not be damned in the commonly accepted terminology but will suffer many limitations and deprivations and fail to reach the highest kingdom, if they do not comply. They become ministering servants to those who complied with all laws and lived all commandments.
>
> "[The Lord] then continues concerning these excellent people who lived worthily but failed to make their contracts binding:
>
> "'For these angels did not abide my law; therefore, they cannot be enlarged, but remain separately and singly, without exaltation, in their saved condition, to all eternity; and from henceforth are not gods, but are angels of God forever and ever.' (D&C 132:17.)
>
> "How conclusive! How bounded! How limiting! And we come to realize again as it bears heavily upon us that this time, this life, this mortality is the time to prepare to meet God. How lonely and barren will be the so-called single blessedness throughout eternity! How sad to be separate and single and apart through countless ages when one could, by meeting requirements, have happy marriage for eternity in the temple by proper authority and continue on in ever-increasing joy and happiness, growth and development toward godhood....
>
> "Are you willing to jeopardize your eternities, your great continuing

happiness, your privilege to see God and dwell in his presence? For the want of investigation and study and contemplation; because of prejudice, misunderstanding, or lack of knowledge, are you willing to forego these great blessings and privileges? Are you willing to make yourself a widow for eternity or a widower for endless ages—a single, separate individual to live alone and serve others? Are you willing to give up your children when they die or when you expire, and make them orphans? Are you willing to go through eternity alone and solitary when all of the greatest joys you have ever experienced in life could be 'added upon' and accentuated, multiplied, and eternalized? Are you willing, with the Sadducees, to ignore and reject these great truths? I sincerely pray you stop today and weigh and measure and then prayerfully proceed to make your happy marriage an eternal one. Our friends, please do not ignore this call. I beg of you, open your eyes and see; unstop your ears and hear" ("Temples and Eternal Marriage," *Ensign*, August 1974, 6).

Verses 19–21, next, are one of the most powerful sets of verses in all the scriptures. In them, we are clearly taught the law of celestial marriage.

Doctrine
The law of celestial marriage.

19 And again, verily I say unto you, if a man **marry** a wife **by my word**, which is **my law**, and **by the new and everlasting covenant** [*according to the law of celestial marriage*], **and it is sealed** unto them **by the Holy Spirit of promise,** [*and it is performed*] **by him who is anointed** [*authorized*], **unto whom I have appointed this power and the keys of this priesthood** [*in other words, who has the authority to seal on earth and in heaven*]; and it shall be said unto them—Ye shall come forth in the first resurrection [*by basic definition, first resurrection means those who enter celestial glory*]; and if it be after the first resurrection, in the next resurrection [*no matter when you are resurrected*]; and **shall inherit thrones, kingdoms, principalities,** and **powers, dominions, all heights and depths** [*these are all terms that refer to gods*]—**then shall it be written in the Lamb's Book of Life** [*the record in heaven in which the names of the exalted are written—compare with D&C 88:2, Revelation 3:5; see also Bible Dictionary under "Book of Life," as well as the notes for D&C 131:5 in this study guide*], **that he shall commit no murder whereby to shed innocent blood** [*the sin against the Holy Ghost—see verse 27; in other words, if he does not commit an unpardonable sin and deeply and sincerely repents of all* other sins he commits], and **if ye abide in my covenant** [*if you keep the law of celestial marriage, keep all of the commandments, and repent of your sins*], **and commit no murder whereby to shed innocent blood, it shall be done unto them in all things** [*all the promises of celestial marriage and exaltation will be given them*] **whatsoever my servant** [*authorized priesthood holder*] **hath put upon them** [*through authorized priesthood ordinances*]**, in time, and through all eternity**; and **shall be of full force when they are out of the world**; and **they shall pass by the angels, and the gods,** which are set there [*celestial glory is not intruded upon by unauthorized entry of evil or people who are not qualified to be there*]**, to their exaltation and glory in all things**, as hath been sealed upon their heads, which glory shall be **a fulness** [*exaltation, the Father's lifestyle*] and **a continuation of the seeds** [*powers of procreation*] **forever and ever** [*having spirit children and living in the family unit forever*].

Next, in verse 20, we are clearly taught the equality of the husband and wife as they serve together as gods in their own eternal family unit.

20 **Then shall they** [*the husband and wife*] **be gods,** because they have no end [*among other things, no end of children*]; **therefore shall they be from everlasting to everlasting** [*will be doing the same thing the Father does*], because they continue; **then shall they** [*the husband and wife*] **be above all, because all things are subject unto them. Then shall they be gods, because they** [*the husband and wife*] **have all power, and the angels are subject unto them.**

Bruce R. McConkie explained verse 20, above, as follows (**bold** added for emphasis):

"If righteous men have power through the gospel and its crowning ordinance of celestial marriage to become kings and priests to rule in exaltation forever, it follows that the women by their side (without whom they cannot attain exaltation) will be queens and priestesses. (Rev. 1:6; 5:10.) Exaltation grows out of the eternal union of a man and his wife. Of those whose marriage endures in eternity, the Lord says, "Then shall they be gods" (D. & C. 132:20); that is, **each of them, the man and the woman, will be a god. As such they will rule over their dominions forever**" (*Mormon Doctrine*, 613).

21 Verily, verily, I say unto you, **except ye abide** [*keep, obey*] **my law** [*the law of celestial marriage*] **ye cannot attain to this glory** [*becoming gods, exaltation*].

22 For **strait is the gate, and narrow the way** [*the rules for exaltation are very strictly defined*] that leadeth unto the **exaltation and continuation of the lives** [*becoming gods and having children forever, in the eternal family unit, which is exaltation*], and few there be that find it, because ye receive me not in the world neither do ye know me.

23 But **if ye receive me in the world, then shall ye know me, and shall receive your exaltation**; that **where I am ye shall be also.**

> Note the difference between verse 24, next, and John 17:3.

24 **This is eternal lives** [*this is the privilege of having children forever*]—to know the only wise and true God, and Jesus Christ, whom he hath sent. I am he. Receive ye, therefore, my law.

John 17:3

3 **And this is life eternal**, that they might know thee the only true God, and Jesus Christ, whom thou hast sent.

Question

What will we do with our spirit children if we become gods and have spirit offspring forever?

Answer

We will create worlds for them and send them to them, just as our Father in Heaven has done for us.

Question

Will we use the same plan of salvation for our spirit children as is used by the Father for us?

Answer

Yes. The First Presidency explained this as follows (bold added for emphasis):

"Only resurrected and glorified beings can become parents of spirit offspring. Only such exalted souls have reached maturity in the appointed course of eternal life; and **the spirits born to them in the eternal worlds will pass in due sequence through the several stages or estates by which the glorified parents have attained exaltation**" ("1916 First Presidency Statement," *Improvement Era*, August 1916, 942).

25 **Broad is the gate, and wide the way that leadeth to the deaths** [*the end of the privilege of having children; in other words, they will not become gods and, consequently, will not be privileged to have eternal increase*]; and many there are that go in thereat, **because they receive me not, neither do they abide in my law** [*of celestial marriage*].

Joseph Fielding Smith explained verse 25, above, as follows:

"The term 'deaths' mentioned here has reference to the cutting off of all those who reject this eternal covenant of marriage and therefore they are denied the power of exaltation and the continuation of posterity. To be denied posterity and the family organization, leads to the 'deaths,' or end of increase in the life to come" (*Church History and Modern Revelation*, 2:360).

Verse 26, next, is one of the most misquoted and misunderstood of all the scriptures. Some people take it to mean that as long as a couple can somehow manage to get married in the temple, they have no further worries as far as exaltation is concerned, as long as they don't commit an unpardonable sin. We will use **bold** to suggest how such individuals read this verse.

26 Verily, verily, I say unto you, **if a man marry a wife according to my word** [*in other words, in the temple*]**,** and they are sealed by the Holy Spirit of promise, according to mine appointment, **and he or she shall commit any sin or transgression** of the new and everlasting covenant **whatever**, and all manner of blasphemies, and **if they commit no murder wherein they shed innocent blood**, yet **they shall** come forth in the first resurrection, and **enter into their exaltation**; but they shall be destroyed in the flesh, and shall be delivered unto the buffetings of Satan unto the day of redemption, saith the Lord God.

Obviously, there is something seriously wrong with the above approach leading up to verse 26! No doubt you can see that it is completely contrary to the overall context of the gospel and the scriptures. What this verse is saying is that, upon deep and thorough repentance, all but unforgivable sins can be forgiven. Therefore, if a person is guilty of extremely serious transgression, including adultery, he or she can still be forgiven, and exaltation is still available. The key issue is that deep and life-changing repentance must take place, so that the individual is a "new" person, "born again," with "a mighty change of heart."

Joseph Fielding Smith explained this aspect of verse 26 as follows:

"Verse 26, in Section 132, is the most abused passage in any scripture. The Lord has never promised any soul that he may be taken into exaltation without the spirit of repentance. While repentance is not stated in this passage, yet it is, and must be, implied. It is strange to me that everyone knows about verse 26, but it seems that they have never read or heard of Matthew 12:31–32, where the Lord tells us the same thing in substance as we find in verse 26, section 132. . . .

"So we must conclude that those spoken of in verse 26 are those who, having sinned, have fully repented and are willing to pay the price of their sinning, else the blessings of exaltation will not follow. Repentance is absolutely necessary for the forgiveness, and the person having sinned must be cleansed" (*Doctrines of Salvation*, 2:95–96).

One of the things that people sometimes forget, in verse 26, is that all celestial marriages must be "sealed by the Holy Spirit of promise," and the Holy Ghost would certainly not seal a marriage in which the spouses intentionally do not keep the other commandments of God.

Next, in verse 27, the Lord explains what the "sin against the Holy Ghost" consists of. It is unforgivable and leads to becoming a son of perdition.

27 The blasphemy against the Holy Ghost, which shall not be forgiven in the world nor out of the world, **is in that ye commit murder wherein ye shed innocent blood, and assent unto my death** [*would gladly crucify Christ if given the opportunity*]**, after ye have received my new and everlasting covenant** [*including knowing full well that the gospel is true by the power of the Holy Ghost*]**, saith the Lord God; and he that abideth not this law can in nowise enter into my glory, but shall be damned, saith the Lord.**

Bruce R. McConkie taught more about "murder, wherein ye shed innocent blood"; in other words, the sin against the Holy Ghost, as spoken of in verse 27, above. He said:

"The innocent blood is that of Christ; and those who commit blasphemy against the Holy Ghost, which is the unpardonable sin (Matt. 12:31–32), thereby 'crucify to themselves the Son of God afresh, and put him to an open shame.' (Heb. 6:6.) They are, in other words, people who would have crucified Christ, having the while a perfect knowledge that he was the Son of God" (*Doctrinal New Testament Commentary*, 3:345).

You may wish to read the notes and commentary given in this series of study guides for D&C 76:30–35 for more information about what leads to becoming sons of perdition.

Verses 28–32, next, relate back to verses 1–2 in which the Lord told Joseph that He would answer his question about Abraham and other ancient prophets regarding plural marriage. Thus far, in verses 3–27, He has revealed the law of celestial marriage itself to Joseph. As previously noted, He will give instruction about plural marriage, beginning with verse 34. In the meantime, in verse 28, next, He teaches the Prophet that the law of celestial marriage was presented as part of the plan of salvation in the premortal councils.

28 I am the Lord thy God, and will give unto thee the law of my Holy Priesthood [*the law of celestial marriage*], as **was ordained** [*established*] **by me and my Father before the world was.**

Next, in verses 29–30, Joseph is reminded that Abraham accepted all of God's laws, including the law of celestial marriage, and that this obedience has already led Abraham to exaltation. In other words, Abraham is already a god. And the promises given to him that his posterity would be innumerable are already under way toward being fulfilled.

29 Abraham received all things, whatsoever he received, by revelation and commandment, by my word, saith the Lord, **and hath entered into his exaltation and sitteth upon his throne.**

30 Abraham received promises concerning his seed [*his posterity*], and of the fruit of his loins [*his descendants*]—from whose loins ye are, namely, my servant Joseph [*Joseph Smith is a descendant of Abraham*]—**which were to continue so long as they were in the world; and as touching Abraham and his seed, out of the world they should continue** [*he would continue having children (spirit offspring—compare with Acts 17:28–29) in the next life*]; both in the world and out of the world should they continue **as innumerable as the stars; or, if ye were to count the sand upon the seashore ye could not number them.**

Next, in verses 31–33, Joseph Smith is told that he too can be exalted if he will obey the law of celestial marriage as did Abraham.

31 This promise is yours also, because ye are of Abraham, and the promise was made unto Abraham; and **by this law** [*through the law of celestial marriage, by which we can indeed become like God*] **is the continuation of the works of my Father, wherein he glorifieth himself** [*in other words, it is through bringing His spirit children to the point of becoming gods like He is and having worlds of their own that the Father increases in glory and dominion—compare to Moses 1:39*].

32 Go ye, therefore, and **do the works of Abraham** [*be obedient in all things like Abraham was*]; **enter ye into my law** [*enter into celestial marriage*] **and ye shall be saved** [*exalted, like Abraham is*].

The phrase "do the works of Abraham," in verse 32, above, is explained in the *Doctrine and*

Covenants Student Manual as follows:

"This is not a commandment to engage in plural marriage (that commandment is given [to Joseph Smith] in verses 34 through 37) but rather a commandment for the Saints to receive the covenants and commandments of God in the same faith and righteousness as Abraham did" (*Doctrine and Covenants Student Manual*, 1981, 332).

33 But if ye enter not into my law [*celestial marriage*] ye cannot receive the promise of my Father, which he made unto Abraham [*in other words, you cannot attain exaltation*].

Verses 34–66
Plural Marriage

As stated several times in the notes and commentary for verses 3–33, the explanation of plural marriage requested by Joseph Smith (according to verses 1–2) began with the Lord's teaching the Prophet the law of celestial marriage in verses 3–33.

Now, having done that, the Savior will answer the specific question regarding why it was approved by the Lord for Abraham and other ancient prophets to have more than one wife.

Before we go farther with this topic, we will quote Bruce R. McConkie, wherein he teaches that plural marriage is not required for exaltation.

"Plural marriage is not essential to salvation or exaltation. Nephi and his people were denied the power to have more than one wife [*see Jacob 2:27*] and yet they could gain every blessing in eternity that the Lord ever offered to any people. In our day, the Lord summarized by revelation the whole doctrine of exaltation and predicated it upon the marriage of one man to one woman. (D. & C. 132:1–28.) Thereafter he added the principles relative to plurality of wives with the express stipulation that any such marriages would be valid only if authorized by the President of the Church (D. & C. 132:7, 29–66.)" (*Mormon Doctrine*, 578).

Now, to the Lord's answer to the Prophet's question about plural marriage.

By way of review, remember that Abraham and Sarah were not able to have children for many years (Isaac was finally born to them when Abraham was a hundred years old and Sarah was ninety—see Genesis 21:1–5). Abraham had been promised that his posterity would be great (see Genesis 12:2), but the years came and went with no child. Finally, when Abraham was eighty-five, Sarah requested that he marry her servant, Hagar, and have children for them. This was according to the custom of the day (Genesis 16:1–3).

Consequently, a son, Ishmael (see Genesis 16:11) was born to them.

This comes into play, now, as the Lord explains plural marriage to Joseph Smith.

34 God commanded Abraham, and Sarah gave Hagar to Abraham to wife. And why did she do it? Because this was the law; and from Hagar sprang many people. This, therefore, was fulfilling, among other things, the promises.

35 Was Abraham, therefore, under condemnation? Verily I say unto you, **Nay; for I, the Lord, commanded it.**

Next, the Lord teaches Joseph a principle; namely, that whatever He commands is right, regardless of any other issues involved.

36 Abraham was commanded to offer his son Isaac; nevertheless [*even though*], **it was written: Thou shalt not kill** [*one of the Ten Commandments—see Exodus 20:13*]. **Abraham, however, did not refuse,** and **it was accounted unto him for righteousness** [*Abraham was given credit for being obedient*].

Verse 37, next, informs us that Abraham, Isaac, and Jacob have already become gods. This, of course, means that their righteous wives have likewise attained their exaltation (compare with verses 19–20).

The Lord is illustrating to Joseph Smith the principle that obedience to God's commands brings exaltation.

37 Abraham received concubines [*legally married secondary wives according to the customs of the day*], and **they bore him children; and it was accounted unto him for righteousness, because** they were given unto him, and **he abode in my law**; as **Isaac also and Jacob** did none other things than that which they were commanded; and **because they did none other things than that which they were commanded, they have entered into their exaltation**, according to the promises, and sit upon thrones, **and are not angels but are gods.**

Next, in verse 38, the Lord uses David and others as examples of those who were authorized to practice plural marriage, with the caution that it must be authorized by Him; otherwise, it is sin.

38 David also received many wives and concubines, and **also Solomon and Moses** my servants, as **also many others** of my servants, from the beginning of creation until this time; and

in nothing did they sin save in those things which they received not of me.

In verse 39, next, King David is used as an example of one who started out faithful but who lost his exaltation through disobedience.

By way of quick review before studying verse 39, it is helpful to recall that Uriah was Bathsheba's husband. While Uriah was away in the army serving the King faithfully, King David pursued an illicit relationship with Bathsheba, resulting in her being with child. In an attempt to cover up his adultery, David commanded Uriah to come home on leave from the army, obviously in the hopes that it would appear that Uriah was the father of Bathsheba's child.

David's plot did not work. Uriah would not go home while his men were giving their lives on the battlefield. Consequently, King David commanded that Uriah be placed in battle where he would be killed. He was (see 2 Samuel 11:2–17). Thus, David attempted to cover up a forgivable sin, adultery, with murder.

In verse 39, next, the Lord tells what happened to David as a result.

39 **David's wives and concubines were given unto him of me** [were authorized by the Lord], **by the hand of Nathan** [an Old Testament prophet—see 2 Samuel 7:2], my servant, **and others** of the prophets **who had the keys of this power;** and **in none of these things did he sin against me save** [except] **in the case of Uriah and his wife** [Bathsheba]; and, **therefore he hath fallen from his exaltation**, and received his portion [punishment]; and **he shall not inherit them** [his wives] **out of the world** [in the next life], **for I gave them unto another**, saith the Lord.

As you can see from verse 39, above, David has tragically "fallen from his exaltation."

We must be extremely careful not to misinterpret the phrase "I gave them unto another," in verse 39, above, to mean that David's wives, who were worthy of exaltation, are treated as mere property without consideration of their feelings on the matter of being eternal mates.

This is one of those cases where we must look at the larger context of the scriptures and the words of the brethren for correct understanding. From them, we know that individual agency is always respected by God. Thus, we know that in exaltation, each spouse, whether husband or wife, will be in that eternal relationship by agency choice. And we can with full confidence apply this principle to David's worthy wives. It will be interesting someday to meet them and see whom they chose to marry for eternity.

In verse 40, next, the Savior encourages Joseph to keep asking questions.

40 I am the Lord thy God, and I gave unto thee, my servant Joseph, an appointment, and restore all things [*the Lord called Joseph Smith to be the Prophet of the Restoration*]. **Ask what ye will, and it shall be given unto you according to my word.**

As we read verses 41–45, next, it is apparent that the Prophet had asked whether people involved in plural marriage were committing adultery as far as the laws of God are concerned. The answer is clearly that plural marriage, when approved by God, is not adultery. But violating the marriage covenant through illicit sex does constitute adultery and brings spiritual destruction.

41 And as ye have asked concerning adultery, verily, verily, I say unto you, **if a man receiveth a wife in the new and everlasting covenant** [*if a man and his wife are married for time and eternity*], **and if she be with another man,** and I have not appointed unto her by the holy anointing, **she hath committed adultery and shall be destroyed** [*spiritually—compare with D&C 42:23 which tells us that lustful thinking drives the Spirit away*].

Next, we are informed that anyone who is unfaithful to his or her spouse, whether married in the temple or having a civil marriage, is guilty of adultery.

42 If she be not in the new and everlasting covenant, and she be with another man, she has committed adultery.

43 And **if her husband be with another woman**, and he was under a vow, **he hath** broken his vow and hath **committed adultery.**

44 And **if she** [*referring to the man's wife in verse 43, above, whose husband has been unfaithful*] **hath not committed adultery**, but is innocent and hath not broken her vow, and she knoweth it, and I reveal it unto you, my servant Joseph, then shall you have power, by the power of my Holy Priesthood, to take her and give her unto him that hath not committed adultery but hath been faithful [*in other words, the doctrine here is that a man or a woman can be sealed to someone else in the temple if his or her marriage is broken up because of unfaithfulness on the part of the spouse*]; for he shall be made ruler over many.

The doctrine taught in verse 44, above, is an important insight into a correct understanding of Matthew 5:32, which, if misunderstood, could lead one to believe that to marry a divorced person is committing adultery. Obviously, worthy individuals whose marriage was broken up by adultery may marry worthily in the temple.

Next, Joseph is taught more about the sealing power.

45 For I have conferred upon you the keys and power of the priesthood, wherein I restore all things, and make known unto you all things in due time.

46 And verily, verily, I say unto you, that whatsoever you seal on earth shall be sealed in heaven; and whatsoever you bind on earth, in my name and by my word, saith the Lord, it shall be eternally bound in the heavens; and **whosoever sins you remit on earth shall be remitted eternally in the heavens; and whosoever sins you retain on earth shall be retained in heaven.**

We know that ultimately God is the only one who can forgive sins. Bruce R. McConkie explained verse 46, above, as follows:

"Revelation from the Lord is always required to retain or remit sins. Since God is the one who must cleanse and purify a human soul, the use of his priestly powers to do so must be authorized and approved by him, and this approval comes by revelation from his Holy Spirit. In many cases in this dispensation the Lord by revelation announced that the sins of certain persons were forgiven. (D. & C. 60:7; 61:2; 62:3; 64:3.) Accordingly, if by revelation he should tell his apostles to act for him, using his power which is priesthood, and to thus retain or remit sins, they would do so, and their acts would in effect be his. See Matt. 16:13–20; 17:1–9; 18:18.

"This same apostolic power is always found in the true Church, and hence we find the Lord saying to Joseph Smith: 'I have conferred upon you the keys and power of the priesthood, . . . and whosesoever sins you remit on earth shall be remitted eternally in the heavens; and whosesoever sins you retain on earth shall be retained in heaven' (D. & C. 132:45–46.)" (*Doctrinal New Testament Commentary*, 1:857–58).

Continuing, the Master gives additional examples of the sealing power which He has restored through Joseph Smith.

47 And again, verily I say, **whomsoever you bless I will bless, and whomsoever you curse I will curse**, saith the Lord; for I, the Lord, am thy God.

48 And again, verily I say unto you, my servant Joseph, that

whatsoever you give on earth, and **to whomsoever you give** [*in marriage*] **any one on earth, by my word and according to my law** [*in compliance with the gospel and the sealing power of the priesthood*], **it shall be visited with blessings and not cursings** [*in other words, it is approved by God*], and with my power, saith the Lord, **and shall be without condemnation on earth and in heaven.**

> Next, in verse 49, the Lord seals the Prophet Joseph Smith up to exaltation. In other words, his calling and election is made sure. And in verse 50, He gives the reasons that this blessing can come upon Joseph at this time.

49 For I am the Lord thy God, and will be with thee even unto the end of the world, and through all eternity; for verily **I seal upon you your exaltation**, and prepare a throne for you in the kingdom of my Father, with Abraham your father [*Joseph's ancestor, who has already received his exaltation—see verses 29 and 37*].

50 Behold, **I have seen your sacrifices**, and will forgive all your sins; **I have seen your sacrifices in obedience** to that which I have told you. Go, **therefore, and I make a way for your escape, as I accepted the offering of Abraham of his son Isaac.**

> As far as the next several verses are concerned, there is much more that we do not know than there is that we do know. We will have to wait for further clarification. When it comes to verse 51, for example, we do not know what the test was. All we know is that they passed the test.

51 Verily, I say unto you: **A commandment I give unto mine handmaid, Emma Smith,** your wife, whom I have given unto you, **that she stay herself and partake not of that which I commanded you to offer unto her** [*stop and do not go ahead with whatever it was that the Lord asked her to do*]; for **I did it, saith the Lord, to prove you all, as I did Abraham**, and that I might require an offering at your hand, by covenant and sacrifice.

> Verses 52–54 briefly summarize the fact that Joseph Smith practiced plural marriage.

52 And **let mine handmaid, Emma Smith, receive all those** [*wives*] **that have been given unto my servant Joseph**, and who are virtuous and pure before me; and those who are not pure, and have said they were pure, shall be destroyed [*spiritually*], saith the Lord God.

53 For I am the Lord thy God, and ye shall obey my voice; and **I give unto my servant Joseph that he shall be made ruler over many things; for he hath been faithful over a few things, and from henceforth I will strengthen him.**

54 And **I command mine handmaid, Emma Smith, to abide and cleave unto my servant Joseph**, and to none else. But if she will not abide [*keep*] this commandment she shall be destroyed [*spiritually as far as exaltation is concerned*], saith the Lord; for I am the Lord thy God, and will destroy her if she abide not in my law.

Occasionally, you may run into claims that Joseph Smith did not participate in plural marriage and that Emma Smith made statements to that effect. President Wilford Woodruff discussed these claims. He said:

"Emma Smith, the widow of the Prophet, is said to have maintained to her dying moments that her husband had nothing to do with the patriarchal order of marriage, but that it was Brigham Young that got that up. I bear record before God, angels and men that Joseph Smith received that revelation, and I bear record that Emma Smith gave her husband in marriage to several women while he was living, some of whom are to-day living in this city, and some may be present in this congregation, and who, if called upon, would confirm my words. But lo and behold, we hear of publication after publication now-a-days, declaring that Joseph Smith had nothing to do with these things. Joseph Smith himself organized every endowment in our Church and revealed the same to the Church, and he lived to receive every key of the Aaronic and Melchizedek priesthoods from the hands of the men who held them while in the flesh, and who hold them in eternity" (in *Journal of Discourses*, 23:131).

55 But **if she will not abide this commandment, then shall my servant Joseph do all things for her** [*keep his commitments to her*], even as he hath said; **and I will bless him and multiply him and give unto him an hundredfold in this world** [*in other words, many blessings—compare with Mark 10:29–30*], **of fathers and mothers, brothers and sisters, houses and lands, wives and children, and crowns of eternal lives** [*exaltation*] **in the eternal worlds.**

Next, we see a gentle and tender lesson on what forgiving others can do for us personally, including receiving blessings that will enable us to overcome obstacles to our individual happiness.

56 And again, verily I say, **let mine handmaid** [*Emma Smith*] **forgive my servant Joseph his trespasses**; and **then shall she be forgiven her trespasses**, wherein she has trespassed against me; and **I, the Lord thy God, will bless her**, and **multiply her**, and make **her heart to rejoice**.

> We do not know what "property" is being referred to in verse 57.

57 And again, I say, let not my servant Joseph put his property out of his hands, lest an enemy come and destroy him; for Satan seeketh to destroy; for I am the Lord thy God, and he is my servant; and behold, and lo, I am with him, as I was with Abraham, thy father, even unto his exaltation and glory.

> Next, the Savior reminds the Prophet that there are yet many things for him to learn (verse 58). Among other things, the Master reviews again the fact that if the Lord gives a commandment, it becomes the right thing to do, no matter what is written elsewhere (verse 59). If we fail to understand this principle, we could easily go into apostasy.
>
> For example, there were many instances in the Book of Mormon where individuals and peoples were told by the Lord not to retaliate against their enemies, such as when Alma told his people to surrender to Amulon and the Lamanites (Mosiah 23:29). However, Captain Moroni rallied the Nephites to fight against their enemies (Alma 46:12–21). It was not sin to surrender, and it was not sin to fight, because in both cases it was the commandment of the Lord through His authorized servant in that particular situation.

58 **Now, as touching the law of the priesthood, there are many things pertaining thereunto**.

59 Verily, **if a man be called of my Father**, as was Aaron [*in other words, by proper authority*], by mine own voice, and by the voice of him that sent me, and I have endowed him with the keys of the power of this priesthood, **if he do anything in my name, and according to my law and by my word, he will not commit sin**, and I will justify him.

60 **Let no one, therefore, set on my servant Joseph** [*accuse Joseph Smith of being a fallen prophet*]; **for I will justify** [*support and uphold*] **him**; for **he shall do the sacrifice which I require at his hands for his transgressions** [*Joseph had to repent as needed—for example, after the loss of the 116 manuscript pages (see D&C 3 and 10)—just like everyone else has to in order to be forgiven*], saith the Lord your God.

Perhaps you have heard that before a man could enter into a plural marriage authorized by the Lord through the Prophet, the consent of his first wife was required. This is found in verse 61, next.

61 And again, **as pertaining to the law of the priesthood** [*as it applies to the principle of plural marriage*]—if any man espouse [*marry*] a virgin, and desire to espouse another, and **the first give her consent**, and if he espouse the second, and they are virgins, and have vowed to no other man, then is he justified; he cannot commit adultery for they are given unto him; for he cannot commit adultery with that that belongeth unto him and to no one else.

62 And **if he have ten virgins given unto him by this law** [*the law of the priesthood—see verse 61*]**, he cannot commit adultery** [*the answer to the basic question asked by Joseph—see verses 1–2, 34–35*], for they belong to him, and they are given unto him; therefore is he justified [*he is not committing sin, adultery*].

63 But **if one or either** [*any*] **of the ten virgins, after she is espoused** [*married*]**, shall be with another man, she has committed adultery**, and shall be destroyed [*spiritually*]; for they are given unto him to multiply and replenish the earth, according to my commandment, and to fulfil the promise which was given by my Father before the foundation of the world [*in premortality*], and for their exaltation in the eternal worlds, that they may bear the souls of men [*motherhood is an eternal privilege only for those who attain exaltation*]; for **herein** [*giving spirits the opportunity to attain immortality and eternal life—Moses 1:39*] **is the work of my Father continued**, that he may be glorified.

64 And again, verily, verily, I say unto you, **if any man** have a wife, **who holds the keys of this power**, and he **teaches unto her the law of my priesthood**, as pertaining to these things, then shall she believe and administer unto him, or she shall be destroyed [*spiritually*], saith the Lord your God; for I will destroy her [*probably by withdrawing His Spirit, as is the case anytime we break a commandment*]; for I will magnify my name upon all those who receive and abide in my law.

65 Therefore, it shall be lawful in me, **if she receive not this law**, for him to receive all things whatsoever I, the Lord his God, will give unto him, because she did not believe and administer

unto him according to my word; and **she then becomes the transgressor**; and **he is exempt from the law of Sarah** [*plural marriage*], who administered unto Abraham according to the law when I commanded Abraham to take Hagar to wife.

66 And now, **as pertaining to this law** [*concerning plural marriage*], verily, verily, I say unto you, **I will reveal more unto you, hereafter; therefore, let this suffice for the present**. Behold, I am Alpha and Omega [*Jesus Christ*]. Amen.

SECTION 133

Background

This revelation was given through the Prophet Joseph Smith on November 3, 1831, at Hiram, Ohio, about 15 miles southeast of Kirtland.

As you can see, this section is not placed in the Doctrine and Covenants in chronological order. In fact, it was given during the same conference of the Church at which section one was given. The conference was convened to consider details of publishing the Book of Commandments, which was a collection of several revelations received by the Prophet up to that time. The Book of Commandments was the predecessor to the Doctrine and Covenants.

Joseph Smith gave some background for this section. He recorded:

"It had been decided by the conference that Elder Oliver Cowdery should carry [*copies of*] the commandments and revelations to Independence, Missouri, for printing, and that I should arrange and get them in readiness by the time that he left, which was to be by—or, if possible, before—the 15th of the month [November]. At this time there were many things which the Elders desired to know relative to preaching the Gospel to the inhabitants of the earth, and concerning the gathering; and in order to walk by the true light, and be instructed from on high, on the 3rd of November, 1831, I inquired of the Lord and received the following important revelation [section 133], which has since been added to the book of Doctrine and Covenants, and called the Appendix" (*History of the Church*, 1:229).

Thus, section 1 is the Lord's preface, and section 133 is the Lord's appendix to the Doctrine and Covenants. In effect, these two sections are bookends to the sections between them.

Section 133 contains an unusually large number of major scriptural references and concepts that assume that the reader is already familiar with many scriptural terms and passages. For example, "Go ye out from Babylon" (verse 5) means to flee sin and evil. "Go forth to meet the Bridegroom" (verse 10) means to prepare to meet the Savior. "He that goeth, let him not look back" (verse 15), referring to Lot's wife and her turning into a pillar of salt, means that once you have made commitments to follow Christ, don't look wistfully back at your old worldly lifestyle. Thus, when a familiar scriptural word or phrase is mentioned in this revelation, it brings up a whole concept and message with just a few words.

In fact, if you become familiar with the words and phrases used by the Savior in this revelation, you will be better equipped to understand much more as you read and study the scriptures and the words of Church leaders throughout your life. We will list twenty of them here. You may wish to see how many of them you already understand before we define them in context as we proceed with this section.

1. "Shall suddenly come to his temple" (verse 2).

2. "He shall make bare his holy arm" (verse 3).

3. "Sanctify yourselves" (verse 4).

4. "Go ye out from Babylon" (verse 5).

5. "Be ye clean that bear the vessels of the Lord" (verse 5).

6. "Awake and arise and go forth to meet the Bridegroom" (verse 10).

7. "He that goeth, let him not look back" (verse 15).

8. "Prepare ye the way of the Lord, and make his paths straight" (verse 17).

9. "Having his Father's name written on their foreheads" (verse 18).

10. "And he shall utter his voice out of Zion, and he shall speak from Jerusalem" (verse 21).

11. "Their enemies shall become a prey unto them" (verse 28).

12. "Living water" (verse 29).

13. "Children of Ephraim" (verse 30).

14. "Crowned with glory" (verse 32).

15. "Who is this that cometh down from God in heaven with dyed garments?" (verse 46).

16. "Their blood have I sprinkled upon my garments, and stained all my raiment" (verse 51).

17. "This was the day of vengeance which was in my heart" (verse 51).

18. "Stand on the right hand of the Lamb" (verse 56).

19. "They shall sing the song of the Lamb, day and night forever and ever" (verse 56).

20. "It shall leave them neither root nor branch" (verse 64).

We will define these phrases in context as we study this section verse by verse.

This section is a call from the Savior to the Saints to come unto Him, to repent and separate themselves from the evil ways of the world, to spread the gospel, and to prepare to meet Him. Among other things, He teaches them about the lost ten tribes (verses 26–33), why He will wear red at His Coming (verses 46–51), the first resurrection at the time of His resurrection (verses 54–55), the resurrection of the righteous (verse 56), His purposes for restoring the gospel (verses 57–61), the destruction of the wicked at His coming (verse 64), and the destiny of those who continue to reject Him (verses 65–73).

The Savior begins by requesting the Saints' attention and introducing Himself.

1 **HEARKEN**, O ye people of my church, saith the Lord your God, and **hear the word of the Lord concerning you**—

2 The Lord **who shall suddenly come to his temple** [*can be a reference to the Second Coming—see heading to Malachi 3, but can also be a reference to other appearances of the Savior prior to the Second Coming*]; the Lord **who shall come down upon the world with a curse** [*punishment*] **to judgment**; yea, **upon all the nations that forget God**, and **upon all the ungodly** [*the wicked*] **among you.**

3 For **he shall make bare his holy arm** [*will demonstrate His power; "arm" is symbolic of power in biblical symbolism*] **in the eyes of all the nations** [*it will be obvious that there is a God to those who are willing to see*], and **all the ends of the earth shall see the salvation of their God** [*salvation will be made available to all people on earth*].

4 Wherefore, **prepare ye, prepare ye**, O my people; **sanctify yourselves** [*come unto Christ and become pure, clean, fit to be in the presence of God*]; **gather ye together,** O ye people of my church, **upon the land of Zion** [*gather in Missouri*], **all you that have not been commanded to tarry** [*to stay in the Kirtland, Ohio, area*].

5 **Go ye out from Babylon** [*flee from evil and wickedness; do not join in the wickedness of the world*]. **Be ye clean that bear the vessels of the Lord** [*be clean and pure in heart as members of the Church and holders of the priesthood*].

6 Call your **solemn assemblies** [*sacred meetings attended by invitation by those who wish to keep God's commandments and separate themselves from the evil ways of the world; these include temple dedications and sustaining a new First Presidency of the Church*], and **speak often one to another.** And **let every man call upon the name of the Lord.**

7 Yea, verily I say unto you again, the time has come when the voice of the Lord is unto you: **Go ye out of Babylon** [*separate yourselves from the wickedness of the world*]; **gather ye out from among the nations,** from the four winds [*from every direction*], from one end of heaven to the other.

> Next, the Savior instructs the Church to send missionaries to preach to all the world. He commands that the gospel is to be taken first to the Gentiles (in this context, it means everyone except the Jews), and then to the Jews.
>
> Currently, we are in the stage of missionary work referred to as the "times of the Gentiles," meaning that the gospel is now to be taken to everyone except the Jews. We have not yet been allowed to make an all-out effort to take the gospel to the Jews. It is one of the "signs of the times" that is yet to be fulfilled.

8 **Send forth the elders of my church unto the nations** which are afar off; **unto the islands of the sea**; send forth **unto foreign lands**; call upon all nations, **first** upon **the Gentiles**, and **then** upon **the Jews.**

9 And behold, and lo, **this shall be their cry** [*the missionaries' message*], and **the voice of the Lord unto all people**: Go ye forth unto the land of Zion [*gather to Zion— literally to Missouri, at the time of this revelation; in our day, it means gathering to the stakes of Zion throughout the world*], that the borders of my people may be enlarged, and that her stakes may be strengthened, and **that Zion may go forth** unto the regions round about.

10 Yea, **let the cry** [*message*] **go forth among all people: Awake and arise and go forth to meet the Bridegroom** [*prepare to meet the Savior; a reference to the parable of the ten virgins in Matthew 25:1–13*]; behold and lo, **the Bridegroom cometh** [*the Second Coming is getting close*]; go ye out to meet him. **Prepare yourselves for the great day of the Lord.**

> There are still people in and out of the Church who claim to be able to pinpoint the time of the Second Coming with

considerable accuracy. Verse 11, next, is yet another reminder not to join with them in their false claims.

11 **Watch** [*be constantly prepared by living righteously*], therefore, **for ye know neither the day nor the hour.**

> As mentioned earlier, there are two major gatherings in the last days prior to the Second Coming. We see these in verses 12 and 13, next. First, the Gentiles are to be gathered to the gospel. While this is happening, the Jews are to be gathered to the Holy Land. Then, when the time is right, they will be converted to the Savior in large numbers.

12 **Let them, therefore, who are among the Gentiles flee unto Zion** [*let the non-Jewish converts gather to Zion*].

13 And **let them who be of Judah** [*the Jews*] **flee unto Jerusalem** [*gather to Jerusalem, the Holy Land*], unto the mountains of the Lord's house.

> Babylon is defined for us in verse 14, next.

14 Go ye out from among the nations, even from **Babylon**, from the midst of **wickedness**, which is **spiritual Babylon.**

> By the way, the term "*Babylon*," as used here, comes from the ancient wicked city of Babylon located where modern-day Iraq now is. It was a stronghold of evil and unrighteousness. The city itself was surrounded by 56 miles of walls that were 335 feet high and 85 feet wide (see Bible Dictionary under "Babylon"). It looked to be completely invincible, much the same as Satan's kingdom does to some today. It fell completely. Such will also be the case with the devil's kingdom at the Second Coming.

> Next, the Master reminds the Saints that their gathering is to be undertaken with wisdom and order.

15 But verily, thus saith the Lord, **let not your flight be in haste, but let all things be prepared before you;** and **he that goeth, let him not look back** lest sudden destruction shall come upon him.

> The phrase "he that goeth, let him not look back" is a reference to Lot's wife in the Old Testament. As Lot and his family fled the evil city of Sodom, they were instructed by the Lord not to look back, but his wife did and became a pillar of salt (see Genesis 19:26). We may assume that she looked back longingly at the lifestyle they were abandoning. Thus, to "look back" after an individual has been baptized and become active in the Church, has been sealed in the temple and had children, etc. is symbolic of wishing to participate in some of the evils

and temptations that must be left behind when covenants are made with God.

Next, the Lord emphasizes a major part of the missionary message to all the world.

16 Hearken and hear, O ye inhabitants of the earth. Listen, ye elders of my church together [*in harmony one with another*], and hear the voice of the Lord; for **he calleth upon all men**, and **he commandeth all men everywhere to repent.**

17 For behold, **the Lord God hath sent forth the angel crying through the midst of heaven** [*as prophesied in Revelation 14:6–7; in other words, we are in the last days*], saying: **Prepare ye the way of the Lord, and make his paths straight** [*repent and go straight forward in righteousness*], for the hour of his coming is nigh—

> The 144,000 mentioned in verse 18, next, are high priests, 12,000 out of each tribe of Israel, who will "administer the everlasting gospel" and "bring as many as will come to the church of the Firstborn" (see D&C 77:11).

18 When the Lamb [*Christ*] shall stand upon Mount Zion (the City of New Jerusalem—see D&C 84:2), and with him **a hundred and forty-four thousand**, having his **Father's name written on their foreheads** [*in biblical symbolism, "forehead" means "loyalty"*].

> As indicated in the note at the end of verse 18, above, "forehead" in biblical symbolism means "loyalty." Thus, symbolically speaking, if you were to have the Savior's name on your forehead, it would indicate to God and others your intent and determination to be loyal to Christ. On the other hand, if you were to have the devil's name or any of his front organizations, so-to-speak, on your forehead, you would be indicating that you are loyal to evil and wickedness.

19 Wherefore, **prepare ye for the coming of the Bridegroom** [*the Second Coming*]; go ye, **go ye out to meet him** [*in other words, come unto Christ; be constantly prepared to meet the Savior*].

> Before the actual Second Coming to all the world, the Savior will make some other prophesied appearances, including those spoken of in verse 20, next.

20 For behold, **he shall stand upon the mount of Olivet** [*the Mount of Olives in the Holy Land east of Jerusalem*], and **upon the mighty ocean**, even the great deep, and **upon the islands of the sea**, and **upon the land of Zion** [*which can include appearances at both New Jerusalem and Adam-ondi-Ahman*].

Ezra Taft Benson spoke of two of these appearances as follows (**bold** added for emphasis):

"His first appearance will be to the righteous Saints who have gathered to the **New Jerusalem**. In this place of refuge they will be safe from the wrath of the Lord, which will be poured out without measure on all nations . . .

"The second appearance of the Lord will be **to the Jews**. To these beleaguered sons of Judah, surrounded by hostile Gentile armies, who again threaten to overrun Jerusalem, the Savior—their Messiah—will appear and set His feet on the Mount of Olives, 'and it shall cleave in twain, and the earth shall tremble, and reel to and fro, and the heavens also shall shake' (D&C 45:48).

"The Lord Himself will then rout the Gentile armies, decimating their forces (see Ezek. 38, 39). Judah will be spared, no longer to be persecuted and scattered" ("Five Marks of the Divinity of Jesus Christ," *New Era*, December 1980, 49–50).

Joseph Smith spoke of the appearance of the Savior at a meeting to be held at Adam-ondi-Ahman in Missouri, which is about seventy miles north northeast of Independence.

"Daniel in his seventh chapter speaks of the Ancient of Days; he means the oldest man, our Father Adam, Michael, he [who] will call his children together and hold a council with them to prepare them for the coming of the Son of Man. He (Adam) is the father of the human family, and presides over the spirits of all men, and all that have had the keys must stand before him in this grand council. . . The Son of Man stands before him, and there is given him glory and dominion. Adam delivers up his stewardship to Christ, that which was delivered to him as holding the keys of the universe, but retains his standing as head of the human family" (*Teachings of the Prophet Joseph Smith*, 157).

Bruce R. McConkie also taught about the Savior's appearance at Adam-ondi-Ahman. He said:

"Before the Lord Jesus descends openly and publicly in the clouds of glory, attended by all the hosts of heaven; before the great and dreadful day of the Lord sends terror and destruction from one end of the earth to the other; before he stands on Mount Zion, or sets his feet on Olivet, or utters his voice from an American Zion or a Jewish Jerusalem; before all flesh shall see him together; before any of his appearances, which taken together comprise the second coming of the Son of God—before all these, there is to be a secret appearance to selected members of his Church. He will come in private to his prophet and to the apostles then living. Those who have held keys and powers and authorities in all ages from Adam to the present will also be present [*at the meeting at Adam-ondi-Ahman*]" (*The Millennial Messiah,* 578–79).

21 And **he shall utter his voice out of Zion** [*New Jerusalem, in America*], **and he shall speak from Jerusalem** [*Old Jerusalem; both of these cities will serve as headquarters for the Savior during the Millennium*], and **his voice shall be heard among all people**;

Next, we are taught that there will be changes in the earth's surface in conjunction with the Second Coming and in preparation for the Millennium. It is interesting to note that changes in the earth's surface also accompanied the destruction of the wicked at the time of the resurrected Savior's coming to the Nephites. You may wish to read about these in 3 Nephi 8:17–18.

22 And it shall be a voice as the voice of many waters, and as the voice of a great thunder, which **shall break down the mountains, and the valleys shall not be found.**

23 **He shall command the great deep** [*the water, oceans*], **and it shall be driven back** into the north countries, and **the islands shall become one land;**

24 And **the land of Jerusalem and the land of Zion shall be turned back into their own place** [*returned to their original locations*]**, and the earth shall be like as it was in the days before it was divided.**

Under the direction of the Prophet Joseph Smith, an article was published that helps us understand verses 23–24, above.

"The Eternal God hath declared that the great deep shall roll back into the north countries and that the land of Zion and the land of Jerusalem shall be joined together, as they were before they were divided in the days of Peleg [*Genesis 10:25*]. No wonder the mind starts at the sound of the last days!" ("The Last Days," *Evening and Morning Star,* February 1833, 1).

Joseph Fielding Smith taught:

"If, however, the earth is to be restored as it was in the beginning, then all the land surface will again be in one place as it was before the days of Peleg, when this great division was accomplished. Europe, Africa, and the islands of the sea including Australia, New Zealand, and other places in the Pacific must be brought back and joined together as they were in the beginning" (*Answers to Gospel Questions,* 5:74).

Next, in verse 25, the Savior speaks of His millennial reign.

25 And the Lord, even **the Savior, shall stand in the midst of his people, and shall reign over all flesh** [*during the Millennium, all people will be governed by the Savior; this form of government is called a "theocracy," meaning government by God*].

> Verses 26–33, next, deal with the return of the Lost Ten Tribes.
>
> As recorded in D&C 110:11, Moses restored the keys of "leading the ten tribes from the land of the north" to Joseph Smith and Oliver Cowdery. These keys have been transferred from prophet to prophet and reside with the President of the Church today.
>
> Because of wickedness, the ten tribes of Israel were carried away captive by Shalmaneser about 721 B.C. and taken away into Assyria (2 Kings 17:6–7). Since then, they have been lost to us. They will return from the north (see Jeremiah 23:8). The resurrected Savior told the Nephites that He was to visit the Lost Ten Tribes at that time (3 Nephi 17:4).
>
> In 1831, the Prophet Joseph Smith told some of the brethren that John, the Beloved Apostle, was at that time working with the Ten Tribes, preparing them for their return. The following quote comes from the history kept by John Whitmer:
>
> "The Spirit of the Lord fell upon Joseph in an unusual manner, and he prophesied that John the Revelator was then among the Ten Tribes of Israel who had been led away by Shalmaneser, king of Assyria, to prepare them for their return from their long dispersion, to again possess the land of their fathers" (*History of the Church*, 1:176, footnote).
>
> We do not know where the lost ten tribes are, so it is fruitless to speculate and draw definite conclusions from it.

26 And **they who are in the north countries** [*the Lost Ten Tribes of Israel*] **shall come in remembrance before the Lord** [*the Lord will fulfill His promises to bring them back*]; and **their prophets shall hear his voice**, and shall no longer stay themselves [*will no longer hold back*]; and they shall smite the rocks, and the ice shall flow down at their presence.

27 And **an highway** [*can be literal; "highway" can also mean the gospel*] **shall be cast up in the midst of the great deep.**

28 **Their enemies shall become a prey unto them** [*no one will stop them*],

> From verse 29, next, it appears that geological changes will be made in order to accommodate the travel and arrival of the lost ten tribes.

In addition, there may be considerable symbolism in verse 29 in the sense that barren deserts can symbolize apostasy, and living water usually refers to the Savior and His gospel (see John 4:10). Thus, one possible interpretation of verse 29 may be that the ten tribes will return from the apostasy that led to their being lost spiritually and carried away into captivity. They will once again be nourished by the living water.

29 And **in the barren deserts there shall come forth pools of living water;** and **the parched ground shall no longer be a thirsty land.**

Verses 30–32 indicate that Ephraim will be gathered first. We see this in lineage declarations in many patriarchal blessings. Ephraim is to prepare the way for the return of the others.

30 **And they shall bring forth their rich treasures unto the children of Ephraim** [*descendants of Ephraim*], **my servants.**

The ten tribes will consist of large numbers of people when they arrive, as indicated in verse 31, next.

31 And **the boundaries of the everlasting hills** [*the Rocky Mountains*] **shall tremble at their presence.**

32 And **there shall they** fall down and **be crowned with glory** [*receive their temple blessings*], even in Zion, **by the hands of the servants of the Lord, even the children of Ephraim.**

President Joseph Fielding Smith explained that the tribe of Ephraim will play a prominent role in the gathering of Israel in the last days. He said: "The Lord called upon the descendants of Ephraim to commence his work in the earth in these last days. . . . The keys are with Ephraim. It is Ephraim who is to be endowed with power to bless and give to the other tribes . . . their blessings" (*Doctrines of Salvation*, 2:250–51; see also D&C 113:5–6).

33 And **they shall be filled with songs of everlasting joy.**

34 Behold, **this** [*gathering them again, in the last days*] **is the blessing of the everlasting God upon the tribes of Israel**, and **the richer blessing** [*the birthright blessing—see Genesis 48:13–20*] **upon the head of Ephraim and his fellows.**

Referring back to verse 34, above, in Old Testament culture, the holder of the birthright blessing had the responsibility of taking care of the other family members. Thus, Ephraim has the responsibility of preparing the way for the other tribes of Israel to return to the Savior. Much is being done now by way of missionary work and temple building to prepare for the continued gathering of Israel, including the return of the ten tribes.

Next, the return of the Jews to Christ is prophesied. This will take place after much pain, as stated in verse 35. This can be referred to as the "spiritual gathering" of the Jews and appears to be yet future as far as large-scale conversions are concerned.

35 And **they also of the tribe of Judah, after their pain, shall be sanctified** [*cleansed by the Atonement of Christ*] **in holiness before the Lord** [*they will become righteous, faithful Saints*], to dwell in his presence day and night, forever and ever.

Next, the Master speaks of the Restoration. The angel spoken of in verse 36 appears to be representative of many angelic beings who participated in restoring the gospel to Joseph Smith, including Moroni, John the Baptist, Peter, James and John, Moses, Elias, and Elijah.

36 And now, verily saith the Lord, **that these things might be known among you**, O inhabitants of the earth, **I have sent forth mine angel flying through the midst of heaven** [*Revelation 14:6–7*], having the everlasting gospel, **who hath** appeared unto some and hath **committed it unto man**, who shall appear unto many that dwell on the earth.

37 And **this gospel shall be preached unto every nation, and kindred, and tongue, and people**.

A brief missionary training course is given next, beginning with verse 38.

38 And **the servants of God shall go forth, saying with a loud voice: Fear** [*respect and honor*] **God and give glory to him**, for **the hour of his judgment is come** [*the much-prophesied last days' punishments and calamities are now coming*];

39 And **worship him that made heaven, and earth**, and the sea, and the fountains of waters—

Verses 40–44, next, summarize the prayers of the righteous in the last days as they plead for the coming of the Savior.

40 Calling upon the name of the Lord day and night, saying: O that thou wouldst rend the heavens [*perhaps meaning "tear the veil away" as will be the case at the time of the Second Coming—see D&C 88:95*], that thou wouldst come down, that the mountains might flow down at thy presence [*the Second Coming*].

The unrestrained glory of the Lord at His coming is described in verse 41, next. It is this glory that will destroy the wicked (see D&C 5:19, 2 Nephi 12:10, 19, 21).

41 **And it shall be answered upon their heads** [*their prayers will be answered*]; for **the presence of the Lord shall be as the melting fire that burneth, and as the fire which causeth the waters to boil.**

The plight of the wicked is briefly described in verses 42–43, next.

42 O Lord, **thou shalt come down to make thy name known to thine adversaries, and all nations shall tremble at thy presence—**

43 **When thou doest terrible things, things they look not for** [*the wicked do not expect to be destroyed; most of them do not believe in Christ or His Second Coming*];

The righteous will rejoice when Christ comes, as foretold in verse 44, next.

44 Yea, **when thou comest down,** and the mountains flow down at thy presence, **thou shalt meet him who rejoiceth and worketh righteousness, who remembereth thee in thy ways.**

In verse 45, next, we are informed that we cannot even begin to imagine the wonderful blessings that lie in store for the righteous.

45 For **since the beginning of the world have not men heard nor perceived by the ear, neither hath any eye seen, O God, besides thee, how great things thou hast prepared for him** [*the faithful, righteous*] **that waiteth** [*trusts, relies; waits with faith for promised blessings*] **for thee.**

Next, in verses 46–51, we are taught more about the Second Coming. Among other things, the Savior will wear red at the time of His coming. Whether this color is literal or symbolic, the message is the same. It represents the blood of the wicked (see verse 51) as they are destroyed at the time of his Second Advent.

46 **And it shall be said: Who is this that cometh down from God in heaven with dyed** [*red*] **garments** [*clothing*]; yea, from the regions which are not known [*from heaven*], clothed in his glorious apparel [*in His full glory*], traveling in the greatness of his strength [*this time, He comes in power*]?

47 And he shall say: I am he who spake in righteousness, mighty to save [*in other words, "I am the Messiah"*].

48 And **the Lord shall be red in his apparel**, and his garments like him that treadeth in the wine-vat [*His clothing will be "stained" (like the clothing of a worker who tramples grapes to make wine) with the blood of the wicked, symbolic of their destruction*].

> The Savior's glory will be far more intense than the light of the sun as explained in verse 49, next. Symbolically, the sun and the moon are embarrassed to compete with the Savior as far as glory is concerned.

49 **And so great shall be the glory of his presence that the sun shall hide his face in shame, and the moon shall withhold its light**, and the stars shall be hurled from their places.

> Next, in verses 50–51, the Savior explains why His clothing will be red when He comes.

50 And his voice shall be heard: **I have trodden the wine-press alone** [*He performed the Atonement alone*], **and have brought judgment upon all people** [*through His atoning sacrifice, He qualified to have all people subject to Him, both to His mercy where possible and to His judgments and condemnations where required by the law of justice*]; and **none were with me** [*He had to do the Atonement alone—compare with Matthew 27:46*];

51 And **I have trampled them** [*the wicked*] **in my fury** [*symbolic of the demands of the law of justice*], and I did tread upon them in mine anger, and **their blood have I sprinkled upon my garments, and stained all my raiment** [*the wicked will have been destroyed at this point of His coming*]; for **this was the day of vengeance** [*justice; punishment of the wicked*] **which was in my heart** [*which is part of the plan of salvation*].

> Next, more is said about the happy state of the righteous as the Savior comes on earth to reign for a thousand years. Note the contrast between the state of the wicked in the above verses and the feelings in the hearts of the faithful.

52 And **now** [*when the Savior comes*] **the year of my redeemed is come** [*finally, the righteous are set free from the oppressions they've endured*]; and **they shall mention the loving kindness of their Lord, and all that he has bestowed upon them according to his goodness, and according to his loving kindness**, forever and ever.

> Verse 53, next, speaks of the Atonement.

53 In all their afflictions he was afflicted. And the angel of his presence saved them; and in his love, and in his pity, he redeemed them, and bore them, and carried them all the days of old;

> One of the teachings of the gospel is that the faithful Saints from the time of Adam and Eve up to the time of the Savior's resurrection came forth with Christ at His resurrection. It is found in verses 54–55, next. All these Saints qualified for celestial glory. No terrestrials or telestials have been resurrected yet.
>
> It is interesting to note that the inhabitants of the city of Enoch, who were translated, were resurrected with Christ.

54 Yea, and **Enoch** also, **and they who were with him**; the **prophets who were before him**; and **Noah** also, and they who were before him; and **Moses** also, and they who were before him;

55 And **from Moses to Elijah**, and from **Elijah to John**, who **were with Christ in his resurrection**, and the holy apostles, with Abraham, Isaac, and Jacob, shall be in the presence of the Lamb.

> The resurrection spoken of in verses 54–55, above, is part of what is termed the "first resurrection." First resurrection is, in fact, often used as a general term meaning celestial resurrection regardless of when a particular righteous person is resurrected.
>
> Another major portion of the first resurrection will take place at the time of the Savior's coming, as discussed next in verse 56.

56 And **the graves of the saints shall be opened** [*the righteous who have died since the resurrection of Christ*]; and **they shall come forth** and stand **on the right hand of the Lamb** [*a phrase meaning those worthy of celestial glory; right hand symbolizes having made and kept covenants*], when he shall stand upon Mount Zion [*when He comes*], and upon the holy city, the New Jerusalem; and **they shall sing the song of the Lamb, day and night forever and ever** [*symbolism, in effect, meaning "We are saved, we are saved"*].

> Verses 57–61 review again the purposes of the Restoration of the true gospel through the Prophet Joseph Smith.

57 And for this cause, **that men might be made partakers of the glories which were to be revealed**, the Lord sent forth [*restored*] the fulness of his gospel, his everlasting covenant, reasoning in plainness and simplicity—

58 **To prepare the weak** [*those who are looked down upon by* skeptics and nonbelievers; also can mean that anyone can live the gospel] **for those things which are coming on the earth**, and **for the Lord's errand** [*to do the work of the Lord*] in the day when **the weak shall confound the wise**, and the little one become a strong nation [*from very small beginnings, the Church will grow to very large numbers*], and **two shall put their tens of thousands to flight** [*symbolic of the fact that the small Church will become very influential*].

59 And **by the weak things of the earth** [*the humble, meek members of the Church*] **the Lord shall thrash the nations by the power of his Spirit.**

60 And **for this cause these commandments were given**; they were commanded to be kept from the world in the day that they were given [*see D&C 105:23–24*], but now are to go forth unto all flesh—

61 And **this according to the mind and will of the Lord**, who ruleth over all flesh.

62 And **unto him that repenteth and sanctifieth himself** [*keeps the commandments*] **before the Lord shall be given eternal life** [*exaltation*].

63 And upon **them that hearken not to the voice of the Lord** shall be fulfilled that which was written by the prophet Moses, that **they should be cut off** from among the people [*in other words, the wicked will be destroyed*].

64 And also **that which was written by the prophet Malachi**: For, behold, **the day cometh** [*the Second Coming*] **that shall burn as an oven, and all the proud, yea, and all that do wickedly, shall be stubble** [*dry grain stocks in a field*]; and **the day that cometh shall burn them up**, saith the Lord of hosts, that it shall **leave them neither root nor branch** [*they will have neither ancestors nor descendants in eternity; in other words, they will not be part of a family unit in eternity*].

As the Master Teacher, the Savior sets the stage for the wicked to ask, "Why were we destroyed?" The answer is given in verses 65–67.

65 Wherefore, **this shall be the answer of the Lord unto them** [*the wicked, when they ask why they were burned*]:

66 In that day when I came unto mine own, **no man among you received me,** and you were driven out.

67 **When I called** [*when I invited you to come unto Me*] **again there was none of you to answer**; yet my arm was not shortened at all that I could not redeem, neither my power to deliver [*I still had power to redeem you; it still was not too late*].

> In the last half of verse 67, above, and in verses 68–69, the Savior is quoting Isaiah 50:2–3.
>
> In effect, He is asking why the wicked and foolish, referred to in verses 66–67, above, refused to listen to Him when He brought his gospel to them. He reminds them that He has not lost His power to redeem them, so it does not make sense for them to reject Him.

68 Behold, **at my rebuke** [*command*] **I dry up the sea** [*as in the Red Sea and the children of Israel*]. **I make the rivers a wilderness** [*the Lord has power over nature*]; their fish stink, and die for thirst.

69 **I clothe the heavens with blackness, and make sackcloth their covering** [*the Lord can cause the sky to be dark during the day; in other words, He has power over all things*].

> Next, in verses 70–74, the Savior explains what will happen to the wicked because they reject Him and the saving principles of the gospel after they are given the opportunity to accept it.

70 And **this shall ye have of my hand—ye shall lie down in sorrow.**

71 Behold, and lo, **there are none to deliver you** [*no one other than the Savior can save us*]; for **ye obeyed not my voice when I called to you out of the heavens; ye believed not my servants** [*missionaries, prophets, teachers, parents, and so forth*]**, and when they were sent unto you ye received them not.**

72 **Wherefore** [*this is why*]**, they sealed up the testimony and bound up the law** [*their testimonies are recorded against you—compare with Isaiah 8:16*]**, and ye were delivered over unto darkness.**

73 **These** [*the wicked*] **shall go away into outer darkness, where there is weeping, and wailing, and gnashing of teeth.**

> The "outer darkness" spoken of in verse 73, above, cannot mean "sons of perdition," because it is used with respect to the wicked in general. Rather, it denotes being turned over to Satan to be punished because they would not repent (see Alma 40:13). The qualifications for becoming sons of perdition are given in D&C 76:31–35.

74 Behold the Lord your God hath spoken it. Amen.

SECTION 134

Background

This section is not a revelation in the sense that most other sections in the Doctrine and Covenants are. Rather, it consists of a declaration of the Church's position regarding governments and laws in general, which was prepared for a general meeting of the Saints in Kirtland, Ohio, on August 17, 1835. During that meeting, this article entitled "Of Governments and Laws in General" was read by Oliver Cowdery and sustained by the Saints as a proper representation of the Church's position on the subject.

Be sure to read the heading to this section in your Doctrine and Covenants.

It is important to know that this statement of beliefs about governments was given as a direct response to accusations by bitter enemies of the Church that the Latter-day Saints were opposed to any government other than their own church and that they were opposed to law and order.

We will use **bold** to highlight the main points of this important document. First of all, we do believe in man-made governments and in law and order.

1 **WE believe that governments were instituted of God for the benefit of man**; and **that he holds men accountable for their acts in relation to them, both in making laws and administering them, for the good and safety of society**.

Next, this article on governments states that without appropriate laws and enforcement, God-given agency cannot function as it is intended to (compare with D&C 101:78).

2 We believe that **no government can exist in peace, except such laws are framed and held inviolate [enforced] as will secure to each individual the free exercise of conscience, the right and control of property, and the protection of life**.

3 **We believe that all governments necessarily require civil officers and magistrates to enforce the laws of the same**; and that such as will administer the law in equity and justice should be sought for and upheld by the voice of the people if a republic, or the will of the sovereign.

The issue of separation of church and state is addressed in verse 4, next.

4 We believe that religion is instituted of God; and that men are amenable [accountable] to him, and to him only, for the exercise

of it, unless their religious opinions prompt them to infringe upon the rights and liberties of others; but **we do not believe that human law has a right to interfere in prescribing rules of worship to bind the consciences of men, nor dictate forms for public or private devotion**; that the civil magistrate should restrain crime, but never control conscience; should punish guilt, but never suppress the freedom of the soul.

> Members of the Church are expected to sustain and honor their government wherever they live, no matter what form their government takes, as long as their basic rights are protected.

5 We believe that **all men are bound to sustain and uphold the respective governments in which they reside, while protected in their inherent and inalienable rights** by the laws of such governments; and that **sedition and rebellion are unbecoming every citizen thus protected**, and should be punished accordingly; and that **all governments have a right to enact such laws as in their own judgments are best calculated to secure the public interest**; at the same time, however, **holding sacred the freedom of conscience**.

> Looking back through history, it is clear that almost any government, no matter the form, is better than no government.

6 We believe that every man should be honored in his station, rulers and magistrates as such, being placed for the protection of the innocent and the punishment of the guilty; and that to the laws all men show respect and deference, as **without them peace and harmony would be supplanted by anarchy and terror**; human laws being instituted for the express purpose of regulating our interests as individuals and nations, between man and man; and divine laws given of heaven, prescribing rules on spiritual concerns, for faith and worship, both to be answered by man to his Maker.

> Verse 7, next, is another statement relating to the separation of church and state.

7 We believe that **rulers, states, and governments have a right, and are bound to enact laws for the protection of all citizens in the free exercise of their religious belief; but we do not believe that they have a right in justice to deprive citizens of this privilege,** or proscribe [*attempt to control*] them in their opinions, **so long as a regard and reverence**

are shown to the laws and such religious opinions do not justify sedition nor conspiracy.

> Verse 8, next, is a clear statement that the Church does believe in law and order.

8 **We believe that the commission of crime should be punished** according to the nature of the offense; that murder, treason, robbery, theft, and the breach of the general peace, in all respects, should be punished according to their criminality and their tendency to evil among men, **by the laws of that government** in which the offense is committed; and for the public peace and tranquility **all men should step forward and use their ability in bringing offenders against good laws to punishment.**

> Verse 9, next, is a clear statement of our position on the separation of church and state as far as the state having a "state religion" is concerned. It is common in many nations of the world for the state to have an official religion, which then is given perks and privileges not available to other religious bodies.

9 **We do not believe it just to mingle religious influence with civil government, whereby one religious society is fostered and another proscribed** [*limited*] in its spiritual privileges, and the individual rights of its members, as citizens, denied.

> The right of a church organization to discipline its members, including excommunication (holding a membership council, imposing membership restrictions, or membership withdrawal), is spoken of in verse 10, next. However, such religious organizations must not take it upon themselves to inflict any penalties upon their members other than restrictions in religious privileges. In other words, they must not overlap into the jurisdiction of civil law and punishment.

10 We believe that **all religious societies have a right to deal with their members for disorderly conduct**, according to the rules and regulations of such societies; provided that such dealings be for fellowship and good standing; but **we do not believe that any religious society has authority to try men on the right of property or life**, to take from them this world's goods, or to put them in jeopardy of either life or limb, **or to inflict any physical punishment upon them. They can only excommunicate them from their society, and withdraw from them their fellowship.**

> Verse 11, next, deals with the issue of self-defense when the government cannot protect us or

refuses to protect us according to our rights as citizens.

11 **We believe that men should appeal to the civil law** [*the laws of the land*] **for redress** [*correction and restitution*] of all wrongs and grievances, where personal abuse is inflicted or the right of property or character infringed, where such laws exist as will protect the same; **but we believe that all men are justified in defending themselves, their friends, and property, and the government, from the unlawful assaults and encroachments** of all persons **in times of exigency** [*emergency*]**, where immediate appeal cannot be made to the laws, and relief afforded.**

> Verse 12, next, should be understood in the context in which it was given; namely, 1835 pre-Civil War American society.

12 We believe it just to preach the gospel to the nations of the earth, and warn the righteous to save themselves from the corruption of the world; but **we do not believe it right to interfere with bond-servants, neither preach the gospel to, nor baptize them contrary to the will and wish of their masters, nor to meddle with or influence them in the least to cause them to be dissatisfied with their situations in this life, thereby jeopardizing the lives of men**; such interference we believe to be unlawful and unjust, and dangerous to the peace of every government allowing human beings to be held in servitude [*slavery*].

Joseph Smith taught that it is not the role of the Church and its missionaries to overthrow the established laws of societies and governments:

"It should be the duty of an Elder, when he enters into a house, to salute the master of that house, and if he gain his consent, then he may preach to all that are in that house; but if he gain not his consent, let him not go unto his slaves, or servants, but let the responsibility be upon the head of the master of that house, and the consequences thereof, and the guilt of that house is no longer upon his skirts. . . . But if the master of that house give consent, the Elder may preach to his family, his wife, his children and his servants, his man-servants, or his maid-servants, or his slaves" (*History of the Church,* 2:263).

SECTION 135

Background

The tribute that appears here as section 135 was written based on the eyewitness accounts of John

SECTION 135

Taylor and Willard Richards who were prisoners in the same room with Joseph and Hyrum Smith at the time of the Martyrdom at Carthage Jail, Carthage, Illinois, on June 27, 1844, at about 5:00 p.m.

We will include a copy of the heading to section 135 from the 2013 edition of the Doctrine and Covenants for your information:

Announcement of the martyrdom of Joseph Smith the Prophet and his brother, Hyrum Smith the Patriarch, at Carthage, Illinois, June 27, 1844. This document was included at the end of the 1844 edition of the Doctrine and Covenants, which was nearly ready for publication when Joseph and Hyrum Smith were murdered.

Elder Taylor was in the jail with them, along with Willard Richards at the time the mob entered the jail and carried out their cowardly deeds. Hyrum was shot first and fell dead on the floor. John Taylor was shot several times, including being hit by a lead ball that smashed the pocket watch in his left vest pocket. It no doubt saved his life. The watch was stopped at twenty-two minutes and twenty seconds after 5:00 P.M. The Prophet was shot and fell from the window onto the ground, dead. At about this time, someone shouted, "The Mormons are coming!" (which was not the case), and the mob quickly dispersed. Elder Richards was not hit by any bullets except for a tiny nick on one ear. We read about this as follows:

"Dr. Richards' escape was miraculous; he being a very large man, and in the midst of a shower of balls, yet he stood unscathed, with the exception of a ball which grazed the tip end of the lower part of his left ear. His escape fulfilled literally a prophecy which Joseph made over a year previously, that the time would come that the balls would fly around him like hail, and he should see his friends fall on the right and on the left, but that there should not be a hole in his garment" (*History of the Church*, 6:619).

Thus, the Prophet of the Restoration and his beloved brother sealed their missions with their blood. We will add minimal notes and commentary to this section, letting the inspired words of John Taylor speak for themselves.

1 TO seal the testimony of this book and the Book of Mormon, **we announce the martyrdom** [*being killed because of a specific mission*] **of Joseph Smith the Prophet, and Hyrum Smith the Patriarch**. They were shot in Carthage jail, on the 27th of June, 1844, about five o'clock P.M., by an armed mob—painted black—of from 150 to 200 persons. Hyrum was shot first and fell calmly,

exclaiming: *I am a dead man!* Joseph leaped from the window, and was shot dead in the attempt, exclaiming: *O Lord my God!* They were both shot after they were dead, in a brutal manner, and both received four balls [*bullets*].

2 **John Taylor** and Willard Richards, two of the Twelve, were the only persons in the room at the time; the former **was wounded in a savage manner with four balls**, but has since recovered; the latter, through the providence of God, escaped, without even a hole in his robe.

> Verse 3, next, tells us the relative position of the Prophet Joseph Smith among all the prophets who have ever lived.

3 **Joseph Smith, the Prophet and Seer of the Lord, has done more, save** [*except*] **Jesus only, for the salvation of men in this world, than any other man that ever lived in it**. In the short space of twenty years, he has brought forth the Book of Mormon, which he translated by the gift and power of God, and has been the means of publishing it on two continents; has sent the fulness of the everlasting gospel, which it contained, to the four quarters of the earth; has brought forth the revelations and commandments which compose this book of Doctrine and Covenants, and many other wise documents and instructions for the benefit of the children of men; gathered many thousands of the Latter-day Saints, founded a great city [*Nauvoo*], and left a fame and name that cannot be slain. He lived great, and he died great in the eyes of God and his people; and like most of the Lord's anointed in ancient times, has sealed his mission and his works with his own blood; and so has his brother Hyrum. In life they were not divided, and in death they were not separated!

4 When Joseph went to Carthage to deliver himself up to the pretended requirements of the law, two or three days previous to his assassination, he said: **"I am going like a lamb to the slaughter; but I am calm as a summer's morning; I have a conscience void of offense towards God, and towards all men. I SHALL DIE INNOCENT, AND IT SHALL YET BE SAID OF ME—HE WAS MURDERED IN COLD BLOOD."**—The same morning, after Hyrum had made ready to go—shall it be said to the slaughter? yes, for so it was—he read the following paragraph, near the close of the twelfth chapter of Ether, in the

Book of Mormon, and turned down the leaf upon it:

> We understand from the last of verse 4, above, and the passage quoted in verse 5, next, that Hyrum also was informed by the Lord that he would die in Carthage Jail.

5 And it came to pass that I prayed unto the Lord that he would give unto the Gentiles grace, that they might have charity. And it came to pass that the Lord said unto me: If they have not charity it mattereth not unto thee, thou hast been faithful; wherefore thy garments shall be made clean. And because thou hast seen thy weakness, thou shalt be made strong, even unto the sitting down in the place which I have prepared in the mansions of my Father. And now I . . . bid farewell unto the Gentiles; yea, and also unto my brethren whom I love, until we shall meet before the judgment-seat of Christ, where all men shall know that my garments are not spotted with your blood. The testators are now dead, and their testament is in force.

> The word *testator*, as used in verse 5, above, means "one who has made a legally valid will" (see any dictionary). The will becomes valid after the death of the testator. This word usage here denotes that Joseph and Hyrum have made their testimonies binding and valid by giving their lives for the cause.

6 Hyrum Smith was forty-four years old in February, 1844, and Joseph Smith was thirty-eight in December, 1843; and henceforward **their names will be classed among the martyrs of religion; and the reader in every nation will be reminded that the Book of Mormon, and this book of Doctrine and Covenants of the church, cost the best blood of the nineteenth century to bring them forth** for the salvation of a ruined world; and that if the fire can scathe a green tree for the glory of God, how easy it will burn up the dry trees [*the wicked*] to purify the vineyard [*the earth*] of corruption. They lived for glory; they died for glory; and glory is their eternal reward. **From age to age shall their names go down to posterity as gems for the sanctified.**

7 They were innocent of any crime, as they had often been proved before, and were only confined in jail by the conspiracy of traitors and wicked men; and **their *innocent blood* on the floor of Carthage jail is a broad seal affixed to "Mormonism" that cannot be rejected by any court on earth**, and their *innocent blood* on the

escutcheon [*coat of arms; seal*] of the State of Illinois, with the broken faith of the State as pledged by the governor, is a witness to the truth of the everlasting gospel that all the world cannot impeach [*refute*]; and **their innocent blood** on the banner of liberty, and on the *magna charta* of the United States, is an ambassador for the religion of Jesus Christ, that **will touch the hearts of honest men among all nations**; and their *innocent blood*, with the innocent blood of all the martyrs under the altar that John saw [*which John the Revelator saw, recorded in Revelation 6:9*], will cry unto the Lord of Hosts till he avenges that blood on the earth. Amen.

SECTION 136

Background

This revelation was given through President Brigham Young on January 14, 1847, at Winter Quarters on the west bank of the Missouri River near Council Bluffs, Iowa.

At this point in time, the Saints were preparing to undertake the final stretch of the westward journey to the Salt Lake Valley.

After the death of the Prophet Joseph Smith, Brigham Young led the Church as the President of the Quorum of the Twelve Apostles. Because of continued threats from the enemies of the Church and mob violence, the Saints began leaving Nauvoo and the surrounding area in February 1846. The first group left on February 4, and others followed. The main body of Saints traveling west at this time was called the Camp of Israel. During February alone, over three thousand Saints crossed the Mississippi River and headed west.

With so many preparing now to journey on from Winter Quarters to the Salt Lake Valley, the need for careful and effective organization was met by the Lord through Brigham Young. In addition to the specific organization of these Saints into companies of hundreds, fifties, and tens, the most important consideration of all, as stated in verses 2 and 4, was that the members of the Church and others traveling with them maintain their personal righteousness. This same principle applies to us today, no matter how we are organized in stakes and wards, districts, and branches, and regardless of who is called to preside over us.

1 THE Word and Will of the Lord concerning the Camp of Israel in their journeyings to the West:

2 Let all the people of the Church of Jesus Christ of Latter-day Saints, and those who journey with them, be organized into

companies, **with a covenant and promise to keep all the commandments and statutes of the Lord our God.**

3 Let the companies be organized with captains of hundreds, captains of fifties, and captains of tens, with a president and his two counselors at their head, under the direction of the Twelve Apostles.

4 And **this shall be our covenant**—that **we will walk in all the ordinances of the Lord**.

5 Let each company provide themselves with all the teams, wagons, provisions, clothing, and other necessaries for the journey, that they can.

6 When the companies are organized let them go to with their might, to prepare for those who are to tarry.

7 Let each company, with their captains and presidents, decide how many can go next spring; then choose out a sufficient number of able-bodied and expert men, to take teams, seeds, and farming utensils, to go as pioneers to prepare for putting in spring crops.

> Next, in verse 8, we see the principles of the law of consecration and our modern welfare system of the Church in action.

8 **Let each company bear an equal proportion**, according to the dividend of their property, **in taking the poor, the widows, the fatherless, and the families of those who have gone into the army** [*the Mormon Battalion*], that the cries of the widow and the fatherless come not up into the ears of the Lord against this people.

> As indicated in verse 9, next, fields were planted by these advanced companies to provide for those who would come along later.

9 Let each company **prepare houses, and fields for raising grain**, for those who are to remain behind this season; and this is the will of the Lord concerning his people.

10 Let every man use all his influence and property to remove this people to the place where the Lord shall locate a stake of Zion.

11 And **if ye do this with a pure heart, in all faithfulness, ye shall be blessed**; you shall be blessed in your flocks, and in your herds, and in your fields, and in your houses, and in your families.

12 Let my servants Ezra T. Benson and Erastus Snow organize a company.

13 And let my servants Orson Pratt and Wilford Woodruff organize a company.

14 Also, let my servants Amasa Lyman and George A. Smith organize a company.

15 And appoint presidents, and captains of hundreds, and of fifties, and of tens.

16 And let my servants that have been appointed go and teach this, my will, to the saints, that they may be ready to go to a land of peace.

> Next, in verses 17–18 we have yet another reminder that the enemies of the Saints will not stop the work of the Lord (compare with D&C 121:33 and Daniel 2:35, 44–45).

17 Go thy way and do as I have told you, and **fear not thine enemies; for they shall not have power to stop my work.**

18 **Zion shall be redeemed in mine own due time.**

> Verse 19, next, cautions us that pure motives are essential in serving the Lord.

19 **And if any man shall seek to build up himself,** and seeketh not my counsel, **he shall have no power,** and his folly shall be made manifest.

In verses 20–30, next, some of the Ten Commandments are reemphasized, and other commandments are given that will assist us in having a peaceful journey throughout life as well as lead us to salvation.

20 Seek ye; and keep all your pledges one with another; and **covet not that which is thy brother's.**

21 **Keep yourselves from evil to take the name of the Lord in vain,** for I am the Lord your God, even the God of your fathers, the God of Abraham and of Isaac and of Jacob.

22 **I am he who led the children of Israel out of the land of Egypt**; and my arm [*symbolic of the power of the Lord*] is stretched out in the last days, to save my people Israel.

23 **Cease to contend one with another; cease to speak evil one of another** [*this certainly includes gossip*].

24 **Cease drunkenness** [*the Word of Wisdom was not yet a commandment—see D&C 89:2*]; and **let your words tend to edifying one another.**

25 **If thou borrowest of thy neighbor, thou shalt restore that

which thou hast borrowed; and if thou canst not repay then go straightway and tell thy neighbor, lest he condemn thee.

26 **If thou shalt find that which thy neighbor has lost, thou shalt make diligent search till thou shalt deliver it to him again.**

27 Thou shalt **be diligent in preserving what thou hast** [*don't be wasteful*], that thou mayest be a wise steward; for it is the free gift of the Lord thy God, and thou art his steward.

28 If thou art merry, **praise the Lord with singing, with music, with dancing, and with a prayer of praise and thanksgiving.**

29 If thou art sorrowful, **call on the Lord thy God with supplication, that your souls may be joyful.**

30 **Fear not thine enemies, for they are in mine hands** and I will do my pleasure with them.

> Next, the Savior explains the role of trials and tribulations in the growth and development of the Saints (compare with D&C 58:2–4).

31 **My people must be tried in all things, that they may be prepared to receive the glory that I have for them**, even the glory of Zion; and **he that will not bear chastisement is not worthy of my kingdom.**

32 **Let him that is ignorant learn wisdom by humbling himself and calling upon the Lord his God, that his eyes may be opened that he may see, and his ears opened that he may hear;**

33 For **my Spirit is sent forth into the world to enlighten the humble and contrite** [*those who desire correction from the Lord as needed*], and to the condemnation of the ungodly.

> Next, in verses 34–36, we see that those who drove the Saints out of the United States, including apostates as well as government officials, may still repent if they so chose.

34 **Thy brethren** have rejected you and your testimony, even **the nation that has driven you out;**

35 And now cometh the day of their calamity, even the days of sorrow, like a woman that is taken in travail; and **their sorrow shall be great unless they speedily repent, yea, very speedily.**

36 For **they killed the prophets, and them that were sent unto**

them; and they have shed innocent blood, which crieth from the ground against them.

> Next, in the first half of verse 37, the Savior gives us a formula, in effect, for gaining additional light and knowledge from Him.

37 Therefore, marvel not at [*don't doubt or question*] these things, for **ye are not yet pure; ye can not yet bear my glory**; but **ye shall behold it if ye are faithful in keeping all my words** that I have given you, from the days of Adam to Abraham, from Abraham to Moses, from Moses to Jesus and his apostles, and from Jesus and his apostles to **Joseph Smith, whom I did call upon by mine angels, my ministering servants, and by mine own voice out of the heavens, to bring forth my work**;

> In verse 37, above, and verses 38–39, next, the Savior bears His personal testimony to us as to the calling of the Prophet Joseph Smith.

38 **Which foundation he did lay, and was faithful; and I took him to myself.**

39 Many have marveled because of his death; but **it was needful that he should seal his testimony with his blood**, that he might be honored and the wicked might be condemned.

40 Have I not delivered you from your enemies, only in that I have left a witness of my name?

41 Now, therefore, hearken, O ye people of my church; and ye elders listen together; you have received my kingdom [*the Church has been restored*].

> This revelation started out with the importance and necessity of the Saints' keeping their personal righteousness at a high level (verse 2). It has come full circle now and closes with the same emphasis.

42 **Be diligent in keeping all my commandments**, lest judgments come upon you, and your faith fail you, and your enemies triumph over you. So no more at present. Amen and Amen.

SECTION 137

Background

> This section is the record of a vision given to the Prophet Joseph Smith on January 21, 1836, in the Kirtland Temple. According to the heading for the 2013 edition, "the occasion was the administration of ordinances in preparation for the dedication of the temple."

This section and section 138 were unanimously accepted as scripture in the April 1976 general conference of the Church. They were originally provided as an addition to the Pearl of Great Price and were added as sections 137 and 138 of the Doctrine and Covenants when the next edition of the Latter-day Saint scriptures was printed.

This section contains pleasant insights and powerful doctrines. One of the best-known doctrines from this vision is found in verse ten in which the Prophet saw the salvation of little children.

Vision of the Celestial Kingdom

1 THE heavens were opened upon us, and I beheld the celestial kingdom of God, and the glory thereof, whether in the body or out I cannot tell.

> It is interesting that the Prophet could not tell whether he was "in the body or out" (verse 1). One of the things we learn from this is that spiritual manifestations are given to us through our spirits. Joseph Smith explained this as follows:
>
> "All things whatsoever God in his infinite wisdom has seen fit and proper to reveal to us, while we are dwelling in mortality, in regard to our mortal bodies, are revealed to us in the abstract, and independent of affinity of this mortal tabernacle, but are revealed to our spirits precisely as though we had no bodies at all; and those revelations which will save our spirits will save our bodies. God reveals them to us in view of no eternal dissolution of the body, or tabernacle" (*Teachings of the Prophet Joseph Smith*, 355).

Continuing his account of this vision, the Prophet describes the beauty and glory of the celestial kingdom.

2 I saw the transcendent beauty of the gate through which the heirs [*those who attain celestial glory*] **of that kingdom will enter**, which was **like unto circling flames of fire**;

3 Also **the blazing throne of God**, whereon was seated **the Father and the Son**.

4 I saw the beautiful streets of that kingdom, which had the appearance of being paved with gold.

> In biblical color symbolism, gold represents the very best, the highest blessings from God (see, for example, Revelation 1:13 describing Christ, and Revelation 4:4 describing the reward of the righteous).

5 I saw Father Adam and **Abraham**; and **my father and my mother; my brother Alvin**, that has long since slept [*who had already died*];

At the time of this vision, Joseph's father and mother were still alive. Thus, the vision was showing the Prophet the future status of his parents. However, his oldest brother, Alvin (seven years older than Joseph), had died on November 17, 1823. It had been a source of concern to the Prophet that his beloved brother, Alvin, had not been baptized, knowing that baptism was a requirement for entrance into celestial glory.

Thus, when he saw Alvin in the celestial kingdom in this vision, it caused him to wonder how this could be. The Master Teacher created a question in His young prophet's mind, as evidenced in verse 6, next, and then answered it in verses 7 and 8.

6 **And marveled how it was that he had obtained an inheritance in that kingdom, seeing that he** had departed this life before the Lord had set his hand to gather Israel the second time, and **had not been baptized for the remission of sins.**

Doctrine

All who would have accepted the gospel had they had a sufficient opportunity in this life will accept it in the next life (see section 138) and will attain celestial glory.

Doctrine

God is completely fair to all of His children.

7 Thus came the voice of the Lord unto me, saying: All who have died without a knowledge of this gospel, who would have received it if they had been permitted to tarry [*if they had not died when they did*]**, shall be heirs of the celestial kingdom of God;**

8 Also all that shall die henceforth without a knowledge of it, who would have received it with all their hearts, shall be heirs of that kingdom;

Verse 9, next, is an example of the importance of answering questions in the bigger, overall context of the scriptures. We read often that we will be judged by our works, by our deeds. But what about the faithful member who wants to keep all of God's commandments but is prevented from paying tithing, for example, by a cruel spouse or parent?

What about the spouse who wants to be sealed in the temple but is prevented because the husband or wife is not converted? And what about the faithful single member who is prevented from celestial marriage because of health conditions or lack of finding a mate?

The questions go on and on, but the answer is clearly and simply given in verse 9.

Doctrine

Because of the complete fairness of God, He will judge us by the desires of our hearts as well as our deeds.

9 For I, the Lord, will judge all men according to their works, according to the **desire of their hearts**.

> Thus, the honest and faithful Saint who is prevented from keeping all of the commandments upon which exaltation is contingent during mortality will be given the opportunity to keep them in the next life because of the sincere desires of his or her heart in this life (compare with D&C 124:49).
>
> Verse 10, next, abolishes a terrible false doctrine that is commonly found among the belief systems of some religions.

10 And I also beheld that **all children who die before they arrive at the years of accountability are saved in the celestial kingdom of heaven.**

Question

> Does verse 10, above, mean that little children who die before age eight are saved, at least in the lowest degree within the celestial kingdom (see D&C 131:1–4), or does it mean that they will receive exaltation in the highest degree of that kingdom?

Answer

They will be exalted. President Joseph F. Smith taught this wonderful doctrine, speaking of little children who die. He said **(bold added for emphasis):**

"Under these circumstances, our beloved friends who are now deprived of their little one, have great cause for joy and rejoicing, even in the midst of the deep sorrow that they feel at the loss of their little one for a time. They know he is all right; they have the assurance that their little one has passed away without sin. Such children are in the bosom of the Father. **They will inherit their glory and their exaltation**, and they will not be deprived of the blessings that belong to them; for, in the economy of heaven, and in the wisdom of the Father, who doeth all things well, those who are cut down as little children are without any responsibility for their taking off, they, themselves, not having the intelligence and wisdom to take care of themselves and to understand the laws of life; and, in the wisdom and mercy and economy of God our Heavenly Father, all that could have been obtained and enjoyed by them if they had been permitted to live in the flesh will be provided for them hereafter. **They will lose nothing by being taken away from us in this way**" (*Gospel Doctrine,* 1977, 452–53).

Question

How can they be exalted since they are not married?

Answer

They will choose a mate in the spirit world or during the Millennium. Then they will introduce themselves and their fiancée to mortals during the Millennium who will be sealed for them by proxy in a temple. Joseph Fielding Smith taught this. He said:

"DECEASED CHILDREN
TO CHOOSE MATES
IN MILLENNIUM

"We have people coming to us all the time just as fearful as they can be that a child of theirs who has died will lose the blessings of the kingdom of God unless that child is sealed to someone who is dead. They do not know the wishes of their child who died too young to think of marriage, but they want to go straight to the temple and have a sealing performed. Such a thing as this is unnecessary and in my judgment wrong.

"The Lord has said through his servants that during the millennium those who have passed beyond and have attained the resurrection will reveal in person to those who are still in mortality all the information which is required to complete the work of these who have passed from this life. Then the dead will have the privilege of making known the things they desire and are entitled to receive. In this way no soul will be neglected and the work of the Lord will be perfected" (*Doctrines of Salvation,* 3:65).

SECTION 138

Background

This section is the record of a vision given to President Joseph F. Smith, the sixth president of the Church in this dispensation, on October 3, 1918. It was given to him six weeks before he passed away. (See background notes for section 137 for additional background information.)

In 1979, the First Presidency and the Quorum of the Twelve Apostles announced that President Joseph F. Smith's vision would be added to the Doctrine and Covenants as section 138 in the 1981 edition of the scriptures.

This vision gives much detail about the postmortal spirit world and the work of preaching the gospel to the dead that is going on there. Thus, it is one of the major doctrinal sections of the Doctrine and Covenants.

In verses 1–11, we see the importance of pondering as a means of opening up the channels of communication with heaven, as President Smith provides us with information as to what led up to this vision.

1 ON the third of October, in the year nineteen hundred and eighteen, **I sat in my room pondering over the scriptures**;

2 **And reflecting** upon the great atoning sacrifice that was made by the Son of God, for the redemption of the world;

3 And the great and wonderful love made manifest by the Father and the Son in the coming of the Redeemer into the world;

4 That through his atonement, and by obedience to the principles of the gospel, mankind might be saved.

5 **While I was thus engaged, my mind reverted to the writings of the apostle Peter**, to the primitive saints [*the members of the Church in the New Testament*] scattered abroad throughout Pontus, Galatia, Cappadocia, and other parts of Asia, where the gospel had been preached after the crucifixion of the Lord.

6 **I opened the Bible and read the third and fourth chapters of the first epistle of Peter**, and as **I read I was greatly impressed, more than I had ever been before, with the following passages:**

7 "For Christ also hath once suffered for sins, the just for the unjust, that he might bring us to God, being put to death in the flesh, but quickened by the Spirit:

8 "By which also **he went and preached unto the spirits in prison**;

9 "Which sometime were disobedient, when once the long-suffering of God waited in the days of Noah, while the ark was a preparing, wherein few, that is, eight souls were saved by water." (1 Peter 3:18–20.)

10 "**For for this cause was the gospel preached also to them that are dead, that they might be judged according to men in the flesh, but live according to God in the spirit.**" (1 Peter 4:6.)

11 **As I pondered** over these things which are written, **the eyes of my understanding were opened**, and **the Spirit of the Lord rested upon me, and I saw the hosts of the dead, both small** [*relatively unknown*] **and great** [*well-known, powerful, influential*].

The Vision of Paradise

12 And there were gathered together in one place [*paradise*] an innumerable company of **the spirits of the just** [*those who are worthy of celestial glory—see D&C 76:69–70*], **who had been faithful in the testimony of Jesus while they lived in mortality;**

13 And who had offered sacrifice in the similitude of the great sacrifice of the Son of God, and had suffered tribulation in their Redeemer's name.

> Bruce R. McConkie described paradise as follows:
>
> "Paradise—the abode of righteous spirits, as they await the day of their resurrection; paradise—a place of peace and rest where the sorrows and trials of his life have been shuffled off, and where the saints continue to prepare for a celestial heaven; paradise—not the Lord's eternal kingdom, but a way station along the course leading to eternal life, a place where the final preparation is made for that fulness of joy which comes only when body and spirit are inseparably connected in immortal glory!" (*The Mortal Messiah*, 4:222).

14 **All these had departed the mortal life, firm in the hope of a glorious resurrection** [*the celestial resurrection—see D&C 88:28–29, 97–98*], **through the grace of God the Father and his Only Begotten Son, Jesus Christ** [*because of the Father's plan and the Atonement of Christ*].

Doctrine

The righteous spirits in paradise were anxiously awaiting their resurrection, knowing that Christ had been crucified and would soon be visiting them prior to their resurrection with Him.

15 I beheld that **they were filled with joy and gladness**, and were rejoicing together **because the day of their deliverance** [*resurrection—see verses 16 and 50*] **was at hand.**

16 **They were assembled awaiting the advent** [*coming*] **of the Son of God into the spirit world, to declare their redemption from the bands of death.**

17 Their sleeping dust [*their dead mortal body*] was to be restored unto its perfect frame [*compare with Alma 40:23*], bone to his bone, and the sinews and the flesh upon them, **the spirit and the body to be united never again to be divided**, that they might receive a fulness of joy.

SECTION 138

Doctrine

When the Savior visited the postmortal spirit world after His crucifixion, He visited the righteous spirits in paradise.

18 While this vast multitude [*of righteous postmortal spirits*] waited and conversed, rejoicing in the hour of their deliverance from the chains of death, **the Son of God appeared**, declaring liberty to the captives who had been faithful;

> Imagine the tenderness and joy in the Savior's heart at this time! He had just left an environment of cruelty, deep evil, and vile hypocrisy in which He had been crucified. Now, he was among humble, righteous people who had already died and who welcomed Him with all their hearts and listened to His every word.

19 And **there he preached to them** the everlasting gospel, the doctrine of the resurrection and the redemption of mankind from the fall, and from individual sins on conditions of repentance.

> As you know, "We believe the Bible to be the word of God as far as it is translated correctly" (eighth article of faith). The version of Peter's teachings that we have in the Bible leaves us with the idea that Christ personally preached to the spirits in prison.

1 Peter 3:18–19

18 For Christ also hath once suffered for sins, the just for the unjust, that he might bring us to God, being put to death in the flesh, but quickened by the Spirit:

19 By which also he went and preached unto the spirits in prison;

Verses 20–22, next, show that this was not the case.

Doctrine

Christ did not preach personally to the wicked in spirit prison.

20 But unto the wicked he did not go, **and among the ungodly and the unrepentant who had defiled themselves while in the flesh, his voice was not raised;**

21 Neither did the rebellious who rejected the testimonies and the warnings of the ancient prophets **behold his presence** [*see Him*], **nor look upon his face.**

22 Where these were, darkness reigned, but among the righteous there was peace;

> On occasions, a student will ask why we refer to it as spirit prison. The answer is simple and important. Sin and ignorance of truth

place a person in "prison" in the sense that they cannot progress. For example, without knowledge of the gospel, we cannot live the gospel and pursue eternal joy and happiness in exaltation. If individuals get caught up in worldliness and evil, they are in bondage, because there are eternal limits placed upon them unless they repent. Thus, they are in "prison."

President Smith continues now with his description of the righteous spirits in paradise as he saw the Savior visit them and prepare them to be resurrected (verse 19).

23 And **the saints rejoiced in their redemption, and bowed the knee and acknowledged the Son of God** as their Redeemer and Deliverer from death and the chains of hell.

24 **Their countenances shone**, and the radiance from the presence of the Lord rested upon them, and **they sang praises unto his holy name**.

Next, in verses 25–28, a question comes up in President Smith's mind, which will lead to additional answers given in the vision.

25 I marveled [*became curious*], for **I understood that the Savior spent about three years in his ministry among the Jews and those of the house of Israel**, endeavoring to teach them the everlasting gospel and call them unto repentance;

26 And yet, notwithstanding his mighty works, and miracles, and proclamation of the truth, in great power and authority, there were but few who hearkened to his voice, and rejoiced in his presence, and received salvation at his hands.

27 **But his ministry among those who were dead was limited to the brief time intervening between the crucifixion and his resurrection;**

28 **And I wondered at the words of Peter—wherein he said that the Son of God preached unto the spirits in prison**, who sometime were disobedient, when once the long-suffering of God waited in the days of Noah—and **how it was possible for him to preach to those spirits and perform the necessary labor among them in so short a time**.

Doctrine

The righteous spirits in paradise are sent on missions into the spirit prison (the spirit world mission field) to teach the gospel to them.

29 And **as I wondered, my eyes were opened**, and my

understanding quickened, **and I perceived that the Lord went not in person among the wicked** and the disobedient who had rejected the truth, to teach them;

30 **But** behold, **from among the righteous, he organized his forces** and appointed messengers, clothed with power and authority, **and commissioned them to go forth and carry the light of the gospel to them that were in darkness**, even **to all** the spirits of men [*everyone will ultimately be given a perfect opportunity to understand and then accept or reject the gospel, before final judgment*]; and **thus was the gospel preached to the dead.**

Doctrine

All will receive a perfect opportunity to understand and then accept or reject the gospel of Jesus Christ before they are brought before the judgment bar of God.

> Of course, children who die before the "years of accountability" (D&C 137:10) will be saved in celestial glory; thus, they do not need the opportunity to receive the gospel spoken of above. They already have it. The intellectually handicapped are in the same category as children who die before the age of accountability (see D&C 29:50 and 137:7).

31 And the chosen messengers went forth **to declare the acceptable day of the Lord** [*Isaiah 61:1–2, meaning that it was time to begin preaching the gospel to the dead according to the timetable predetermined in the plan of salvation*] and proclaim liberty to the captives who were bound, even unto all who would repent of their sins and receive the gospel.

> According to verse 32, next, there are two major categories of people in the spirit world mission field (spirit prison).

32 Thus was the gospel preached to **(1) those who had died** in their sins, **without a knowledge of the truth, or (2) in transgression, having rejected the prophets.**

> From verse 32, above, we understand that there are good and honorable people in the spirit world mission field who have not had the gospel adequately preached to them or have not heard it at all. Also, there are intentionally wicked individuals. Obviously, there are also many people who fit somewhere in between these two categories. It is much the same as here on earth as far as missionary work is concerned. They all need to have the gospel preached to them, and

that takes place in the spirit prison. Joseph Fielding Smith addressed the topic of who goes to paradise and who goes to the spirit world mission field as follows:

"As I understand it, *the righteous—meaning* **those who have been baptized and who have been faithful**—are gathered **in one part [paradise] and all the others in another part of the spirit world**. This seems to be true from the vision given to President Joseph F. Smith [See D&C 138]" (*Doctrines of Salvation,* 2:230).

This whole doctrine should be very comforting to those who worry about good and honorable loved ones and friends who have died but are not yet in paradise. They realize that these loved ones are not being punished by being sent to the spirit prison or mission field; rather, they are being given an opportunity to hear, understand, and accept the gospel, just as is the case with people on the earth. Furthermore, they must accept it in an environment of opposition and diversity of thinking and belief systems, just as we here on earth must. If they accept it and are faithful there, they have every opportunity of obtaining the highest degree of glory in the celestial kingdom (exaltation) that we here on earth have once their temple work is done by mortals, either here or during the Millennium.

Next, in verses 33–34, we see that the very same gospel principles are taught in the spirit world mission field as are taught by missionaries here on earth.

33 These were taught **faith** in God, **repentance** from sin, vicarious **baptism** for the remission of sins, **the gift of the Holy Ghost** by the laying on of hands,

34 And **all other principles of the gospel** that were necessary for them to know in order to qualify themselves that they might be judged according to men in the flesh, but live according to God in the spirit [*in other words, they will be judged by the same standards as mortals who have the opportunity to live the gospel here*].

Verse 35, next, summarizes the fact that all the dead are given the opportunity to hear and understand the gospel of Jesus Christ.

35 **And so it was made known among the dead**, both small and great, the unrighteous as well as the faithful, **that redemption had been wrought through the sacrifice of the Son of God upon the cross.**

Verses 36–37, next, summarize the fact that the spirits of the righteous were organized into a mighty missionary force to preach the gospel to all the dead who had not yet qualified for the privilege of being in the presence of the Savior.

36 Thus was it made known that **our Redeemer spent his time during his sojourn in the world of spirits, instructing and preparing the faithful spirits** of the prophets who had testified of him in the flesh;

37 **That they might carry the message of redemption unto all the dead, unto whom he could not go personally, because of their rebellion and transgression**, that they through the ministration of his servants might also hear his words.

> Next, in verses 38–49, President Smith points out a number of ancient prophets whose spirits he saw in the vision as they awaited the Savior's arrival to visit them in the spirit world paradise.

38 Among the great and mighty ones who were assembled in this vast congregation of the righteous were Father **Adam**, the Ancient of Days and father of all,

39 And our glorious **Mother Eve**, with **many of her faithful daughters** who had lived through the ages and worshiped the true and living God.

40 **Abel**, the first martyr, was there, and his brother **Seth**, one of the mighty ones, who was in the express image of his father, Adam.

41 **Noah**, who gave warning of the flood; **Shem**, the great high priest; **Abraham**, the father [*ancestor*] of the faithful; **Isaac**, **Jacob**, and **Moses**, the great law-giver of Israel;

42 And **Isaiah**, who declared by prophecy that the Redeemer was anointed to bind up the broken-hearted, to proclaim liberty to the captives, and the opening of the prison to them that were bound, were also there.

43 Moreover, **Ezekiel**, who was shown in vision the great valley of dry bones, which were to be clothed upon with flesh [*who were to be resurrected*], to come forth again in the resurrection of the dead, living souls;

44 **Daniel**, who foresaw and foretold the establishment of the kingdom of God in the latter days, never again to be destroyed nor given to other people;

45 **Elias** [*Elijah—see Bible Dictionary under "Elias"*], who was with Moses on the Mount of Transfiguration;

46 And **Malachi**, the prophet who testified of the coming of Elijah—of whom also Moroni spake to the Prophet Joseph Smith, declaring that he should come before the ushering in of the great and dreadful day of the Lord—were also there.

> In verses 47–48, next, President Smith briefly explains the role and mission of Elijah in restoring the sealing power (see D&C 110:13–15) so that work for the dead can be performed in temples during our dispensation.

47 The Prophet Elijah was to plant in the hearts of the children the promises made to their fathers,

48 Foreshadowing the great work to be done in the temples of the Lord in the dispensation of the fulness of times [*our dispensation*], for the redemption of the dead, and the sealing of the children to their parents, lest the whole earth be smitten with a curse and utterly wasted at his coming.

49 **All these and many more, even the prophets who dwelt among the Nephites** and testified of the coming of the Son of God, **mingled in the vast assembly and waited for their deliverance,**

Doctrine

We will miss our mortal bodies after we die. We will consider the limitations of not having a physical body to be a type of bondage.

50 For **the dead had looked upon the long absence of their spirits from their bodies as a bondage**.

> Next, in verse 51, President Smith teaches that the Savior gave these righteous spirits in paradise, to whom He appeared during the time His body lay in the tomb, the power to be resurrected with Him.

51 These [*the spirits in paradise*] the Lord taught, and **gave them power to come forth, after his resurrection from the dead,** to enter into his Father's kingdom, there to be crowned with immortality [*living forever with a resurrected body of flesh and bone*] and eternal life [*exaltation*],

> Among other things, verse 52, next, teaches us that we can continue to progress in celestial glory.

52 **And continue thenceforth their labor** as had been promised by the Lord, and be partakers of all blessings which were held in reserve for them that love him.

The Prophet Joseph Smith also taught that the faithful can continue to progress after they have died. He said (**bold** added for emphasis):

"When you climb up a ladder, you must begin at the bottom, and ascend step by step, until you arrive at the top; and so it is with the principles of the Gospel—you must begin with the first, and go on until you learn all the principles of exaltation. But **it will be a great while after you have passed through the veil before you will have learned them. It is not all to be comprehended in this world; it will be a great work to learn our salvation and exaltation even beyond the grave**" (*Teachings of the Prophet Joseph Smith,* 348).

Next, in verses 53–56, President Joseph F. Smith sees many modern prophets, including his own father, and other righteous spirits in the spirit world. He explains that many righteous spirits were reserved to come forth in the dispensation of the fullness of times.

Doctrine

Many choice spirits were reserved to come to earth during the last days.

53 The Prophet Joseph Smith, and my father, **Hyrum Smith, Brigham Young, John Taylor, Wilford Woodruff**, and **other choice spirits who were reserved to come forth in the fulness of times** to take part in laying the foundations of the great Latter-day work,

54 Including the building of the temples and the performance of ordinances therein for the redemption of the dead, **were also in the spirit world.**

55 I observed that they were also among the noble and great ones who were **chosen in the beginning to be rulers** [*leaders—see Abraham 3:25*] **in the Church of God.**

As you know, we were taught the gospel of Jesus Christ in premortality, given agency (see D&C 29:35–36), and allowed to make agency choices that led to growth and progress, or to rebellion (as was the case with the devil and his one third; see Revelation 12:4, 7–9). Verse 56, next, is one of the places in scripture in which we see the doctrine that we were taught the gospel in premortality.

Doctrine

We were taught the gospel of Jesus Christ during our premortal lives as spirit children of God.

56 Even before they were born, they, with many others, received their first lessons in the world of

spirits and were prepared to come forth in the due time of the Lord to labor in his vineyard for the salvation of the souls of men.

> Next, in verse 57, we find the doctrine that after faithful men die, they serve as missionaries in the spirit world, preaching to the spirits in the spirit world mission field.

Doctrine

After faithful men die, they serve as missionaries in the spirit world.

57 I beheld that the faithful elders of this dispensation, when they depart from mortal life, continue their labors in the preaching of the gospel of repentance and redemption, through the sacrifice of the Only Begotten Son of God, **among those who are in darkness and under the bondage of sin in the great world of the spirits of the dead.**

Question

> Do faithful sisters, after they die, also serve as missionaries in the spirit world?

Answer

> Yes. President Joseph F. Smith taught (**bold** added for emphasis):
>
> "Now, among all these millions of spirits that have lived on the earth and have passed away, from generation to generation, since the beginning of the world, without the knowledge of the gospel—among them you may count that at least one-half are women. Who is going to preach the gospel to the women? Who is going to carry the testimony of Jesus Christ to the hearts of the women who have passed away without a knowledge of the gospel? Well, to my mind, it is a simple thing. **These good sisters** who have been set apart, ordained to the work, called to it, authorized by the authority of the holy Priesthood to minister for their sex, in the House of God for the living and for the dead, **will be fully authorized and empowered to preach the gospel and minister to the women** while the elders and prophets are preaching it to the men. The things we experience here are typical of the things of God and the life beyond us. There is a great similarity between God's purposes as manifested here and his purposes as carried out in his presence and kingdom. **Those who are authorized to preach the gospel here and are appointed here to do that work will not be idle after they have passed away, but will continue to exercise the rights that they obtained here under the Priesthood of the Son of God to minister for the salvation of those who have died without a knowledge of the truth**" (*Gospel Doctrine,* 461).

Next, in verses 58–59, we see that the dead must repent of their sins and be cleansed by the Atonement of Christ in order to accept the ordinance work which is done for them by us in the temples.

58 The **dead who repent will be redeemed, through obedience to the ordinances of the house of God** [*temples*],

59 And **after they have paid the penalty of their transgressions, and are washed clean**, shall **receive a reward according to their works**, for they are heirs of salvation.

President Smith closes by bearing his testimony to us of the truthfulness of his marvelous vision of the redemption of the dead.

60 **Thus was the vision of the redemption of the dead revealed to me**, and **I bear record, and I know that this record is true**, through the blessing of our Lord and Savior, Jesus Christ, even so. Amen.

OFFICIAL DECLARATION—1

Background

The heading for Official Declaration—1, used in the 2013 edition of the Doctrine and Covenants, is as follows:

The Bible and the Book of Mormon teach that monogamy is God's standard for marriage unless He declares otherwise (see 2 Samuel 12:7–8 and Jacob 2:27, 30). Following a revelation to Joseph Smith, the practice of plural marriage was instituted among Church members in the early 1840s (see section 132). From the 1860s to the 1880s, the United States government passed laws to make this religious practice illegal. These laws were eventually upheld by the U.S. Supreme Court. After receiving revelation, President Wilford Woodruff issued the following Manifesto, which was accepted by the Church as authoritative and binding on October 6, 1890. This led to the end of the practice of plural marriage in the Church.

The Official Declaration—1 is sometimes referred to as the "Manifesto" and is the official document from the Church announcing the end of the practice of plural marriage.

The practice of plural marriage had been revealed to the Prophet Joseph Smith as early as 1831 (see heading to section 132) and had first been publicly preached in the Salt Lake Valley on August 29, 1852, by Elder Orson

Pratt under the direction of President Brigham Young (see *Doctrine and Covenants Student Manual,* 1981 edition, page 327).

Although the Saints and the Church had been severely persecuted because of this practice, President Wilford Woodruff, the president of the Church at the time plural marriage was discontinued, clearly stated that public pressure was not the reason for its discontinuance. Rather, it was commanded by the Lord that it be stopped. In a minute, we will use **bold** to point this out in the excerpts from addresses by President Woodruff, which follow Official Declaration—1 in the Doctrine and Covenants.

We will now read the Manifesto, using **bold** at times for emphasis.

To Whom It May Concern:

Press dispatches having been sent for political purposes, from Salt Lake City, which have been widely published, to the effect that the Utah Commission, in their recent report to the Secretary of the Interior, allege that plural marriages are still being solemnized and that forty or more such marriages have been contracted in Utah since last June or during the past year, also that in public discourses the leaders of the Church have taught, encouraged and urged the continuance of the practice of polygamy—

I, therefore, as President of the Church of Jesus Christ of Latter-day Saints, do hereby, in the most solemn manner, declare that these charges are false. **We are not teaching polygamy or plural marriage, nor permitting any person to enter into its practice**, and I deny that either forty or any other number of plural marriages have during that period been solemnized in our Temples or in any other place in the Territory.

One case has been reported, in which the parties allege that the marriage was performed in the Endowment House, in Salt Lake City, in the Spring of 1889, but I have not been able to learn who performed the ceremony; whatever was done in this matter was without my knowledge. In consequence of this alleged occurrence the Endowment House was, by my instructions, taken down without delay.

Inasmuch as laws have been enacted by Congress forbidding plural marriages, which laws have been pronounced constitutional by the

court of last resort, I hereby declare my intention to submit to those laws, and to use my influence with the members of the Church over which I preside to have them do likewise.

There is nothing in my teachings to the Church or in those of my associates, during the time specified, which can be reasonably construed to inculcate or encourage polygamy; and when any Elder of the Church has used language which appeared to convey any such teaching, he has been promptly reproved. And **I now publicly declare that my advice to the Latter-day Saints is to refrain from contracting any marriage forbidden by the law of the land.**

WILFORD WOODRUFF
President of the Church of Jesus Christ
of Latter-day Saints.

President Lorenzo Snow offered the following:

"I move that, recognizing Wilford Woodruff as the President of the Church of Jesus Christ of Latter-day Saints, and the only man on the earth at the present time who holds the keys of the sealing ordinances, we consider him fully authorized by virtue of his position to issue the Manifesto which has been read in our hearing, and which is dated **September 24th, 1890**, and that as a Church in General Conference assembled, we accept his declaration concerning plural marriages as authoritative and binding."

The vote to sustain the foregoing motion was unanimous.

Salt Lake City, Utah, October 6, 1890.

EXCERPTS FROM THREE ADDRESSES BY PRESIDENT
WILFORD WOODRUFF REGARDING THE MANIFESTO
[*Official Declaration—1*]

The Lord will never permit me or any other man who stands as President of this Church to lead you astray. It is not in the programme. It is not in the mind of God. If I were to attempt that, the Lord would remove me out of my place, and so He will any other man who attempts to lead the children of men astray from the oracles of God and from their duty. (Sixty-first Semiannual General Conference of the Church, Monday, October 6, 1890, Salt Lake City, Utah. Reported in *Deseret Evening News,* October 11, 1890, p. 2.)

It matters not who lives or who dies, or who is called to lead this Church, they have got to lead it by the inspiration of Almighty God. If they do not do it that way, they cannot do it at all. . . .

I have had some revelations of late, and very important ones to me, and I will tell you what the Lord has said to me. Let me bring your minds to what is termed the manifesto. . . .

The Lord has told me to ask the Latter-day Saints a question, and He also told me that if they would listen to what I said to them and answer the question put to them, by the Spirit and power of God, they would all answer alike, and they would all believe alike with regard to this matter.

The question is this: Which is the wisest course for the Latter-day Saints to pursue—to continue to attempt to practice plural marriage, with the laws of the nation against it and the opposition of sixty millions of people, and at the cost of the confiscation and loss of all the Temples, and the stopping of all the ordinances therein, both for the living and the dead, and the imprisonment of the First Presidency and Twelve and the heads of families in the Church, and the confiscation of personal property of the people (all of which of themselves would stop the practice); or, after doing and suffering what we have through our adherence to this principle to cease the practice and submit to the law, and through doing so leave the Prophets, Apostles and fathers at home, so that they can instruct the people and attend to the duties of the Church, and also leave the Temples in the hands of the Saints, so that they can attend to the ordinances of the Gospel, both for the living and the dead?

The Lord showed me by vision and revelation exactly what would take place if we did not stop this practice. If we had not stopped it, you would have had no use for . . . any of the men in this temple at Logan; for all ordinances would be stopped throughout the land of Zion. Confusion would reign throughout Israel, and many men would be made prisoners. This trouble would have come upon the whole Church, and we should have been compelled to stop the practice. Now, the question is, whether it should be stopped in this manner, or in the way the Lord has manifested to us, and leave our Prophets and Apostles and fathers free men, and the temples in the hands of the people, so that the dead may be redeemed. A large number has already been delivered from the prison house in the spirit world by this people, and shall the work go on or stop? This is the question I lay before the Latter-day Saints. You have to judge for yourselves. I want you to answer it for yourselves. I shall not answer it; but I say to you that that is exactly the condition we as a people would have been in had we not taken the course we have.

. . . I saw exactly what would come to pass if there was not something done. I have had this spirit upon me for a long time. But **I want to say this: I should have let all the temples go out of our hands; I should have gone to prison myself, and let every other man go there, had not the God of heaven commanded me to do what I did do**; and when the hour came that I was commanded to do that, it was all clear to me. **I went before the Lord, and I wrote what the Lord told me to write.** . . .

I leave this with you, for you to contemplate and consider. The Lord is at work with us. (Cache Stake Conference, Logan, Utah, Sunday, November 1, 1891. Reported in *Deseret Weekly,* November 14, 1891.)

Now I will tell you what was manifested to me and what the Son of God performed in this thing. . . . All these things would have come to pass, as God Almighty lives, had not that Manifesto been given. Therefore, **the Son of God felt disposed to have that thing presented to the Church and to the world for purposes in his own mind**. The Lord had decreed the establishment of Zion. He had decreed the finishing of this temple. He had decreed that the salvation of the living and the dead should be given in these valleys of the mountains. And Almighty God decreed that the Devil should not thwart it. If you can understand that, that is a key to it. (From a discourse at the sixth session of the dedication of the Salt Lake Temple, April 1893. Typescript of Dedicatory Services, Archives, Church Historical Department, Salt Lake City, Utah.)

OFFICIAL DECLARATION—2

Background

The heading for Official Declaration—2, used in the 2013 edition of the Doctrine and Covenants, is as follows:

The Book of Mormon teaches that "all are alike unto God," including "black and white, bond and free, male and female" (2 Nephi 26:33). Throughout the history of the Church, people of every race and ethnicity in many countries have been baptized and have lived as faithful members of the Church. During Joseph Smith's lifetime, a few black male members of the Church were ordained to the priesthood. Early in its history, Church leaders stopped conferring the priesthood on black males of African descent. Church records offer no clear insights into the origins of this practice. Church leaders believed that a revelation from God was needed to alter this practice and prayerfully sought guidance. The revelation came to Church President Spencer W. Kimball and was affirmed to other Church leaders in the Salt Lake Temple on June 1, 1978. The revelation removed all restrictions with regard to race that once applied to the priesthood.

Official Declaration—2 is the official statement of the Church that the priesthood can now be given to any worthy man. It is marvelous to live in the day and age when this blessing is given to all the world.

As we read this declaration, we will use **bold** for emphasis:

To Whom It May Concern:

On September 30, 1978, at the 148th Semiannual General Conference of The Church of Jesus Christ of Latter-day Saints, the following was presented by President N. Eldon Tanner, First Counselor in the First Presidency of the Church:

In early June of this year, the First Presidency announced that a revelation had been received by President Spencer W. Kimball extending priesthood and temple blessings to all worthy male members of the Church. President Kimball has asked that I advise the conference that after he had received this revelation, which came to him after extended meditation and prayer in the sacred rooms of the holy temple, he presented it to his counselors, who accepted it and approved it. It was then presented to the Quorum of the Twelve Apostles, who unanimously approved it, and was subsequently presented to all other General Authorities, who likewise approved it unanimously.

President Kimball has asked that I now read this letter:

June 8, 1978

To all general and local priesthood officers of The Church of Jesus Christ of Latter-day Saints throughout the world:

Dear Brethren:

As we have witnessed the expansion of the work of the Lord over the earth, we have been grateful that people of many nations have responded to the message of the restored gospel, and have joined the Church in ever-increasing numbers. This, in turn, has inspired us with a desire to extend to every worthy member of the Church all of the privileges and blessings which the gospel affords.

Aware of the promises made by the prophets and presidents of the Church who have preceded us that at some time, in God's eternal plan, all of our brethren who are worthy may receive the priesthood, and witnessing the faithfulness of those from whom the priesthood has been withheld, we have pleaded long and earnestly in behalf of these, our faithful brethren, spending many hours in the Upper Room of the Temple supplicating the Lord for divine guidance.

He has heard our prayers, and **by revelation** has confirmed that the long-promised day has come when **every faithful, worthy man in the Church may receive the holy priesthood**, with power to exercise its divine authority, and enjoy with his loved ones every blessing that flows therefrom, including the blessings of the temple. Accordingly, **all worthy male members of the Church may be ordained to the priesthood without regard for race or color**. Priesthood leaders are instructed to follow the policy of carefully interviewing all candidates for ordination to either the Aaronic or the Melchizedek Priesthood to insure that they meet the established standards for worthiness.

We declare with soberness that the Lord has now made known his will for the blessing of all his children throughout the earth who will hearken to the voice of his authorized servants, and prepare themselves to receive every blessing of the gospel.

> Sincerely yours,
>
> SPENCER W. KIMBALL
> N. ELDON TANNER
> MARION G. ROMNEY
>
> The First Presidency

Recognizing Spencer W. Kimball as the prophet, seer, and revelator, and president of The Church of Jesus Christ of Latter-day Saints, it is proposed that we as a constituent assembly accept this revelation as the word and will of the Lord. All in favor please signify by raising your right hand. Any opposed by the same sign.

The vote to sustain the foregoing motion was unanimous in the affirmative.

> Salt Lake City, Utah, September 30, 1978.

SOURCES

Anderson, Richard Lloyd. *Investigating the Book of Mormon Witnesses.* Salt Lake City: Deseret Book, 1981.

Barrett, Ivan J. *Joseph Smith and the Restoration.* Provo, UT: Brigham Young University, 1982.

Black, Susan Easton. *Who's Who in the Doctrine and Covenants.* Salt Lake City: Bookcraft, 1997.

Book of Mormon Student Manual. Salt Lake City: The Church of Jesus Christ of Latter-day Saints (Institutes of Religion), 1982.

Cannon, George Q. *Life of Joseph Smith the Prophet.* Salt Lake City: Deseret News Press, 1907.

Church History in the Fulness of Times. Salt Lake City: The Church of Jesus Christ of Latter-day Saints (Institutes of Religion), 1989, 2003.

Clark, James R. (Compiler.) *Messages of the First Presidency of The Church of Jesus Christ of Latter-day Saints.* 6 vols. Salt Lake City: Bookcraft, 1965–75.

Conference Reports of The Church of Jesus Christ of Latter-day Saints. Salt Lake City: The Church of Jesus Christ of Latter-day Saints, 1898 to the present.

Cowan, Richard. *Temples to Dot the Earth.* Salt Lake City: Deseret Book, 1989.

Cowley, Matthias F. *Wilford Woodruff: History of His Life and Labors.* 2d ed. Salt Lake City: Bookcraft, 1964.

Doctrine and Covenants and Church History: Gospel Doctrine Teacher's Manual. Salt Lake City: The Church of Jesus Christ of Latter-day Saints, 1999.

Doctrine and Covenants Student Manual. Salt Lake City: The Church of Jesus Christ of Latter-day Saints (Institutes of Religion), 1981, 2018.

Doctrines of the Gospel Student Manual. Salt Lake City: The Church of Jesus Christ of Latter-day Saints (Institutes of Religion), 1981.

Doxey, Roy W. (Compiler.) *Latter-day Prophets and the Doctrine and Covenants.* Salt Lake City: Deseret Book, 1978.

"The Family: A Proclamation to the World." *Ensign or Liahona,* Nov. 2010, 129.

Hancock, Levi Ward. Autobiography. Typescript. L. Tom Perry Special Collections, Harold B. Lee Library, Brigham Young University, Provo, Utah.

Hinckley, Bryant S. *Sermons and Missionary Services of Melvin J. Ballard.* Salt Lake City: Deseret Book, 1949.

Joseph Smith Papers, The. Salt Lake City: Church Historian's Press. See also josephsmithpapers.org. (These books consist of several volumes now [2020] and will consist of more than 30 volumes when they are complete.)

Journal of Discourses. 26 vols. London: Latter-day Saints' Book Depot, 1854–86.

Kimball, Spencer W. *The Teachings of Spencer W. Kimball.* Edited by Edward L. Kimball. Salt Lake City: Bookcraft, 1982.

Lang, W. *History of Seneca County [Ohio], from the Close of the Revolutionary War to July, 1880.* Woburn, MA: Unigraphic, 1973.

Latter-day Saints' Millennial Star, The. Manchester, Liverpool, and London, England: The Church of Jesus Christ of Latter-day Saints, 1840–1970.

Life and Teachings of Jesus and His Apostles: New Testament Student Manual, The. Salt Lake City: The Church of Jesus Christ of Latter-day Saints, 1979.

Ludlow, Daniel H. *Encyclopedia of Mormonism.* Edited by Daniel H. Ludlow. 5 vols. New York: Macmillan, 1992.

Lundwall, N. B. *Temples of the Most High.* Salt Lake City: Bookcraft, 1971.

Matthews, Robert J. *A Plainer Translation: Joseph Smith's Translation of the Bible—A History and Commentary.* Provo, Utah: Brigham Young University Press, 1975.

McConkie, Bruce R. *Doctrinal New Testament Commentary.* 3 vols. Salt Lake City: Bookcraft, 1965–73.

———. *The Millennial Messiah: The Second Coming of the Son of Man.* Salt Lake City: Deseret Book, 1982.

———. *Mormon Doctrine.* 2d ed. Salt Lake City: Bookcraft, 1966.

———. *The Mortal Messiah: From Bethlehem to Calgary.* 4 vols. Salt Lake City: Deseret Book, 1979–81.

———. *The Promised Messiah: The First Coming of Christ.* Salt Lake City: Deseret Book, 1978.

McGavin, Cecil E. *Historical Background of the Doctrine and Covenants.* Salt Lake City: Literary Licensing, 2011.

Murdock, John. Typescript of the Journal of John Murdock. Harold B Lee Library, Brigham Young University.

Otten, L. G. *Historical Background and Setting for each section of the Doctrine and Covenants.* Privately published, 1970.

Pratt, Parley P. *Autobiography of Parley P. Pratt.* Edited by Parley P. Pratt Jr. Salt Lake City: Deseret Book, 1938–1985.

Proctor, Scott and Maurine. *The Revised and Enhanced History of Joseph Smith by His Mother.* Salt Lake City: Bookcraft, 1996.

"Special Witnesses of the Name of Christ," *The Religious Educator: Perspectives on the Restored Gospel,* vol. 12, no. 2. BYU Religious Studies Center. Provo, UT: Brigham Young University, 2011.

Revelations in Context. Edited by Matthew McBride and James Goldberg (2016). See history.lds.org.

Roberts, B. H. *A Comprehensive History of The Church of Jesus Christ of Latter-day Saints, Century One.* 6 vols. Salt Lake City: Deseret Press, 1930.

Smith, Hyrum M. and Janne M. Sjodahl. *Doctrine and Covenants Commentary.* Salt Lake City: Deseret Book, 1951.

Smith, Joseph. *History of The Church of Jesus Christ of Latter-day Saints.* Edited by B. H. Roberts. 2d ed. rev., 7 vols. Salt Lake City: The Church of Jesus Christ of Latter-day Saints, 1932–51.

―――. *Teachings of the Prophet Joseph Smith.* Selected by Joseph Fielding Smith. Salt Lake City: Deseret Book, 1976.

Smith, Joseph F. *Gospel Doctrine.* Salt Lake City: Deseret Book, 1939.

Smith, Joseph Fielding. *Answers to Gospel Questions.* Compiled by Joseph Fielding Smith Jr. 5 vols. Salt Lake City: Deseret Book, 1957–66.

―――. *Church History and Modern Revelation—A Course Study for Melchizedek Priesthood Quorums.* Salt Lake City: The Council of the Twelve Apostles of The Church of Jesus Christ of Latter-day Saints, 1946.

―――. *Doctrines of Salvation.* Compiled by Bruce R. McConkie. 3 vols. Salt Lake City: Bookcraft, 1954–56.

―――. *Way to Perfection.* Salt Lake City: Deseret Book, 1975.

Smith, Hyrum M. and Janne M. Sjodahl. *Doctrine and Covenants Commentary.* Salt Lake City: Deseret Book, 1951.

Smith, Lucy Mack. *History of Joseph Smith by His Mother, Lucy Mack Smith.* Salt Lake City: Bookcraft, 1958.

Sperry, Sidney B. *Doctrine and Covenants Compendium.* Salt Lake City: Bookcraft, 1960.

Tait, Lisa Olsen and Brent Rogers. "A House for Our God." *Revelations in Context.* See churchofjesuschrist.org/study/manual/revelations-in-context/a-house-for-our-god?lang=eng.

Talmage, James E. *The Articles of Faith.* Salt Lake City: Deseret Book, 1984.

———. *Jesus the Christ.* Salt Lake City: Deseret Book, 1977.

Teachings of Presidents of the Church—Wilford Woodruff. Salt Lake City: The Church of Jesus Christ of Latter-day Saints, 2004.

Times and Seasons. Commerce (later Nauvoo), Illinois, 1839–46.

Widtsoe, John A. *Evidences and Reconciliations.* Salt Lake City: Bookcraft, 1943.

———. *Priesthood and Church Government.* Salt Lake City: Deseret Book, 1962.

———. *The Message of the Doctrine and Covenants.* Salt Lake City: Bookcraft, 1978.

———. *The Word of Wisdom: A Modern Interpretation.* Salt Lake City: Deseret Book, 1938.

Whitney, Orson F. *The Life of Heber C. Kimball.* Salt Lake City: Steven and Wallis, 1945.

Young, Brigham. *Discourses of Brigham Young.* Selected by John A. Widtsoe. Salt Lake City: Deseret Book, 1954.

Additional sources for the notes given in this work are as follows:

- The Standard Works of The Church of Jesus Christ of Latter-day Saints.
- Footnotes in the Latter-day Saint version of the King James Bible.
- The Joseph Smith Translation of the Bible.
- The Bible Dictionary in the back of the Latter-day Saint version of the King James Bible.
- Various dictionaries.
- Various student manuals provided for our institutes of religion.
- Other sources as noted in the text.

About the Author

David J. Ridges was raised in southeastern Nevada until his family moved to North Salt Lake City, Utah, when he was in fifth grade. He is the second of eight children.

Brother Ridges graduated from Bountiful High, served a two-and-a-half-year German-speaking mission to Austria, attended the University of Utah and BYU, and then graduated from BYU with a major in German and a physics minor. He later received a master's degree in educational psychology with a Church History minor from BYU.

He taught seminary and institute of religion as his chosen career for thirty-five years. He taught BYU Campus Education Week, Especially for Youth, Adult Religion, and Know Your Religion classes for over twenty-five years.

ABOUT THE AUTHOR

Brother Ridges has served as a Sunday School and seminary curriculum writer. He has had many callings, including Gospel Doctrine teacher, bishop, stake president, and patriarch. He and Sister Ridges have served two full-time, eighteen-month CES missions. He has written over forty books, which include several study guides for the standard works, Isaiah, Revelation, and many doctrinal publications on gospel topics such as the signs of the times, plan of salvation, and temples.

Brother and Sister Ridges met at the University of Utah. They were married in the Salt Lake Temple, are the parents of six children, and have sixteen grandchildren and one great-granddaughter so far. They make their home in Springville, Utah.

Scan to visit

www.davidjridges.com

Notes

Notes

Notes

Notes